2nd International Workshop on Natural Language Processing for Digital Humanities (NLP4DH)

Online
20 November 2022

ISBN: 978-1-7138-6317-5

Printed from e-media with permission by:

Curran Associates, Inc.
57 Morehouse Lane
Red Hook, NY 12571

proceedings.com

Some format issues inherent in the e-media version may also appear in this print version.

Printed with permission by Curran Associates, Inc. (2023)

For permission requests, please contact the Association for Computational Linguistics at the address below.

Association for Computational Linguistics
209 N. Eighth Street
Stroudsburg, Pennsylvania 18360

Phone: 1-570-476-8006
Fax: 1-570-476-0860

acl@aclweb.org

Additional copies of this publication are available from:

Curran Associates, Inc.
57 Morehouse Lane
Red Hook, NY 12571 USA
Phone: 845-758-0400
Fax: 845-758-2633
Email: curran@proceedings.com
Web: www.proceedings.com

NLP4DH 2021

The 2nd International Workshop on Natural Language Processing for Digital Humanities

Proceedings of the Workshop

November 20, 2022

Preface

Textual sources are essential for research in digital humanities. Especially when larger datasets are analyzed, the use of natural language processing (NLP) technologies is essential. However, NLP is still often focused to written standard languages, which customarily differs from specific genres and text types that may interest a digital humanist today. The situation is even more complicated when the research is done on minority languages, or historical and dialectal materials.

Natural language processing has usually a strong computer science focus, which means that methods are developed to cater for higher numerical results and to solve some rather abstract level tasks such as machine translation, poem generation or sentiment analysis. Digital humanities, on the other hand, has usually a strong humanities focus which means that the research questions are typically more concrete, diving deeper to understanding some phenomena rather than solving a problem. Natural language processing also seeks to validate the methods, whereas digital humanities takes the validity of the methods for granted. This is due to the fact that a method is often the end goal in natural language processing, where as a method is just a tool in the digital humanities. The two fields work from very different starting points, and therefore we believe that more venues are needed where scholars from both fields can come together and learn from each other.

We believe that digital humanists recognize the shortcomings of the contemporary natural language processing tools, and the NLP community has already come up with various fully functional solutions. However, these communities would benefit from further communication. For example, model fine tuning and retraining are among useful technologies in NLP that could be applied to efficiently improve the result on these divergent varieties. Similarly work in digital humanities often results in open datasets that could be used to compare different strategies. In this workshop we aimed to foster and initiate wider conversation and sharing of examples of how NLP tools are best leveraged to the research questions that are relevant in humanities.

The Workshop on Natural Language Processing for Digital Humanities (NLP4DH) was organized for the second time in November 20, 2022 with AACL IJCNLP 2022: The 2nd Conference of the Asia-Pacific Chapter of the Association for Computational Linguistics and the 12th International Joint Conference on Natural Language Processing. Our workshop received a plethora of submissions, out of which 22 were accepted to be presented in the workshop. We are especially excited about the upcoming special issue in the Journal of Data Mining & Digital Humanities that will feature extended versions of some of the papers accepted in the workshop.

rootroo

https://rootroo.com

Organizing Committee

- Mika Hämäläinen, University of Helsinki and Rootroo Ltd
- Khalid Alnajjar, University of Helsinki and Rootroo Ltd
- Niko Partanen, University of Helsinki
- Jack Rueter, University of Helsinki
- Thierry Poibeau, École normale supérieure and CNRS

Program Committee

- Iana Atanassova, Université de Bourgogne Franche-Comté
- Yuri Bizzoni, Aarhus University
- Miriam Butt, University of Konstanz
- Won Ik Cho, Seoul National University
- Quan Duong, University of Helsinki
- Hugo Gonçalo Oliveira, University of Coimbra
- Kenichi Iwatsuki, ARIKTTA
- Heiki-Jaan Kaalep, University of Tartu
- Enrique Manjavacas, Leiden University
- Matej Martinc, Jozef Stefan Institute
- Flammie Pirinen, UiT The Arctic University of Norway
- Tyler Shoemaker, University of California, Davis
- Liisa Lotta Tarvainen-Li, Acolad
- Jörg Tiedemann, University of Helsinki
- Jouni Tuominen, Aalto University
- Shuo Zhang, Bose Corporation
- Emily Öhman, Waseda University
- Frederik Arnold, Humboldt-Universität zu Berlin
- Nicolas Gutehrlé, Université de Bourgogne Franche-Comté
- Thibault Clérice, Université PSL
- Aynat Rubinstein, The Hebrew University of Jerusalem
- Lama Alqazlan, University of Warwick
- Gechuan Zhang, University College Dublin
- Moshe Stekel, Ariel University
- Alejandro Sierra-Múnera, University of Potsdam
- Avinash Tulasi, IIIT Delhi

Table of Contents

Conference Program

Sunday, November 20, 2022

17:00–17:00 Workshop opening

17:00–18:30 Poster session 1

17:00–18:30 *A Stylometric Analysis of Amadís de Gaula and Sergas de Esplandián*
Yoshifumi Kawasaki

17:00–18:30 *Computational Exploration of the Origin of Mood in Literary Texts*
Emily Öhman and Riikka H. Rossi

17:00–18:30 *Sentiment is all you need to win US Presidential elections*
Sovesh Mohapatra and Somesh Mohapatra

17:00–18:30 *Interactive Analysis and Visualisation of Annotated Collocations in Spanish (AVAnCES)*
Simon Gonzalez

17:00–18:30 *Fractality of sentiment arcs for literary quality assessment: The case of Nobel laureates*
Yuri Bizzoni, Kristoffer Laigaard Nielbo and Mads Rosendahl Thomsen

17:00–18:30 *Style Classification of Rabbinic Literature for Detection of Lost Midrash Tanhuma Material*
Solomon Tannor, Nachum Dershowitz and Moshe Lavee

17:00–18:30 *Use the Metadata, Luke! – An Experimental Joint Metadata Search and N-gram Trend Viewer for Personal Web Archives*
Balázs Indig, Zsófia Sárközi-Lindner and Mihály Nagy

Sunday, November 20, 2022 (continued)

18:30–19:30 Lunch break

19:30–21:00 Poster session 2

19:30–21:00 *MALM: Mixing Augmented Language Modeling for Zero-Shot Machine Translation*
Kshitij Gupta

19:30–21:00 *ParsSimpleQA: The Persian Simple Question Answering Dataset and System over Knowledge Graph*
Hamed Babaei Giglou, Niloufar Beyranvand, Reza Moradi, Amir Mohammad Salehoof and Saeed Bibak

19:30–21:00 *Enhancing Digital History – Event discovery via Topic Modeling and Change Detection*
King Ip Lin and Sabrina Peng

19:30–21:00 *A Parallel Corpus and Dictionary for Amis-Mandarin Translation*
Francis Zheng, Edison Marrese-Taylor and Yutaka Matsuko

19:30–21:00 *Machines in the media: semantic change in the lexicon of mechanization in 19th-century British newspapers*
Nilo Pedrazzini and Barbara McGillivray

19:30–21:00 *Optimizing the weighted sequence alignment algorithm for large-scale text similarity computation*
Maciej Janicki

19:30–21:00 *Domain-specific Evaluation of Word Embeddings for Philosophical Text using Direct Intrinsic Evaluation*
Goya van Boven and Jelke Bloem

Sunday, November 20, 2022 (continued)

21:00–21:30 Coffee break

21:30–23:00 Poster session 3

21:30–23:00 *Towards Bootstrapping a Chatbot on Industrial Heritage through Term and Relation Extraction*
Mihael Arcan, Rory O'Halloran, Cécile Robin and Paul Buitelaar

21:30–23:00 *Non-Parametric Word Sense Disambiguation for Historical Languages*
Enrique Manjavacas Arevalo and Lauren Fonteyn

21:30–23:00 *Introducing a Large Corpus of Tokenized Classical Chinese Poems of Tang and Song Dynasties*
Chao-Lin Liu, Ti-Yong Zheng, Kuan-Chun Chen and Meng-Han Chung

21:30–23:00 *Creative Text-to-Image Generation: Suggestions for a Benchmark*
Irene Russo

21:30–23:00 *The predictability of literary translation*
Andrew Piper and Matt Erlin

21:30–23:00 *Emotion Conditioned Creative Dialog Generation*
Khalid Alnajjar and Mika Hämäläinen

21:30–23:00 *Integration of Named Entity Recognition and Sentence Segmentation on Ancient Chinese based on Siku-BERT*
Sijia Ge

21:30–23:00 *(Re-)Digitizing Ngôo Siú-lé's Mandarin – Taiwanese Dictionary*
Pierre Magistry and Afala Phaxay

A Stylometric Analysis of *Amadís de Gaula* and *Sergas de Esplandián*

Yoshifumi Kawasaki
The University of Tokyo
ykawasaki@g.ecc.u-tokyo.ac.jp

Abstract

Amadís de Gaula (AG) and its sequel *Sergas de Esplandián* (SE) are masterpieces of medieval Spanish chivalric romances. Much debate has been devoted to the role played by their purported author Garci Rodríguez de Montalvo. According to the prologue of AG, which consists of four books, the author allegedly revised the first three books that were in circulation at that time and added the fourth book and SE. However, the extent to which Montalvo edited the materials at hand to compose the extant works has yet to be explored extensively. To address this question, we applied stylometric techniques for the first time. Specifically, we investigated the stylistic differences (if any) between the first three books of AG and his own extensions. Literary style is represented as usage of parts-of-speech n-grams. We performed principal component analysis and k-means to demonstrate that Montalvo's retouching on the first book was minimal, while revising the second and third books in such a way that they came to moderately resemble his authentic creation, that is, the fourth book and SE. Our findings empirically corroborate suppositions formulated from philological viewpoints.

1 Introduction

Amadís de Gaula (AG), which is a medieval Spanish chivalric romance published at the beginning of the sixteenth century, has long been considered a masterpiece of the genre. Its sequel *Sergas de Esplandián* (SE) came out a few years after. Both works have been attributed to Garci Rodríguez de Montalvo, a lower-class aristocrat from Medina del Campo in the present-day Valladolid prefecture. Note that no other work has been ascribed to him.

AG consists of four books. Together with its sequel SE, there are a total of five books in the series, even though the latter was published separately. According to the prologue of AG, the author revised the first three books that were in circulation at that time, and *translated* the fourth book and SE from a Greek manuscript he had encountered. In reality, however, they are both considered his own creation; feigning a *translation* was a literary commonplace back then. Still, the extent to which the author modified the materials at hand to compose the extant version has yet to be extensively explored.

To delve into the enigmatic composition of Montalvo's works, we applied stylometric analysis for the first time, to the best of our knowledge. Stylometry is a field of study that, among other goals, aims to identify authorship of disputed or anonymous documents (Juola, 2006; Grieve, 2007; Zhao and Zobel, 2007; Stamatatos, 2009; Jockers and Witten, 2010). Specifically, we investigated the stylistic differences (if any) between the first three books of AG and his own extensions, that is, the fourth book of AG and SE. Literary style is represented as usage of parts-of-speech (POS) n-grams. Since the employment of syntactic features is supposed to be fairly unconscious and hardly imitable, POS n-grams, which capture partial syntactic information, can reasonably serve as stylistic fingerprints. We performed principal component analysis (PCA) and k-means to demonstrate that Montalvo's retouching on the first book was minimal, while revising the second and third books in such a way that they came to moderately resemble his original contributions, that is, the fourth book and SE. Our findings empirically corroborate suppositions formulated from philological viewpoints by Cacho Blecua (Rodríguez de Montalvo, 2020a).

The rest of the paper is organized as follows. In Section 2, we review related research. Section 3 describes the methodology utilized. In Section 4, we present experimental results, followed by a discussion in Section 5. Section 6 concludes the study by discussing future research directions.

The 2nd International Workshop on Natural Language Processing for Digital Humanities (NLP4DH), pages 1–7
November 20, 2022.

2 Related Work

Research on the genesis of the Amadisian oeuvre has been conducted by Hispanic philologists including Cacho Blecua (Rodríguez de Montalvo, 2020a,b), Domingo del Campo (1982), and Sainz de la Maza (Rodríguez de Montalvo, 2003). However, few scholars have exhaustively inspected the linguistic usage therein. Labrousse (2021) studied a variation of nominal phrases containing possessives in the first and fourth books of AG and found discrepancies between them. However, the second and third books of AG as well as SE were not included in her scope of study. Moreover, the analysis was restricted to the first 500 occurrences of the construction in question. To gain a more complete picture, a comprehensive scrutiny is needed.

Over the past few years, Spanish Philology has witnessed an increasing number of stylometric studies (Fradejas Rueda, 2016; Rißler-Pipka, 2016; de la Rosa and Suárez, 2016; Rojas Castro, 2017; Cerezo Soler and Calvo Tello, 2019; García-Reidy, 2019; Hernández Lorenzo, 2019). The style markers used have been mostly limited to functional words and frequent words. POS *n*-grams have been rarely adopted even though its effectiveness has been confirmed by various studies addressing literary works in multiple languages including English (Koppel et al., 2002; Clement and Sharp, 2003; Juola, 2006; Hirst and Feiguina, 2007; Eder, 2015; Pokou et al., 2016; Savoy, 2017), French (Kocher and Savoy, 2019), Japanese (Uesaka and Murakami, 2015), and recently in Spanish (Kawasaki, 2021).

The advantages of leveraging POS sequences are multi-fold: (i) their numerous occurrences provide reliable statistics; (ii) they are relatively independent from content; (iii) being out of conscious control of the author, they are supposed to be hardly imitable; and (iv) they partially capture syntactic patterns, which have been shown to be reliable style markers (Baayen et al., 1996).

3 Methods

The digitized texts of AG and SE were retrieved from *Corpus of Hispanic Chivalric Romances*[1]. For AG, we used the version published in Seville in 1539 by the printer Juan Cromberger[2]. For SE, we employed the version published in Rome in 1525 by the printers Jacobo de Junta and Antonio de Salamanca[3]. They were the only digitized texts available, although the first edition of AG goes back to 1508 and SE back to 1510.

AG consists of 133 chapters arranged across four books: AG1, AG2, AG3, and AG4. The token size amounts to 530,000 words. SE is composed of 184 chapters forming a single book. The token size adds up to 190,000 words. Since the chapter length varies considerably from one another, we decided to generate equal-length pieces of 10,000 words from respective books. The prologues and epistolary passages were omitted in advance. Note that book division was maintained for the subsequent analyses, while chapter division was disregarded. As for the final part of a book, where the piece length was below 10,000, it was treated as an independent one if it exceeded 6,000 words; otherwise, it was merged into the penultimate piece. Thus, AG1 resulted in 13 pieces, AG2 in 9, AG3 in 11, AG4 in 16, and SE in 18.

For stylistic features, we leveraged POS *n*-grams. The tags were assigned using a tagger designed for present-day Spanish `spaCy 3.3.1`[4]. The model employed was `es_dep_news_trf`, which is larger and more accurate. We utilized this tagger because there are no publicly available ones designed for Medieval Spanish, in which the Amadisian works are written. Based on the philological expertise, we modified extensively the texts prior to tagging to facilitate correct parsing; specifically, we applied as much orthographic modernization as possible. For instance, *auer* "to have" was transformed into its modern counterpart *haber* and certain words were separated, like *acostose* was separated into *acostó se* "he/she lay down".

AUX and PROPN were merged into VERB and NOUN respectively as their correct identification proved to be hardly feasible. For frequent functional words including auxiliary verbs, adverbs, conjunctions, and prepositions, we adopted surface forms in lieu of the assigned tags to make the most of their differing usage, for example, the preposition *de* "of" was not converted into ADP but maintained as such. As for verbs, we distinguished among infinite forms, that is, infinitives (INF), gerunds (GERUND), and past participles (PPART) and gave them distinct labels. In contrast,

[1] https://textred.spanport.lss.wisc.edu/chivalric/index.html

[2] https://textred.spanport.lss.wisc.edu/chivalric/textsoriginal/ama-text.txt

[3] https://textred.spanport.lss.wisc.edu/chivalric/textsoriginal/ag5-text.txt

[4] https://spacy.io/

the finite forms were uniformly given an identical label regardless of mode, tense, grammatical person, and number. In addition, we differentiated highly frequent verbs *haber* "to have" and *ser* "to be" by tagging the relevant forms with their infinitival forms. As for punctuation, we only retained periods and question marks representing sentence boundaries and omitted commas, colons, and semicolons that could stem from editorial interventions. These measures resulted in 54 tag types in total. Tagging performance was evaluated by computing an accuracy rate on randomly chosen five hundred-word passages: one from each of the four books of AG and another from SE. The mean accuracy was almost perfect at 0.99 ± 0.01. Note that, without manual modification of the texts and tags, the mean accuracy declined to 0.83 ± 0.02.

Every piece was represented as a vector whose elements represent z-transformed relative frequencies of the n-grams. We considered only the most frequent POS n-grams above a given rank threshold, while the remainder was aggregated under the label of OTHERS. To assess the robustness of our analyses, we varied the n-gram size n for $n \in \{1, 2, 3, 4\}$ and the rank threshold r for $r \in \{100, 300, 500\}$. For $n = 1$, r was fixed to 54, which was the number of unigram types.

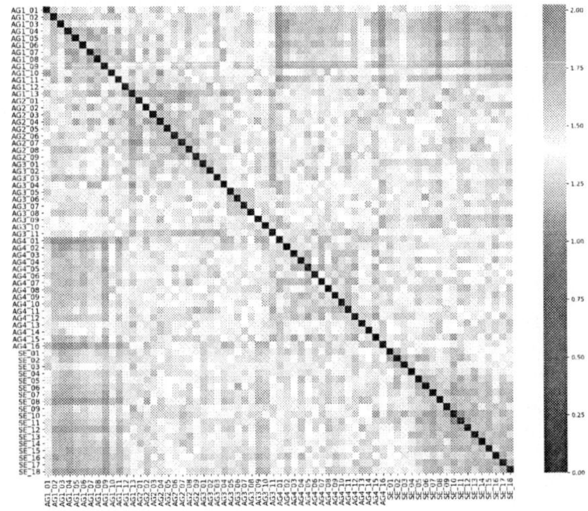

Figure 1: Pair-wise distance scores between the pieces computed with $(n, r) = (3, 300)$. The bluer (redder) the cell, the more (less) similar the pair of pieces.

4 Analysis

For illustrative purposes, we present the results obtained with $(n, r) = (3, 300)$. Figure 1 displays the pair-wise distance scores between the pieces, computed as $\sqrt{\frac{\|\boldsymbol{x}_i - \boldsymbol{x}_j\|^2}{r}}$, where $\boldsymbol{x}_i$ represents the feature vector for the i-th piece. The bluer (redder) the cell, the more (less) similar the pair of pieces. Overall, we observe lower *intra*-book distance scores in contrast to larger *inter*-book ones. However, it is worth noting that the distance scores between AG2 and AG3 are relatively low and that these two books exhibit less dissimilarity with AG4 and SE.

Next, we conducted two types of exploratory multivariate analyses, PCA and k-means, to examine whether any stylistic difference was found across the books.

4.1 PCA

The first two PC scores obtained with $(n, r) = (3, 300)$ are plotted in Figure 2. Contribution ratios for PC1 and PC2 were 16.9% and 8.3%, respectively. PC1 can be reasonably interpreted as a representation of Montalvo's degree of contribution; on the left side are AG4 and SE, which are assumed to be his original creations, on the right side is AG1, which presumably best conserves the primitive appearance, and in between are AG2 and AG3, which were allegedly modified to some degree (Rodríguez de Montalvo, 2020a). PC2, which roughly dissociates AG4 and SE, can be regarded as reflecting Montalvo's internal stylistic variation. That the rest of books are found in between might be ascribed to their different origin, thereby remaining immune to Montalvo's literary style.

4.2 *k*-means

We conducted k-means clustering using `sklearn.cluster.KMeans` with default setting (Pedregosa et al., 2011)[5]. The number of clusters k was varied for $k \in \{2, 3, 4, 5\}$. As the algorithm was sensitive to the initial centroids selected, we ran it 100 times and computed the mean concordance rate, which was defined as the average number of times a pair of pieces was classified into the same cluster. We supposed that no clear-cut pattern would emerge without stylistic differences across the books.

Figure 3 illustrates the pair-wise mean concordance rates obtained with $(k, n, r) = (2, 3, 300)$. The darker the cell, the more often the pair of pieces belonged to the same cluster and are judged as similar. We can discern two clusters, one formed by

[5] `https://scikit-learn.org/stable/modules/generated/sklearn.cluster.KMeans.html`

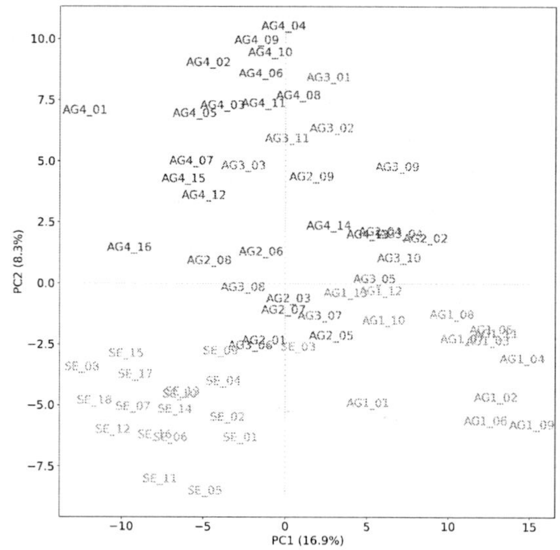

Figure 2: Scatter plot of PC1 and PC2 calculated with $(n, r) = (3, 300)$. PC1 can be understood as a representation of Montalvo's degree of contribution, whereas PC2 can be understood as reflecting his internal stylistic variation.

AG1 only and the other by Montalvo's genuine writings, AG4 and SE. Meanwhile, AG2 and AG3 vacillated between the two clusters, which implies Montalvo's more extensive revisions there compared to AG1, which he might have retouched minimally. Our findings empirically corroborate suppositions formulated by Cacho Blecua (Rodríguez de Montalvo, 2020a).

5 Discussion

5.1 Sensitivity analysis of hyper-parameters

We examined the effects of the hyper-parameters and confirmed that the results were scarcely affected by n or r, which verifies the robustness of our findings. With respect to k-means, it is noteworthy that, even for $k = 5$, equal to the number of books, AG2 and AG3 jointly constituted a cluster instead of forming distinct individual groups, whereas AG1, AG4, and SE formed an individual one as shown in Figure 4. This result suggests that Montalvo accommodated AG2 and AG3 to his own literary style, to the point that they diverged from AG1, which seems almost intact.

5.2 Characteristic POS n-grams

We inspected n-grams whose frequency scores varied notably across the books and thus played a crucial role in the multivariate analyses. Figure 5 shows the trigrams among the top 300 for which the mean z-transformed relative frequency scores were above 1.0 or below -1.0 for any of the five books. Some of the sequences deserve special mention from the philological viewpoint:

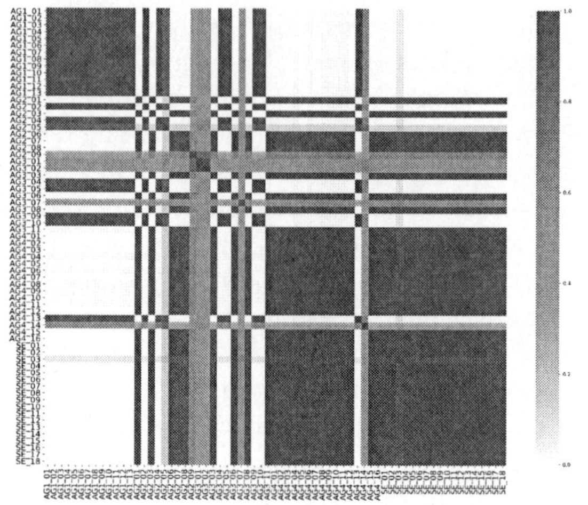

Figure 3: Pair-wise mean concordance rates computed from 100 iterations of k-means performed with $(k, n, r) = (2, 3, 300)$. The darker the cell, the more similar the pair of pieces.

CCONJ_VERB_PRON This trigram typically represents postposition of the pronoun to the finite verb (e.g., *y abrió lo* "and he/she opened it"). Its ratio was 0.63% in AG1, 0.44% in AG2, 0.52% in AG3, 0.32% in AG4, and 0.20% in SE. In his genuine creation, Montalvo apparently abstained from this syntactic pattern used recurrently in the first three books.

PRON_haber_PPART This trigram entails the use of the perfect tense (e.g., *lo he hecho* "I have done it"). Its ratio was 0.09% in AG1, 0.15% in AG2, 0.15% in AG3, 0.24% in AG4, and 0.16% in SE. We can see that Montalvo more frequently employed the perfect tense in his own works.

PUNCT_ADV_VERB This trigram represents the sentence beginning with an adverb followed by a finite verb (e.g., *Entonces dijeron* "Then they said"). Its ratio was 0.10% in AG1, 0.07% in AG2, 0.04% in AG3, 0.05% in AG4, and 0.05% in SE. This pattern was adopted more often in the first two books.

VERB_CCONJ_VERB This trigram typically represents two verbs joined with a coordinate conjunction (e.g., *cenaron y durmieron* "they had dinner and slept"). Its ratio was 0.36% in AG1, 0.28% in AG2, 0.32% in AG3, 0.29% in AG4, and 0.19%

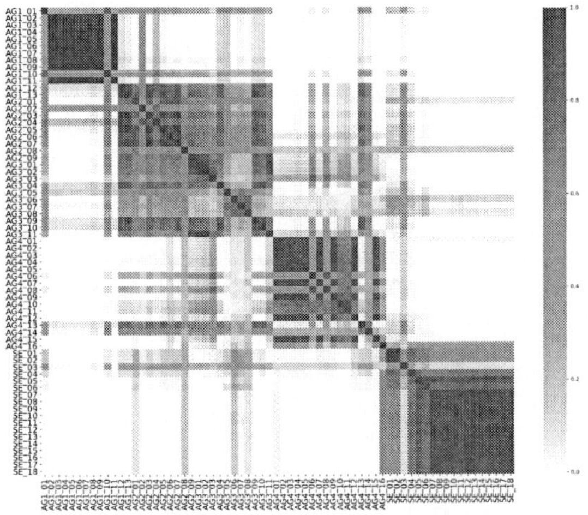

Figure 4: Pair-wise mean concordance rates computed from 100 iterations of k-means performed with $(k, n, r) = (5, 3, 300)$. The darker the cell, the more similar the pair of pieces.

in SE. This syntagma might have been more frequently employed in the older versions of AG to which Montalvo had access.

VERB_PUNCT_NOUN This trigram represents closing a sentence with verb and opening the following one with (proper) noun. Its ratio was 0.25% in AG1, 0.15% in AG2, 0.14% in AG3, 0.14% in AG4, and 0.11% in SE. Montalvo seems to have avoided disposing verbs at sentence-final position.

grande_NOUN_que This trigram represents the noun preceded by adjective *grande* "great" and followed by relative pronoun *que* (e.g., *gran fatiga que* "great fatigue that"). Its ratio was 0.06% in AG1, 0.11% in AG2, 0.10% in AG3, 0.15% in AG4, and 0.14% in SE. Montalvo tended to utilize the syntagma more frequently in his own creation.

muy_ADJ_NOUN This trigram represents the nominal phrase of the type *muy leal caballero* "very loyal knight." Its ratio was 0.04% in AG1, 0.05% in AG2, 0.06% in AG3, 0.06% in AG4, and 0.13% in SE. This construction is found prominently in SE.

6 Conclusions

This study addressed a long-standing enigma concerning the genesis of the two monumental works authored by Montalvo. Applying stylometric techniques, we demonstrated that Montalvo's retouching on AG1 was minimal, while revising AG2 and AG3 to such an extent that they came to moderately resemble his authentic creations, AG4 and SE. Our findings empirically corroborate suppositions formulated from philological viewpoints by Cacho Blecua (Rodríguez de Montalvo, 2020a).

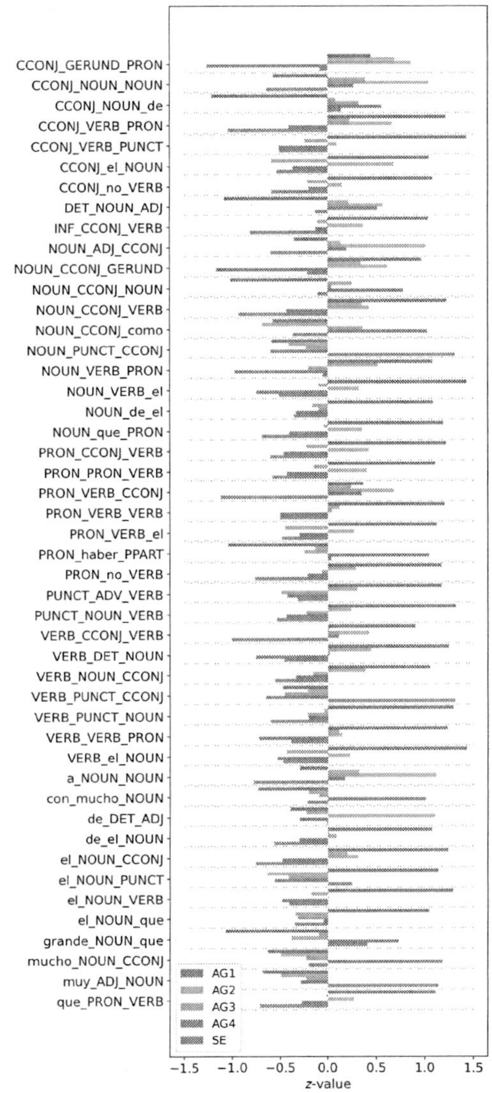

Figure 5: Trigrams among the top 300 for which the mean z-transformed relative frequency scores were above 1.0 or below -1.0 for any of the five books.

One limitation of our study is the lack of distinction between narration and conversation. The distinction is desirable, because varying proportions of the two components across the books could potentially affect the study's outcome. In so doing, we can also examine if authorial fingerprints are more clearly detectable in one part than in the other.

Acknowledgments

This work was supported by JSPS KAKENHI Grant Number JP18K12361.

References

Harald Baayen, Hans van Halteren, and Fiona Tweedie. 1996. Outside the Cave of Shadows: Using Syntactic Annotation to Enhance Authorship Attribution. *Literary and Linguistic Computing*, 11(3):121–132.

Juan Cerezo Soler and José Calvo Tello. 2019. Autoría y estilo. Una atribución cervantina desde las humanidades digitales. El caso de *La conquista de Jerusalén*. *Anales Cervantinos*, 51:231–250.

Ross Clement and David Sharp. 2003. Ngram and Bayesian Classification of Documents for Topic and Authorship. *Literary and Linguistic Computing*, 18(4):423–447.

Francisca Domingo del Campo. 1982. *El lenguaje en el* Amadís de Gaula. Tesis doctoral, Universidad Complutense de Madrid, Madrid.

Maciej Eder. 2015. Does Size Matter? Authorship Attribution, Small Samples, Big Problem. *Digital Scholarship in the Humanities*, 30(2):167–182.

José Manuel Fradejas Rueda. 2016. El análisis estilométrico aplicado a la literatura española: Las novelas policiacas e históricas. *Caracteres. Estudios culturales y críticos de la esfera digital*, 5(2):196–245.

Alejandro García-Reidy. 2019. Deconstructing the Authorship of *Siempre ayuda la verdad*: A Play by Lope de Vega? *Neophilologus*, 103:493–510.

Jack Grieve. 2007. Quantitative Authorship Attribution: An Evaluation of Techniques. *Literary and Linguistic Computing*, 22(3):251–270.

Laura Hernández Lorenzo. 2019. Fernando de Herrera y la autoría de Versos: Un primer acercamiento al drama textual desde la Estilometría. *Romanische Studien*, 6:75–90.

Graeme Hirst and Ol'ga Feiguina. 2007. Bigrams of Syntactic Labels for Authorship Discrimination of Short Texts. *Literary and Linguistic Computing*, 22(4):405–417.

Matthew L. Jockers and Daniela M. Witten. 2010. A Comparative Study of Machine Learning Methods for Authorship Attribution. *Literary and Linguistic Computing*, 25(2):215–223.

Patrick Juola. 2006. Authorship Attribution. *Foundations and Trends in Information Retrieval*, 1(3):233–334.

Yoshifumi Kawasaki. 2021. Stylometric Analysis of Avellaneda's *Don Quijote*. In *12th International Conference on Corpus Linguistics*, Universidad de Murcia (Online). Spanish Association for Corpus Linguistics.

Mirco Kocher and Jacques Savoy. 2019. Evaluation of Text Representation Schemes and Distance Measures for Authorship Linking. *Digital Scholarship in the Humanities*, 34(1):189–207.

Moshe Koppel, Shlomo Argamon, and Anat Rachel Shimoni. 2002. Automatically Categorizing Written Texts by Author Gender. *Literary and Linguistic Computing*, 17(4):401–412.

Mallorie Labrousse. 2021. Los sistemas de los posesivos en el *Amadís de Gaula*, reflejo de un cambio lingüístico. *Revista de Historia de la Lengua Española*, 16:35–66.

Fabian Pedregosa, Gael Varoquaux, Alexandre Gramfort, Vincent Michel, Bertrand Thirion, Olivier Grisel, Mathieu Blondel, Peter Prettenhofer, Ron Weiss, Vincent Dubourg, Jake Vanderplas, Alexandre Passos, David Cournapeau, Matthieu Brucher, Matthieu Perrot, and Édouard Duchesnay. 2011. Scikit-learn: Machine learning in Python. *Journal of Machine Learning Research*, 12:2825–2830.

Yao Jean Marc Pokou, Philippe Fournier-Viger, and Chadia Moghrabi. 2016. Authorship Attribution Using Variable Length Part-of-Speech Patterns. In *Proceedings of the 8th International Conference on Agents and Artificial Intelligence*, volume 2, pages 354–361.

Nanette Rißler-Pipka. 2016. Avellaneda y los problemas de la identificación del autor: Propuestas para una investigación con nuevas herramientas digitales. In *El otro Don Quijote. La continuación de Fernández de Avellaneda y sus efectos*, pages 27–51, Augsburgo. Institut für Spanien-, Portugal- und Lateinamerikastudien.

Garci Rodríguez de Montalvo. 2003. *Sergas de Esplandián*. Editorial Castalia, Madrid.

Garci Rodríguez de Montalvo. 2020a. *Amadís de Gaula I*, 12th edition. Cátedra, Madrid.

Garci Rodríguez de Montalvo. 2020b. *Amadís de Gaula II*, 12th edition. Cátedra, Madrid.

Antonio Rojas Castro. 2017. Luis de Góngora y la fábula mitológica del Siglo de Oro: clasificación de textos y análisis léxico con métodos informáticos. *Studia Aurea*, 11:111–142.

Javier de la Rosa and Juan Luis Suárez. 2016. The Life of *Lazarillo de Tormes* and of His Machine Learning Adversities. *Lemir*, 20:373–438.

Jacques Savoy. 2017. Analysis of the Style and the Rhetoric of the American Presidents over Two Centuries. *Glottometrics*, 38:55–76.

Efstathios Stamatatos. 2009. A Survey of Modern Authorship Attribution Methods. *Journal of the American Society for Information Science and Technology*, 60(3):538–556.

Ayaka Uesaka and Masakatsu Murakami. 2015. Verifying the authorship of Saikaku Ihara's work in early modern Japanese literature; A quantitative approach. *Digital Scholarship in the Humanities*, 30(4):599–607.

Ying Zhao and Justin Zobel. 2007. Searching With Style: Authorship Attribution in Classic Literature. In *Proceedings of the Thirtieth Australasian Computer Science Conference*, volume 62 of *CRPIT*, pages 59–68, Ballarat. Australian Computer Society.

Computational Exploration of the Origin of Mood in Literary Texts

Emily Öhman
Waseda University
ohman@waseda.jp

Riikka Rossi
University of Helsinki
riikka.rossi@helsinki.fi

Abstract

This paper is a methodological exploration of the origin of mood in early modern and modern Finnish literary texts using computational methods. We discuss the pre-processing steps as well as the various natural language processing tools used to try to pinpoint where mood can be best detected in text. We also share several tools and resources developed during this process. Our early attempts suggest that overall mood can be computationally detected in the first three paragraphs of a book.

1 Introduction

This paper aims to provide a short exploratory study into a very specific literary concept: *mood*. *Mood* is the general atmosphere that the author creates through their word choices, style and use of imagery and can sometimes even include *tone*. *Mood* is about how the reader feels about the text, and the related concept of *tone* is about how the implied author feels about it and uses words to convey their attitude towards a topic or subject[1] (Turco, 2020).

We use various natural language processing (NLP) tools and methods to attempt to identify the origins and location of mood. For this purpose we have collected a corpus of 975 literary works written in Finnish. Our paper utilizes many tried and tested NLP and computational literary studies methods, but to our knowledge it is the first to combine emotion detection / sentiment analysis with traditional literary affect studies exploring tone and mood.

Since the choice of words is of the utmost importance when creating both of these sometimes entangled concepts in literary works, mood, and to some extent tone, detection are perfect subjects for analyzing the use of emotion-associated words in text. It is not easy to determine where specifically mood is created in a text. Does mood reside everywhere, or is it most strongly present in the first chapter of books, or perhaps the first few paragraphs of each chapter? In a larger sense *mood* is not reducible to a single aspect, but generated by a set of textual elements.

We suggest that the computational study of the valence of the lexicon can be valuable in providing an accurate picture on the distribution of the positive and negative valence in a text-continuum, and thus help us to better understand the relationship between the linguistic qualities of a text and its perceived emotional effects, particularly the mood of a text.

2 Previous Work

Literature can be considered a domain where the affective functions of language are of principal importance (Hogan, 2011). Research on literature and emotions is an active field in traditional literary studies, particularly after the "affective turn"; a shift in attitude towards how affect is perceived in literary theory that took place about two decades ago (see e.g Smith, 2011 and Armstrong, 2014). Research topics range from the study of literature and empathy (Keen, 2007) to the study of literature and cognition (Hogan, 2011)), negative affects and tone in texts (Ngai, 2005) to empirical perspectives (Sklar, 2013; Van Lissa et al., 2018), and even emotions specific to Finnish literature (Rossi, 2020; Rossi and Lyytikäinen, 2022).

Recently, the question of a text's overall emotional tone or mood has aroused vivid interest (e.g. Ngai (2005), Lyytikäinen (2017), and Rossi (2020)). Yet a systematic theory of how tone and mood are created and triggered is still under construction. We suggest that a study of the emotional valence of the lexicon measured quantitatively provides a new approach that can help with understanding the components of a text's mood (Öhman and Rossi, 2021).

The field of computational literary studies (CLS)

[1] On the concepts of tone and mood in literary studies, see Richards (1929); Ngai (2005); Flatley (2008).

The 2nd International Workshop on Natural Language Processing for Digital Humanities (NLP4DH), pages 8–14
November 20, 2022.

can generally be considered a field within digital humanities that uses NLP tools to analyze and make new discoveries in texts by quantitative means. It is somewhat rare for studies within the field of CLS to have literary experts working on the project, and many such projects rely heavily on the analysis of the quantitative results also conducted by experts of NLP rather than experts of literature as is true for many other interdisciplinary fields (Bartlett et al., 2018). Kim and Klinger (2018) provide a substantive overview of sentiment analysis as it is used in CLS. Very few, if any, of the different types of such studies discussed in their survey deal with topics that are common in traditional literary analysis. We hope to rectify this situation by bringing CLS and affect studies in literature closer together and this paper will hopefully be a small part of that process.

3 Data

We downloaded the first 1000 books from Project Gutenberg[2], where (1) the language was Finnish, and (2) the text was in utf-8 plain text format. As far as we are aware, there is no way of filtering out texts by their original language, so our dataset includes many translated works. We used the simple gutenberg-cleaner[3] to get rid of the preamble and the legal text at the end of the book, then we created a regex to extract key information such as the title, the name of the author, the year of publication, and whether the book was originally written in Finnish. The translation status of the book was extracted based on whether the terms *suomentaja*, *suomennettu*, *suomentanut*, or any version of *kääntäjä/käännös/käännetty* etc. were present within the first ten lines of text after the preamble was removed.

Due to encoding issues, our final corpus consists of 975 books of which roughly half were originally written in Finnish. A vast majority (95+%) were written or translated between the years 1850 and 1925 and over 90% after 1880, with only a few instances of older texts meaning that the language used in the texts can be considered Modern Finnish (Forsman Svensson, 2011). The final data consists of 2,938,032 sentences and 41,417,116 tokens.

[2]`https://www.gutenberg.org/`

[3]`https://libraries.io/pypi/gutenberg-cleaner`

3.1 The Emotion Intensity Lexicon

We used the Finnish Emotion Intensity Lexicon (FEIL) (Öhman, 2022) as a base for our emotion lexicon. FEIL is based on the NRC emotion lexicons (Mohammad and Turney, 2013) adapted for Finnish and lists words alongside the emotions they are associated with as well as the intensity of the associated emotion as a number between 0 and 1. It is roughly based on Plutchik's wheel of emotions (Plutchik, 1980) and contains the emotions *anger, anticipation, disgust, fear, joy, sadness*, and *trust*.

4 Method

Finnish is a great language to work with in terms of NLP. Numerous resources not only exist but are also well-curated. There are several researchers and research groups who actively develop new tools and improve upon old ones, and most of these tools are open source (Hämäläinen and Alnajjar, 2021). Thus we had the opportunity to test several different lemmatizers and tokenizers. We further add to this list of tools by having created a Finnish version of the chapterize[4] package.

After the Project Gutenberg added information was removed, the texts were lemmatized, split into paragraphs, and tokenized. First, we tried fine-tuning Finnish BERT (Virtanen et al., 2019) to work with our texts (as per Gururangan et al., 2022), but the results were not promising and require further work (particuarly the vocabulary was not improved sufficiently). We subsequently tried multiple different lemmatization tools, including the Turku Neural Parser (Kanerva et al., 2019), murre (Partanen et al., 2019; Hämäläinen et al., 2021), and both the *experimental* and *news* Finnish spaCy models. In the end we settled for the Turku Neural Parser as the results were the most accurate (see table 1 for an example) and all words were parsed, and parsed correctly in context as well (in the example it was the only one able to correctly parse the nonstandard form *kahvians* – standard form: *kahviansa* – partitive case of 3rd. pers. sing./plur. coffee).

Incidentally, in the dissertation of Airio (2009) *kahviansa* is discussed as an example of "parasite words" since it can be mistakenly split into *kahvi* (coffee) and *ansa* (trap), something none of the lemmatizers did. With careful optimism, we take this

[4]The original: `https://pypi.org/project/chapterize/` and the Finnish version: `https://github.com/esohman/chapterize-fi`

as a demonstration of how good lemmatizers for morphologically complex languages have become in the past decade.

After pre-processing the texts, we identified the first three paragraphs of each book. This was trickier than expected as despite removing the preambles/headers, some metadata remains in the text files and this metadata is of various shapes without uniformity or even commonly recurring pattern of where the actual text of the book starts. For this reason, we created a Finnish version of the chapterize package for Python and used the chapter splits to help recognize opening paragraphs together with sentence and paragraph ids provided by the conllu metadata.We used two different text sections as targets for overall mood detection: the first three paragraphs of each book, and the first 200 tokens from each chapter in each book.

From previous studies (Öhman and Rossi, 2021) we know that certain words can quickly overwhelm the results; when analyzing the novel *Rautatie* by *Juhani Aho*, the term *rautatie* (railroad) in the lexicon was associated with *trust* and because the store takes place on the railroad and is about the railroad the levels of *trust* in the results were not representative of the level of *trust* in the novel itself. As FEIL contains mostly contemporary words and their contemporary emotion associations we needed to make sure that (1) the most common words in our texts that in our opinion have an emotion association are indeed in the lexicon, and (2) that the most common emotion word matches represent the correct emotions at reasonable intensities. These steps are iterative and continuous in that they should be repeated whenever the lexicon or lemmatization is altered.

The removal of non-emotion associated words is straightforward and fairly uncontroversial. However, re-labeling emotion words or adding new words to the lexicon should be done with utmost care, ideally using multiple annotators who are not the authors and cross-checking the results using inter-annotator agreement scores (van Atteveldt et al., 2021). In this vein, we did not want to bias the lexicon with our own interpretations of emotion intensities so instead we created a large word2vec model of our corpus and used it to look up words in the lexicon with high cosine similarity to the words we wanted to introduce to the lexicon (as per e.g. Maas et al., 2011; Yu et al., 2017; Ye et al., 2018). This lead to the association for e.g. the words *kirkas, valkoinen, and valkea* to be identical. As the words that needed to be added were relatively few, we manually checked that the emotion associations and intensities made sense. For future projects we intend to employ human annotators in addition to this approach, however, this approach alone showed a lot of promise and was very accurate within the small sample size.

After completing steps (1) and (2), we removed 128 entries from the lexicon and added 203 tokens including *rakastaa*, to love. The exclusion of such an important term from the lexicon exemplifies some of the issues with using a lexicon that was originally created for English where the noun and verb forms are often the same unlike in Finnish where the forms are distinct (cf. to love/ a love, to run/a run vs. rakastaa/rakkaus, juosta/juoksu). Some of these issues were fixed in FEIL by adding both the Finnish noun and verb forms of a single English entry, but many such examples remain (Öhman, 2022). We used this domain- and period-specific version of FEIL to tabulate normalized (per token count for inter-text comparability), intensity scores for each target text. Other future projects should include checking that both noun and verb forms are found in the lexicon.

If we are looking at purely the word choices of the author, tone and mood can be difficult to distinguish from each other and can be intertwined to different degrees. However, the tone of a literary text tends to shift much more even within a chapter and therefore by focusing on the first paragraphs of each chapter, or even the opening paragraphs of the first chapter only, we can get a fairly accurate idea of the mood of the text, with less of a risk of it being confused with tone.

Although the tone of the text may vary within one work (due to e.g. changes in the narrative point of view or mover from description to dialogue narration) the analysis of the beginnings of a text may be indicative of the overall tone of a text. Namely from the perspective of the reader, the beginnings tend to shape the experience of reading. Theories of perception (e.g. Perry 1979) argue that the openings play a crucial role in creating a text's overall emotional disposition: as in everyday life, the first impression matters in reading, too. The emotion effects created in the beginning of a text modify and adjust the reader's general emotional orientation by shaping up modes of perception and organization of information. For instance, the melancholic

<table>
<tr><td>Translation</td><td>The provost sits down in his rocking chair, stands his pipe on the floor against the table leg, and starts drinking his coffee</td></tr>
<tr><td>Original</td><td>Rovasti istuutuu keinutuoliinsa, panee piippunsa lattialle pöydän jalkaa vasten pystyyn ja rupeaa juomaan kahvians</td></tr>
<tr><td>Murre (hist)</td><td>(öljy)movasti istua keinutuoli panna pippu latija pöytä jalka vaste pystyä ja ruveta juoma kahvis</td></tr>
<tr><td>spaCy (news_lg)</td><td>Rovasti istuutua keinutuoliinsa panee piippu lattia pöytä jalka vasten pystyyn ja rupeata juoda kahvians</td></tr>
<tr><td>spaCy (exp. /w voikko)</td><td>rovasti istuutua keinutuoli panna piippu lattia pöytä jalka vasten pystyyn ja ruveta juoda kahvians</td></tr>
<tr><td>UralicNLP</td><td>Rovasti|rovasti istuutua panna piippu lattia pöytä jalka vasten pystyyn|pysty ja ruveta juoma|juoda</td></tr>
<tr><td>Turku Neural Parser</td><td>rovasti istuutua keinu#tuoli panna piippu lattia pöytä jalka vasten pystyyn ja ruveta juoda kahvi</td></tr>
</table>

Table 1: Example of lemmatization using different lemmatizers for Finnish.

mood created in the beginning of Aho's *Rautatie*, or the strong effects of disgust in the beginning of Sillanpää's *Hurskas kurjuus*, are likely to influence the reader experiences later reactions and feelings triggered by narrative events.

5 The Mood in Selected Texts

The results are difficult to present in a small space as they list all the emotion scores per text, therefore we are focusing here on qualitatively evaluating a small subset of the data. The selection is pragmatic, and based on the second author's area of expertise.

5.1 An overview of the selected texts

The first one is Juhani Aho's breakthrough novel *Rautatie* (tr. as *The Railroad*, 1884). In this text, from the perspective of the implied reader, the novel evokes emotional effects of melancholia and nostalgia, which are characteristic of Aho's work.

The second one is Minna Canth's *Kauppa-Lopo* (no translation, the title refers to the protagonist's nickname, 1889), a tragic story of poverty and illness. The beginning of the novella, set in prison, underlines the anti-hero's ugly appearance, but the narrative contrasts the physical ugliness with an inner goodness: she is described as good-hearted and compassionate towards other people. Canth's naturalism was considered "poor art" by her contemporaries and she was accused of being an admirer of disgust, "destroying the laws of beauty, unfolding ugliness in every sense" (Rossi, 2007, 52).

The third one is Frans Emil Sillanpää's *Hurskas kurjuus* (tr. as *Meek Heritage*, literally "Sacred Misery", 1919), which begins with a shocking prologue which anticipates the death of the protagonist: it describes the execution of a poor tenant farmer who had ended up as a Red Guard soldier in the Finnish Civil War (1918). Despite the negative emotions and the tragic events the narrator also expresses trust and comfort in the future of the Finnish nation.

The last one is *Putkinotko* (no translation, 1919-20) by Joel Lehtonen. Like Sillanpää's *Sacred Misery*, this novel tracks the tensions that escalated in the Finnish Civil War in 1918. The novel's protagonist, a good-hearted yet self-willed tenant farmer resigns to obey the landlord and instead resorts to illegal distillery to support the family. The novel is emotionally ambivalent: the idyllic descriptions of Finnish summer nature and the comic elements are likely to arouse positive emotions, while the unembellished description of poverty intends to evoke moral anger and sadness for the social inequality.

5.2 Results

The results for the texts are presented in figures 1 and 2.

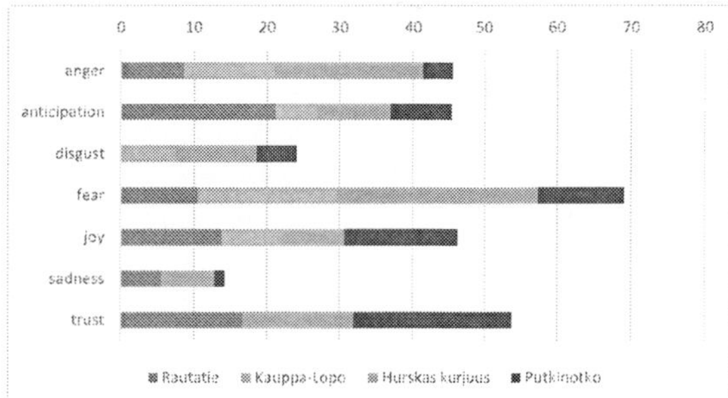

Figure 1: Emotion word distribution in first three paragraphs per 1000 words

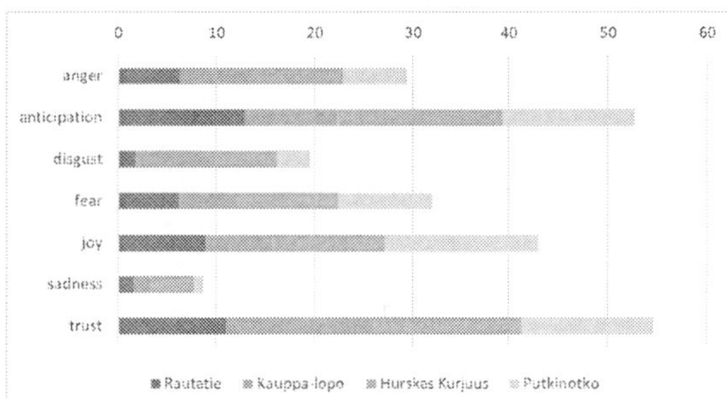

Figure 2: Emotion word distribution in the first 200 tokens of each chapter per 1000 words

From figure 1 it is possible to see some patterns emerge. In particular, the laconism of *Rautatie* is evident when compared to some of the other authors and the strong emotional impact of *Hurskas Kurjuus* becomes very apparent, with *fear* and *anger*, but also *sadness* being particularly notable. *Fear* and to some extent *anger* are also very present in *Kauppa-lopo*, likely due to the described prison environment and appearance of the protagonist. *Trust* and *joy* are the most notable emotions in *Putkinotko*, perhaps due to the detailed descriptions of the idyllic landscape that dominate the opening chapter.

In general, when comparing the two approaches, first paragraph-only vs. opening paragraphs of each chapter, in the latter the positive emotions are much more prevalent. This indicates that the intended opening mood for these novels is built on negative emotions intended to evoke strong feelings in the reader. In the former, the openings of each chapter are more varied.

6 Discussion

We find that the preliminary results correspond well with established interpretations of mood in select texts when comparing to the emotion word distribution of the first three paragraphs of a literary text. Comparing the valency and intensity of emotions in the opening paragraphs of the book and the opening paragraphs of all chapters, we can see that when looking at all chapters, the emotions approach the distribution of emotion in the lexicon, i.e. they become muddled even though there are some idiosyncrasies that can be assumed to be because of the author's style. Furthermore, the differences between the different texts are also evened out in the all-chapters approach. This could also be in part because the focus becomes more varied and therefore the results average out and start to converge on the distribution of emotions in the lexicon. We recommend that the quest for mood should begin with the opening paragraphs of a text.

It is important to note that evoking emotional effects in literature is not restricted to emotion words or to direct descriptions of the character's emotions. All aspects of the narrative, from description of objects to narrative point of view and style, including tropes and even the rhythm of the text are important aspects in triggering emotional effects in the reader. For instance, the melancholic tone of Juhani Aho's text is not generated by themes of separation and loss alone but also by Aho's style, which favors fragmentation and loosening of syntax, with a recurring mannerism of three points "..." , as a sign of hesitation and withdrawal, even evoking a depressive loss of contact.

The qualitative analysis demonstrates that the selected texts depict and trigger negative emotions in particular: feelings of deception, fear, anxiety, disgust and hatred, anger, moral indignation and melancholia. On one hand, this can be explained by genre-specific emotional effects: a critical naturalist novel tends to shock and challenge its reader by representing and inciting strong negative emotions, which confirm the effect of reality of a text and direct the reader's attention to the social defects described. For instance, the emotion of disgust, which is a genre-specific emotion of the naturalist novel, is a named emotion and salient in Sillanpää's and Canth's novels in particular (Rossi, 2007, 2017, 2020).

The salience of negative emotions can be explained by the importance of negative emotions in literature and art in general. As discussed by Menninghaus et al. (2017) negative emotions are an important resource for the arts, since negative emotions have been shown to be particularly powerful in securing attention, intense emotional involvement, and high memorability, and hence is precisely what artworks strive for.

This dataset will be used for more robust detection of tone and mood in Finnish literature. Our preliminary studies show that the "big data" results support qualitative analyses and further justifies the use of purely lexicon-based methods when dealing with larger collections of text where word choice is an important factor of creating affective states in the reader. Specifically, we can see that the choice of emotion associated words in the first three paragraphs correlates highly with established analyses of mood in the selected texts. We hope to add established emotion categories from literary affect studies (see e.g. Hogan 2011) to the lexicon as a measure to further improve the usability of the FEIL lexicon for the literary domain (Öhman, 2020). Additionally, we would like to expand on the methodologies used in this exploratory study and hopefully create more and more robust approaches to tone and mood detection in literature.

Acknowledgements

This work was supported by JSPS KAKENHI Grant Number 22K18154 and the Waseda University Tokutei-kadai Grant 2022C-544.

References

Eija Airio. 2009. *Morphological Problems in IR and CLIR. Applying linguistic methods and approximate string matching tools*. Tampere University Press.

Nancy Armstrong. 2014. The affective turn in contemporary fiction. *Contemporary Literature*, 55(3):441–465.

Andrew Bartlett, Jamie Lewis, Luis Reyes-Galindo, and Neil Stephens. 2018. The locus of legitimate interpretation in Big Data sciences: Lessons for computational social science from-omic biology and high-energy physics. *Big Data & Society*, 5(1):2053951718768831.

Jonathan Flatley. 2008. *Affective mapping: melancholia and the politics of modernism*. Harvard University Press Cambridge, MA.

Pirkko Forsman Svensson. 2011. Virtuaalinen vanha kirjasuomi. *http://www. vvks. info/aanne-_ja_muoto-oppi/heittyminen/.*

Suchin Gururangan, Mike Lewis, Ari Holtzman, Noah Smith, and Luke Zettlemoyer. 2022. DEMix layers: Disentangling domains for modular language modeling. In *Proceedings of the 2022 Conference of the North American Chapter of the Association for Computational Linguistics: Human Language Technologies*, pages 5557–5576, Seattle, United States. Association for Computational Linguistics.

Mika Hämäläinen and Khalid Alnajjar. 2021. The current state of Finnish NLP. In *Proceedings of the Seventh International Workshop on Computational Linguistics of Uralic Languages*, pages 65–72, Syktyvkar, Russia (Online). Association for Computational Linguistics.

Mika Hämäläinen, Niko Partanen, and Khalid Alnajjar. 2021. Lemmatization of historical old literary Finnish texts in modern orthography. In *Actes de la 28e Conférence sur le Traitement Automatique des Langues Naturelles. Volume 1 : conférence principale*, pages 189–198, Lille, France. ATALA.

Patrick Colm Hogan. 2011. *What literature teaches us about emotion*. Cambridge University Press.

Jenna Kanerva, Filip Ginter, and Tapio Salakoski. 2019. Universal Lemmatizer: A Sequence to Sequence Model for Lemmatizing Universal Dependencies Treebanks. *arXiv preprint arXiv:1902.00972*.

Suzanne Keen. 2007. *Empathy and the Novel*. Oxford University Press on Demand.

Evgeny Kim and Roman Klinger. 2018. A survey on sentiment and emotion analysis for computational literary studies. *arXiv preprint arXiv:1808.03137*.

Pirjo Lyytikäinen. 2017. How to Study Emotion Effects in Literature: Written Emotions in Edgar Allan Poe's "The Fall of the House of Usher. In *Writing Emotions: Theoretical Concepts and Selected Case Studies in Literature*, pages 247–64. Bielefeld: Transcript Verlag.

Andrew L. Maas, Raymond E. Daly, Peter T. Pham, Dan Huang, Andrew Y. Ng, and Christopher Potts. 2011. Learning word vectors for sentiment analysis. In *Proceedings of the 49th Annual Meeting of the Association for Computational Linguistics: Human Language Technologies*, pages 142–150, Portland, Oregon, USA. Association for Computational Linguistics.

Winfried Menninghaus, Valentin Wagner, Julian Hanich, Eugen Wassiliwizky, Thomas Jacobsen, and Stefan Koelsch. 2017. The distancing-embracing model of the enjoyment of negative emotions in art reception. *Behavioral and Brain Sciences*, 40.

Saif M. Mohammad and Peter D. Turney. 2013. Crowdsourcing a word-emotion association lexicon. *Computational Intelligence*, 29(3):436–465.

Sianne Ngai. 2005. *Ugly feelings*, volume 6. Harvard University Press Cambridge, MA.

Emily Öhman. 2020. Emotion annotation: Rethinking emotion categorization. In *DHN Post-Proceedings*, pages 134–144.

Emily Öhman. 2022. SELF & FEIL: Emotion Lexicons for Finnish. In *Proceedings of the 6th Digital Humanities in the Nordic and Baltic Countries conference*. CEUR Workshop Proceedings.

Emily Öhman and Riikka Rossi. 2021. Affect and Emotions in Finnish Literature: Combining Qualitative and Quantitative Approaches. In *The Language of Emotions: Building and Applying Computational Methods for Emotion Detection for English and Beyond*.

Niko Partanen, Mika Hämäläinen, and Khalid Alnajjar. 2019. Dialect text normalization to normative standard Finnish. In *Proceedings of the 5th Workshop on Noisy User-generated Text (W-NUT 2019)*, pages 141–146, Hong Kong, China. Association for Computational Linguistics.

Menakhem Perry. 1979. Literary dynamics: how the order of a text creates its meanings [with an analysis of faulkner's" a rose for emily"]. *Poetics today*, 1(1/2):35–361.

Robert Plutchik. 1980. A general psychoevolutionary theory of emotion. *Theories of emotion*, 1:3–31.

I.A. Richards. 1929. *Practical Criticism*, volume 1964. Routledge: London.

Riikka Rossi. 2007. *Le naturalisme finlandais. Une conception entropique du quotidien*. Suomalaisen Kirjallisuuden Seura.

Riikka Rossi. 2017. Writing disgust, writing realities. *Sabine Schönfellner, Gudrun Tockner (eds.) Writing Emotions*, page 277.

Riikka Rossi. 2020. *Alkukantaisuus ja tunteet — Primitivismi 1900-luvun alun suomalaisessa kirjallisuudessa*. Number 1456 in Suomalaisen Kirjallisuuden Seuran toimituksia. Suomalaisen Kirjallisuuden Seura.

Riikka Rossi and Pirjo Lyytikäinen. 2022. Pohjoisia tunteita. *AVAIN-Kirjallisuudentutkimuksen aikakauslehti*, 19(1):3–9.

Howard Sklar. 2013. *The Art of Sympathy in Fiction : Forms of Ethical and Emotional Persuasion*. Linguistic Approaches to Literature. John Benjamins Publishing Company.

Rachel Greenwald Smith. 2011. Postmodernism and the affective turn. *Twentieth Century Literature*, 57(3/4):423–446.

Lewis Turco. 2020. *The book of literary terms: the genres of fiction, drama, nonfiction, literary criticism, and scholarship*. University of New Mexico Press.

Wouter van Atteveldt, Mariken ACG van der Velden, and Mark Boukes. 2021. The validity of sentiment analysis: Comparing manual annotation, crowd-coding, dictionary approaches, and machine learning algorithms. *Communication Methods and Measures*, 15(2):121–140.

Caspar J Van Lissa, Marco Caracciolo, Thom van Duuren, and Bram van Leuveren. 2018. Difficult Empathy-The Effect of Narrative Perspective on Readers' Engagement with a First-Person Narrator.

Antti Virtanen, Jenna Kanerva, Rami Ilo, Jouni Luoma, Juhani Luotolahti, Tapio Salakoski, Filip Ginter, and Sampo Pyysalo. 2019. Multilingual is not enough: BERT for Finnish. *arXiv preprint arXiv:1912.07076*.

Zhe Ye, Fang Li, and Timothy Baldwin. 2018. Encoding sentiment information into word vectors for sentiment analysis. In *Proceedings of the 27th International Conference on Computational Linguistics*, pages 997–1007, Santa Fe, New Mexico, USA. Association for Computational Linguistics.

Liang-Chih Yu, Jin Wang, K Robert Lai, and Xuejie Zhang. 2017. Refining word embeddings using intensity scores for sentiment analysis. *IEEE/ACM Transactions on Audio, Speech, and Language Processing*, 26(3):671–681.

Sentiment is all you need to win US Presidential elections

Sovesh Mohapatra*
University of Massachusetts Amherst
soveshmohapa@umass.edu

Somesh Mohapatra*
Massachusetts Institute of Technology
someshm@mit.edu

Abstract

Election speeches play an integral role in communicating the vision and mission of the candidates. From lofty promises to mud-slinging, the electoral candidate accounts for all. However, there remains an open question about what exactly wins over the voters. In this work, we used state-of-the-art natural language processing methods to study the speeches and sentiments of the Republican candidates and Democratic candidates fighting for the 2020 US Presidential election. Comparing the racial dichotomy of the United States, we analyze what led to the victory and defeat of the different candidates. We believe this work will inform the election campaigning strategy and provide a basis for communicating to diverse crowds.

1 Introduction

In a democracy, elections serve as the people's mandate. They speak for what the people think and who they want to represent their voices. However, the mandate is not without bias and is often swayed by the communication at election rallies, on social media, and at dinner table conversations (Anderson and Tverdova, 2001). Understanding what reinforces people's opinions, or changes them, is a complex question (Johnston, 1992).

Election campaign of a candidate attempts to decode what the people want and focuses the messaging around that (Dupont et al., 2019). The audience strategy is usually based on heuristics like the assumption that voters vote based on their economic interests leads them to change the economy for the better, for instance, by introducing support funds or creating new jobs, especially shortly before an election (Powell Jr and Whitten, 1993; Whitten and Palmer, 1999). These are also being dominated by people who happen to know the intricacies of the ground (McClurg, 2004). With the rise in usage of *post hoc* analysis of strategies, elections have started to become less heuristic-driven and more data-driven (Anstead, 2017). One of the most prominent and mobilizing parts of the elections are the speeches, and the use of language, by the running candidates (Steffens and Haslam, 2013; Ikeanyibe et al., 2018). The sentiments and statements in speeches are often described as an art.

In this paper, we attempted to decode the art of speeches by focusing on the sentiment classification of speeches across various states and demographics, and how their effect on the election results. A survey was also conducted to analyze people's responses to snippets of the speeches.

2 Related Work

In the social sciences field, there have been multiple approaches to analyze the US Presidential election speeches. Populism framing in the speeches has been explored to analyze speeches in a novel database comprising of speeches from 1896 to 2016 in Fahey (2021), and a more recent focus with active metaphors in Keating (2021). Political rhetoric (Bull and Miskinis, 2015; Conway III et al., 2012), deception strategies (Al-Hindawi and Al-Aadili, 2017), and metrical analysis (Ban and Oyabu, 2009), amongst other linguistic approaches have been used to study Presidential elections for different years. However, these approaches do not leverage the significant advances in artificial intelligence to push forth their analyses.

The rise of sentimental analysis and widespread availability of Twitter data have contributed to more computational analysis in the recent years. Several studies analyzed the Twitter responses, tweets by Donald Trump, and their aftermath using NLP tools (Liu, 2017; Yaqub et al., 2017; Caetano et al., 2018; Siegel et al., 2021). Political sentiment anal-

* Authors contributed equally

The 2nd International Workshop on Natural Language Processing for Digital Humanities (NLP4DH), pages 15–20
November 20, 2022.

ysis and the use of sentiment analysis to predict election results has been attempted (Nausheen and Begum, 2018; Elghazaly et al., 2016; Liu and Lei, 2018). Finity et al. (2021) provide a text analysis of the 2020 US election speeches. We believe that the extension of these approaches to more recent emnotion-based approaches, along with human surveys could provide a robust method of understanding the effect that the speeches have.

In 2021, GoEmotions, a database of fine-grained emotions, labeled for 27 emotion categories was released by a team of researchers from Google, Amazon and Stanford Linguistics Department (Demszky et al., 2020). Sequence to emotion models were developed in Huang et al. (2021), visualization of the emotions was done in Dumont and Facen, and these models were applied to text sentiment analysis and essay analysis (Thainguan et al., 2021; Maheshwari and Varma, 2022). More advanced models, such as Emoroberta, have been recently developed (Kamath et al., 2022), and limitations of the text-based emotion detection have also been discussed (Alvarez-Gonzalez et al., 2021).

3 Methodology

3.1 Data Collection and Processing

We have collected the transcripts from 61 election rally speeches that Republican candidate Donald Trump had given in various states between 2018 and 2020. Considering the Democrats, we have collected around 85 rally speeches by Barack Obama, Kamala Harris, and Joe Biden. The transcripts of the speeches were web-scrapped from various online news and transcripts such as `USNews.com` (accessed on May 15, 2022), `CNN.com` (accessed on June 10, 2022), and `Rev.com` (accessed on June 15, 2022).

Each speech was then classified based on the state they were delivered. After which, we labelled the states into two different race categories: Black or White states. The state's label was based on the statistics that in the US, 14.9% identified as Black or African American from `blackdemographics.com` (accessed on July 4, 2022). So, a state with a population of more than 14.9% of people identifying themselves as Black or African Americans is considered a Black state. Later, it was again categorized into four new categories: loss in White (White state where the party has lost the elections), win in White (White state where the party has won the elections), loss in Black (Black state where the party has lost the elections) and win in Black (Black state where the party has won the elections).

Further, we clustered all the classified White state's speeches into one and all the Black state's speeches into the other. Then, we tokenized each sentence and passed it through our fine-tuned BERT model to classify the different sentences into the twenty seven selected emotions.

3.2 Human Survey Collection

Along with the machine categorisation of the sentences in the speeches, we took fifteen sentences representing a mix of nine types of emotions. These fifteen sentences were snippets from the various speeches delivered by candidates of both parties. Out of fifteen snippets, nine snippets didn't have information about the speaker, and the remaining six snippets had information about who is the speaker of the snippet. Out of the six, the last two snippets presented with interchanging the speakers' names. (see Table 1).

The survey was a digital form which had a geographical location question to understand the demographics of the people taking the survey and two questions per snippet: whether the individual would vote for the candidate by just listening to this snippet, and from which party the speaker of the snippet was. We collected 68 responses, with the age of people ranging from 18 to 60. All participants in the survey were randomly selected from a pool of professors, students and staffs from various departments of the university which helped in getting survey takers from various states of the United States. This helped in giving us the idea required for the geographic location specific ideologies that require the local government to govern in a better way.

3.3 Model Training

We used a BERT model, given its ability to provide context-dependent token-level representations from whole sentences (Devlin et al., 2018; Suhr et al., 2018), unlike word-by-word and context-independent GloVebased or Word2Vec embeddings (Miaschi and Dell'Orletta, 2020; Dev et al., 2020).

3.4 Fine-tuning of the Model

The model's downstream performance is essential for activities for specific usages, such as sentimental analysis of human conversations, thereby requiring fine-tuning of generic models for specific actions (Devlin et al., 2018). We fine-tuned the

Table 1: Examples of snippets used in the survey.

Snippets from Speeches	Party	Emotion
As I personally told the Taliban leader if anyone ever double crossed the USA it would be the last thing they ever did	Republican	Negative, Anger, Optimism
I'll never forget what President Kennedy said about going to the moon	Democratic	Positive, Optimism
Would be good to talk to him rather than nuclear war wouldn't it be nice? Anyway through a series of events I did talk to him and it was nasty at the beginning remember	Republican	Positive, Optimism, Gratitude
Think about what it takes to be a Black person who loves America today	Democratic	Positive, Admiration, Love

BERT model using the GoEmotions dataset, a corpus of sentences classified into 27 different emotions (Demszky et al., 2020). Using a transfer learning strategy, the model parameters were updated by training over the GoEmotions labeled corpus for 25 epochs.

4 Results and Discussion

4.1 Republicans and Democrats use similar sentiments, on average

We noted that the top 10 emotions (sentence-wise) used in the speeches in both White and Black states delivered by both parties follow a similar template, which could sometimes create a bias for the public in choosing their candidate (Figures 1A, 1B). This result also demonstrates how both parties attempt to use similar sentiments to attract voters.

4.2 Comparison in Speech wins in Black states, loses in White states for Republicans

The sentences with comparison and sadness emotions played a significant role in the speeches delivered in the Black states that were won by the Republicans (Figure 1C). However, they had to face a loss in the White states with a higher frequency of the same category. This difference shows the different aspirations of the White and Black population. Comparison includes disapproval, approval and confusion; while sadness clusters remorse, grief and disappointment emotions.

4.3 Approval and Desire in Speech win in Black states, lose in White states for Democrats

The sentences based on emotions such as approval and happiness played a significant role in all the speeches delivered in the Black states that were won by the Democrats, in line with the liberal ideology (Figure 1D). In contrast, they had to face a loss in the White states with a higher frequency of the same category, owing to the strong Republican pull. Happiness clusters amusement, excitement and joy, and desire includes gratitude emotions.

4.4 Curiosity and Disapproval leads to loses in both Black and White states for Republicans

The sentences categorized as curiosity and disapproval in speeches led the Republicans to lose in both Black and White states. Interestingly, disapproval sentences are one of the top three kinds of sentences that Republicans used in their speeches (Figure 1E). It is also one of the top negative emotions used by the Republicans. This difference in the results may be attributed to the influence of the Democrats during the election campaigns, and the results coming in from the swing states.

4.5 Anger and Disgust lead to loses in both Black and White states for Democrats

The sentences categorized as anger and disgust in speeches led the Democrats to lose in both the Black and White states. As with the observation in the case of Democrats, anger sentences are one of the top four kinds of sentences used by Democrats. It is also one of the top negative emotions used by the Democrats. This anomaly shows us the expectation of the people from the Democrats not to show negative emotions like anger and disgust towards any matter and instead come up with a solution to dissolve the situation. (Figure 1F).

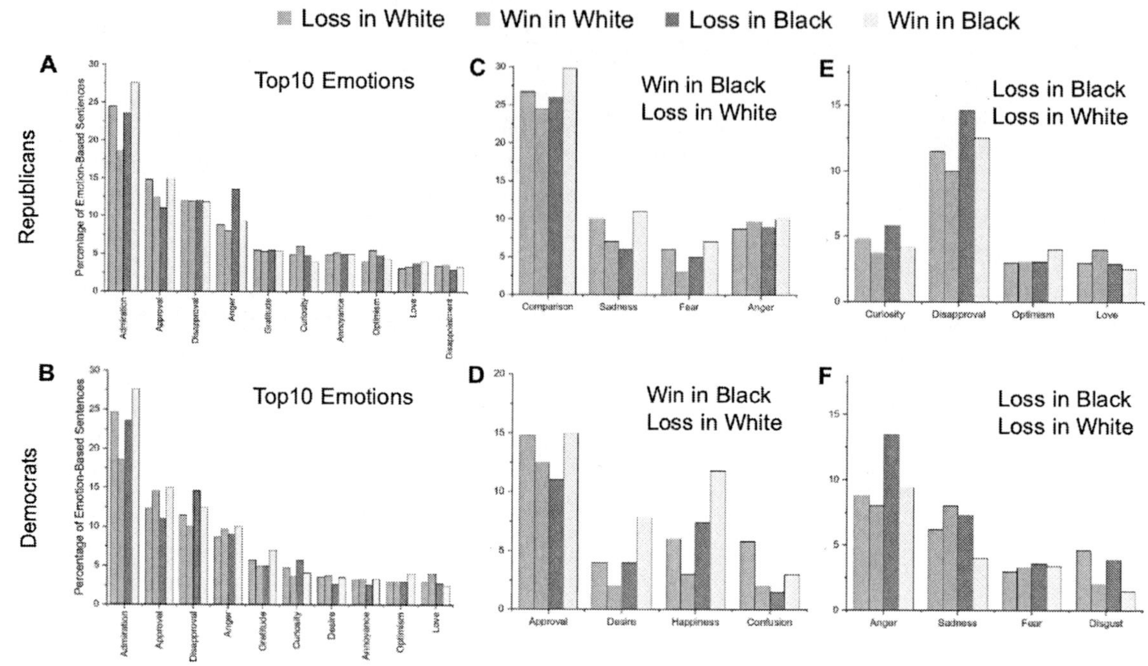

Figure 1: Top 10 Emotions in the Speech by A. Republicans and B. Democrats. Emotions that led to win in Black and loss in White states for C. Republicans and D. Democrats; and loss in both states for E. Republicans and F. Democrats.

4.6 Positivity wins in White states, loses in Black states for Republicans, and vice-versa for Democrats

We observed that when the overall notion of the speech was positive, it favored the Republicans and not the Democrats to win elections in the White states. In contrast, this is reversed when the overall notion of the speech becomes negative. The Republicans won the elections in the Black states, but the Democrats had to face loss (Figure 2). The reversal of notions in the speeches and wins in Black versus White states for Republicans and Democrats highlights their approach to the different demographies, and how it played out in the results.

The positive notion of a speech was calculated by clustering the frequencies of the positive emotions: gratitude, optimism, love, excitement, caring, joy, and amusement. Similarly, the negative notion of the speech was calculated by clustering the frequencies of negative emotions: annoyance, disappointment, anger, fear, sadness, disgust, and embarrassment.

4.7 Survey Findings

Along with observing various sentiments swaying the results of an election, we found that the sentiments are not the only factor behind deciding the influence of the speech. From the survey, we found the emotions like desire and happiness categorized sentences when given to the people by indicating to them that the snippet is from the Democrats, then the individual's choice to vote increased. In contrast, when a similar emotion-based snippet was given by blinding the information about the candidate, the individual opinion to vote varied. Similar results were observed when the emotion of curiosity-based snippets were provided that led the individual's choice to vote for Republicans decreased. However, when we blinded the information about the candidate, the similar emotion-based snippets got different opinions. This result explains why it is crucial to understand an individual's expectations from the candidate they hear to.

From our machine categorization of snippets, we also saw that the emotion curiosity-based sentences were not also in favor of the Republicans when delivered in either Black or White states.

5 Limitations, and Future Work

The small lexicon considering just speeches targeting the 2020 Presidential elections results in detecting a relatively narrow understanding of how

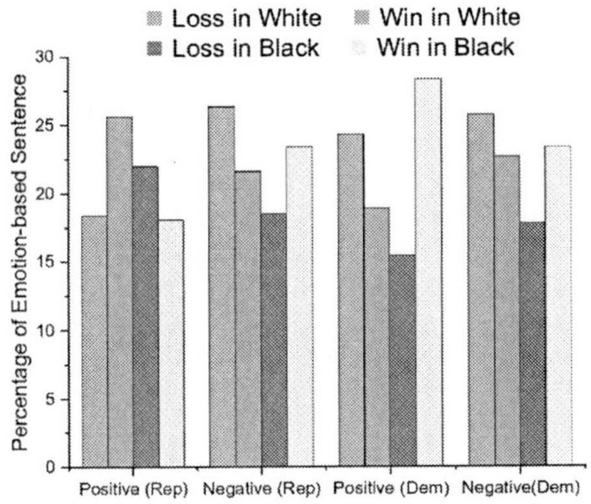

Figure 2: Net impact of sentiments, positive and negative, for Republicans and Democrats.

the sentiments used in the speeches affect the individuals. Furthermore, the idea behind voting for an individual comes with many prejudices against the candidate and the party representing. This was observed in the survey when we put forward the same snippet and attributed it to a different speaker. In our study, we nevertheless saw an interesting set of emotions that have driven the 2020 Presidential elections for either party, such as Section 4.6, where we noted how positivity and negativity notions had impacts when used by either party, and Section 4.4 and 4.5, where we noted that when the parties used particular emotion-based sentences, they had to face a loss.

Future work, including understanding the impact of emotions on voters from different backgrounds, such as immigrants, white- and blue-collar workers, and other demographics, can shed light on the relationship between how the particular emotion-based sentences can sway the elections. Considering multiple years of Presidential elections rally speeches and understanding the opinions biased by the individual's background would be vital in understanding the changing landscape of people's aspirations and how they are catered to by the candidates.

6 Conclusion

We collected a large-scale political rally speech of the 2020 Presidential elections to understand how speeches and sentiments have influenced the opinion of people voting for a particular candidate. Our analysis confirmed that different kinds of emotion-based sentences sway people's views about voting for a candidate. In contrast, we also observed that people wanted to listen to a particular party about a specific topic using a set of emotion-based sentences. Our analysis demonstrated that if the emotion could be identified *a priori* and delivered by a specific candidate, the election strategy could be targeted and aligned to the voters' bias.

References

F Al-Hindawi and N Al-Aadili. 2017. The pragmatics of deception in american presidential electoral speeches. *International Journal of English Linguistics*, 7(5):207–219.

Nurudin Alvarez-Gonzalez, Andreas Kaltenbrunner, and Vicenç Gómez. 2021. Uncovering the limits of text-based emotion detection. *arXiv preprint arXiv:2109.01900*.

Christopher J Anderson and Yuliya V Tverdova. 2001. Winners, losers, and attitudes about government in contemporary democracies. *International political science review*, 22(4):321–338.

Nick Anstead. 2017. Data-driven campaigning in the 2015 united kingdom general election. *The International Journal of Press/Politics*, 22(3):294–313.

Hiromi Ban and Takashi Oyabu. 2009. Metrical analysis of the speeches of 2008 american presidential election candidates. In *NAFIPS 2009-2009 Annual Meeting of the North American Fuzzy Information Processing Society*, pages 1–5. IEEE.

Peter Bull and Karolis Miskinis. 2015. Whipping it up! an analysis of audience responses to political rhetoric in speeches from the 2012 american presidential elections. *Journal of Language and Social Psychology*, 34(5):521–538.

Josemar A Caetano, Hélder S Lima, Mateus F Santos, and Humberto T Marques-Neto. 2018. Using sentiment analysis to define twitter political users' classes and their homophily during the 2016 american presidential election. *Journal of internet services and applications*, 9(1):1–15.

Lucian Gideon Conway III, Laura Janelle Gornick, Chelsea Burfeind, Paul Mandella, Andrea Kuenzli, Shannon C Houck, and Deven Theresa Fullerton. 2012. Does complex or simple rhetoric win elections? an integrative complexity analysis of us presidential campaigns. *Political Psychology*, 33(5):599–618.

Dorottya Demszky, Dana Movshovitz-Attias, Jeongwoo Ko, Alan Cowen, Gaurav Nemade, and Sujith Ravi. 2020. Goemotions: A dataset of fine-grained emotions. *arXiv preprint arXiv:2005.00547*.

Sunipa Dev, Tao Li, Jeff M Phillips, and Vivek Srikumar. 2020. Oscar: Orthogonal subspace correction and rectification of biases in word embeddings. *arXiv preprint arXiv:2007.00049*.

Jacob Devlin, Ming-Wei Chang, Kenton Lee, and Kristina Toutanova. 2018. Bert: Pre-training of deep bidirectional transformers for language understanding. *arXiv preprint arXiv:1810.04805*.

Felix Dumont and Taylor Facen. Visualing fine-grained emotions in reddit posts through the goemotions dataset.

Julia C Dupont, Evelyn Bytzek, Melanie C Steffens, and Frank M Schneider. 2019. Which kind of political campaign messages do people perceive as election pledges? *Electoral Studies*, 57:121–130.

Tarek Elghazaly, Amal Mahmoud, and Hesham A Hefny. 2016. Political sentiment analysis using twitter data. In *Proceedings of the International Conference on Internet of things and Cloud Computing*, pages 1–5.

James J Fahey. 2021. Building populist discourse: An analysis of populist communication in american presidential elections, 1896–2016. *Social Science Quarterly*, 102(4):1268–1288.

Kevin Finity, Ramit Garg, and Max McGaw. 2021. A text analysis of the 2020 us presidential election campaign speeches. In *2021 Systems and Information Engineering Design Symposium (SIEDS)*, pages 1–6. IEEE.

Chenyang Huang, Amine Trabelsi, Xuebin Qin, Nawshad Farruque, Lili Mou, and Osmar R Zaiane. 2021. Seq2emo: a sequence to multi-label emotion classification model. In *Proceedings of the 2021 conference of the North American chapter of the association for computational linguistics: human language technologies*, pages 4717–4724.

Okey Marcellus Ikeanyibe, Christian Chukwuebuka Ezeibe, Peter Oluchukwu Mbah, and Chikodiri Nwangwu. 2018. Political campaign and democratisation: Interrogating the use of hate speech in the 2011 and 2015 general elections in nigeria. *Journal of Language and Politics*, 17(1):92–117.

Richard Johnston. 1992. *Letting the people decide: Dynamics of a Canadian election*. Stanford University Press.

Rohan Kamath, Arpan Ghoshal, Sivaraman Eswaran, and Prasad B Honnavalli. 2022. Emoroberta: An enhanced emotion detection model using roberta. In *IEEE International Conference on Electronics, Computing and Communication Technologies*.

John Keating. 2021. Populist discourse and active metaphors in the 2016 us presidential elections. *Intercultural Pragmatics*, 18(4):499–531.

Chang Liu. 2017. Reviewing the rhetoric of donald trump's twitter of the 2016 presidential election.

Dilin Liu and Lei Lei. 2018. The appeal to political sentiment: An analysis of donald trump's and hillary clinton's speech themes and discourse strategies in the 2016 us presidential election. *Discourse, context & media*, 25:143–152.

Himanshu Maheshwari and Vasudeva Varma. 2022. An ensemble approach to detect emotions at an essay level. In *Proceedings of the 12th Workshop on Computational Approaches to Subjectivity, Sentiment & Social Media Analysis*, pages 276–279.

Scott D McClurg. 2004. Indirect mobilization: The social consequences of party contacts in an election campaign. *American Politics Research*, 32(4):406–443.

Alessio Miaschi and Felice Dell'Orletta. 2020. Contextual and non-contextual word embeddings: an in-depth linguistic investigation. In *Proceedings of the 5th Workshop on Representation Learning for NLP*, pages 110–119.

Farha Nausheen and Sayyada Hajera Begum. 2018. Sentiment analysis to predict election results using python. In *2018 2nd international conference on inventive systems and control (ICISC)*, pages 1259–1262. IEEE.

G Bingham Powell Jr and Guy D Whitten. 1993. A cross-national analysis of economic voting: taking account of the political context. *American Journal of Political Science*, pages 391–414.

Alexandra A Siegel, Evgenii Nikitin, Pablo Barberá, Joanna Sterling, Bethany Pullen, Richard Bonneau, Jonathan Nagler, Joshua A Tucker, et al. 2021. Trumping hate on twitter? online hate speech in the 2016 us election campaign and its aftermath. *Quarterly Journal of Political Science*, 16(1):71–104.

Niklas K Steffens and S Alexander Haslam. 2013. Power through 'us': Leaders' use of we-referencing language predicts election victory. *PloS one*, 8(10):e77952.

Alane Suhr, Srinivasan Iyer, and Yoav Artzi. 2018. Learning to map context-dependent sentences to executable formal queries. *arXiv preprint arXiv:1804.06868*.

Piyathida Thainguan, Nithiwat Thanasrisawat, and Pawarit Sripiboon. 2021. Text sentiment analysis from goemotions.

Guy D Whitten and Harvey D Palmer. 1999. Cross-national analyses of economic voting. *Electoral Studies*, 18(1):49–67.

Ussama Yaqub, Soon Ae Chun, Vijayalakshmi Atluri, and Jaideep Vaidya. 2017. Analysis of political discourse on twitter in the context of the 2016 us presidential elections. *Government Information Quarterly*, 34(4):613–626.

Interactive Analysis and Visualisation of Annotated Collocations in Spanish (AVAnCES)

Simon Gonzalez
The Australian National University / Canberra, ACT, Australia
u1037706@anu.edu.au

Abstract

Phraseology studies have been enhanced by Corpus Linguistics, which has become an interdisciplinary field where current technologies play an important role in its development. Computational tools have been implemented in the last decades with positive results on the identification of phrases in different languages. One specific technology that has impacted these studies is social media. As researchers, we have turned our attention to collecting data from these platforms, which comes with great advantages and its own challenges. One of the challenges is the way we design and build corpora relevant to the questions emerging in this type of language expression. This has been approached from different angles, but one that has given invaluable outputs is the building of linguistic corpora with the use of online web applications. In this paper, we take a multidimensional approach to the collection, design, and deployment of a phraseology corpus for Latin American Spanish from Twitter data, extracting features using NLP techniques, and presenting it in an interactive online web application. We expect to contribute to the methodologies used for Corpus Linguistics in the current technological age. Finally, we make this tool publicly available to be used by any researcher interested in the data itself and also on the technological tools developed here.

1 Introduction

Advances in current technologies have played a pivotal role in the development of academic fields, such as corpus-based phraseology. One of the most tangible results is the development of corpora based on digitised books (Michel et al., 2011), Google books (Zieba, 2018), and social media (Caselli et al.). Contributions from Corpus Linguistics have also been invaluable. Corpus Linguistics has been identified as one of the fastest growing linguistic methods in language studies (Abdumanapovna, 2018). This growth has gone hand in hand with advances in technologies, and it is clearly tangible in the tools that are now available for us as linguistic researchers to create exhaustive corpora to be accessed all around the world (a comprehensive list can be found in Tools for Corpus Linguistics). This has made Corpus Linguistics strongly dependent on the internet, where many websites have been deployed specifically for this purpose. All these factors render working with linguistic corpora a very interdisciplinary field, combining linguistics, data processing, data visualisation, and app development.

Another technological development that has influenced corpus-based phraseology has been the birth and development of social media platforms since the early 2000s. With these, we can create corpora that are based on natural language, from text to speech sources. Among these social media platforms, Twitter is one of the most influential ones and most widely used around the globe for the last two decades. A positive take on this is that Twitter offers free APIs that can be used to build tools for linguistic purposes. Researchers have made positive use of this and have maximised the potential to collect data and use it for language research (Dijkstra et al., 2021; Goel et al., 2016; Shoemark, 2020).

Within the field of Computational Linguistics, language studies have also found invaluable tools that have positively influenced the way we approach phraseology studies. Natural Language Processing techniques allow us to do a wide range of tasks on a large amount of data in relatively quick time. This has changed the focus from analysing small amounts of data, generally limited to the time human coders could process data, to processing massive amounts of data, where the limit is now on

The 2nd International Workshop on Natural Language Processing for Digital Humanities (NLP4DH), pages 21–30
November 20, 2022.

the computational capability.

Taking these technological contributions, namely social media, and open-source computational tools, we present in this paper the development of an online tool for the querying, analysis, and visualisation of collocations in Latin American Spanish based on a social media corpus. We discuss the emerging challenges when creating a corpus from social media and propose methodological processes appropriate for building digital language corpora to efficiently analyse collocations. The main motivation is to bring more depth to the presentation and analysis of linguistic patterns in a more interactive way. This type of implementation gives users powerful tools oriented towards finding patterns in available corpora. The final product aims to give researchers full control of the corpus by combining linguistic analysis, Natural Language Processing outputs, and visualisation techniques. With this holistic approach, we offer a deeper understanding of the complexity of collocations through exploration tools.

The goal of this research is then to present a new approach to analyse collocations. In this paper, we focus on Spanish, but this methodology can be used for any language that has outputs in social media platforms. We apply the analytical framework of Network Analysis to the study of collocations, and we also look at syntactic relationships and statistical measurements. In this sense, we aim to bridge the gap between the Continental tradition (Hausmann, 1991; Melcuk, 2007) and the British Contextualists tradition (Sinclair, 1991; Sinclair et al., 1970; Jones and Sinclair, 1974).

This paper is organised as follows. In Section 2, we present the technologies implemented in a more contextualised way, relevant to our study. We also present related work and our approach to the analysis and app development. We present the Methodology in Section 3 and the Analysis in Section 4. The Final product is presented in Section 5, with the Conclusions in Section 6.

2 Background and Rationale

The development of this new technology is created within three frameworks: Social Media, Computational Linguistics, and Internet Technologies. These are briefly discussed in the next sections below.

2.1 Social Media and Corpus Linguistics

One relevant premise in Corpus Linguistics is to collect reliable representative data, and this is achieved by selecting resources that allow language expression in a natural context (Abdumanapovna, 2018), and social media allows the study of language in contexts used for everyday communication (Rudiger and Dayter, 2020). This integration of social media on Corpus Linguistics is becoming more common practice, and it has been implemented, explored, and documented (Dunn, 2022; Rudiger and Dayter, 2020; Sun et al., 2021). Because of the complexity that social media language entails, it has not been widely explored, despite its prevalence in current communication processes (Sardinha, 2022). It has been therefore suggested to implement multidimensional (MD) analysis to approach the study of language in social media platforms, so we can capture its complexities. MD approaches were initially proposed by Biber (1988) and they are still widely implemented in current studies (Gardner et al., 2019; Jin, 2021; Sardinha, 2022). This method consists of analysing multiple linguistic characteristics of texts in a comprehensive way, examining a range of linguistic features across sources, which in turn helps identify correlations across features in whole corpora. The nature of this task requires the appropriate tools for achieving the correct results. That is why, the implementation of Natural Language Processing (NLP) tools helps in this methodological approach.

2.2 The Role of NLP in Corpus Linguistics

NLP allows Corpus Linguistics to have more statistical (Gerlach and Font-Clos, 2020; Lafferty et al., 2001; Manning and Schütze, 1999; Schmid, 1994) and machine learning (Karkaletsis et al., 2015) approaches to analyse language. This growing overlap between these two fields has experienced strong consolidation in the last decade. It is now common practice to implement NLP techniques in the design, modelling, and querying of linguistic corpora (Almujaiwel, 2018; Amri et al., 2017; Gentzkow et al., 2018), especially, in the analysis of linguistic forms within large datasets. This has positively contributed to more established corpus analysis approaches that focus on frequency counts, which helps us examine patterns of individual words and words in contact with other words. Other established methodologies that have been reinforced with NLP techniques include analysis of collocations, n-grams, and word distributions. But NLP techniques can also provide other layers of analysis beyond word features. With NLP approaches, we can also analyse syntactic relationships and dependencies in sentences, examine semantic relationships, and automate identification of specific words in large corpora. A common application is the recognition of Named Entities, which consider textual distributions, word relationships, and syntactical positions. This is particularly useful when tagging geographic locations, proper names and institutions mentioned in the corpus. In summary, NLP tools are generally implemented for text chunking, word sense disambiguation, Named Entity Recognition, syntactic parsing, semantic role labelling, and semantic parsing (Amri et al., 2019). A clear advantage of NLP techniques is that they facilitate the quantification of features, which is the bases for statistical approaches to language data analysis. This does not substitute qualitative approaches to Corpus Linguistics, but rather complements the way we explore and analyse our linguistic data.

2.3 The Internet and Corpus Linguistics

The advancement of the internet and the computational power of current resources allow Corpus Linguistics to carry out tasks with intensive processing power and storage capacity. These help in both the processing and retrieval of large datasets (Abdumanapovna, 2018; Biber et al., 2006; Kennedy, 1998). In fact, Fisas et al. (2016) argue that this gives Corpus Linguistics more outcome feasibility and real-time access to corpora, regardless of physical location. The use of internet technologies has already been exploited for corpus purposes (Andersen, 2012; Collins, 2019; Hardie, 2012) and there are available corpora maximising this technology, e.g. *The Corpus of Contemporary American English (COCA)* (Davies, 2008), *The British National Corpus* (Clear, 1993), and the *Czech National Corpus* (Hnatkova et al., 2014).

2.4 Purpose of Current Corpus

The aim of our corpus is to capture the linguistic complexities of collocations in Spanish used on Twitter and explore the differences between the structures and patterns across users in thirteen Latin American countries. There has been a growing interest in linguistic studies using Twitter data for different purposes. The areas include phonological variation (Dijkstra et al., 2021; Eisenstein, 2013), stylistic and lexical variation on writing (Blodgett et al., 2016; Nguyen, 2017; Shoemark, 2020; Wurschinger, 2021; Pavalanathan and Eisenstein, 2015), dialectal studies (Eisenstein, 2017; Jorgensen et al., 2015), and language change (Goel et al., 2016). In this corpus, we prepare the data holistically, in such a way that it gives opportunities for users to focus their analysis on a wide range of linguistic features. This is explained in the following sections.

The focus of this study is on collocations, which can be defined as words occurring together in high frequencies with their semantic properties (Corpas-Pastor, 2017). In the computational sense, collocations are described as a distinct type of *multi-word expression (MWE)* which occurs in high frequency relative to the individual words that make the expression (Baldwin and Kim, 2010). In this sense, this is based on statistical quantification for all combinations (Jones and Sinclair, 1974; Stubbs, 2002). Apart from statistical approaches to identifying MWEs, other methods have been proposed in the literature. One of this is based on n-gram frequencies, also known as collocational networks. A limitation of this approach is that it can only identify continuous co-occurrences. The statistical approaches aim to overcome this limitation and are purposed to discover discontinuous co-occurrences. Hybrid models have therefore been developed to capture both continuous and discontinuous occurrences. These can combine measurements of linguistic features (e.g., semantic patterns), statistical calculations, and psychological approaches (Stefanowitsch, 2013). In this paper, we implement a multi-modal approach based on the hybrid models previously proposed, where we combine syntactic dependencies and n-gram patterns.

3 Methodology

Among other computational languages and software available, shiny R (Chang et al., 2019), within R (R Core Team, 2022), offers an invaluable infrastructure that, if well implemented, can facilitate the integration of the necessary methods mentioned above to produce high quality linguistic corpora. The app developed as part of this study and all its functionality were developed in R, which has been widely used for Corpus Linguistics development and related tasks (Abeille and Godard, 2000; S.Th., 2009). The main framework was within

Filter	Count	Percentage
URLs	$\sim 10,000$	1.3%
Re-tweets	$\sim 258,000$	35%
Quote tweets	$\sim 60,000$	8%
Non-Spanish tweets	$\sim 95,000$	13%
Less than 10 Words	$\sim 137,000$	19%

Table 1: Filters applied to the raw data, showing the type of filter, the total number of tweets filtered, and the percentage from the total extracted corpus.

Country	Females (120)	Males (119)
Argentina	210 (33%)	425 (67%)
Bolivia	513 (27%)	1397 (73%)
Chile	160 (28%)	410 (72%)
Colombia	711 (39%)	1130 (61%)
Costa Rica	745 (59%)	518 (41%)
Cuba	313 (31%)	703 (69%)
Ecuador	669 (49%)	680 (51%)
Mexico	762 (52%)	715 (48%)
Panama	848 (54%)	727 (46%)
Peru	437 (57%)	335 (43%)
Puerto Rico	606 (40%)	911 (60%)
Dominican Rep.	1177 (55%)	952 (45%)
Venezuela	633 (44%)	801 (56%)
TOTAL	**7784**	**9694**

Table 2: Total number of sentences per country and gender in the corpus.

shiny R. Shiny apps allow great interactivity and responsiveness. Interactivity allows users to explore visualisations in effective ways, and responsiveness allows users to navigate contents in real time, with the use of clicks and dropdown menus. Other libraries that we used for the creation of visuals were *ggplot2* (Wickham, 2016) and *echarts4r* (Coene, 2022). *echarts4r* is used to create a wide variety of interactive visuals, and *ggplot2* allows a great degree of flexibility when creating figures, which is relevant to explore complex linguistic data. But this allows complex ideas to be presented in a digestible way. Another advantage of this is that it allows users to see data points within the general context, as well as being able to narrow down into more specific analysis. This creates a seamless navigation of linguistic data in an efficient way.

3.1 Corpus

A preliminary research was done to identify relevant Twitter accounts to build the corpus from. For this, we aimed to choose Latin American users whose accounts had a relatively large number of posts. The reason was to gather as much data as allowed in the free API (3,250 tweets per account at a given moment). The filters below show that there is a lot of data that is lost to keep more comparable content. The second criterion was that the posts had to be in Spanish, and finally, the accounts had to be active at the moment of the data extraction. The motivation was to capture synchronous language use. This is especially relevant when analysing the use of phrases, which can be compared across sociolinguistically related groups of speakers in similar timeframes. Initially, there was a total of over 744,000 tweets. From this, we applied the filters presented in Table 1.

The final output was a total of 307,000 tweets. This is the main body of the corpus. For the demonstration of the app, we chose a subset of the whole corpus. Large corpora require substantial computational power to process the data in real time. For this reason, we selected approximately 17,000 sentences from the original corpus, distributed across all users from the thirteen countries. We left in only sentences with 15 to 17 words. The motivation was to select tweets with similar structures and character length. The final data contains 239 individual users, with an average of 73 sentences per user. The distributions per country and gender are shown in Table 2. Due to the limitations on the use of Twitter data for individual identification, account usernames are not presented, and the source data is not available for download. We only present analysis on the phrases, n-grams, and syntactic dependencies, which encompasses the aim of the tool. However, following Twitter regulations, we can only share the Tweet IDs as a request sent to the author of this paper.

The data extraction was done through an R script developed by the first author. We used the *rTweet* (Kearney, 2019) package, which allows users to gather Twitter posts by the free Twitter API. After collecting the data, the next step was the development of computational algorithms used to create linguistic annotations. This is described in the following sections.

3.2 Corpus Processing

The corpus was processed for two separate yet related tasks. The first one was to extract all the morphological and syntactic information. The main purpose was to give morphosyntactic infor-

Country	ADJ	ADP	ADV	AUX	DET	NOUN	PRON	VERB
Argentina	9%	20%	7%	5%	15%	24%	10%	14%
Bolivia	8%	21%	4%	4%	17%	26%	6%	14%
Chile	9%	20%	6%	4%	15%	25%	8%	13%
Colombia	8%	22%	5%	4%	16%	25%	7%	13%
Costa Rica	9%	22%	5%	4%	14%	24%	8%	14%
Cuba	9%	20%	5%	5%	16%	25%	7%	13%
Ecuador	8%	21%	5%	5%	15%	24%	8%	14%
Mexico	8%	22%	4%	4%	17%	25%	7%	13%
Panama	8%	21%	5%	4%	15%	25%	8%	14%
Peru	8%	19%	6%	4%	16%	23%	10%	14%
Puerto Rico	7%	23%	5%	4%	16%	25%	7%	13%
Dominican Rep.	8%	21%	4%	4%	17%	26%	7%	13%
Venezuela	8%	22%	5%	4%	15%	24%	8%	14%
TOTAL	**16129**	**42810**	**9735**	**8348**	**32122**	**49745**	**14649**	**26609**

Table 3: Total number and percentages of Parts of Speech per country in the corpus.

mation to collocations and the contexts in which they appear. The second task carried out statistical measurements on the collocations to be displayed through the corresponding visualisations.

3.2.1 Morphosyntactic Tagging

The morphosyntactic processing of this dataset was preprocessed outside the app and before launching it. For each sentence, we tagged each word and added their morphological and syntactic information. We implemented a wide range of NLP techniques for the data processing and analysis. The data was processed using the *UDPipe* (Straka and Strakova, 2017) package as the main tool for the NLP tasks. We used the *Spanish Ancora* model available in the package. The algorithm tokenises each sentence, identifies word lemmas, and then assigns a range of features based on the positions and functions of words in the sentence. Three main features extracted were the part of speech, morphological information (e.g., gender and number for nouns, tense and aspect for verbs), and their syntactic function in the given sentence (e.g., subject, object). The total distribution per country of Parts of Speech tagging is shown in Table 3. As observed, their distributions are similar across all countries.

3.2.2 Statistical Analysis of the Data

Unlike the morphosyntactic tagging, the statistical processing of this dataset is done interactively within the app. The user chooses the corresponding country, and then all the calculations are made. This is done following the processes from (Schweinberger, 2022) and using the *quanteda* (Benoit et al., 2018) and text mining – *tm* (Feinerer and Hornik, 2020) – packages. The first step is to concatenate all sentences in a single vector and then tokenise all words. From this point onwards, the process splits into two workflows. The first one is to calculate collocations across all words in the data, and the second one is to calculate all the collocations that can occur with a word selected in the app by the user. These processes are expanded below.

3.2.3 Overall Collocations Processing

In this process, the user first has the option to filter out stop words in Spanish using the *stopwords* (Benoit et al., 2021) package. The default option is to include stops words to capture collocations where stop words are included, for example, prepositions. We calculate the stats for the collocations running the function `textstat_collocations()` in the *quanteda* package, which calculates the lambda value as computed in Blaheta and Johnson (2001). Here, the user selects two parameters. The first one is the size of the collocations, e.g., number of words in the unit, from two to five. The second parameter is the minimum count. This refers to the number of times the collocation appears. The larger the size of the data, the more rigorous it can be to capture more frequent collocations. On the other hand, for smaller datasets, higher minimum counts could filter out relevant collocations. Here we maximise the power of interactivity, where users choose their

Collocation	Lambda	z
Golpe De Estado	4.87003	2.30594
Estado De Derecho	4.41775	2.04069
Democracia Y Libertad	3.1469	1.72487
Abuso De Poder	1.95931	0.87952
Libertad De Expresion	1.72231	0.73930
Poder Y Placer	1.24259	0.54335
Ministro De Gobierno	1.22566	0.7563
TOTAL	**7784**	**9694**

Table 4: Three-word collocations for tweets from Bolivia in the Overall Collocations.

Term	Strength	Term	Strength
abuso	18.42	consultiva	5.53
placer	12.85	quiso	5.53
estrategia	9.99	avenidas	5.53
segundo	9.99	casas	5.53
corrupcion	9.65	conductores	5.53
médicos	8.41	semáforo	5.53
horas	7.82	vuelven	5.53
opinión	7.82	sola	5.53
luis	5.80	públicos	5.53
ejerciendo	5.53	ruta	5.53

Table 5: Collocation strength for the term "poder" ("power"). Top 20 collocations shown. Note that the term "abuso" ("abuse) is the strongest term, and the strength stabilises at term "ejerciendo" ("exercising").

parameters to better explore the corpus.

3.2.4 Word-based Collocations Processing

The first step in this process is to convert the sentences into a quanteda *Corpus* object. It contains the original sentences, document-level variables and metadata, corpus-level metadata, and features that are used for subsequent processing of the corpus. Like the **3.2.3 Overall Collocations Processing**, users can choose to filter out stop words. The non-optional filters are removing punctuation characters and numbers. This corpus is then converted to a *Document Term Matrix* object, which contains a sparse term-document matrix. This is a mathematical matrix that stores information on the frequency of terms that occur in the sentences, where rows correspond to the sentences in the collection and columns correspond to the terms. For statistical purposes, this is used to calculate co-occurrences counts from the word selected to all the other words in the data, as shown in Table 4. Table 5 shows the strength of specific words in relation to a reference word, which adds another layer of information for collocations.

4 Analysis and Visualisation

In this paper, we implement an analysis approach driven by visualisations of collocations. The visualisations are based on the mathematical measures done in the data processing stage, for both overall collocations and word-based selections. The driving approach is on ***Network Analysis (NA)***, which has been widely implemented in different fields, including causal distribution research (Kelly, 1983), archaeology (Golitko and Feinman, 1981; Orengo and Livarda, 2016), psychological studies (Jones et al., 2021; Mullarkey et al., 2019), and social network research (Clifton and Webster, 2017). The main purpose of NA is to identify relationships within the components of a network. The assumption is that meaningful relationships between two or more elements will always reflect better and stronger connections than random or weaker relationships. The working components from which NA operates are based on relational data organised in a matrix form. This is where the relationship between the matrix output from the data processing and the methods in NA converge. We take the numeric output of the matrix and feed it into a network analysis visualisation function from the *visNetwork* (Almende, 2021) package. An example of a Network is shown in Figure 1.

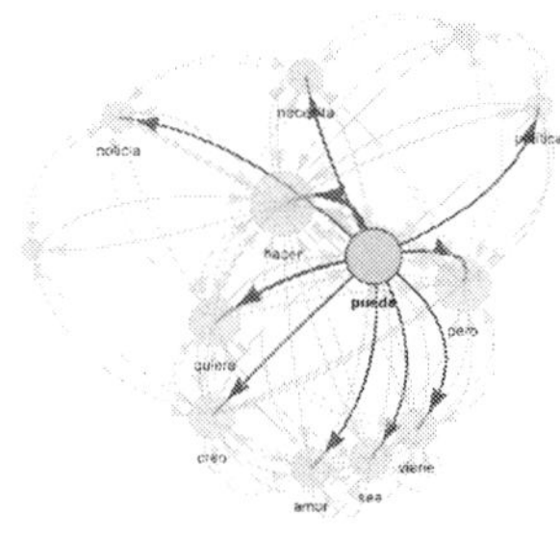

Figure 1: Network for the term "puede".

4.1 Parts of Speech Networks

Network Analysis is also applied to the parts of speech tagging of the data. This can be used to observe relationships at the morphological level. It complements the analysis of collocations and provides another perspective to examine. Like in the collocations' visualisation, we use the functionality from the *visNetwork* package, and users can change the parameters of analysis, including the number of links between nodes, and the base frequency for all the tags, as shown in Figure 2.

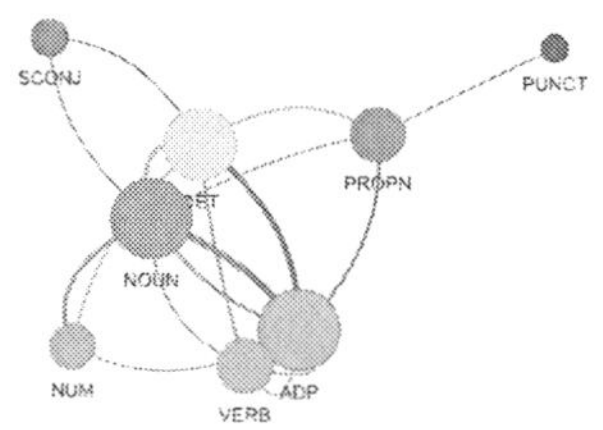

Figure 2: Network Analysis of Parts of Speech relationships in data selected.

4.2 Syntactic Dependencies

Another relevant implementation of the analysis targets syntactic dependencies. Here we use the output from the Morphosyntactic tagging step. The visualisation is done using the *textplot* (Wijffels et al., 2021) package. The main functionality of this package is to read the syntactic information from *UDPipe* outputs and then plot the dependencies in a text visualisation output. This can be done for all the sentences in the corpus. This is a powerful functionality that can be used to explore syntactic patterns of all collocations, and to understand all their contexts, as shown in Figure 3.

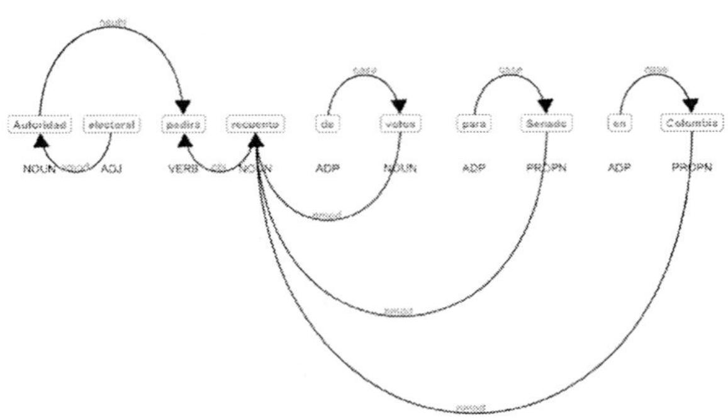

Figure 3: Syntactic Dependencies visualisation output, showing morphological and syntactic relationships between words.

4.3 Other Visualisations

Other visualisations are provided to examine a range of parameters that are important in understanding patterns and distributions of collocations in the corpus (See Figure 4). This gives users more tools to understand the patterns. These are presented in bar plots and radius pie charts from the *eachrts4r* package, which are used for examining of n-grams and parts of speech patterns.

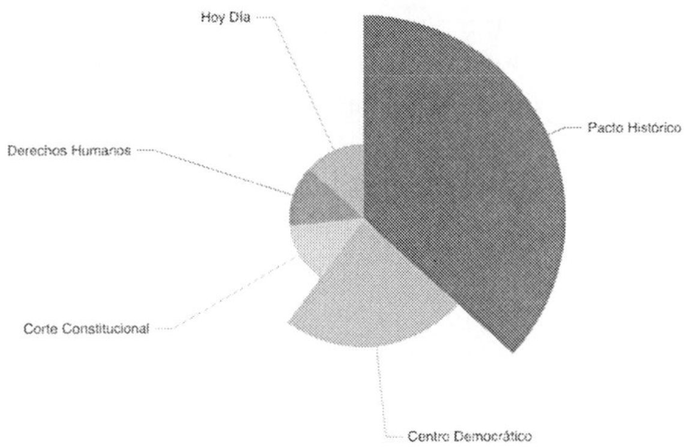

Figure 4: Radius Pie Chart of top five collocations within selected data.

5 Final Product

The final product is an app that gives users the opportunity to explore all the data, and the results from the different analyses. The code and application can be accessed through the GitHub repository: https://github.com/simongonzalez/AVANCES. The app is organised into five main sections. The first one is the visualisation of the distributions of speakers based on countries and occupations in the data. The second section shows the distributions of n-grams and parts of speech through network visualisations, pie charts, and bar plots. The third section presents results from the Network Analysis, looking at overall and word-based collocations. The fourth section shows the syntactic dependencies plots, and the sentences are selected by the user. The fifth and final section has a searching capability. In this tab, users can search for syntactic patterns in the data. The source tagging comes from the *UDPipe* output, showing the morphosyntactic patterns. The main usability is to allow users to identify in advance the potential sequences that can be relevant to explore in more depth. All these five sections then gather all the pre-processed data and also process the data based on user requests. This gives a full control on the data processing to have sophisticated exploration tools.

6 Conclusions and future work

In this paper, we have presented the development and deployment of a Spanish linguistic corpus built from Twitter posts. We combined NLP techniques, linguistic analysis, and app development approaches to create a holistic framework to analyse and explore collocations across Twitter users from thirteen Latin American countries. In future versions of the app, we aim to include more language features, as well as more data from other Spanish-speaking countries. We also aim to carry out more linguistic analysis relevant for corpus research, such as language variation, stylistics, sentiment analysis, for example. Finally, this is an open-source tool with the potential to be expanded and customised based on user needs.

References

S.A. Abdumanapovna. 2018. The contemporary language studies with corpus linguistics. In *Proceedings of the 2nd International Conference on Digital Technology in Education (ICDTE 2018)*, pages 82–85, New York, NY, USA.

A. Abeille and D. Godard. 2000. French word order and lexical weight. *Syntax and Semantics*, pages 325–358.

B.V. Almende. 2021. visnetwork: Network visualization using 'vis.js' library. *R Package*. Version 2.1.0.

S. Almujaiwel. 2018. Integrating nlp with corpus linguistics and vice versa. In *Proceedings of the International Conference on Learning and Optimization Algorithms: Theory and Applications (LOPAL '18)*, pages 1–6, New York, NY, USA.

S. Amri, L. Zenkouar, and R. Benkhouya. 2019. A comparative study on the efficiency of pos tagging techniques on amazigh corpus. In *Proceedings of the 2nd International Conference on Networking, Information Systems Security (NISS19)*, pages 1–5, New York, NY, USA.

S. Amri, L. Zenkouar, and M. Outahajala. 2017. Build a morphosyntaxically annotated amazigh corpus. In *Proceedings of the 2nd international Conference on Big Data, Cloud and Applications (BDCA'17)*, pages 1–7, New York, NY, USA.

G. Andersen. 2012. *Exploring Newspaper Language: Using the web to create and investigate a large corpus of modern Norwegian*, volume 49. John Benjamins Publishing.

T. Baldwin and S.N. Kim. 2010. Multiword expressions. *Handbook of Natural Language Processing*, pages 267–292. 2nd edn.

K. Benoit, D. Muhr, and K. Watanabe. 2021. stopwords: Multilingual stopword lists. *R package*.

K. Benoit, K. Watanabe, H. Wang, P. Nulty, A. Obeng, S. Müller, and A. Matsuo. 2018. quanteda: An r package for the quantitative analysis of textual data. *Journal of Open Source Software*, 3(30).

D. Biber. 1988. *Variation across speech and writing*. Cambridge University Press.

D. Biber, Conrad S., and R. Reppen. 2006. *Corpus Linguistics: investigating language structure and use*. Cambridge University Press.

D. Blaheta and M. Johnson. 2001. Unsupervised learning of multi-word verbs. In *ACLEACL Workshop on the Computational Extraction, Analysis and Exploitation of Col-locations*.

S.L. Blodgett, L. Green, and B.T. O'Connor. 2016. Demographic dialectal variation in social media: A case study of african-american english. In *Proceedings of the 2016 Conference on Empirical Methods in Natural Language Processing*, pages 1119–1130.

Tommaso Caselli, Arjan Schelhaas, Marieke Weultjes, Folkert Leistra, Hylke van der Veen, Gerben mmerman, and Malvina Nissim. Dalc: the dutch abusive language corpus. In *Proceedings of the 5th Workshop on Online Abuse and Harms (WOAH)*. Association for Computational Linguistics.

W. Chang, J. Cheng, J. Allaire, Y. Xie, and J. McPherson. 2019. shiny: Web application frame-work for r. *R Package Version 1.3.2*.

J.H. Clear. 1993. *The British national corpus. The digital word: text-based computing in the humanities*. MIT Press.

A. Clifton and G. D. Webster. 2017. An introduction to social network analysis for personality and social psychologists. *Social Psychological and Personality Science*, 8(4):442–453.

J. Coene. 2022. echarts4r: Create interactive graphs with 'echarts javascript'. *R Package Version 5*.

L.C. Collins. 2019. *Corpus Linguistics for Online Communication: A Guide for Research*. Routledge.

G. Corpas-Pastor. 2017. Collocational constructions in translated spanish: What corpora reveal. In *Euphoria 2017, LNAI*, pages 29–40.

M. Davies. 2008. *The Corpus of Contemporary American English (COCA): 560 million words, 1990-present*.

J. Dijkstra, W. Heeringa, L. Jongbloed-Faber, and H. Van de Velde. 2021. Using twitter data for the study of language change in low-resource languages. a panel study of relative pronouns in frisian. *Frontiers in Artificial Intelligence*.

J. Dunn. 2022. *Natural Language Processing for Corpus Linguistics (Elements in Corpus Linguistics)*, volume 1. Cambridge University Press, Cambridge.

J. Eisenstein. 2013. Phonological factors in social media writing. In *Proceedings of the Workshop on Language in Social Media (LASM 2013)*, pages 11–19.

J. Eisenstein. 2017. Identifying regional dialects in online social media. *The Handbook of Dialectology*.

I. Feinerer and K. Hornik. 2020. tm: Text mining package. *R Package Version 0.7-8.*

B. Fisas, F. Ronzano, and H. Saggion. 2016. A multilayered annotated corpus of scientific papers. In *LREC.*

S. Gardner, H. Nesi, and D. Biber. 2019. Discipline, level, genre: Integrating situational perspectives in a new md analysis of university student writing. *Applied Linguistics*, 40(4):646–674.

M. Gentzkow, J. Shapiro, and M. Taddy. 2018. Congressional record for the 43rd–114th congresses: Parsed speeches and phrase counts (tech. rep.). In *Palo Alto, CA: Stanford Libraries.*

M. Gerlach and F. Font-Clos. 2020. A standardized project gutenberg corpus for statistical analysis of natural language and quantitative linguistics. *Entropy*, 22(1):126–132.

R. Goel, S. Soni, N. Goyal, J. Paparrizos, H.M. Wallach, F.D. Diaz, and J. Eisenstein. 2016. The social dynamics of language change in online networks. *ArXiv.*

M. Golitko and G. M. Feinman. 1981. Procurement and distribution of prehispanic mesoamerican obsidian 900 bc-ad 1520: A social network analysis. *Journal of Archaeological Method and Theory*, 22(1):206–247.

A. Hardie. 2012. Cqpweb – combining power, flexibility and usability in a corpus analysis tool. *International Journal of Corpus Linguistics*, 17(3):380–409.

F.J. Hausmann. 1991. Collocations in the bilingual dictionary. In *An International Encylopedia of Lexicography*, pages 2775–2778.

M. Hnatkova, M. Kren, P. Prochazka, and H. Skoumalova. 2014. The syn-series corpora of written czech. In *Proceedings of LREC2014*, pages 160–164.

B. Jin. 2021. A multi-dimensional analysis of research article discussion sections in an engineering discipline: Corpus explorations and scientists' perceptions. *SAGE Open*, 28(1):114–133.

P.-J. Jones, R. Ma, and R.-J. McNally. 2021. Bridge centrality: A network approach to under-standing comorbidity. *Multivariate Behavioral Research*, 56(2):353–367.

S. Jones and J. Sinclair. 1974. English lexical collocations. a study in computational linguistics. *Cahiers de Lexicology*, 24:15–21.

A.K. Jorgensen, D. Hovy, and A. Sogaard. 2015. Challenges of studying and processing dialects in social media. In *Proceedings of the ACL 2015 Workshop on Noisy User-generated Text*, pages 9–18.

G. Karkaletsis, G. Petasis, and V. Paliouras. 2015. *Using machine learning techniques for part-of-speech tagging in the Greek language.* World Scientific Publishing Company, Singapore.

M.W. Kearney. 2019. rtweet: Collecting and analyzing twitter data. *Journal of Open Source Software*, 4(42). 0.7.0.

H. H. Kelly. 1983. Perceived causal structures. *Attribution theory and research: Conceptual, developmental and social dimensions.*

G. Kennedy. 1998. *An Introduction to Corpus Linguistics.* Longman, London.

J. Lafferty, A. McCallum, and F. Pereira. 2001. Conditional random fields: Probabilistic models for segmenting and labeling sequence data. In *Proceedings of the ICML-01*, pages 282–289.

C. Manning and H. Schütze. 1999. *oundations of Statistical Natural Language Processing.* The MIT Press.

I. Melcuk. 2007. Lexical functions. *Phraseology. An International Handbook of Contemporary Research*, 1:119–131.

J. Michel, Y. Shen, and et al. 2011. Quantitative analysis of culture using millions of digitized books. *Science*, 331(6014):176–182.

M.-C. Mullarkey, I. Marchetti, and C.-G. Beevers. 2019. Using network analysis to identify central symptoms of adolescent depression. *Journal of Clinical Child Adolescent Psychology*, 48(4):656–668.

D. Nguyen. 2017. *Text as social and cultural data : a computational perspective on variation in text.* University of Twente, The Netherlands. PhD Dissertation.

H.A. Orengo and A. Livarda. 2016. The seeds of commerce: A network analysis-based approach to the romano-british transport system. *Journal of Archaeological Science*, 66:21–35.

U. Pavalanathan and J. Eisenstein. 2015. Audience-modulated variation in online social media. *American Speech*, 90:187–213.

R Core Team R Core Team. 2022. *R: A language and environment for statistical computing.* R Foundation for Statistical Computing, Vienna, Austria.

S. Rudiger and D. Dayter. 2020. *Corpus Approaches to Social Media.* John Benjamins.

T. B. Sardinha. 2022. Corpus linguistics and the study of social media: a case study using multi-dimensional analysis. *The Routledge Handbook of Corpus Linguistics*, pages 656–674.

H. Schmid. 1994. Probabilistic part-of-speech tagging using decision trees. In *International Conference on New Methods in Language Processing*, Manchester, UK.

M. Schweinberger. 2022. Analyzing co-occurrences and collocations in r. *R Tutorial*. 2022.05.04.

P. Shoemark. 2020. *Discovering and analysing lexical variation in social media text*. The University of Edinburgh. PhD Dissertation.

J. Sinclair. 1991. *Corpus, Concordance, Collocation*. Oxford University Press, Oxford.

J. Sinclair, S. Jones, and R. Daley. 1970. *English lexical studies: report to OSTI on project C/LP/08*. Department of English, University of Birmingham. Final report for period January 1967-September 1969.

A. Stefanowitsch. 2013. Collostructional analysis. *The Oxford Handbook of Construction Grammar*, pages 290–306.

Gries. S.Th. 2009. *Quantitative Corpus Linguistics with R*, volume 1. Routledge, London and New York.

M. Straka and J. Strakova. 2017. Pos tagging, lemmatizing and parsing ud 2.0 with udpipe. In *Proceedings of the CoNLL 2017 Shared Task: Multilingual Parsing from Raw Text to Universal Dependencies*, pages 88–99, Vancouver, Canada. Association for Computational Linguistics.

M. Stubbs. 2002. Two quantitative methods of studying phraseology in english. *International Journal of Corpus Linguist*, 7(12):215–244.

Y. Sun, G. Wang, and H. Feng. 2021. Linguistic studies on social media: A bibliometric analysis. *SAGE Open*.

H. Wickham. 2016. ggplot2: Elegant graphics for data analysis. *R Package*.

J. Wijffels, S. Epskamp, I. Feinerer, and K. Hornik. 2021. textplot: Visualise complex relations in texts. *R Package*. 0.2.0.

Q. Wurschinger. 2021. Social networks of lexical innovation. investigating the social dynamics of diffusion of neologisms on twitter. *Frontiers in Artificial Intelligence*.

A. Zieba. 2018. Google books ngram viewer in sociocultural research. *Res. Lang.*, 16:357–376.

The fractality of sentiment arcs for literary quality assessment: The case of Nobel laureates

Yuri Bizzoni
Aarhus University
yuri.bizzoni@cc.au.dk

Kristoffer Nielbo
Aarhus University
kln@cas.au.dk

Telma Peura
University of Helsinki
telma.peura@gmail.com

Mads Rosendahl Thomsen
Aarhus University
madsrt@cc.au.dk

Abstract

In the few works that have used NLP to study literary quality, sentiment and emotion analysis have often been considered valuable sources of information. At the same time, the idea that the nature and polarity of the sentiments expressed by a novel might have something to do with its perceived quality seems limited at best. In this paper, we argue that the fractality of narratives, specifically the long-term memory of their sentiment arcs, rather than their simple shape or average valence, might play an important role in the perception of literary quality by a human audience. In particular, we argue that such measure can help distinguish Nobel-winning writers from control groups in a recent corpus of English language novels. To test this hypothesis, we present the results from two studies: (i) a probability distribution test, where we compute the probability of seeing a title from a Nobel laureate at different levels of arc fractality; (ii) a classification test, where we use several machine learning algorithms to measure the predictive power of both sentiment arcs and their fractality measure. Our findings seem to indicate that despite the competitive and complex nature of the task, the populations of Nobel and non-Nobel laureates seem to behave differently and can to some extent be told apart by a classifier.

1 Introduction

The question of what defines the perception of quality in literature is probably as old as narrative itself, but the ability to process and analyze large quantities of literary texts, and to perform complex statistical experiments on them (Moretti, 2013), has recently made new ways of studying this question possible. This does not mean that the riddle has become easy at all: first of all, studying literary quality with methods from corpus linguistics means that one has to create a dataset of "high quality" texts, usually to contrast against "lower quality" texts; second, while it is possible to analyze a larger number of texts in a shorter time, we need to know where to look to find possible, non-obvious correlations with the perception of quality. Recently, a series of studies have looked into the possibility of correlating some fractal properties of a text - the degree of fractality of its sentences' length, sentiment arc, or succession of topics - with its literary quality. These studies have been using as a proxy to define the quality of a text either canons defined by a single scholar, or majority-vote measures taken by large reader platforms, where the aggregated score given by a large number of readers is used as the value of the book, often with a threshold to transform it into a binary problem. Other similar works have used the number of sales of a book to approximate its "quality".

In this work, we try to use a perhaps more daring, less explored metric to define quality: we apply an already tested measure: the fractality of the sentiment arc of a text, which is the curve that represents the changes in sentiment throughout the text. We compute this metric for a group of texts written by authors who won the Nobel Prize for Literature, and we ask whether this simple measure can help tell such texts from a highly competitive control group.

Despite the difficulty of the task - in the best cases, Nobel Prizes are assigned to only one among many valid competitors, which means that several high quality writers will fall in the negative class - our results seem to indicate that a weak but reliable signal is present, and that it can be exploited by classic machine learning algorithms to predict whether a narrative's arc belongs to a Nobel laureate or not.

The paper is organized as follows: in Section 2, we describe some of the most relevant related works in sentiment analysis and fractal theory for

The 2nd International Workshop on Natural Language Processing for Digital Humanities (NLP4DH), pages 31–41
November 20, 2022.

studies in literary quality. In Section 3 we present the corpus and discuss the idea of using Nobel Prize winners; Section 4 gives a detailed overview of the concept of series fractality for sentiment arcs. Finally, Section 5 details the settings of our experiments and Section 6 presents our main results. In Section 7 we discuss our conclusions and possible future works.

2 Related Works

2.1 Sentiment Arcs of Narratives

Drawing the sentiment arc of a story is one of the simplest methods to abstract a narrative's shape. At the same time the sentiment or emotional aspect of communication is often regarded as one of the most relevant in narrative, especially "artistic" narrative (Drobot, 2013), as it is linked with the central and somewhat unique property of literary texts of evoking, rather than describing, experiences and inner states. As Hu et al. (2021) argues, readers have to emotionally engage with the evolution of the story, and a sentiment arc is an index of those engagement "prompts". For this reason, sentiment analysis models (Alm, 2008; Jain et al., 2017), at the word (Mohammad, 2018), sentence (Mäntylä et al., 2018) or paragraph (Li et al., 2019) level, have often been employed in computational literary studies (Cambria et al., 2017; Kim and Klinger, 2018; Brooke et al., 2015; Jockers, 2017). Sentiment analysis usually draws its scores from human annotations of single words (Mohammad and Turney, 2013) or from lexicons induced from labelled documents (Islam et al., 2020). Several studies have tried to complement the essentiality of sentiment analysis with algorithms for textual emotion detection (Alm et al., 2005), or by developing more complex SA tools (Xu et al., 2020). Scholars usually analyse sentiment arcs in terms of their overall shape (Reagan et al., 2016), but recent developments have looked for more complex mathematical properties (Gao et al., 2016).

2.2 Fractality

The study of fractals (Mandelbrot and Ness, 1968; Mandelbrot, 1982, 1997), especially applied to long series (Beran, 1994; Eke et al., 2002; Kuznetsov et al., 2013) offers a new way of looking into the properties of narrative and literary texts, exploring their degree of predictability or self-similarity (Cordeiro et al., 2015), following links with fractal properties already found in visual arts and musics. Recently, Mohseni et al. (2021) have looked into the degree of fractality of canonical and non-canonical literary texts using a series of classical stylometric features such as sentence length, type-token ratio and part of speech ratio, while Hu et al. (2021) applied fractal analysis to a novel's sentiment arc. Bizzoni et al. (2022) explore this possibility further, showing that sentiment arcs' fractality appears to correlate with the perceived quality of literary fairy tales. Nonetheless, not all studies on literary quality have relied on sentiments or fractality: important results have also been obtained with much simpler measures such as bigram frequency (van Cranenburgh and Koolen, 2015).

2.3 Quality

The idea that readers' perception of what is pleasant or engaging could be found in complex statistical patterns has given rise to a series of attempts to approach literary quality using quantitative models (Moretti, 2013). While it is hardly meaningful to define an absolute measure for something like the apperception of quality, this line of research has had to define strategies to approximate a value of quality for a dataset of texts. To "measure quality", most works to this date have looked for large scale collections of readers' preferences, from books' sales to average scores on reading platforms such as GoodReads (Kousha et al., 2017), while a smaller number of work has instead tried to rely on established literary canons (Wilkens, 2012). Although these two concepts of quality are distinct and often retrieve different collections of titles, Walsh and Antoniak (2021) have observed that their overlap might be much larger than expected. In both cases, the possibility of comparing different canons and different aggregations of readers' preferences has opened the possibility of expanding the scope and reliability of aesthetic studies of literature (Underwood, 2019; Wilkens, 2012).

3 A dataset of Nobel literature

The first problem in determining the relationship between sentiment arcs and literary quality is finding a metric for literary quality itself; and it could be argued that the problem of finding a reliable source of quality judgments is the same that every individual reader has when faced with an amount of literature too large to read and evaluate alone (Underwood, 2019) - it's one of the main reasons why literary awards exist at all. While several previ-

	N. Authors	N. Titles
Whole corpus	7000	9089
Nobel group	18	85
Control group	738	1312

Table 1: Overall titles and authors in the corpus, number of Nobel laureates and dimensions of the control group.

ous works attempting to classify or measure some aspect of literary quality have relied on quantitative metrics such as number of copies sold or average reviews on large scale platforms - or even in newspapers - few attempts have been made, to the best of our knowledge, to use high prestige literary awards as a central metrics to approximate the quality of a work. In this paper we try to use arguably the most prestigious international literary award, the Nobel Prize for Literature, as our sole guide to select literary quality. Naturally, this setting is a deliberate extremization: no literary award can possibly be considered the unique indicator of what literary quality is, and questions on the sensibility of the Nobel committee's choices, both in terms of who got the prize and in terms of who did not receive it, rise almost every year. At the same time, high level literary prizes can work as imperfect guidelines for one kind of quality, and it would be interesting to find out whether, on a larger scale than single books or authors, a "signal" telling Nobel-winning texts from a control population can be found.

Unfortunately, no comprehensive corpus of Nobel-winning authors exists to date. To carry out our experiment, we used a recent corpus of literary texts, the Chicago Corpus, compiled by Hoyt Long and Richard Jean So, composed of 9089 novels published in the US between 1880 and 2000. The corpus contains key works of US Nobel laureates, seminal works from mainstream literature as well as relevant works in genres such as Mystery and Science Fiction (Long and Roland, 2016). [1]

The US Nobel laureates in the corpus make the relative majority of the group of Nobel laureates, e.g. John Galsworthy, Sinclair Lewis, William Faulkner, Ernest Hemingway, John Steinbeck, Saul Bellow and Toni Morrison. Works by non-US writers like for example Knut Hamsun, Samuel Beckett and Nadine Gordimer are represented with a more limited selection of their work.

As noted, the corpus is highly curated and contains high quality fiction from authors who have received other prizes, like the National Book Award, e.g. Don DeLillo, Joyce Carol Oates, and Philip Roth. Our expectation is therefore not that Nobel laureates will be completely different from the rest of the corpus, also in terms of literary quality.

Finally it is worth noting that the whole corpus is heavily skewed towards the Anglosaxon literature, and that both the Nobel laureates and their control group are mainly constituted by Anglophone writers. This naturally moves the whole contest on the plain of a well refined "Anglo-centric" canon. While it does not damage our experiments per se, given that the same imbalance happens among the Nobel laureates as among the remaining writers, it is a distortion that we have to keep in mind.

4 Fractality of sentiment arcs

To estimate the long-term memory of sentiment arcs we combine non-linear adaptive filtering with fractal analysis, specifically adaptive fractal analysis (Gao et al., 2011; Tung et al., 2011). Non-linear adaptive filtering is used because of the inherent noisiness of story arcs. First, the signal is partitioned into segments (or windows) of length $w = 2n + 1$ points, where neighboring segments overlap by $n + 1$. The time scale is $n + 1$ points, which ensures symmetry. Then, for each segment, a polynomial of order D is fitted. Note that $D = 0$ means a piece-wise constant, and $D = 1$ a linear fit. The fitted polynomial for ith and $(i + 1)th$ is denoted as $y^{(i)}(l_1), y^{(i+1)}(l_2)$, where $l_1, l_2 = 1, 2, ..., 2n + 1$. Note the length of the last segment may be shorter than w. We use the following weights for the overlap of two segments.

$$y^{(c)}(l_1) = w_1 y^{(i)}(l + n) + w_2 y^{(i)}(l), \quad l = 1, 2, \ldots, n + 1 \quad (1)$$

where $w_1 = (1 - \frac{l-1}{n}), w_2 = 1 - w_1$ can be written as $(1 - \frac{d_j}{n}), j = 1, 2$, where d_j denotes the distance between the point of overlapping segments and the center of $y^{(i)}, y^{(i+1)}$. The weights decrease linearly with the distance between the point and center of the segment. This ensures that the filter is continuous everywhere, which ensures that non-boundary points are smooth.

We use the Hurst exponent to measure long-term memory. Assuming that stochastic process $X =$

[1]Several quantitative literary studies have used the corpus (Underwood et al., 2018; Cheng, 2020), which can be found at https://textual-optics-lab.uchicago.edu/us_novel_corpus.

$X_t : t = 0, 1, 2, ...$, with stable covariance, mean μ and σ^2, the process' autocorrelation function for $r(k), k \geq 0$ is:

$$r(k) = \frac{E\left[X(t)X(t+k)\right]}{E\left[X(t)^2\right]} \sim k^{2H-2}, \text{as} \quad k \to \infty \tag{2}$$

where H is called the Hurst exponent (Mandelbrot, 1982). For $0.5 < H < 1$ the story arc is characterized by persistent such that increments are followed by increases and decreases by further decreases. For $H = 0.5$ the story arc only has short-range correlations; and when $H < 0.5$ the story arc is anti-persistent such that increments are followed by decreases and decreases by increments. For the specific application domain (i.e., narratives) persistent story arcs are characteristic of coherent narratives, where the emotional intensity evolves at longer time scales. Story arcs' that only show short memory lack coherence and appear like a collection of short stories. Anti-persistent story arcs will appear bland and rigid narratives oscillating around an average emotional state (Hu et al., 2021).

Detrended fluctuation analysis (DFA) is the most widely used method for estimating the Hurst parameter, but DFA may involve discontinuities at the boundaries of adjacent segments. Such discontinuities can be detrimental when the data contain trends (Hu et al., 2001), non-stationarity (Kantelhardt et al., 2002), or nonlinear oscillatory components (Chen et al., 2005; Hu et al., 2009). Adaptive fractal analysis is a more robust alternative to DFA (Gao et al., 2011; Tung et al., 2011). AFA consists of the following steps: first, the original process is transformed to a random walk process through first-order integration $u(n) = \sum_{k=1}^{n}(x(k) - \overline{x}), n = 1, 2, 3, ..., N$, where $\overline{x}$ is the mean of $x(k)$. Second, we extract the global trend $(v(i), i = 1, 2, 3, ..., N)$ through the nonlinear adaptive filtering. The residuals $(u(i) - v(i))$ reflect the fluctuations around a global trend. We obtain the Hurst parameter by estimating the slope of the linear fit between the residuals' standard deviation $F^{(2)}(w)$ and w window size as follows:

$$F^{(2)}(w) = \left[\frac{1}{N}\sum_{i=1}^{N}(u(i) - v(i))^2\right]^{\frac{1}{2}} \sim w^H \tag{3}$$

All our sentiment arcs are sentence based, extracted using the VADER model (Hutto and Gilbert, 2014) in NLTK's implementation (Bird, 2006). While VADER is not the most recent Sentiment Analysis model, we chose it for its transparency, since it is possible to reconstruct the reasons of its judgments based on its systems of rules, as well as its popularity, as its underlying dictionary and set of rules has proven the weapon of choice for a large number of previous works. The sentiment arc is obtained by first computing the sentiment of each word in the text, and then by computing the average sentiment of each sentence. The sentiment of a word is in turn obtained using an ad-hoc lexicon, which links a sentiment score to each word and takes care of morphological variations. The sentiment of a sentence is then computed as the average of the sentiment scores of all the words in that sentence, by taking care of tricky structures like negations, intensifiers and so forth.

5 Experiments

We present the results for two experiments:

1. Without directly testing the predictive power of narrative sentiment arcs and their Hurst exponent, we analyzed its distribution in both Nobel-winning and non-Nobel-winning populations, to test whether the two populations might differ in their average score;

2. To directly test the predictive power of our Hurst exponent, we ran a series of classifiers to check whether sentiment arcs and their Hurst score can provide a degree of predictive power on telling whether or not a given text is likely to belong to a Nobel-winning author.

In both cases, we decided to design the non-Nobel-winning class (or control group) in order to be as contextual to the Nobel population as possible: for each book belonging to an author who won the Nobel prize, we took all novels published between one year before and one year after its publication date, and we considered them as the "control group" for that book. All the control groups for all books of one author work as the control group for that author, and all control groups together combine into the overall control group for the Nobel prize population. We did this also to mimic as much as possible the logic of the prize itself, that selects between contemporary candidates. A detailed summary of this selection process can be seen in Table 2.

Nobel	N. titles	Control
S. Beckett	1	32
S. Bellow	5	228
W. Churchill	4	125
W. Faulkner	15	332
J. Galsworthy	9	105
W. Golding	2	6
N. Gordimer	2	3
K. Hamsun	1	1
E. Hemingway	7	170
R. Kipling	3	19
D. Lessing	3	34
S. Lewis	8	137
T. Morrison	5	192
A. Munro	1	2
J. Steinbeck	15	81
R. Tagore	1	19
S. Undset	2	32
P. White	1	0
Total	85	1518

Table 2: Number of titles per Nobel and control group. Notice that the control group's total number is higher than the one reported in Table 1 since one title can figure in more than a subgroup.

5.1 Probability distribution

In the first experiment, we simply focused on the possibility that the Nobel-winning population might have a different Hurst score distribution than the control group, and that such difference might be statistically significant on the large scale. To further test this idea, we divided our corpus in Hurst classes (e.g. all titles having a Hurst score of 0.51, 0.52, etc.) and we looked at the probability of seeing a title from a Nobel laureate in each of these classes. To deal with the problem of having a heavily imbalanced dataset, since the control authors are much more numerous in any class than Nobel winning authors, we computed the probabilities on a sub-sampled portion of the control group as large as the Nobel group, so that both populations sum up to the exact same amount. Finally, in order to avoid relying on random lucky or unlucky sub-samplings from the majority class, and in general to increase the representativity of our comparison, we repeated the random majority class sub-sampling 100 times and drew the average probability for each Hurst class. The result is that for each class of Hurst values, we compute the probability of seeing a Nobel author's title and the average probability of seeing a non-Nobel author's title as computed over several subsamples.[2]

5.2 Classification

In the second experiment, we trained four different classifiers:

- **Quadratic Discriminant Analysis** classifier (Bose et al., 2015): a generative model that is particularly apt to classify data when the decision boundaries are non-linear;
- **Gaussian Naive Bayes** classifier (Chan et al., 1982): we chose this model particularly for its ability to handle small and complex training data;
- **Random Forest** classifier (Ho, 1995): this algorithm is well suited to make fine-grained predictions on data that are not necessarily linearly divisible;
- **Decision Tree** classifier, which has the benefits of being simple and able to handle relatively small datasets (Swain and Hauska, 1977).

As features, we used the Hurst score and a condensed version of the sentiment arc for each novel.

The large difference in our classes' sizes represents an additional difficulty. The sparsity of Nobel titles makes training on the dataset as is a seemingly meaningless task, since classifiers systematically ignore or misrepresent the minority class. To contrast that dataset's imbalance, we tried three resampling techniques:

- **Random** subsampling: this is the easiest resampling technique, and it simply means that we randomly drew from the majority class a number of data points equal to the size of the minority class, as we did in Section 5.1;
- **Near Miss** subsampling (Mani and Zhang, 2003; Bao et al., 2016), specifically the so called *Near-Miss 1* method: this is a more sophisticated undersampling technique based on the distance between items from the majority and items from the minority class, where the elements from the majority class with the smallest average distance to three minority class examples are selected for comparison.

[2]This naturally means that the probabilities do not necessarily sum up to 1.

	Score	p-value
T-test	2.57	0.01
Anova	6.63	0.01
Mann-Whitney U	55106	0.023
Kruskal-Wallis	5.166	0.023

Table 3: Difference between Nobel laureates and control group as tested by four significance measures (the first two assume that the populations have a normal distribution, the last two do not make such assumption). In all cases, the difference in Hurst score distributions is statistically significant.

In this way, the algorithm selects datapoints that are closest to the decision boundary;

- **SMOTE** upsampling (Chawla et al., 2002), a upsampling technique widespread in machine learning, often used in cases of severely imbalanced datasets (Liu et al., 2019; Rustogi and Prasad, 2019). SMOTE has the considerable benefit of creating not simple duplicates of the observed datapoints, but rather slightly different synthetic datapoints, increasing the ability of a classifier of modeling a minority class.

6 Results

6.1 Probability distribution

The difference between the distributions of Hurst scores for the Nobel and the control group is statistically significant according to several measures, as can be seen in Table 3.

The probability of seeing a text from a Nobel laureate peaks at a different point than the probability of seeing a text from the control group (see Figure 1). The distribution of the two groups reinforces the hypothesis, laid by Hu et al. (2021), that high literary quality might lie in a specific area on the Hurst continuum - in other words, that there might be a specific interval of Hurst values where high quality narrative texts are most likely to fall. Naturally we should not ignore the fact that the two probability distributions have a considerable overlap; that the statistical significance, while being strong, does not mean that the two groups are completely separable; and that the number of control titles is higher than the number of titles from Nobel-winning authors for any Hurst interval. In other words, any text has a lower probability of belonging to a Nobel laureate than of belonging to an author that did not win the Nobel prize - after all it's possible to award the Nobel prize to just one person every year. At the same time, if we take equal-sized classes for the two groups, texts having a Hurst score ranging approximately between 0.53 and 0.61 seem to have a higher probability of belonging to a Nobel laureate than of belonging to a control author, while texts falling outside of this range have a higher probability of belonging to a control author than of belonging to a Nobel laureate: again, the Nobel population and the control population display statistically different behaviours on the Hurst continuum. Figure 1 offers a visualization of our results.

A cursory qualitative examination of the results for different authors proved that these results often (but not always) correspond to what we might expect from a given title or author. For example John Steinbeck, one of the best represented writers in the corpus with 15 novels, has an average Hurst exponent of 0.598, and thus differs insignificantly from the 90 works in its control group, that score an average of 0.606, but with a more significant standard deviation (0.41 vs. 0.25). While Steinbeck's novels Hurst scores range from 0.56 to 0.64, the two novels that get by far the highest average grades on GoodReads (*Mice and Men* and *The Grapes of Wrath* with *Cannery Row* as a very distant third) both have a Hurst exponent of exactly 0.58, at the apex of the probability curve for Nobel titles. Similar observations can be made for the works for other popular Nobel laureates, such as Hemingway, with his most renowned titles (such as for example *The Old Man and the Sea* or *For whom the bell tolls*) roughly falling within what we considered a fuzzy Goldilocks interval for literary quality, while less acclaimed texts such as *To have and have not* are clearly out of it (Figure 1). Many other factors play into the success of these prominent novels, but their location in the middle of what seems to be a "Goldilocks"-zone for variability is significant, also when studied on the level of the individual authorship.

6.2 Classification

Among the three techniques we adopted to resample our dataset, we found that randomly undersampling the majority class does not yield particularly strong results, while Near Miss understampling and SMOTE oversampling both bring the models to better performances (see Figure 2). The reason for this lies probably in the fact that the difference between

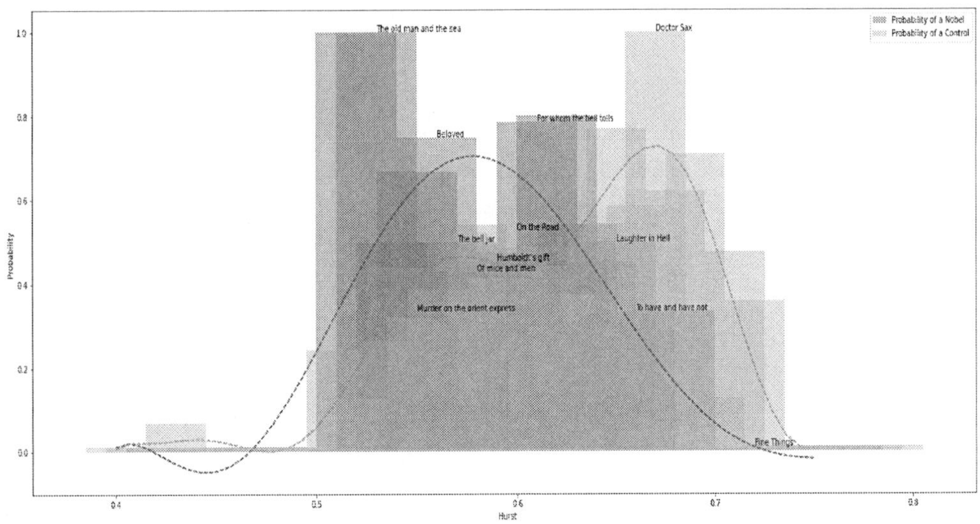

Figure 1: Probability distribution of the Nobel group and of the control group. The control population's probabilities are averaged over 100 different selections. We added some titles for reference. Not all works from Nobel laureates fall in the Hurst "sweet spot": for example, *The Old Man and The Sea* has a Hurst score of 0.53, while the less acclaimed *To Have and Have Not* from the same author has a Hurst score of 0.69.

the two populations, while present, is quite difficult to pick up even when we control for size: after all, we are using a corpus with a large number of high quality authors that did not win a Nobel prize, so the control group is both much larger than the Nobel group and bound to have several elements similar to its members. Just randomly subsampling from the majority class to create a small group of non-Nobels to learn from makes the task very difficult, while an algorithm like Near Miss, that selects data with the least distance to the negative classe's samples, essentially selecting learning cases that is most fruitful for the classifier to model, brings significantly better results. Finally, it's worth noting how SMOTE upsampling brings about the highest performances of the group (excluding the "All dataset" case): while this technique does not create completely dependable results, since it relies on the synthetic generation of new data points for the minority class, its effectiveness can make us more confident in postulating that a difference between the Nobel and the control populations does indeed exist.

In Table 4 we provide a summary of the performances, adding in parenthesis the performance of the classifiers when they are only fed information from the sentiment arcs, without accessing the Hurst exponent. The comparison seems to us quite interesting: the sentiment arcs seem to suffice in bringing about better-than-chance performances, and in some cases even quite high scores; on the other hand, all classifiers trained on a feature set enriched by the single dimension of the arcs' Hurst exponent perform better than when they do not have access to such information, with no exception, and in some cases the single presence of the Hurst exponent increases the F scores significantly.

7 Discussion and Conclusions

In this paper we have tried to use a measure of fractality for sentiment arcs to distinguish Nobel-winning writers in a corpus of selected literary texts in the English language, as a case for the relevance of this metric in literary quality evaluation. We are not interested in the overall valence of a literary work as such, but in its patterns of variation and repetition throughout the narrative arc, although the underlying argument for using sentiment analysis (and not just, for example, PoS tagging) is that it can be linked to the evocation of emotions in the work. Even if it is far from catching the expressions of emotions perfectly, as there are many way to express them, also through words with a neutral sentiment, we believe it remains a strong

	Original dataset	Random Subs.	Near Miss	SMOTE Ups.
Quadratic Discr. An.	0.90 (0.90)	0.55 (0.51)	0.56 (0.51)	0.57 (0.50)
Gaussian Naive Bayes	0.91 (0.90)	0.52 (0.49)	0.80 (0.67)	0.67 (0.53)
Decision Tree Cl.	0.88 (0.88)	0.57 (0.52)	0.69 (0.60)	0.87 (0.82)
Random Forest	0.91 (0.90)	0.53 (0.51)	0.79 (0.62)	**0.90 (0.86)**
Average				

Table 4: Weighted F scores, averaged from a 10-fold cross-validation, for four classifiers trained on different versions of the dataset. Notice how the results on the "all dataset" column are effects of the majority class being overwhelmingly larger than the minority class. In parenthesis, we add the performances when only using information from the sentiment arcs. The other three columns, reporting results based on resampled versions of the dataset, do not resent of the distortion.

indicator of the work's rhetoric appeal structure. Overall, the best attitude towards this kind of metric is probably similar to the attitude we can have towards the aesthetic properties of fractals in music or visual arts: it is never *necessary* for a work of art to contain anything fractal, but on the large scale we could expect fractal patterns to hold a correlation with the perception of beauty. In the same way, we should not imagine a systematic relationship between quality and a given range of Hurst exponents: first of all because there is no single way to measure literary quality, and second because a "good" Hurst exponent can hardly be the single factor in high quality textual narrative. Nonetheless, we have found that the distribution of Hurst exponents, as computed on the sentiment arcs of whole novels, for the titles of authors who won a Literature Nobel Prize is different from the distribution of Hurst exponents for the titles of the control group. This is particularly relevant considering that the control group still included several high-level writers, from Nabokov to Woolf, who can be said to rival the Nobel population in terms of both fame and critical acclaim. What this difference in distribution seems to indicate is that there might be a "sweet spot" of self-similarity in sentiment arcs, roughly between 0.53 and 0.61, where the probability of seeing a text from a Nobel laureate grows and the probability of seeing a title from a non-Nobel laureate decreases. Following on this finding, we tried to create a classifier that would tell whether a text came from a Nobel laureate or not based on its Hurst exponent and a representation of its sentiment arc only. What we found is that when we control for data imbalance by using Near Miss subsampling or SMOTE upsampling, classifiers appear to perform well above chance, while if we subsample randomly their performance suffers considerably. We consider this a indication that a "signal" for Nobel laureates exists, despite the highly competitive control group, and that it falls in line with previous studies on the Hurst exponent for sentiment arcs.

8 Future Work

Given the scope and complexity of the concept of literary quality, there are several interesting directions this research can take. A sensible next step would be to increase the size of our corpus to include more texts, in order to see if the signal for Nobel laureates becomes more pronounced. Specifically, we aim at increasing the number of titles in the minority class, both by looking at other prestigious awards and by including not only the winners, but also the list of nominees. Being pre-selected for a prestigious award, nominees could help creating a larger "quality class" and might even temper the random or political factors playing in the choice of a single individual winner. The Chicago corpus does not offer such information in its metadata, but it is still possible and even relatively easy to access it for the Nobel prize. Other large English language prizes like the Pulitzer Prize would also be of great interest to create a larger subset. Another goal worth striving for, albeit on a longer time scale, is to include a more diverse range of titles. The Chicago corpus is constituted mainly of Anglophone writers - both the Nobel group and its control are heavily skewed towards the Anglo-Saxon literature. Finally, the internal imbalance in the amount of titles that different Nobel laureates hold in our selection might play a role in the be-

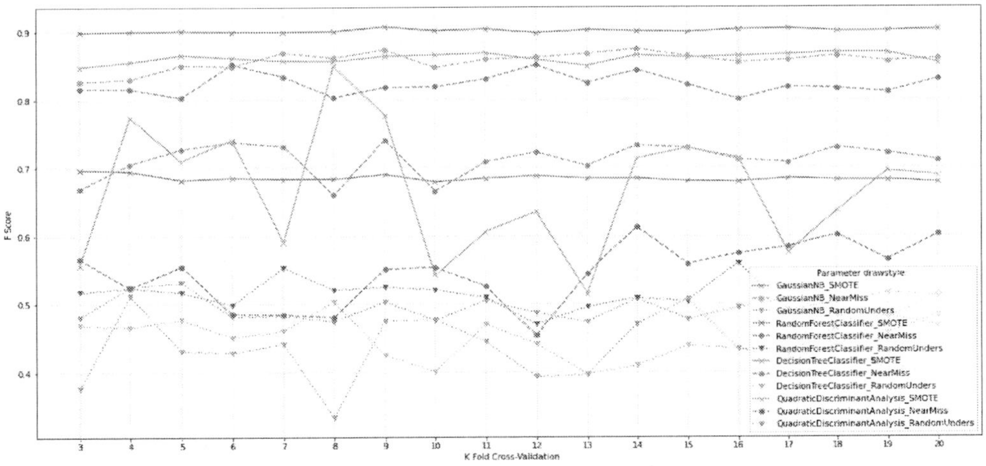

Figure 2: Classification results for our 4 classifiers under three different assumptions: random undersampling, Near Miss undersampling and SMOTE upsampling, with increasing number of folds in a K-folds cross-validation.

haviour of the systems. While we are comforted by the fact that the same metrics have proved useful with completely different authors in previous works, in future we would like to design ablation experiments aimed at checking the performance of the machine learning models on the less represented names. Finally, it would be interesting to see if this signal is specific to English-language texts or if it appears in other languages as well.

References

Cecilia Ovesdotter Alm, Dan Roth, and Richard Sproat. 2005. Emotions from text: machine learning for text-based emotion prediction. In *Proceedings of human language technology conference and conference on empirical methods in natural language processing*, pages 579–586.

Ebba Cecilia Ovesdotter Alm. 2008. *Affect in* text and speech*. University of Illinois at Urbana-Champaign.

Lei Bao, Cao Juan, Jintao Li, and Yongdong Zhang. 2016. Boosted near-miss under-sampling on svm ensembles for concept detection in large-scale imbalanced datasets. *Neurocomputing*, 172:198–206.

Jan Beran. 1994. *Statistics for Long-Memory Processes*, 1 edition. Chapman and Hall/CRC, New York.

Steven Bird. 2006. Nltk: the natural language toolkit. In *Proceedings of the COLING/ACL 2006 Interactive Presentation Sessions*, pages 69–72.

Yuri Bizzoni, Telma Peura, Kristoffer Nielbo, and Mads Thomsen. 2022. Fractal sentiments and fairy tales-fractal scaling of narrative arcs as predictor of the perceived quality of andersen's fairy tales. *Journal of Data Mining & Digital Humanities*.

Smarajit Bose, Amita Pal, Rita SahaRay, and Jitadeepa Nayak. 2015. Generalized quadratic discriminant analysis. *Pattern Recognition*, 48(8):2676–2684.

Julian Brooke, Adam Hammond, and Graeme Hirst. 2015. Gutentag: an nlp-driven tool for digital humanities research in the project gutenberg corpus. In *Proceedings of the Fourth Workshop on Computational Linguistics for Literature*, pages 42–47.

Erik Cambria, Dipankar Das, Sivaji Bandyopadhyay, and Antonio Feraco. 2017. Affective computing and sentiment analysis. In *A practical guide to sentiment analysis*, pages 1–10. Springer.

Tony F Chan, Gene H Golub, and Randall J LeVeque. 1982. Updating formulae and a pairwise algorithm for computing sample variances.

In *COMPSTAT 1982 5th Symposium held at Toulouse 1982*, pages 30–41. Springer.

Nitesh V Chawla, Kevin W Bowyer, Lawrence O Hall, and W Philip Kegelmeyer. 2002. Smote: synthetic minority over-sampling technique. *Journal of artificial intelligence research*, 16:321–357.

Zhi Chen, Kun Hu, Pedro Carpena, Pedro Bernaola-Galvan, H. Eugene Stanley, and Plamen Ch. Ivanov. 2005. Effect of nonlinear filters on detrended fluctuation analysis. *Phys. Rev. E*, 71(1):011104.

Jonathan Cheng. 2020. Fleshing out models of gender in english-language novels (1850–2000). *Journal of Cultural Analytics*, 5(1):11652.

João Cordeiro, Pedro R. M. Inácio, and Diogo A. B. Fernandes. 2015. Fractal beauty in text. In *Progress in Artificial Intelligence*, Lecture Notes in Computer Science, pages 796–802. Springer International Publishing.

Andreas van Cranenburgh and Corina Koolen. 2015. Identifying literary texts with bigrams. In *Proceedings of the Fourth Workshop on Computational Linguistics for Literature*, pages 58–67.

Irina-Ana Drobot. 2013. Affective narratology. the emotional structure of stories. *Philologica Jassyensia*, 9(2):338.

A. Eke, P. Herman, L. Kocsis, and L. R. Kozak. 2002. Fractal characterization of complexity in temporal physiological signals. *Physiological Measurement*, 23(1):R1.

Jianbo Gao, Jing Hu, and Wen-wen Tung. 2011. Facilitating Joint Chaos and Fractal Analysis of Biosignals through Nonlinear Adaptive Filtering. *PLoS ONE*, 6(9):e24331.

Jianbo Gao, Matthew L Jockers, John Laudun, and Timothy Tangherlini. 2016. A multiscale theory for the dynamical evolution of sentiment in novels. In *2016 International Conference on Behavioral, Economic and Socio-cultural Computing (BESC)*, pages 1–4. IEEE.

Tin Kam Ho. 1995. Random decision forests. In *Proceedings of 3rd international conference on document analysis and recognition*, volume 1, pages 278–282. IEEE.

Jing Hu, Jianbo Gao, and Xingsong Wang. 2009. Multifractal analysis of sunspot time series: the effects of the 11-year cycle and Fourier truncation. *Journal of Statistical Mechanics: Theory and Experiment*, 2009(02):P02066.

Kun Hu, Plamen Ch. Ivanov, Zhi Chen, Pedro Carpena, and H. Eugene Stanley. 2001. Effect of trends on detrended fluctuation analysis. *Physical Review E*, 64(1).

Qiyue Hu, Bin Liu, Mads Rosendahl Thomsen, Jianbo Gao, and Kristoffer L Nielbo. 2021. Dynamic evolution of sentiments in never let me go: Insights from multifractal theory and its implications for literary analysis. *Digital Scholarship in the Humanities*, 36(2):322–332.

Clayton Hutto and Eric Gilbert. 2014. Vader: A parsimonious rule-based model for sentiment analysis of social media text. In *Proceedings of the international AAAI conference on web and social media*, volume 8, pages 216–225.

SM Mazharul Islam, Xin Luna Dong, and Gerard de Melo. 2020. Domain-specific sentiment lexicons induced from labeled documents. In *Proceedings of the 28th International Conference on Computational Linguistics*, pages 6576–6587.

Swapnil Jain, Shrikant Malviya, Rohit Mishra, and Uma Shanker Tiwary. 2017. Sentiment analysis: An empirical comparative study of various machine learning approaches. In *Proceedings of the 14th International Conference on Natural Language Processing (ICON-2017)*, pages 112–121, Kolkata, India. NLP Association of India.

Matthew Jockers. 2017. Syuzhet: Extracts sentiment and sentiment-derived plot arcs from text (version 1.0. 1).

Jan W. Kantelhardt, Stephan A. Zschiegner, Eva Koscielny-Bunde, Shlomo Havlin, Armin Bunde, and H. Eugene Stanley. 2002. Multifractal detrended fluctuation analysis of nonstationary time series. *Physica A: Statistical Mechanics and its Applications*, 316(1-4):87–114.

Evgeny Kim and Roman Klinger. 2018. A survey on sentiment and emotion analysis for computational literary studies.

Kayvan Kousha, Mike Thelwall, and Mahshid Abdoli. 2017. Goodreads reviews to assess the wider impacts of books. 68(8):2004–2016. _eprint: https://onlinelibrary.wiley.com/doi/pdf/10.1002/asi.23805.

Nikita Kuznetsov, Scott Bonnette, Jianbo Gao, and Michael A. Riley. 2013. Adaptive Fractal Analysis Reveals Limits to Fractal Scaling in Center of Pressure Trajectories. *Annals of Biomedical Engineering*, 41(8):1646–1660.

Xin Li, Lidong Bing, Wenxuan Zhang, and Wai Lam. 2019. Exploiting bert for end-to-end aspect-based sentiment analysis. *arXiv preprint arXiv:1910.00883*.

Shiyu Liu, Ming Lun Ong, Kar Kin Mun, Jia Yao, and Mehul Motani. 2019. Early prediction of sepsis via smote upsampling and mutual information based downsampling. In *2019 Computing in Cardiology (CinC)*, pages Page–1. IEEE.

Hoyt Long and Teddy Roland. 2016. Us novel corpus. Technical report, Textual Optic Labs, University of Chicago.

Benoit Mandelbrot. 1982. *The Fractal Geometry of Nature*, updated ed. edition edition. Times Books, San Francisco.

Benoit B. Mandelbrot. 1997. *Fractals and Scaling in Finance: Discontinuity, Concentration, Risk. Selecta Volume E*, 1997 edition edition. Springer, New York.

Benoit B. Mandelbrot and John W. Van Ness. 1968. Fractional Brownian Motions, Fractional Noises and Applications. *SIAM Review*, 10(4):422–437.

Inderjeet Mani and I Zhang. 2003. knn approach to unbalanced data distributions: a case study involving information extraction. In *Proceedings of workshop on learning from imbalanced datasets*, volume 126, pages 1–7. ICML.

Saif M. Mohammad. 2018. Obtaining reliable human ratings of valence, arousal, and dominance for 20,000 english words. In *Proceedings of The Annual Conference of the Association for Computational Linguistics (ACL)*, Melbourne, Australia.

Saif M Mohammad and Peter D Turney. 2013. Nrc emotion lexicon. *National Research Council, Canada*, 2.

Mahdi Mohseni, Volker Gast, and Christoph Redies. 2021. Fractality and variability in canonical and non-canonical english fiction and in non-fictional texts. 12.

Franco Moretti. 2013. *Distant reading*. Verso Books.

Mika V. Mäntylä, Daniel Graziotin, and Miikka Kuutila. 2018. The evolution of sentiment analysis—a review of research topics, venues, and top cited papers. 27:16–32.

Andrew J Reagan, Lewis Mitchell, Dilan Kiley, Christopher M Danforth, and Peter Sheridan Dodds. 2016. The emotional arcs of stories are dominated by six basic shapes. 5(1):1–12. Publisher: SpringerOpen.

Rishabh Rustogi and Ayush Prasad. 2019. Swift imbalance data classification using smote and extreme learning machine. In *2019 International Conference on Computational Intelligence in Data Science (ICCIDS)*, pages 1–6. IEEE.

Philip H Swain and Hans Hauska. 1977. The decision tree classifier: Design and potential. *IEEE Transactions on Geoscience Electronics*, 15(3):142–147.

Wen-wen Tung, Jianbo Gao, Jing Hu, and Lei Yang. 2011. Detecting chaos in heavy-noise environments. *Physical Review E*, 83(4).

Ted Underwood. 2019. *Distant Horizons: Digital Evidence and Literary Change*. University of Chicago Press. Publication Title: Distant Horizons.

Ted Underwood, David Bamman, and Sabrina Lee. 2018. The transformation of gender in english-language fiction. *Journal of Cultural Analytics*, 3(2):11035.

Melanie Walsh and Maria Antoniak. 2021. The goodreads 'classics': A computational study of readers, amazon, and crowdsourced amateur criticism. *Journal of Cultural Analytics*, 4:243–287.

Matthew Wilkens. 2012. Canons, close reading, and the evolution of method. *Debates in the digital humanities*, pages 249–58.

Hu Xu, Bing Liu, Lei Shu, and Philip S Yu. 2020. Dombert: Domain-oriented language model for aspect-based sentiment analysis. *arXiv preprint arXiv:2004.13816*.

Style Classification of Rabbinic Literature for Detection of Lost Midrash Tanḥuma Material

Shlomo Tannor
School of Computer Science
Tel Aviv University
shlomotannor@mail.tau.ac.il

Nachum Dershowitz
School of Computer Science
Tel Aviv University
nachum@tau.ac.il

Moshe Lavee
Department of Jewish History
Haifa University
mlavee@univ.haifa.ac.il

Abstract

Midrash collections are complex rabbinic works that consist of text in multiple languages, which evolved through long processes of unstable oral and written transmission. Determining the origin of a given passage in such a compilation is not always straightforward and is often a matter of dispute among scholars, yet it is essential for scholars' understanding of the passage and its relationship to other texts in the rabbinic corpus.

To help solve this problem, we propose a system for classification of rabbinic literature based on its style, leveraging recently released pretrained Transformer models for Hebrew. Additionally, we demonstrate how our method can be applied to uncover lost material from Midrash Tanḥuma.

1 Introduction

Midrash anthologies are multi-layered works that consist of text in multiple languages, composed by different authors spanning different generations and locations. The midrash collator often merges and quotes various earlier sources, sometimes paraphrasing previous material. These complex processes can make it hard for scholars to clearly separate and detect the different sources which the collection is composed of. Identifying sections which originate in one source or another can shed light on many scholarly debates and help researchers gain a better understanding of the historical development of the rabbinic corpus.

The ability to analyze and classify rabbinic texts in an automated way has tremendous potential. Placing old manuscripts, uncovering lost material that is quoted in later works (e.g. parts of Midrash Tanḥuma, *Mekhilta Deuteronomy*), and determining authorship or dating of a text are examples for such uses. This great potential motivated us to turn to current state-of-the-art natural language processing (NLP) methods to determine whether we can currently solve any such high-impact problem.

We propose a system for classification of rabbinic literature by detecting unique stylistic patterns in the language of the text. Additionally, we demonstrate how our classifier can be used to uncover lost midrashic material that is quoted in later works. As a test case, we apply our method to detect lost sections of the Midrash Tanḥuma that are quoted in the *Yalkut Shimoni*.[1]

2 Related Work

Work from recent years on authorship attribution and plagiarism detection has demonstrated the effectiveness of stylometry and literary style classification in general.

Dershowitz et al. (2015) perform automatic biblical source criticism by looking at preferences among synonyms and other stylistic attributes. Siegal and Shmidman (2018) used computational tools to help reconstruct the lost *Mekhilta Deuteronomy*. They start off with a list of candidate texts, and the main problem they focus on is removing quotes or near-quotes of existing material from other sources. Ithaca (Assael et al., 2022) is an impressive toolkit for restoration and classification of ancient Greek epigraphs.

[1]A medieval midrash anthology from the 13th century CE.

The 2nd International Workshop on Natural Language Processing for Digital Humanities (NLP4DH), pages 42–46
November 20, 2022. ©2022 Association for Computational Linguistics

3 Method

3.1 Dataset

Our training dataset was extracted from Sefaria's resources.[2] We use the raw text files and divide them into the following categories:

Mishnah – In this category we include all tractates of the Mishnah and the Tosefta. Both collections are generally dated to the second century CE and consist of rabbinic rulings and debates, organized by topic.

Midrash Halakhah – These collections are dated to around the same time of the Mishnah, but they are organized according to the Pentateuch and focus more on the exegesis of biblical verses. In this class we include: *Mekhilta d'Rabbi Yishmael*, *Mekhilta d'Rashbi*, *Sifra*, *Sifre Numbers*, and *Sifre Deuteronomy*.

Jerusalem Talmud – We include all tractates of the Jerusalem Talmud, omitting the Mishnah passages that provide the basis for discussion. These texts for the most part are written in Palestinian Aramaic and are roughly dated to the 4th c. CE.

Babylonian Talmud – We include all tractates of the Babylonian Talmud, omitting the Mishnah passages that provide the basis for discussion. These texts for the most part are written in Babylonian Aramaic and are roughly dated to the 5th c.

Midrash Aggadah – In this category we include early midrash works assumed to have been composed during the amoraic period (up to the 5th c.) or slightly later. The works included in training are: *Genesis Rabbah*, *Leviticus Rabbah*, and *Pesikta de-Rav Kahanna*. Like midrash halakhah these works follow the order of verses in the Bible, but in contrast they focus less on deriving rulings (halakhah) and more on expounding on the biblical narrative. Other works which we did not use during training but which we partially associate with this category include: Ruth Rabbah, Lamentations Rabbah, and Canticles Rabbah.

Midrash Tanḥuma – In this category we include later midrashic works which make up what is referred to as Tanḥuma-Yelammedenu Literature. The works included in training are: *Midrash Tanḥuma*, *Midrash Tanḥuma Buber*, and *Deuteronomy Rabbah*. Other works that we did not use during training but we partially associate with this category include Exodus Rabbah starting from Section 15[3] and Numbers Rabbah starting from Section 15.[4]

We divide these works into continuous blocks of 50 words. We then clean the text by removing vowel signs, punctuation and metadata. In order to neutralize the effect of orthography differences, we also expand common acronyms and standardize spelling for common words and names.

After cleaning and normalizing the data, we split our dataset into training (80%) and validation (20%) sets. Finally, we downsample all majority classes in the validation set to get a balanced dataset.

3.2 Models

Baseline. For our baseline model we use a logistic regression model over a bag of n-grams encoding. We include unigrams, bigrams, and trigrams. We use the default parameters from scikit-learn (Pedregosa et al., 2011) but set `fit_intercept=False` to reduce the impact of varying text length and set `class_weight="balanced"` in order to deal with class imbalance in the training data. This type of model is highly interpretable, enabling us to see the features associated with each class. Finally, we choose this model as our baseline as it generally achieves reasonable results without the need to tune hyperparameters.

AlephBERT. The next model we evaluate is AlephBERT (Seker et al., 2022) – a Transformer model trained with the masked-token prediction training objective on modern Hebrew texts. While this model obtains state-of-the-art results for various tasks on modern Hebrew, performance might not be ideal on rabbinic Hebrew, which differs significantly from Modern Hebrew. We train the pre-trained model on the downstream task using the Huggingface Transformers framework (Wolf et al., 2020) for sequence classification, using the default parameters for three epochs.

BEREL. The third model we evaluate is BEREL Shmidman et al. (2022) – a Transformer model trained with a similar architecture to that of BERT-base (Devlin et al., 2019) on rabbinic Hebrew texts.

[2] `https://github.com/Sefaria/Sefaria-Export`

[3] See "Exodus Rabbah," *Encyclopaedia Judaica*, for the rationale behind this division.

[4] See "Numbers Rabbah," *Encyclopaedia Judaica*, for the rationale behind this division.

In addition to the potential benefit of using a model that was pretrained on similar text to that of the target domain, BEREL also uses a modified tokenizer that doesn't split up acronyms which would otherwise be interpreted as multiple tokens with punctuation marks in between. (Acronyms marked by double apostrophes [or the like] are very common in rabbinic Hebrew.) We train the pretrained model on our downstream task in an identical fashion to the training of the AlephBERT model.

Morphological. Finally, we also train a model that focuses only on morphological features in the text, in an attempt to neutralize the impact of content words. We expect this type of model to detect more "pure" stylistic features that help discriminate between the different textual sources. To extract features from the text, we use a morphological engine for rabbinic Hebrew created by DICTA (`https://morph-analysis.dicta.org.il/`). We then train a logistic regression model over an aggregation of all morphological features that appear in a given paragraph.

3.3 Text Reuse Detection

To achieve our end goal of detecting lost midrashic material, we combine our style classification model with a filtering algorithm based on text-reuse detection. For reuse detection, we use RWFS (Schor et al., 2021), a system designed for this goal using fuzzy full-text search on windows of n-grams. For our corpus of texts we use all biblical and early rabbinic works using the texts available on Sefaria. We use 3-gram matching and permit a Levenshtein distance of up to 2 for each individual word. The match score for each retrieved document is given by the number of n-gram matches and the results are sorted accordingly.

3.4 Detecting Lost Tanḥuma Candidates

Tanḥuma-Yelammedenu Literature is a name given to a genre of late midrash works, some of which are lost and only scarcely preserved in anthologies or Genizah fragments (Bregman, 2003; Nikolsky and Atzmon, 2021). One of the lost works was called Yelammedenu and we know about it since it is cited in various medieval rabbinic works such as *Yalkut Shimoni* and the *Arukh*.[5] While lost Tanḥuma material is explicitly cited in some works, it is often quoted without citation in various anthologies.

[5] An early dictionary for rabbinic literature from the 11th century CE.

Model	Validation Acc
Baseline	0.867
AlephBERT	0.879
BEREL	**0.922**
Morphological	0.560

Table 1: Model accuracy on validation set.

To find candidates for "lost" Tanḥuma passages, we apply the following process:

1. Extract all passages from the given midrash collection, in our case we used *Yalkut Shimoni*.
2. Split long passages into segments of up to 50 words.
3. Run these segments through the style detection model.
4. Collect segments for which our model gives the highest score to the Tanḥuma class.
5. Run these segments through a text-reuse engine.
6. Keep only segments that do not have a well established source. (Our threshold was $\#n$-gram matches $\leq 0.2 \cdot \#n$-grams in query.)

4 Results

As can be seen in Table 1 our baseline model achieves well over the random guess accuracy of 0.166 on the validation set, and achieves almost the same accuracy as the AlephBERT fine-tuned model. The BEREL-based model leads by a significant margin, nevertheless, we choose to use our baseline model for inference on *Yalkut Shimoni* due to its more calibrated scores, and its higher explainability.[6]

In Figure 2, we can see that the the most common errors are mixing 'Tanḥuma' with 'Midrash Aggadah.' On the other hand, 'Babylonian Talmud' and 'Jerusalem Talmud' seem to be the most distinct classes, perhaps due to their extensive use of Aramaic in addition to Hebrew.

After taking the whole *Yalkut Shimoni* on the Pentateuch and following the process described in Section 3.4, we can analyze the prevalence of each class in the collection. As can be seen in Figure 1, the Babylonian Talmud is the most quoted class, while the Jerusalem Talmud is rarely, if ever, quoted. Our classifier gives a similar distribution to

[6] For logistic regression, the model weights correspond directly to an n-gram's contribution to the score given to a specific class.

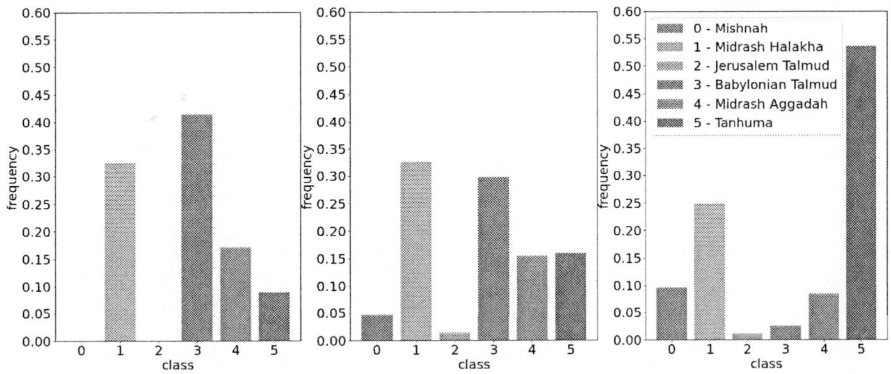

Figure 1: From left to right: (1) class frequencies for passages based on text reuse detection; (2) predicted class frequencies for passages with high text reuse score; (3) predicted frequencies for passages with low reuse score.

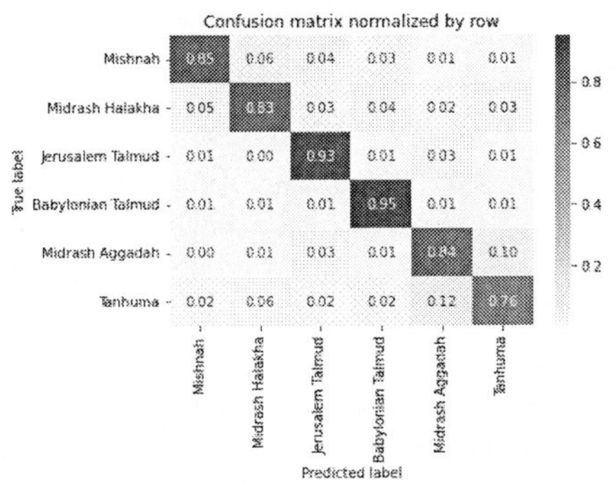

Figure 2: Confusion matrix for baseline model.

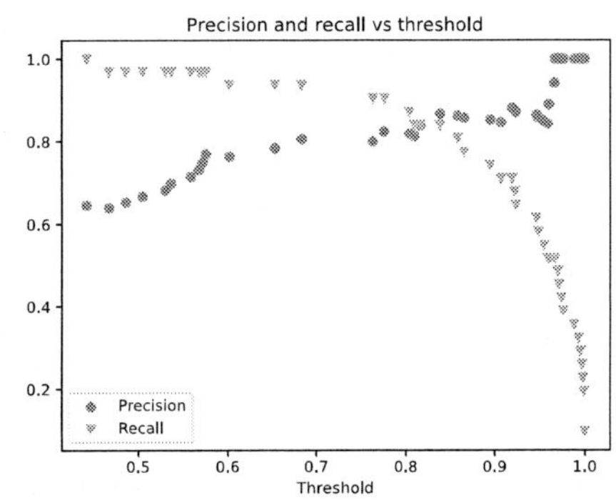

Figure 3: Precision and recall for lost Tanḥuma.

that of the text-reuse engine. However, when looking only at passages with low reuse score we see that the Babylonian Talmud rarely appears while 'Tanḥuma' becomes the most frequent predicted class by far, followed by 'Midrash Halakha.' This aligns with the fact that we know of lost works that belong to these categories, while the Babylonian Talmud was well preserved throughout the generations as the core text of the rabbinic tradition.

To evaluate our classifier on the target task, we sampled for manual labeling a random set of 50 items classified as Tanḥuma. A midrash expert analyzed these passages and looked them up in the early print edition of *Yalkut Shimoni*, which tends to include citations in the margins. Sections that were ascribed to Yelammedenu (ילמדנו) and sections that were recognized as being typical Tanḥuma material were labeled as "positive," while all other passages were labeled "negative." Out of these items, 22 were cited as Yelammedenu, while an additional 8 were recognized as typical Tanḥuma material from lost sources,[7] yielding an approximate precision of 60%.

From Figure 3, we see that the precision grows monotonically with the decision threshold, indicating that the model is useful in recovering lost Tanḥuma material. Furthermore, we see that we can achieve a precision of approximately 80% by setting an appropriate decision threshold without a high cost to recall.

5 Discussion and Future Work

Our results for detecting Tanḥuma sections in *Yalkut Shimoni* demonstrate that our method can be a useful tool for researchers working on recovering lost rabbinic material.

We are planning a digital library of Tanḥuma-Yelammedenu literature and believe our work will be of high value to researchers working on detecting lost material of this genre. We intend to

[7]These latter items are perhaps the more exciting find as they have previously been unidentified.

run our classifier on additional collections such as *Midrash HaGadol* for which we don't currently have ground truth labels to help uncover additional lost Tanḥuma passages.

Our method can be expanded and applied to many more open questions in Jewish studies. An obvious direction involves applying it to other lost midrashic material. Another is exploring the Baraitot[8] that appear in the Babylonian Talmud and the Jerusalem Talmud and their relationship to each other. Also promising would be to apply it to the many fragmentary manuscripts that have been found in collections like the Cairo Geniza. This would require dealing carefully with noisy text with errors originating in handwritten text recognition.

Acknowledgments

This research was supported in part by grant no. 1188 from the Israeli Ministry of Science and Technology.

References

Yannis Assael, Thea Sommerschield, Brendan Shillingford, Mahyar Bordbar, John Pavlopoulos, Marita Chatzipanagiotou, Ion Androutsopoulos, Jonathan Prag, and Nando de Freitas. 2022. Restoring and attributing ancient texts using deep neural networks. *Nature*, 603(7900):280–283.

Marc Bregman. 2003. *The Tanhuma-Yelammedenu Literature: Studies in the Evolution of the Versions*. Gorgias Press.

Idan Dershowitz, Navot Akiva, Moshe Koppel, and Nachum Dershowitz. 2015. Computerized source criticism of biblical texts. *Journal of Biblical Literature*, 134(2):253–271.

Jacob Devlin, Ming-Wei Chang, Kenton Lee, and Kristina Toutanova. 2019. BERT: Pre-training of deep bidirectional transformers for language understanding. In *Proceedings of the 2019 Conference of the North American Chapter of the Association for Computational Linguistics: Human Language Technologies, Volume 1 (Long and Short Papers)*, pages 4171–4186, Minneapolis, Minnesota. Association for Computational Linguistics.

Ronit Nikolsky and Arnon Atzmon. 2021. *Studies in the Tanhuma-Yelammedenu Literature*. Brill.

Fabian Pedregosa, Gaël Varoquaux, Alexandre Gramfort, Vincent Michel, Bertrand Thirion, Olivier Grisel, Mathieu Blondel, Peter Prettenhofer, Ron Weiss, Vincent Dubourg, Jake Vanderplas, Alexandre Passos, David Cournapeau, Matthieu Brucher, Matthieu Perrot, and Édouard Duchesnay. 2011. Scikit-learn: Machine learning in Python. *Journal of Machine Learning Research*, 12(85):2825–2830.

Uri Schor, Vered Raziel-Kretzmer, Moshe Lavee, and Tsvi Kuflik. 2021. Digital research library for multi-hierarchical interrelated texts: from 'tikkoun sofrim' text production to text modeling. *Classics@18*.

Amit Seker, Elron Bandel, Dan Bareket, Idan Brusilovsky, Refael Greenfeld, and Reut Tsarfaty. 2022. AlephBERT: Language model pre-training and evaluation from sub-word to sentence level. In *Proceedings of the 60th Annual Meeting of the Association for Computational Linguistics (Volume 1: Long Papers)*, pages 46–56, Dublin, Ireland. Association for Computational Linguistics.

Avi Shmidman, Joshua Guedalia, Shaltiel Shmidman, Cheyn Shmuel Shmidman, Eli Handel, and Moshe Koppel. 2022. Introducing BEREL: BERT embeddings for rabbinic-encoded language. *Computing Research Repository*, arXiv 2208.01875.

Michal Bar-Asher Siegal and Avi Shmidman. 2018. Reconstruction of the Mekhilta Deuteronomy using philological and computational tools. *Journal of Ancient Judaism*, 9(1):2–25.

Thomas Wolf, Lysandre Debut, Victor Sanh, Julien Chaumond, Clement Delangue, Anthony Moi, Pierric Cistac, Tim Rault, Remi Louf, Morgan Funtowicz, Joe Davison, Sam Shleifer, Patrick von Platen, Clara Ma, Yacine Jernite, Julien Plu, Canwen Xu, Teven Le Scao, Sylvain Gugger, Mariama Drame, Quentin Lhoest, and Alexander Rush. 2020. Transformers: State-of-the-art natural language processing. In *Proceedings of the 2020 Conference on Empirical Methods in Natural Language Processing: System Demonstrations*, pages 38–45, Online. Association for Computational Linguistics.

[8]A tannaitic tradition not incorporated in the Mishnah, see: "Baraita," *The Jewish Encyclopedia*.

Use the Metadata, Luke! – An Experimental Joint Metadata Search and N-gram Trend Viewer for "Personal" Web Archives

Balázs Indig, Zsófia Sárközi-Lindner, Mihály Nagy
Eötvös Loránd University, Department of Digital Humanities
National laboratory for Digital Humanities
Muzeum krt. 6-8., H-1088, Budapest, Hungary
{indig.balazs,lindner.zsofia,nagy.mihaly}@btk.elte.hu

Abstract

Many digital humanists (philologists, historians, sociologists, librarians, the audience for web archives) design their research around metadata (publication date ranges, sources, authors, etc.). However, current major web archives are limited to technical metadata while lacking high quality, descriptive metadata allowing for faceted queries. As researchers often lack the technical skill necessary to enrich existing web archives with descriptive metadata, they increasingly turn to creating personal web archives that contain such metadata, tailored to their research requirements. Software that enable creating such archives without advanced technical skills have gained popularity, however, tools for examination and querying are currently the missing link. We showcase a solution designed to fill this gap.

1 Introduction

The potential of the vast amount of data generated on the World Wide Web (as a corpus of text) has taken the lead from printed media and is constantly evolving (e.g. the U.S. presidential tweets). For example, sociologists and linguists must use online sources to gain insight into recent trends (temporal, ideological standpoints) in social topics and language as the print media can not keep up the pace and provide real-time updates (e.g. COVID-19 news, social media). Luckily, the state of major web archives indicates that all important data will likely be preserved. Therefore, beyond tackling the difficulties of web harvesting, meeting the needs of researchers has become the most recent goal of archivists (Major and Gomes, 2021, 13).

However, the quantity of data in major archives does not counteract deficiencies and negligence in quality. The aforementioned direction of research requires quality descriptive metadata (publication date, author, column, portal name, keywords, etc.) for specific portals with complete and up-to-date archives, to for example assess source dependent standpoints. Unfortunately, major web archives are limited to full-text or URL searching, even more advanced ones only include filters on technical metadata (e.g. file format, crawl date), and a rare few such as `https://webarchives.ca/` have facets on descriptive metadata.

As Hale et al. (2017), Indig et al. (2020) and Costa (2021) have pointed out, for a more detailed overview of sources, a uniform format for metadata and text would be needed because websites are typically neither consistent nor well-structured. Nevertheless, the complexity and time-consuming nature of isolating the useful text, identifying the segments along with metadata (e.g. title, headings, image), preprocessing (e.g. tokenization and parsing) and postprocessing (e.g. filtering, deduplication, curation of metadata) in existing web archives make it an unattainable promise of future AI solutions. This is especially relevant for those without technical skills or sufficient infrastructure[1].

Fortunately, many workflows (e.g. crawling, text extraction, NLP, plotting) can be conducted sufficiently well with a few clicks on free, easy-to-use software or services that work on uploaded data or prepared data sets (see examples in Section 3.). Researchers with insufficient funds (e.g. PhD students) are therefore limited to creating "personal" web archives using such tools to gian at least preliminary results through exploratory analysis and test their ideas before going further. These attempts usually get stuck at the aggregation and visualisation stages, as available tools and tutorials do not facilitate the freedom to experiment, instead only showcasing basic, and typical workflows. With our tool these scholars can find answers to detailed questions involving metadata based on their gathered data with at most a few line of code needed

[1] Downstream projects e.g. *the OSCAR corpus* (Ortiz Suárez et al., 2019) discard metadata in favour of deduplication and filtering.

The 2nd International Workshop on Natural Language Processing for Digital Humanities (NLP4DH), pages 47–52
November 20, 2022. ©2022 Association for Computational Linguistics

for the collecting and preprocessing steps.

Such archives must be created manually and in many cases cannot be published or shared due to conservative legal regulations. This puts pressure on website operators, as everyone is forced to create an archive of their own, the very issue that was intended to be avoided by shared archives such as *Common Crawl* that have become trapped in a rivalry of quantity over quality. On top of that, the *Internet Archive* does not support downloading and restoring pages[2], and as of yet does not contain a faceted query and visualisation interface for descriptive metadata. In the future, large web archives may catch up and support querying quality uniform descriptive metadata out of the box, but until then scholars must individually experiment with the available tools on a smaller scale. Here we find the eternal struggle to strike a balance between precision and recall in a non-standardised open domain.

2 Background

Ruest et al. (2020) developed *The Archives Unleashed Toolkit*[3] which generalised typical scholarly activities into the *Filter-Extract-Aggregate-Visualize (FEAV) cycle*. This model features a chain of independent tasks where each task can be adapted separately to the technological developments and different goals on different scales. Nonetheless, existing tools are not yet sufficiently easy-to-use and integrated for individual researchers, who opt for simpler ones which are easier to setup, use and adapt.

Off-the-shelf services are too dependent on the provider. Moreover, they are constantly growing and developed, which means that these services will inevitably change over time[4] (e.g. shut down or being extended), and become volatile[5]. This hinders the reproducibility of obtained results, forcing researchers not to trust such sources, since it is essential to ensure the citation and long-term preservation of research data and final research results (Barats et al., 2020). In the long term, research material should be suitable for the widest possible research community, and should stand the test of time to facilitate reproducibility. This requires web archivists to resist the siren voices of merely increasing size, and strive to democratise and further reduce the complexity of the tools involved.

3 Tools for a Modular FEAV Cycle

Tools such as *Trafilatura* (Barbaresi, 2021) serve as good examples, as they are adequate for creating custom, "personal" web archives and have unique features compared to existing major web archives (e.g. extracting descriptive metadata and text in a uniform format with sufficient quality and quantity). In a few lines of Python code one can create enough research data for preliminary analysis, and by combining such data sets more complicated advanced research questions can be answered in depth.

Processing such text with NLP pipelines (e.g. *SpaCy* (Montani et al., 2022)) with another few lines of code to extract lemmas and named entities is easy even for non-technical researchers. On the visualisation front there exist a large number of tools and libraries providing quick and elegant solutions (e.g. *D3.js* (Bostock, 2012)), often implicitly handling most parameters, however, their functionality either focuses on ease-of-use or modularity, rarely both. Their popularity – judging by their download and citation counts – shows that people tend to prefer them. They may also appear as building blocks of some full-fledged compact applications as well. The last remaining part is the aggregation of data, which is either done with predefined workflows limiting its scope or is completely left to the user with all of its complexity.

Following from the design of such pipelines, if any of these tools are not yielding satisfactory results, they can be changed independently (maintaining the FEAV cycle) as their output is in simple and standard format. We take these tools as granted, and focus on the missing part, the ground-up design of an ideal trend viewer as the aggregation module for the desired tool chain.

4 Trend Viewer Trends

The history of n-gram trend viewers starts with the *Google Books N-gram Viewer* (Michel et al., 2011) which has an exceptionally large corpus, but its software is not freely available to try on custom

[2] `https://wiki.archiveteam.org/index.php?title=Restoring`

[3] `https://github.com/archivesunleashed/aut`

[4] For example `https://archivesunleashed.org/cloud/` has "shut down on 30 June 2021, and will be replaced by a similar service ".

[5] For example *Warcbase*, `https://github.com/lintool/warcbase` (Lin et al., 2017) is unmaintained since September 2017 in favour of *The Archives Unleashed Toolkit*.)

data. Another similar example is the *Microsoft Web N-gram Services*, which has been shut down[6].

The National Library of Norway also established an elaborate n-gram trend search service (Birkenes et al., 2015) on their collection of books, but the source code[7] has not been updated for 7 years and is written in the now deprecated *Python 2* language. Its *SQLite* database back end can handle 34 billion words from books and newspapers in a remarkable way. The project is still relevant as the *Icelandic Gigaword Corpus* utilises the code in their recent work (Steingrímsson et al., 2020).

The most versatile existing solution is *Shine*[8] (Jackson et al., 2016), an experimental faceted search engine and trend viewer tool based on *Solr* in its early stages, however, it has not shown signs of development since 2020. It has similar goals to those of our project (see Section 1.), including faceted search over various metadata, however, it fails to cover descriptive metadata other than publication date when it comes to aggregation and visualisation. The *Web Archives for Longitudinal Knowledge (WALK)*[9] project is a good demonstration of applying Shine to facilitate DH research.

These examples suggests that there is an emerging trend in the DH and NLP of using descriptive metadata for diachronic corpora (created from e.g. web archives) where available. Such data augmented with modern NLP (e.g. sentiment analysis, wikification (Brank et al., 2017)), aggregated and displayed in the context of not just time, but all other accessible factors can help digital humanists focus and gain insight on new previously nonexistent scopes of their research. Our aggregation module works independently on the output of existing crawling and NLP tools, and uses an existing visualisation tool, therefore maintaining ease of use and sufficient generality.

5 Method: Redesign from the Ground Up

We encourage future researchers to utilise e.g. Trafilatura to create their own research data in standard format (e.g. *TEI XMLs*) that can be lemmatised effectively with e.g. SpaCy to get preprocessed data in decent quality and quantity in almost any language[10]. We also provide example scripts, however, for the sake of reproducibility we used an existing data set containing descriptive metadata for our experiments: Indig et al. (2020) developed a pilot web archive described as a *complete, reliable* and *versatile* representation of archived content (recorded in *WARC* files) for Hungarian news portals while *maintaining archive content authenticity* (Lendák et al., 2022). It contains around 1 billion words from about 2.8 million news articles written in the last 20 years composed of roughly 20 different Hungarian news portals with a standardised layout and descriptive metadata in *TEI XML* format. The whole archive is available with DOI links on the *Zenodo.org* repository[11] which is maintained by *CERN* ensuring the reproducibility of further downstream research and making a positive example of legally sharing "personal" web archives for non-profit research purposes.

Building on the various types of available metadata in the input data set (publication date, author, column, portal name, keywords, etc.), we designed an extensible hybrid query service. On one hand, the retrieved records can be viewed as a list of links to the original pages as in traditional search engines, and the query can be refined with filters on metadata fields. Additionally authorised non-profit researchers can view – legally, without copyright infringement – the full article in our standardised HTML format which contains the original text formatting generated on-the-fly from the stored *TEI XMLs*. This allows access even if the original link is broken or its content has changed, which also helps manual work and gathering examples. On the other hand, the features of the retrieved documents can be visualised with different kinds of graphs (e.g. line and bar charts) by setting the appropriate parameters (e.g. the fields for the axes), allowing the user to create custom views of the data filtered by the represented features (see Figure 1.) opening possibilities for non-technical users to express research questions (see Section 7. for more examples).

All retrieved data and plotted graphs can be downloaded for use e.g. in research papers or additional processing. As an example, bundling such a tool with a research paper can enable readers to cross-check and further examine the presented results and enhance reproducibility and reusability,

[6] https://www.microsoft.com/en-us/research/project/web-n-gram-services/

[7] https://github.com/NationalLibraryOfNorway/NB-N-gram

[8] https://github.com/ukwa/shine

[9] https://webarchives.ca/

[10] see the evaluation in the respective papers

[11] https://zenodo.org/communities/elte-dh/search?page=1&size=20&q=TEI

increasing the impact of the paper.

6 Technical Evaluation and Details

Existing search engine platforms e.g. *Solr* or *ElasticSearch* provide a solid foundation, however, their complexity and possible vulnerabilities are prone to hacking attempts and require continuous maintenance. Their complexity also discourages external developers from customisation attempts. The same holds for deep learning frameworks, which also require advanced technical skills and machinery.

Birkenes et al. (2015) have shown that storing n-grams in *SQLite* can be fast enough even for databases extending over 34 billion tokens and yield correct results. However, they use separate tables for uni-, bi- and trigrams. Our approach was to add padding tokens at the end of text segments and create only a table with 5-grams, as we can represent lower-order n-grams using only the first n tokens, thus creating fewer rows overall. The actual frequencies come from grouping the matching lower-order n-grams (*GROUP BY* statement in SQL) and *SUM*ming the frequencies for each group[12]. So one can easily use wider search patterns e.g. "[first name] [surname] [job title] [organisation]".

Each n-gram has a frequency and is linked to a document while the metadata (publication date, sources, authors, etc.) for each document – identified by a document ID – are stored in a row in a separate table along with the path for the TEI XML document on the file system. We distinguish three types of fields: a) simple text (e.g. portal name, column), b) multi-valued text (e.g. author, keywords), c) date (e.g. publish date) which can specified as an interval when used as a filter.

Our import script requires a *CoNLL-U* like vertical TSV format used by Sketch Engine (Kilgarriff et al., 2014). The possible lemmas for each word are acquired by lemmatising the text prior to database creation with a common lemmatiser. We only store the lemma n-grams in the database, because their disambiguation in the query string is done by a look-up table using all possibilities in *conjunctive normal form (CNF)* as ambiguous n-grams are unlikely and results close to real lemmatisation can be achieved.

Our pipeline uses *AWK* and standard *Unix* tools, allowing to create and count lemma 5-grams for 1 billion words while retaining their source document IDs, in about an hour. The user has to write a configuration file and run a single command to import the data into the database. We provide example scripts to help users from the crawling through to the importing stages. To allow rewriting or different development paths, we decoupled the front end and the back end which communicate with a stable REST API. The application is available as a docker image to facilitate operating system independence and long term usage.

The only limiting factor we experienced is the quality of the used data, as regarding performance even low-end hardware can handle databases with the the expected size.

7 Examples

Search engines for web archives or interfaces for visualising trends usually help researchers navigate through data sets, allowing quick assessment of the usefulness of materials for current research (e.g. cross-check data to reveal artefacts), possibly verifying simpler claims or filtering useful parts (saving time by not processing unused segments). We would like to illustrate how, thanks to more detailed preprocessing, a few tiny adjustments can expand the possibilities for answering more complex research questions. We provide presets in the WebUI for users to show the examples given below.

One can observe the emergence and rivalry of new terms across different news portals, e.g. in relation to the climate crisis[13], or the way how medical jargon[14] became common language during the COVID-19 pandemic (Varga et al., 2022a,b), and how the correlation between its key issues (e.g. *restriction*, *quarantine* vs. *vaccination*) have changed over time by the start of the third wave. Another example demonstrates how one can get a quick answer to the question "Which values (*national*, *chatolic*, *european*) are more prominent in the articles of the selected news portals?", which can then be nuanced through more detailed examination (e.g. their ideological standpoints). A small but important detail is that distortions due to the size of each portal can be mitigated by expressing the occurrences of n-grams as a percentage (e.g. percentage

[12] A prefix trie or perfect hash based approaches could potentially yield more compact storage format, but they would increase complexity as metadata still would require a database.

[13] e.g. *climate change*, *climate emergency*, *climate strike*, *climate hysteria*

[14] e.g. *social distancing*, *spike protein*, *long covid*, *PCR test*, *super-spreader*

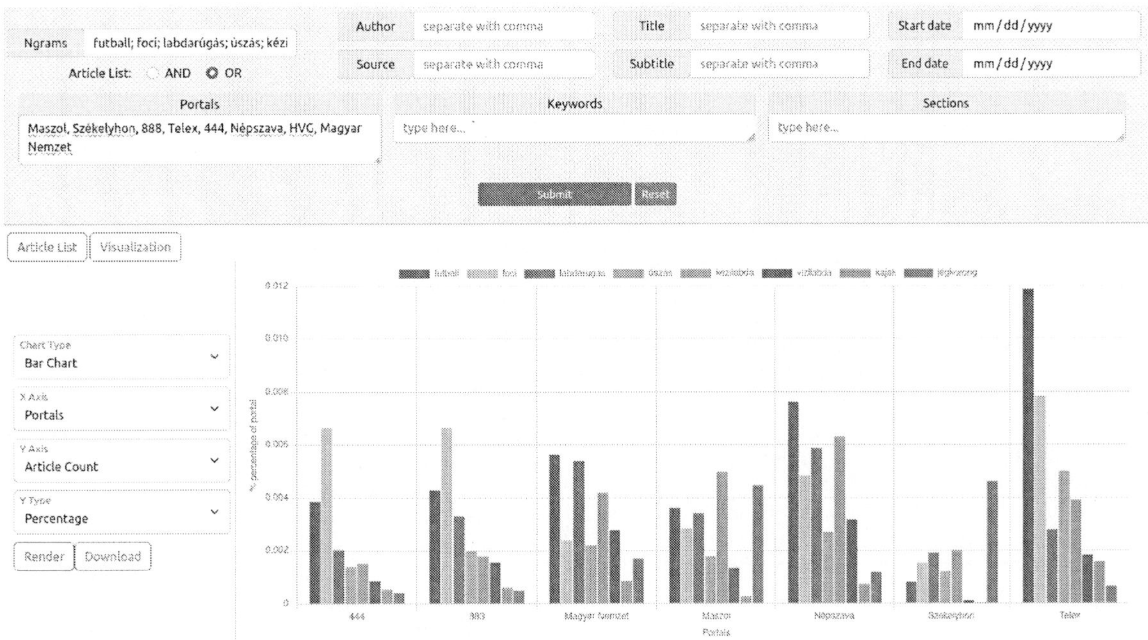

Figure 1: The distribution of mentions of different kinds of sport across portals on the WebUI.

of articles per portal). When listing relevant articles the logical operators applied to the n-gram can be used to separate the trend of co-occurrence and independent occurrences of the listed n-grams. Thanks to accurate metadata extraction, the use of hashtags by online newspapers and journalists can be tested, the variety and consistency of keywords and phrases associated with topics can be a telling feature, and it helps to improve the accuracy of the search and the weighting of the topic. In the field of sports, we can investigate the interest of some Hungarian news portals in Hungary and abroad, by querying articles about different sports (see Figure 1). We would expect that portals in Hungary would be predominantly concerned with football results and in Romania *hockey* (*jégkorong*) would be more prominent (e.g. on *maszol.ro*). The fact that in Hungarian three synonyms of almost equal rank are typically used to describe football (*labdarúgás, futball, foci*) makes interpretation difficult, because synonyms sometimes complement each other and sometimes overlap, which is reflected in the number of results. This can be clarified with the downloadable TSV files. Future plans include making it even easier to do this directly in the search engine by utilising vector space models to unify synonyms if enabled. A further point to note is the importance of context. If researchers want to quantify traces of hate speech or ethnic exclusion, they need to be familiar with the background and the attitudes of the sources used. A simple but striking example is the occurrence of the term *gypsy* (*cigány*). In two of the newspapers studied, the results are very prominent, but one is an avowedly extremist medium (far-right wing), while the other deals specifically with social issues, education and inclusion.

8 Conclusion and Discussion

We introduced a search and visualisation engine for viewing n-gram trends in light of different descriptive metadata implemented in a lightweight SQL-based framework. A custom data set can be imported with a few lines of Python code, and the customised visualisation can be exported to be used directly in research papers. This helps researchers express their questions freely or share their data through a query and visualisation interface (e.g. as anonymous supplementary material for research papers) and enable further examination and possible new discoveries on the same data set.

We plan to add more NLP modules (e.g. sentiment analysis to study hate speech and wikification for semantic results) for different layers of annotation and support for CQL expressions. The source code[15] and docker image is published under a copyleft license and a public pilot service is available.

[15] https://github.com/ELTE-DH/meta-trend-viewer

References

Christine Barats, Valérie Schafer, and Andreas Fickers. 2020. Fading Away... The challenge of sustainability in digital studies. *Digital Humanities Quarterly*, 014(3).

Adrien Barbaresi. 2021. Trafilatura: A web scraping library and command-line tool for text discovery and extraction. In *Proceedings of the 59th Annual Meeting of the Association for Computational Linguistics and the 11th International Joint Conference on Natural Language Processing: System Demonstrations*, pages 122–131, Online. Association for Computational Linguistics.

Magnus Breder Birkenes, Lars G. Johnsen, Arne Martinus Lindstad, and Johanne Ostad. 2015. From digital library to n-grams: NB n-gram. In *Proceedings of the 20th Nordic Conference of Computational Linguistics (NODALIDA 2015)*, pages 293–295, Vilnius, Lithuania. Linköping University Electronic Press, Sweden.

Mike Bostock. 2012. D3.js - data-driven documents.

Janez Brank, Gregor Leban, and Marko Grobelnik. 2017. Annotating documents with relevant wikipedia concepts. In *Proceedings of the Slovenian Conference on Data Mining and Data Warehouses (SiKDD 2017)*, Ljubljana, Slovenia.

Miguel Costa. 2021. *Full-Text and URL Search Over Web Archives*, pages 71–84. Springer International Publishing, Cham.

Scott A. Hale, Grant Blank, and Victoria D. Alexander. 2017. *Live versus archive: Comparing a web archive to a population of web pages*, pages 45–61. UCL Press.

Balázs Indig, Árpád Knap, Zsófia Sárközi-Lindner, Mária Timári, and Gábor Palkó. 2020. The ELTE.DH pilot corpus – creating a handcrafted Gigaword web corpus with metadata. In *Proceedings of the 12th Web as Corpus Workshop*, pages 33–41, Marseille, France. European Language Resources Association.

Andrew Jackson, Jimmy Lin, Ian Milligan, and Nick Ruest. 2016. Desiderata for exploratory search interfaces to web archives in support of scholarly activities. In *Proceedings of the 16th ACM/IEEE-CS on Joint Conference on Digital Libraries*, JCDL '16, page 103–106, New York, NY, USA. Association for Computing Machinery.

Adam Kilgarriff, Vít Baisa, Jan Bušta, Miloš Jakubíček, Vojtěch Kovář, Jan Michelfeit, Pavel Rychlý, and Vít Suchomel. 2014. The Sketch Engine: ten years on. *Lexicography*, pages 7–36.

Imre Lendák, Balázs Indig, and Gábor Palkó. 2022. WARChain: Consensus-based trust in web archives via proof-of-stake blockchain technology. *Journal of Computer Security*, pages 1–17.

Jimmy Lin, Ian Milligan, Jeremy Wiebe, and Alice Zhou. 2017. Warcbase: Scalable analytics infrastructure for exploring web archives. *Journal on Computing and Cultural Heritage*, 10(4).

Daniela Major and Daniel Gomes. 2021. *Web Archives Preserve Our Digital Collective Memory*, pages 11–19. Springer International Publishing, Cham.

Jean-Baptiste Michel, Yuan Kui Shen, Aviva Presser Aiden, Adrian Veres, Matthew K Gray, Google Books Team, Joseph P Pickett, Dale Hoiberg, Dan Clancy, Peter Norvig, et al. 2011. Quantitative analysis of culture using millions of digitized books. *science*, 331(6014):176–182.

Ines Montani, Matthew Honnibal, Matthew Honnibal, Sofie Van Landeghem, Adriane Boyd, Henning Peters, Paul O'Leary McCann, Maxim Samsonov, Jim Geovedi, Jim O'Regan, Duygu Altinok, György Orosz, Søren Lind Kristiansen, Daniël de Kok, Lj Miranda, Roman, Explosion Bot, Leander Fiedler, Grégory Howard, Edward, Wannaphong Phatthiyaphaibun, Richard Hudson, Yohei Tamura, Sam Bozek, murat, Ryn Daniels, Peter Baumgartner, Mark Amery, and Björn Böing. 2022. explosion/spaCy: New Span Ruler component, JSON (de)serialization of Doc, span analyzer and more.

Pedro Javier Ortiz Suárez, Benoît Sagot, and Laurent Romary. 2019. Asynchronous pipelines for processing huge corpora on medium to low resource infrastructures. In *Proceedings of the 8th Workshop on Challenges in the Management of Large Corpora (CMLC-7)*, Proceedings of the Workshop on Challenges in the Management of Large Corpora (CMLC-7) 2019. Cardiff, 22nd July 2019, pages 9 – 16, Mannheim. Leibniz-Institut für Deutsche Sprache.

Nick Ruest, Jimmy Lin, Ian Milligan, and Samantha Fritz. 2020. *The Archives Unleashed Project: Technology, Process, and Community to Improve Scholarly Access to Web Archives*, Joint Conference on Digital Libraries 2020 (JCDL 2020), page 157–166. Association for Computing Machinery, New York, NY, USA.

Steinþór Steingrímsson, Starkaður Barkarson, and Gunnar Thor Örnólfsson. 2020. Facilitating corpus usage: Making Icelandic corpora more accessible for researchers and language users. In *Proceedings of the Twelfth Language Resources and Evaluation Conference*, pages 3399–3405, Marseille, France. European Language Resources Association.

Éva Katalin Varga, Emese Márton, Balázs Indig, Zsófia Sárközi-Lindner, and Gábor Palkó. 2022a. Erdélyi és anyaországi orvosi terminológia pandémia idején. *Alkalmazott Nyelvtudomány*, page in press.

Éva Katalin Varga, Ákos Zimonyi, Balázs Indig, Zsófia Sárközi-Lindner, and Gábor Palkó. 2022b. Durva influenza vagy veszélyes világjárvány? a covid-19 terminológiája a médiában. *XXVIII. Magyar Alkalmazott Nyelvészeti Kongresszus : Nyelvek, Nyelvváltozatok, Következmények*, page in press.

MALM: Mixing Augmented Language Modeling for Zero-Shot Machine Translation

Kshitij Gupta
Department of Electrical and Electronics Engineering
BITS Pilani, Pilani Campus
Rajasthan, India
mailguptakshitij@gmail.com

Abstract

Large pre-trained language models have brought remarkable progress in NLP. Pre-training and Fine-tuning have given state-of-art performance across tasks in text processing. Data Augmentation techniques have also helped build state-of-art models on low or zero resource tasks. Many works in the past have attempted at learning a single massively-multilingual machine translation model for zero-shot translation. Although those translation models are producing correct translations, the main challenge is those models are producing the wrong languages for zero-shot translation. This work and its results indicate that prompt conditioned large models do not suffer from off-target language errors i.e. errors arising due to translation to wrong languages. We empirically demonstrate the effectiveness of self-supervised pre-training and data augmentation for zero-shot multi-lingual machine translation.

1 Introduction

Machine Translation is one of the classic problems in Natural Language Processing(NLP). Several products like Google Translate, Bing Translate provide services to millions of translation requests across a diversity of language pairs. While the requests for these services come in almost all language pairs imaginable, the quality of translation for low-resource language pairs like German-Arabic is especially low. This is prompted due to a lack of quality training data for such locale pairs compared to high-resource languages like English-French etc.

Specifically, for few-shot machine translation, there have been many successful techniques proposed. Zoph et al. (2016) demonstrated that transfer learning from high-resource languages to low-resource languages can be used to achieve remarkably high BLEU scores. Building on top of it, Gu et al. (2018) showed that universal lexical representations achieve better alignment of lexical and syntactic relations between languages. Similarly, (Fadaee et al., 2017) have been successfully used to utilize computer vision leanings in augmentation to low-resource translation.

Success due to techniques like transfer-learning, data augmentation, etc. has also provided great progress in building large multi-lingual neural machine translation models (Johnson et al., 2017). The objective here is to build a single high-capacity model that is able to generate translations for any language pair and can be trained at the same time. Zhang et al. (2021) have used conditional specific language routing for achieving impressive performance across low resource language pairs. Similar to this work, Xia et al. (2019) utilized data augmentation strategies and Zhang et al. (2020) used random online back translation to achieve state-of-the-art performance for low-resource machine translation. In their work, Arivazhagan et al. (2019a) encourage parameter sharing across language by implementing an auxiliary loss function. Similarly, de-noising objective (Liao et al., 2021) and distillation techniques (Sun et al., 2020) have also been shown to have boosted zero translation learning.

Recently, research direction in massively multilingual translation models(MMT) (Aharoni et al., 2019) has also been popularized to build zero-shot translation systems. Arivazhagan et al. (2019b) provides a survey of challenges associated with MMT models, while also emphasizing the importance of preprocessing and vocabulary in knowledge transfer across language pairs. Although, Gonzales et al. (2020) detail the lack of robustness of zero-shot models across training runs, we do not notice it in our training runs and find that augmentation techniques help stabilize the training process.

Neural models like Transformer (Vaswani et al.,

The 2nd International Workshop on Natural Language Processing for Digital Humanities (NLP4DH), pages 53–58
November 20, 2022. ©2022 Association for Computational Linguistics

2017) have brought significant advances in tasks across NLP. Pre-trained language models like BERT (Devlin et al., 2018), BART (Lewis et al., 2019), T5 (Raffel et al., 2019) have achieved state-of-art performance across the NLP spectrum. Similarly, generative models like GPT-2 (Brown et al., 2020) have shown few and zero-shot abilities on many tasks. The wide success across tasks has not only been limited to high-resource languages like English, and French but has indeed been shared with low-resource languages like Azerbaijani, Belarussian, Galician, Urdu, etc (Lakew et al., 2021). It has also brought significant progress in single large multi-lingual models mBERT (Devlin et al., 2018), mBART (Liu et al., 2020), mT5 (Xue et al., 2020) that learn universal representation across languages. This is responsible for remarkable zero and few-shot performance across tasks for languages that lack supervised training data.

In this paper, we will investigate language modeling pre-training and data augmentation strategy for zero-shot translation Our work provides 2 major and concise pieces of contributions:

1. *Prompt Conditioned* models like mT5 do not suffer from off-target translation and a language tag in the task prompt is sufficient for the model to generate output in the right language.

2. *SeqMix* style data augmentation technique on top of large pre-trained language models like mT5 is a simple yet competitive approach against a strong baseline on zero-shot translation.

2 Problem

We will first look at the challenge of off-target translation. For all the zero-shot language pairs, we construct a random test dataset of 1000 examples[1] from the source language that may or may not be part of the original test dataset. We then run the translation system over those examples and identify all the output that corresponds to the wrong target language.

Say, a translation model(M) generates for data instances($x_1...x_n$) translations as ($y'_1...y'_n$) and reference translations as ($y_1...y_n$) for source language(s) and target language(t). Also, given a language identification oracle as L, where $L(x)$ is the predicted language M for data instance$x$. In this work, we will utilize Salcianu et al. (2016)'s Language Identification system to measure language performance. We then describe *off-target translation error rate*(OTTER) as:

$$OTTER(M) = \frac{\sum_i L(y'_i) \neq t}{\sum_i L(y_i) = t} \quad (1)$$

In the original paper, Zhang et al. (2020) used the accuracy of translation language as a metric to compare. We argue that any language identification system is noisy and thus accuracy on just translation output doesn't take into account errors of the language identification system. OTTER, on the other hand, is a noisy measure that measures language accuracy over both reference and translation output text of the translation system.

The main question that we investigate is improving the quality of zero-resource translation. The problem at hand is learning a single model that is able to learn translation across language pairs that are unseen during the training time. This is motivated by human language learning experience, that if a person knows German, English, and Arabic and can translate over German $\rightarrow$ English and Arabic $\rightarrow$ English then they should be able to translate with sufficiently good quality between German $\rightarrow$ Arabic without any formal training. This is true for us because beneath all the lexical and grammatical differences across languages, we share the grounding of various concepts in the same representation. Basically, the representation of the concept 'cat' is the same as the word 'Katze' in German.

Traditionally, a pivot language has been prominently used to achieve this task. For example; if a German-to-Arabic translation is required then the original text is passed through the first German-to-English translation engine, and then the output English sentence is passed through the English-to-Arabic translation system.

This simple yet effective strategy has been shown to achieve state-of-art performance across zero-resource settings in many language pairs. Currey and Heafield (2019) use data augmentation with pivot language to generate pseudo-parallel data across zero-shot language pairs and then re-train a system. Recently, Dabre et al. (2021) have even utilized multi-pivot languages and simultaneous translation as a method to improve zero-shot performance. While Kim et al. (2019) combined pivoting with transfer learning and an adapter module, Siddhant et al. (2020) leveraged monolingual data

[1]We choose 1000 as a good compromise across languages irrespective of their original test size

with self-supervision for low resource languages to achieve impressive performance.

3 Experimental Setup

For the purpose of this study, we will constrain the study and experiments to OPUS-100 by Zhang et al. (2020). OPUS-100 is an English-centric dataset with over 100 language pairs that have either source/target language as English. It also consists of several other non-English-centric pairs that are available for zero-shot translation objectives. We should emphasize that while previous and related work on this dataset has been centered around massively-multilingual translation as well as zero-shot translation, the objective of the current work is only on zero-shot translation. As part of zero-shot languages, OPUS-100 provides 15 language pairs that are combinations of French, German, Arabic, Russian, Chinese and Dutch. For the evaluation of our translation model, we shall use the BLEU score, which is a standard metric of automatic evaluation across machine translation.

We run our experiments using the mT5 implementation available in the Transformers library provided by HuggingFace (Wolf et al., 2019) and use pre-trained mT5 models(small, large, and xx-large) from Xue et al. (2020). For reproducibility purposes, we use the Adam optimizer and run our experiments on a Google TPU v2-32 instance for 64,000 steps with 256 max length, 512 batch size, 0.0001 learning rate and we use a beam size of 4 at inference time.

For baseline experiments, we consider 2 strong baselines – (i) First, for any language pair say XX-YY, we train 2 Transformer models XX-En and En-YY, and run zero shot inference for any new sentence from language XX through XX-En and then through En-YY, note that we do not pre-train these models (ii) Second, we consider the model from Zhang et al. (2020) which implements random online back translation to recover from off-target translation.

4 Methodology

4.1 Large Pre-trained Model with Prompt Conditioning

First, we provide a brief introduction to the T5 architecture. T5 or Text-to-Text Transfer Transformer is a recently introduced framework that frames all the NLP tasks as a text-to-text problem. While the model architecture is vanilla Transformer architecture (Vaswani et al., 2017), it has been pretrained on the C4 dataset (Raffel et al., 2019) on a Masked Language Modeling objective (Devlin et al., 2018). Any new task could be provided as a brief prompt to the model along with the input, for example, translation from German to English could be specified as `translate German to English: This is a test input sentence`, while the output is generally not formatted. This is the default prompt style used by (Raffel et al., 2019) as well as by this work.

Recently, Xue et al. (2020) introduced the multilingual version of this model which is pre-trained on the mC4 dataset. They have shown that mT5 exhibits zero-shot capabilities, as learning a task in one language is directly transferable to the same task in a different language without any further training. They also highlight that the model suffers from unexpected translation in the output space. For example, a model trained on English Part-of-speech and when inference is run on French input outputs an English translation of the French input. This issue is similar to what (Zhang et al., 2020) has suggested that the massively multilingual translation models suffer from. The lack of language signals to the model results in although correct output but in an incorrect target language.

4.2 Data Augmentation

We run experiments on 2 main techniques in this work:

- *Sentence Concatenation*
- *Seq2Mix*

In the first set, if our objective is to run translation from German to Arabic, then at each training time, we choose a data point from the German-English dataset and a random data point from the English-Arabic dataset. We then concatenate the source sentence and target sentence for both language pairs with a simple `<sep>` token. This results in a training sentence whose input has the first half as a German sentence and the second half as an English sentence. Similarly, the output has the first half in English and the Second half as Arabic sentences. We modify the input prompt slightly here to identify the languages present in the new input and output, as `translate German and English to English and Arabic`. We hypothesize that the model is intelligent enough to pick up the right words and context from the

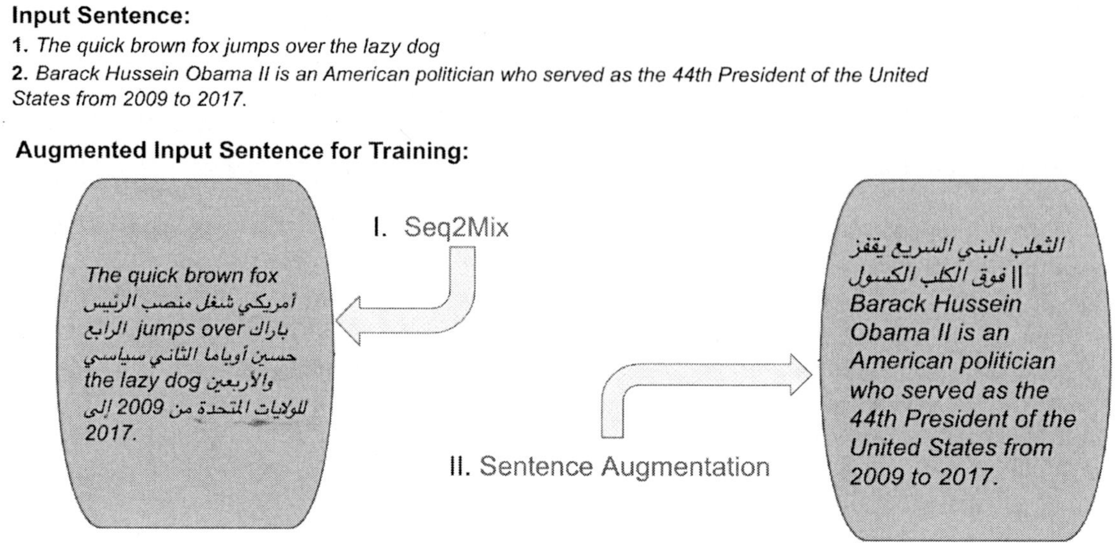

Figure 1: Example of Data Augmentation

prompt to produce the right output.

Secondly, we used Seq2Mix as introduced by Guo et al. (2020). They propose 2 variants of the Seq2Mix algorithm – hard and soft Seq2Mix. For the purpose of this work, we will only focus on the hard version. In essence, for 2 input sentences of equal sequence length[2], from German $(Gx_1, ..., Gx_n)$ and English $(Ex_1, ..., Ex_n)$, we construct a German-English sentence $(GEx_1, ..., GEx_n)$, where GEx_i is a token taken randomly from either (Gx_i, Ex_i) with a sample probability from Binomial(λ).[3] A similar process is run over to obtain an English-Arabic sentence which serves as output to the German-English input.

Figure 1 depicts both the augmentation techniques for the input sentences in the same. It is noteworthy that we need not merge sentences that are similar to each other, thus we could select any two sentences from our dataset for creating the augmented data. All of these data augmentation strategies work to create synthetic datasets that are employed along with the original bilingual datasets at training time with equal weighting. We hypothesize that while the model learns translation from both synthetic and original datasets, the prompt conditioning along with the mixed vocab is learned better at training time.

[2]otherwise use padding to ensure the sequences are of equal length

[3]where λ itself is sampled from $\beta(0.5, 0{,}5)$

5 Results & Analysis

We find that a mixed data augmentation training regime helps bring down OTTER to an extremely low range as referenced in 1. We attribute this to the compositional relationships learned by the large language model on the mixed vocabulary as well as the language tag we use as part of the task prompt.

	OTTER	BLEU
Transformer + Pivot	-	12.98
Zhang et al. (2020)	-	14.78
Ours (small mT5)	27.1%	4.9
Ours (large mT5)	24.2%	5.1
Ours (XXL mT5)	19.4%	7.2
XXL mT5 + input concat	0.9%	15.4
XXL mT5 + Seq2Mix	**0.7%**	**15.7**

Table 1: OTTER and BLEU scores for zero-shot language pairs; results are average across all the 15 language pairs in the zero-shot setting

Similarly, we find that data augmentation techniques like Seq2Mix (Guo et al., 2020), can substantially improve zero-shot performance when used on top of large pre-trained language models. We explain the performance using the following reasoning:

- Mixing vocabulary in the same sentence during training force the internal representation of tokens to align themselves in similar clusters across languages.

- Using XX-English and English-YY translation objective along with data augmentation smoothens the loss landscape to facilitate better representation for zero-shot translation

6 Conclusion

In this paper, we utilized mixing augmentation techniques along with large sequence-to-sequence models to generate high-quality zero-shot translation models for language pairs that have no training data available. We successfully demonstrate that large pre-trained language models are able to learn the semantic spaces between languages and are already good at zero-shot machine translation. However, data augmentation techniques can further boost this performance to achieve impressive results on zero-shot translation.

7 Future Work

We plan on running further experiments with improved data augmentation strategies at pre-training time which we think will benefit downstream zero-shot translation.

References

Roee Aharoni, Melvin Johnson, and Orhan Firat. 2019. Massively multilingual neural machine translation. *arXiv preprint arXiv:1903.00089*.

Naveen Arivazhagan, Ankur Bapna, Orhan Firat, Roee Aharoni, Melvin Johnson, and Wolfgang Macherey. 2019a. The missing ingredient in zero-shot neural machine translation. *arXiv preprint arXiv:1903.07091*.

Naveen Arivazhagan, Ankur Bapna, Orhan Firat, Dmitry Lepikhin, Melvin Johnson, Maxim Krikun, Mia Xu Chen, Yuan Cao, George Foster, Colin Cherry, et al. 2019b. Massively multilingual neural machine translation in the wild: Findings and challenges. *arXiv preprint arXiv:1907.05019*.

Tom B Brown, Benjamin Mann, Nick Ryder, Melanie Subbiah, Jared Kaplan, Prafulla Dhariwal, Arvind Neelakantan, Pranav Shyam, Girish Sastry, Amanda Askell, et al. 2020. Language models are few-shot learners. *arXiv preprint arXiv:2005.14165*.

Anna Currey and Kenneth Heafield. 2019. Zero-resource neural machine translation with monolingual pivot data. In *Proceedings of the 3rd Workshop on Neural Generation and Translation*, pages 99–107, Hong Kong. Association for Computational Linguistics.

Raj Dabre, Aizhan Imankulova, Masahiro Kaneko, and Abhisek Chakrabarty. 2021. Simultaneous multi-pivot neural machine translation. *arXiv preprint arXiv:2104.07410*.

Jacob Devlin, Ming-Wei Chang, Kenton Lee, and Kristina Toutanova. 2018. Bert: Pre-training of deep bidirectional transformers for language understanding. *arXiv preprint arXiv:1810.04805*.

Marzieh Fadaee, Arianna Bisazza, and Christof Monz. 2017. Data augmentation for low-resource neural machine translation. *arXiv preprint arXiv:1705.00440*.

Annette Rios Gonzales, Mathias Müller, and Rico Sennrich. 2020. Subword segmentation and a single bridge language affect zero-shot neural machine translation. In *Proceedings of the Fifth Conference on Machine Translation*, pages 528–537.

Jiatao Gu, Hany Hassan, Jacob Devlin, and Victor OK Li. 2018. Universal neural machine translation for extremely low resource languages. *arXiv preprint arXiv:1802.05368*.

Demi Guo, Yoon Kim, and Alexander Rush. 2020. Sequence-level mixed sample data augmentation. In *Proceedings of the 2020 Conference on Empirical Methods in Natural Language Processing (EMNLP)*, pages 5547–5552, Online. Association for Computational Linguistics.

Melvin Johnson, Mike Schuster, Quoc V Le, Maxim Krikun, Yonghui Wu, Zhifeng Chen, Nikhil Thorat, Fernanda Viégas, Martin Wattenberg, Greg Corrado, et al. 2017. Google's multilingual neural machine translation system: Enabling zero-shot translation. *Transactions of the Association for Computational Linguistics*, 5:339–351.

Yunsu Kim, Petre Petrov, Pavel Petrushkov, Shahram Khadivi, and Hermann Ney. 2019. Pivot-based transfer learning for neural machine translation between non-english languages. *arXiv preprint arXiv:1909.09524*.

Surafel M. Lakew, Matteo Negri, and Marco Turchi. 2021. Zero-shot neural machine translation with self-learning cycle. In *Proceedings of the 4th Workshop on Technologies for MT of Low Resource Languages (LoResMT2021)*, pages 96–113, Virtual. Association for Machine Translation in the Americas.

Mike Lewis, Yinhan Liu, Naman Goyal, Marjan Ghazvininejad, Abdelrahman Mohamed, Omer Levy, Ves Stoyanov, and Luke Zettlemoyer. 2019. Bart: Denoising sequence-to-sequence pre-training for natural language generation, translation, and comprehension. *arXiv preprint arXiv:1910.13461*.

Junwei Liao, Yu Shi, Ming Gong, Linjun Shou, Hong Qu, and Michael Zeng. 2021. Improving zero-shot neural machine translation on language-specific encoders-decoders. *arXiv preprint arXiv:2102.06578*.

Yinhan Liu, Jiatao Gu, Naman Goyal, Xian Li, Sergey Edunov, Marjan Ghazvininejad, Mike Lewis, and Luke Zettlemoyer. 2020. Multilingual denoising pre-training for neural machine translation. *Transactions of the Association for Computational Linguistics*, 8:726–742.

Colin Raffel, Noam Shazeer, Adam Roberts, Katherine Lee, Sharan Narang, Michael Matena, Yanqi Zhou, Wei Li, and Peter J Liu. 2019. Exploring the limits of transfer learning with a unified text-to-text transformer. *arXiv preprint arXiv:1910.10683*.

Alex Salcianu, Andy Golding, and Anton Bakalov. 2016. Compact language detector v3. *https://github.com/google/cld3*.

Aditya Siddhant, Ankur Bapna, Yuan Cao, Orhan Firat, Mia Chen, Sneha Kudugunta, Naveen Arivazhagan, and Yonghui Wu. 2020. Leveraging monolingual data with self-supervision for multilingual neural machine translation. *arXiv preprint arXiv:2005.04816*.

Haipeng Sun, Rui Wang, Kehai Chen, Masao Utiyama, Eiichiro Sumita, and Tiejun Zhao. 2020. Knowledge distillation for multilingual unsupervised neural machine translation. *arXiv preprint arXiv:2004.10171*.

Ashish Vaswani, Noam Shazeer, Niki Parmar, Jakob Uszkoreit, Llion Jones, Aidan N Gomez, Lukasz Kaiser, and Illia Polosukhin. 2017. Attention is all you need. *arXiv preprint arXiv:1706.03762*.

Thomas Wolf, Lysandre Debut, Victor Sanh, Julien Chaumond, Clement Delangue, Anthony Moi, Pierric Cistac, Tim Rault, Rémi Louf, Morgan Funtowicz, et al. 2019. Huggingface's transformers: State-of-the-art natural language processing. *arXiv preprint arXiv:1910.03771*.

Mengzhou Xia, Xiang Kong, Antonios Anastasopoulos, and Graham Neubig. 2019. Generalized data augmentation for low-resource translation. *arXiv preprint arXiv:1906.03785*.

Linting Xue, Noah Constant, Adam Roberts, Mihir Kale, Rami Al-Rfou, Aditya Siddhant, Aditya Barua, and Colin Raffel. 2020. mt5: A massively multilingual pre-trained text-to-text transformer. *arXiv preprint arXiv:2010.11934*.

Biao Zhang, Ankur Bapna, Rico Sennrich, and Orhan Firat. 2021. Share or not? learning to schedule language-specific ca-pacity for multilingual translation. In *International Conference on Learning Representations*.

Biao Zhang, Philip Williams, Ivan Titov, and Rico Sennrich. 2020. Improving massively multilingual neural machine translation and zero-shot translation. In *Proceedings of the 58th Annual Meeting of the Association for Computational Linguistics*, pages 1628–1639, Online. Association for Computational Linguistics.

Barret Zoph, Deniz Yuret, Jonathan May, and Kevin Knight. 2016. Transfer learning for low-resource neural machine translation. *arXiv preprint arXiv:1604.02201*.

ParsSimpleQA: The Persian Simple Question Answering Dataset and System over Knowledge Graph

Hamed Babaei Giglou*, **Niloufar Beyranvand***, **Reza Moradi***,
Amir Mohammad Salehoof, **Saeed Bibak**
Natural Language Processing Department, Part AI Research Center, Tehran, Iran
{hamedbabaeigiglou,nilou.beyranvand,rezymo,
a.m.salehoof}@gmail.com
saeed.bibak@partdp.ai

Abstract

The simple question answering over the knowledge graph concerns answering single-relation questions by querying the facts in the knowledge graph. This task has drawn significant attention in recent years. However, there is a demand for a simple question dataset in the Persian language to study open-domain simple question answering. In this paper, we present the first Persian single-relation question answering dataset and a model that uses a knowledge graph as a source of knowledge to answer questions. We create the ParsSimpleQA dataset semi-automatically in two steps. First, we build single-relation question templates. Next, we automatically create simple questions and answers using templates, entities, and relations from Farsbase. To present the reliability of the presented dataset, we proposed a simple question-answering system that receives questions and uses deep learning and information retrieval techniques for answering questions. The experimental results presented in this paper show that the ParsSimpleQA dataset is very promising for the Persian simple question-answering task.

1 Introduction

A knowledge graph (KG) represents a network of real-world entities, with a massive semantic net that integrates various, inconsistent and heterogeneous information resources to represent knowledge about different domains (Stroh and Mathur, 2016). Some KGs contain information from multiple domains to permit machine learning applications to operate on various tasks such as question answering (QA), recommender systems, and search systems by allowing them to retrieve and reuse comprehensive answers for a given query over KG. Many studies used well-structured KGs as external resources to support open-domain QA, whereas the Knowledge Graph-based Question Answering (KGQA) system aims to answer Natural Language Questions (NLQs) automatically.

KG as a data structure underpins digital information systems, assists users in finding and retrieving resources, and serves navigation and visualization purposes. In the humanities, knowledge graphs are usually rooted in knowledge organization systems that have a centuries-old tradition and have undergone a digital transformation with the advent of web-connected data (Haslhofer et al., 2018). This work addresses the Persian language, which in general is underrepresented in NLP and also within digital humanities. Considering open-domain QA in low resources languages such as Persian, this work certainly benefits also the research on digital humanities. Generally, knowledge graphs and applications could be vehicles for formalizing and connecting findings and insights derived from the analysis of possibly large-scale corpora in the digital humanities domain. Where with help of such applications we can digitize archive collections for librarians or social science research.

In the English language, there are more valuable research works, but there is limited work that has been carried out for the Persian KGQA. The Farsbase (Asgari-Bidhendi et al., 2019) is the first Persian KGs that uses hybrid techniques to extract knowledge from various sources, such as Wikipedia, Web tables, and unstructured texts. The Farsbase was published in 2018; since then, only a few research works have been published to incorporate the Farsbase in NLP tasks due to the unavailability of datasets that refer to the KG. This also limited research on digitalizing datasets for open-domain QA tasks, since, human readers often rely on a certain amount of broad background knowledge obtained from sources outside of the text. It is perhaps not surprising then, that machine readers also require knowledge external to the text itself to perform well on QA tasks where KGs are the best source of such information. To overcome these

*These authors contributed equally to this work.

The 2nd International Workshop on Natural Language Processing for Digital Humanities (NLP4DH), pages 59–68
November 20, 2022. ©2022 Association for Computational Linguistics

concerns, (Etezadi and Shamsfard, 2020) were the first researchers who proposed the PeCoQ dataset as the first dataset for Persian complex QA over KG. Although the existing dataset is very well developed for complex QA, many general-purpose KGQA systems in other languages (e.g English) are designed to deal with complex QA by decomposing complex questions into simple questions. The Knowledge Graph Simple Question Answering (KGSQA) is a key building block for complex QA, and its performance depends on KGSQA (Yani and Krisnadhi, 2021). So putting more emphasis on KGSQA is necessary for KGQA. To facilitate research on Persian KGQA, the first simple QA dataset and system have been introduced in this work. To the best of our knowledge, this is the first step toward Persian KGSQA. In this work, we first proposed the ParsSimpleQA dataset, a simple QA dataset in Persian. Next, we proposed a simple QA framework for the Persian KGSQA.

The rest of the article is organized as follows. We first describe the problem statements and definitions in section 2. The KGQA studies are studied in section 3. Section 4 presents the ParsSimpleQA dataset. The first Persian simple QA model is presented in section 5. Section 6 describes experimental setups, and results are covered in section 7. Finally, in section 8 we conclude the article.

2 Problem Statement and Definitions

Our study aims to design the first simple QA dataset and system for the Persian language that can map a simple NLQ q to a matching query Q consisting of the subject and relation to be executed in the KG G to retrieve answers. KG G comprises triples in the form of (s, r, o) where s, r, and o denote the head entity, predicate/relation, and the tail entity, respectively. In this work, G is Farsbase KG, the first Persian multi-source KG. A simple question is a question that contains a single relation that can be queried through G to extract facts. For example, the question "*who is the director of Alone in Berlin?*" contains a director relation which can be answered using G fact that "*Vincent Perez*" is the director.

The KGSQA task is defined as (Buzaaba and Amagasa, 2021): given a KG $G = \{(s_i, r_i, o_i)\}$ that represents a set of triples, and a NLQ $q = \{w_1, w_2, \ldots, w_T\}$, where $w_i \in q$ is a sequence of words, the simple QA task is to find a triple $(s', r', o') \in G$, such that o' is the answer to the question.

3 Related Works

The KGQA has attracted a considerable body of research in recent years, and increasingly, researchers are building end-to-end neural network models for this task. A straightforward decomposition of the KGQA pipeline is entity recognition, relation prediction, entity linking, and evidence integration. This work explored relationship prediction, entity linking, and evidence integration to transform natural language into queries to extract simple factoid question answers from KGs.

3.1 Relation Prediction

Relation prediction (RP) can be considered a classification task since the simple QA assumes only a single relation is mentioned in the question. (Mohammed et al., 2018) and (Buzaaba and Amagasa, 2021) investigated various models including BiLSTM, BiGRU, CNN, and logistic regression for RP. Similarly, (Li et al., 2021) tried the BiGRU model for the RP task. Overall, (Mohammed et al., 2018) and (Li et al., 2021) concluded that BiGRU is the best model for RP in their KGSQA pipelines. Moreover, (Sidiropoulos et al., 2020) used a combination of word2vec (Mikolov et al., 2013) with LSTM to solve the RP task. However, (Lukovnikov et al., 2019) took advantage of pre-trained language models and fine-tuned BERT (Devlin et al., 2019) for the RP task.

3.2 Entity Linking

Entity linking (EL) is the task of linking a set of entities mentioned in a text to a KG. (Buzaaba and Amagasa, 2021; Lukovnikov et al., 2019; Mohammed et al., 2018) used an inverted index to retrieve entity mentions from KG and then ranked mentions using *fuzzywuzzy*, a string-based similarity method. Additionally, (Fu et al., 2020) proposed a low-resource cross-lingual EL (XEL) that supports 25 languages, including Persian. They proposed a simple yet effective zero-shot XEL system, *QuEL*, that utilizes the search engine's query logs. (Asgari-Bidhendi et al., 2020) proposed the ParsEL-Social, the first Persian EL dataset which is constructed from social media contents. Next, they utilize context-dependent and context-independent features to propose the first EL model called ParsEL 1.0 in Persian using Farsbase KG. Moreover, in (Asgari-Bidhendi et al.) they proposed the ParsEL 1.1, which is an improved version of the previously proposed EL model, by adding graph-based features. In the latest work in EL at Persian, (Asgari-Bidhendi et al., 2021) introduced an unsupervised language-independent entity disambiguation (ULIED), which uses disambiguate and linked named entities. The proposed entity disambiguation uses different similarity measurements for candidate entity weighting and aggregation. The ULIED showed promising results in languages other than English, such as Persian.

3.3 Evidence Integration

Evidence integration (EI) is the final task to integrate evidence to reach a single (entity, relation) prediction. (Sidiropoulos et al., 2020) used a heuristic based on popularity, that chooses entities that appear among the facts in KG either as a subject or as an object. (Mohammed et al., 2018) used the top m entities and r relations to generate $m * r$ tuples where scores are the product of their component scores. After pruning meaningless combinations, they used graph-based features such as popularity nodes to select the final answers. (Lukovnikov et al., 2019) ranked the given entity-relation pairs by considering string-based similarity for entity and higher prediction probability using the BERT language model (Devlin et al., 2019) for relation. Next, they took top-scored pairs, which can easily generate a query to retrieve the answer from the KG.

3.4 Datasets

In (Bordes et al., 2015), the SimpleQuestions benchmark was first introduced, and this benchmark consists of 108,442 simple questions annotated with the correct Freebase knowledge base fact, where facts have exactly one relation. This allowed a significant improvement in English KGSQA research, where (Petrochuk and Zettlemoyer, 2018) reported an empirical analysis and concluded the SimpleQuestions dataset is nearly solved. However, researchers continued to analyze this benchmark further. Since neural network models require appropriate data for end-to-end training, the demand for a dataset in a new language is increased. Due to this concern, for the Persian language, the first KGQA dataset, which supports the complex QA, was introduced by (Etezadi and Shamsfard, 2020).

4 ParsSimpleQA Dataset

To construct a KGQA system in the practical environment, we should solve the following tasks: entity detection, EL, RP, and EI where each task can be addressed in a supervised or unsupervised learning fashion using an appropriate dataset. The proposed dataset is suited for training and evaluation of models for suitable and optimal queries to extract answers from KG G. For automated QA dataset generation, we had to deal with two challenges: creating high-quality templates and creating logical/correct QAs which the ParsSimpleQA datasets consider these challenges properly. Figure 1 depicts the process of creating the dataset. In the following, we discussed the details for ParsSimpleQA creation.

1. **Relationship Selection:** Farsbase consists of many relationships and considering all of them for dataset creation is computationally costly. For this reason, we filtered almost 100 most common relationships from G. Next, we analyzed chosen relationships based on two criteria: (1) whether they are meaningful in Persian or not, and (2) whether they meet Persian NLP dataset creation needs. In the final, we obtained 35 relationships for dataset creation.

2. **Generating Templates:** In this step, we used three annotators who were familiar with KGQA techniques for building templates and asked them to build templates for each relationship collaboratively. Templates are questions that only require an entity to be complete. By using specified entities, we were able to generate QAs. For example, for the template *Who is the author of* $< ENT >$*?*, we may consider the following samples: *Who is the author of Harry Potter?* and *Who is the author of Blindness?* where *Harry Potter* and *Blindness* are entities.

3. **Template Evaluations and Cleaning:** For creating high-quality templates, we asked three NLP researchers with at least a master's degree to check templates and find the inappropriate templates for relationships. During this process, we kept evaluations blind for researchers. To obtain high-quality templates, we applied hard voting for researcher decisions about accepting or rejecting templates. Next, the rejected template was removed from the final list to obtain 149 templates. Then, we asked annotators to analyze templates to see whether there are relationships that share the same information or not. Thereby, we

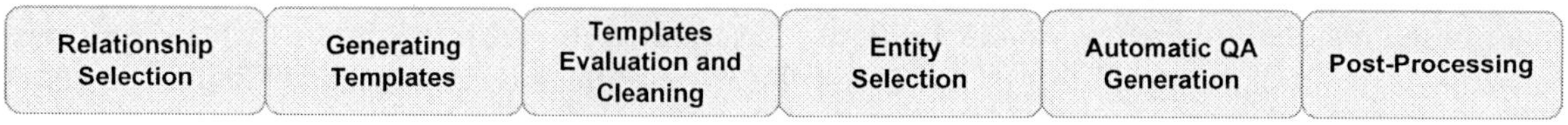

Figure 1: The ParsSimpleQA dataset generation procedure

combined multiple relationships to obtain 32 relationships in total. On average, 4.65 templates per relationship were constructed for the ParsSimpleQA dataset.

4. **Entity Selection:** Two ranges of data sources have been used to build the Farsbase knowledge base. The first source involves extracting rule-based information from dumped *Wikipedia* data, and the other source includes other knowledge bases such as *Yago* and *Wikidata*. Rule-based information extracted from the *Wikipedia* dumps naturally contains a lot of noise, including meaningless words, as well as information from other knowledge bases, including entities from different languages such as Chinese and Korean. None of them are appropriate for this task. Therefore, we considered the following three conditions in the entity selection for dataset creation: 1) The entity must have a URI field (a unique ID in KG), 2) Ignoring entities from *dbpedia*, *yago-knowledge.org*, *ecowlim.tfri.gov.tw*, *data.linkedmbd.org*, *data.linkedopendata.it*, and 3) Considering only entities with Persian letters.

5. **Automatic QA Generation:** All selected KG entities are inserted into template slots with condition that they have that template relation. So, we can say that template markings such as author/actor allow for natural sentences to be generated. We used all entities as subject entities and relationships for each template to run a Cypher query (Francis et al., 2018) – a Neo4j query language – over KG to generate object entities. Subsequently, we constructed (s, r, o) triples. Next, we constructed the samples using subject s and relationship templates where we know that answer is an object entity o. The constructed samples contain information such as relation type, template, question entity (subject), question (combination of template and question entity), question entity URI (identified entity in KG), answer entity (object), and answer entities URIs. At the end, the $n_{templates} * n_{relationships} * n_{entities}$ samples were obtained (n is number of items).

6. **Post-Processing:** The goal of this step is to create a final dataset for KGSQA by performing grouping, processing, and doing train-validation-test set splits. The following steps were performed for post-processing where the train/validation/test split with respect to relationship type and entities to avoid leakage.

   (a) Grouping data based on relation types. So, we clustered the samples for relation templates for each relation group.

   (b) Aggregation of groups based on question entity URIs. For each entity, we may have multiple samples with different answers (multiple answers for a question). In this step, we list the answers to each question.

   (c) Combining similar relations that annotators identified.

   (d) Train, validation, and test splits. We performed a train-validation-test split on question entity URIs and templates separately for each relation group. Next, the final train-validation-test sets for relation types were generated using divided questions entity URI and templates. This process was done by looking for pair entities and templates in the divided lists. After obtaining train-validation-test sets individually for relations, we merged them to form the final train, validation, and test sets.

We employed 60% train, 20% validation, and 20% test split rates while creating datasets. Table 1 presents the stats of the proposed datasets. Overall 36,122 samples for 32 relationship types using 149 templates and 16,772 unique entities were created.

5 Method

Our methodology for the Persian KGSQA uses the ParsSimpleQA dataset and comprises the following components: relation prediction (RP), entity linking (EL), and evidence integration (EI). Figure 2 depicts a proposed framework. In the proposed

Sets	# of samples	# of templates	# of question entities
Train	29,360	78	10,945
Validation	2,261	34	1,898
Test	4,501	37	3,929
Overall	36,122	149	16,772

Table 1: ParsSimpleQA dataset stats

KGSQA, a deep learning model is presented to identify the relation type of the questions. Next, the EL module uses a hybrid method for candidate entity generation and rankings for URI identification of entities from KG. Finally, the EI module uses question relation type, obtained URIs from entity linker, and KG to generate the answers using a Cypher query.

5.1 Relation Prediction

This module's goal is to identify the question relation type r' using a supervised approach. In recent years, transformer-based language models, such as BERT, have achieved state-of-the-art performance on many tasks (Min et al., 2021). Transformers encode context bidirectionally and require minimal architecture changes for a wide range of NLP tasks. Since the nature of KGSQA is open-domain specific, and to solve RP, a general-purpose representation such as BERT is a logical choice due to the advantages of contextualized representations. For relation type identification, we used ParsBERT (Farahani et al., 2021) a BERT variant for the Persian language as a pre-trained language model. To modify the output of ParsBERT for the RP task, we added an extra layer for fine-tuning. In ParsSimpleQA, samples appear to be imbalanced, which affects the RP fine-tuning since during the training, weights flow toward the majority class. To overcome this issue, we applied the focal loss function (Lin et al., 2017) which is an improved version of cross-entropy loss by focusing on hard learning of misclassified examples.

5.2 Entity Linking

The EL aims to link a set of entities mentioned in a text to a KG. EL consists of candidate generation (CG) and candidate ranking (CR). For CG, we applied a keyword-based search engine to retrieve the entities, where it uses a string-based BM25 scoring function as the similarity scoring function. For CR, most of the approaches tried to use node context information to perform CR. However, the Farsbase (Asgari-Bidhendi et al., 2019) contains only 14% of abstract context information which can be encoded in the form of contextualized representation for EL using transformers. However, in this way, we may lose nodes that do not contain context information but are the key object nodes for the question to form the answer triples. To overcome this limitation, we proposed a graph-based features ranking mechanism as a second ranking function that considers node connections instead of context information. Assessing EL with graph-based and context-based rankings boosts the performance of the EL rankings, regardless of the question itself. We acknowledge that the question itself must be taken into consideration since it plays an essential role in candidate entity generation. So, CR contains information about string-based features. Finally, a string-based ranking method that has been used for CG is incorporated with graph-based and context-based rankings as a hybrid CR for EL. The proposed hybrid CR takes advantage of each other for the final appropriate candidate ranking. The final CR has been calculated in the following manner:

String-based ranking: Entities in KG are indexed into the search engine using an inverted index data structure. Next, with BM25 scoring function (Robertson and Zaragoza, 2009), relative entities are retrieved as a CG for CR. BM25 is based on the bag-of-words approach. The score of a subject s' given a query q which contains the words $w_1, w_2, ..., w_T$ is given by:

$$R_{bm25}(s', q) = \sum_{i=1}^{n} IDF(w_i) \cdot QT(s', w_i)$$

$$QT(s', w_i) = \frac{f(w_i, s') \cdot (k_1 + 1)}{f(w_i, s') + k_1 \cdot (1 - b + b \cdot \frac{|s'|}{avgdl})}$$

where $f(w_i, s')$ is q's term frequency in the s', $|s'|$ is the length of the s' in words, and $avgdl$ is the average length in the text collection from KG. k_1 and b are free parameters.

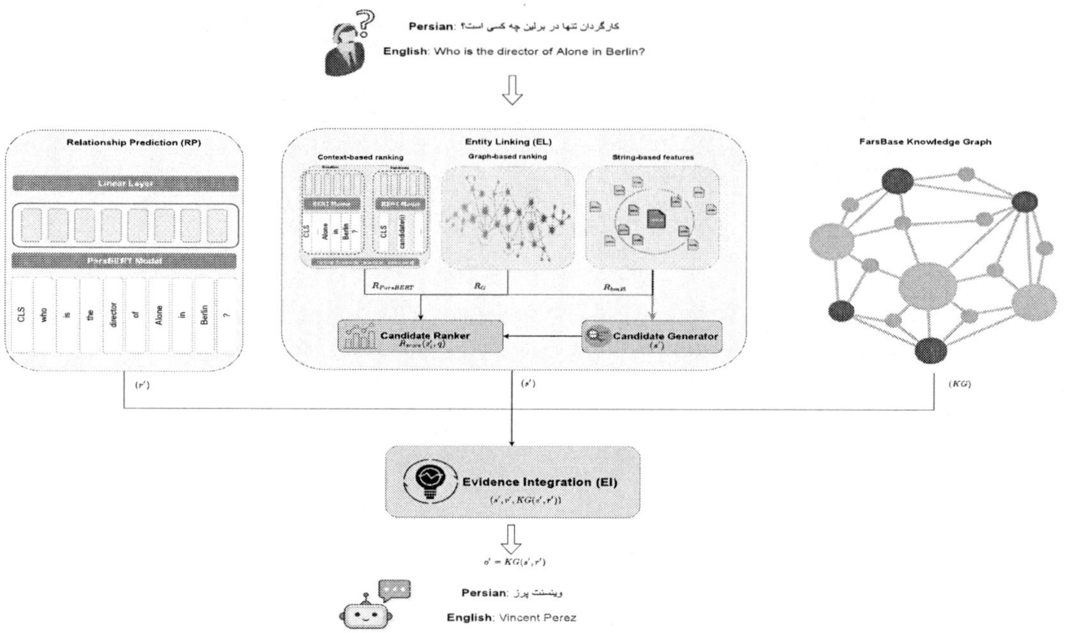

Figure 2: The workflow of SimpleQA model

Context-based ranking: Since the question conveys a better level of meaning, first, the embeddings of the question q and candidates s' are obtained using the ParsBERT language model. Next, we calculated cosine similarity between $V_{s'}$ and V_q vectors to obtain $R_{ParsBERT}(V_{s'}, V_q)$, where $V_{s'}$ and V_q are embeddings of s' and V_q, respectively.

$$R_{ParsBERT}(s', q) = Similarity(V_{s'}, V_q)$$

Graph-based ranking: Assuming that a node with more connections is also more popular, the degree of each node is used as its popularity score to calculate $R_G(s')$.

$$R_G(s', q) = degree(s')$$

Finally, for each candidate s'_i where $s'_i \in s'$, we calculate the probability $P(R, k, q)$ for ranking outputs $R \in \{R_{bm25}, R_{ParsBERT}, R_G\}$ using the following formula:

$$P(R, s'_i, q) = \frac{R(s'_i, q)}{\sum_{j=1}^{n_{s'}} R(s'_j, q)}$$

where $n_{s'}$ is the number of candidates s'_i. In the final, the average of ranked probabilities was calculated to obtain the final $R_{score}(s'_i, q)$ ranking score for candidates, where we pick the top_e ELs with the highest probability score.

$$R_{score}(s'_i, q) = \frac{P_{R_{bm25}} + P_{R_{ParsBERT}} + P_{R_G}}{3}$$

5.3 Evidence Integration

In evidence integration (EI), once we have a list of candidate entities, each candidate node is used as a starting point to reach candidate answers o'. We limit our search to a single hop and retrieve all nodes that are reachable from the candidate node s' where the relation path is consistent with the predicted relation r'. Due to the high performance of the EL model, we used EL final scoring R_{score} as a sorting function for answers o'. During EI, since EL and RP models are independent, the triples may appear to be meaningless because EL can produce s' that does not have the r' that the RP model predicted. In this case, the (s', r') pairs are ignored from EI.

6 Experimental Setups

Metrics: Commonly used performance measures include accuracy, precision, recall, and F-measure (Diefenbach et al., 2018). Since For each question there is an expected set of correct answers, these are called the gold standard answers. we can define the metrics as followings (n is a number of samples):

$$accuracy(q) = \frac{n_{correct\ predictions}}{n_{dataset\ samples}}$$

$$precision(q) = \frac{n_{correct\ system\ answers\ for\ q}}{n_{system\ answers\ for\ q}}$$

$$recall(q) = \frac{n_{correct\ system\ answers\ for\ q}}{n_{gold\ standard\ answers\ for\ q}}$$

$$F - measure = 2 * \frac{precision(q) * recall(q)}{precision(q) + recall(q)}$$

Where precision indicates how many of the answers are correct, recall indicates how many of the returned answers are in the gold standard. F-measure is the weighted average between the (macro) precision and recall.

Training Setups: We have used the ParsSimpleQA dataset for training and evaluating the first Persian KGSQA model. We imported Farsbase KG into the Neo4j database. Next, after tuning several hyperparameter models, the final model was trained. Training and hyperparameter tuning was done using the NVIDIA Tesla V100 GPU machine.

7 Results

7.1 Results and Hyperparameter Tunings

Regarding imbalanced nature of the data, results for RP, EL, and EI tasks are demonstrated in Tables 2, 3, and 4, respectively. In the following, we presented a more detailed analysis.

Relation Prediction: For comparison of the proposed method for RP, we implemented the BiGRU baseline, which was proposed in (Mohammed et al., 2018). We did the hyperparameter tuning for BiGRU and ParsBERT models using the validation set. The optimal values for the BiGRU are $\alpha = 1e - 4$, $batch - size = 16$, $optimizer = adam$, and $loss = cross - entropy$. The optimal values for ParsBERT are $\alpha = 1e - 5$, $batch - size = 4$, and $optimizer = adam$. For loss function in fine-tuning ParsBERT, we examined cross-entropy, Inverse of Square Root of Number of Samples (ISNS) (Mahajan et al., 2018), and FL loss functions which experimental results showed the superiority of the focal loss function for RP task. Table 2 presents the experimental results over validation and final results over the test set. The experiment with three loss functions showed that hard learning of misclassified classes using the focal loss function is an appropriate choice for this task.

Entity Linking: The results for the proposed EL method over the validation and test set are presented in Table 3, and the optimal top_e parameter is the number of top candidates for EL prediction and it is set into 1.

Evidence Integration: After entering RP, EL, and KG into EI, the final hyperparameters needed to be tuned for the final system. The final parameters are 1) top_a, the number of top answers in the final system, 2) top_r, the number of top relations, and 3) top_e, the number of top ELs. We run the two-step tuning by considering F1-score as a judgment metric for optimal parameters. In the first step we tried to find optimal values for top_r and top_e since both top_r and top_e are effects the final system response. As a result, according to the Figure 3, the optimal values for (top_r, top_e) pair are (2, 5). Next, we used optimal top_r and top_e to tune the top_a. Figure 4 shows the tuning results for top_a, where the results after $top_a = 5$ remains unchanged. In the end, we used optimal values for the final system evaluation, where the results are presented in Table 4 for the test set.

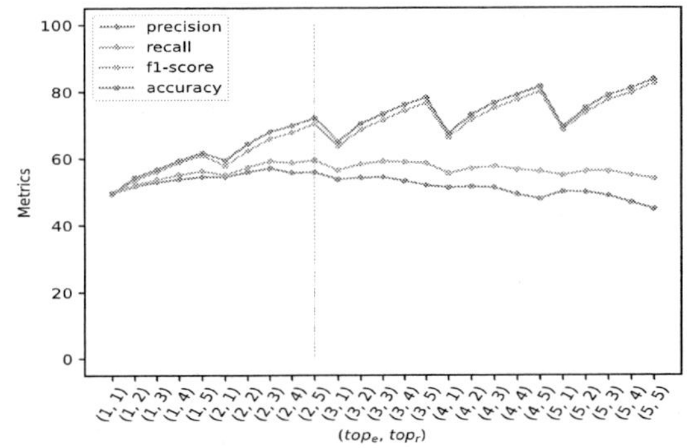

Figure 3: Hyperparameter tuning for (top_e, top_r) set using validation set

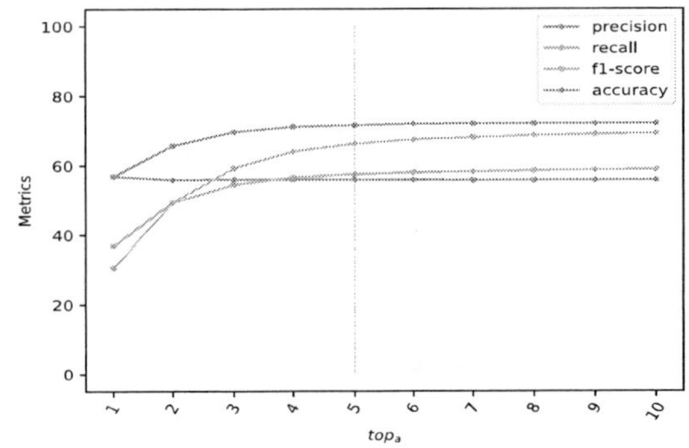

Figure 4: Hyperparameter tuning for top_a using validation set

7.2 Analysis

All models under comparison have all their components fixed, except RP. Therefore, any improvement observed is due to RP.

Effect of RP: RP uses the ParsBERT model, and in the experimental result, ParsBERT recognizes the relations more accurately than the baseline. However, we observed two concerns:

Model	Loss Function	Precision	Recall	F1-score	Accuracy	Dataset
BiGRU	cross entropy	34.33	36.36	33.61	60.15	Validation
ParsBERT	cross entropy	60.8	64.56	60.87	77.62	Validation
ParsBERT	ISNS	62.97	61.79	55.85	75.36	Validation
ParsBERT	FL	60.18	65.88	61.14	77.39	Validation
ParsBERT	FL	53.99	59.22	54.25	54.61	Test

Table 2: Relation prediction results

top_e Entities	Precision	Recall	F1-score	Accuracy	Dataset
1	68.02	67.18	67.38	68.02	Validation
1	68.23	66.77	67.18	68.23	Test

Table 3: Entity linking results

top_e	top_r	top_a	Precision	Recall	F1-score	Accuracy	Dataset
2	5	5	55.94	66.20	57.52	71.56	Validation
2	5	5	48.56	63.93	52.27	68.30	Test

Table 4: Final system results

- *Imbalanced Relations:* The weighting technique solved this issue somehow, but the issue isn't completely solved. Still, we can see the model does not work accurately for some relations.
- *Relations Similarity:* This happened due to the similarity in templates, and asking annotators to find similar relations wasn't enough since the experimental analysis showed that some templates might have common words in templates that lead to misclassification.

However, regarding both weaknesses, the model performs promisingly regarding the baseline model and positively helps the rest of the pipeline. This shows that producing this kind of data could help better identification of relation types.

KGSQA Performance Analysis:

- According to Table 3, the proposed EL strongly generalized well on unseen questions.
- Figures 3 and 4 for hyperparameter tunning showed the effect of low performance on RP affect on the other tasks such as ELs in the system. This is obvious in (top_e, top_r) pairs, e.g $(4, 1)$, $(3, 1)$. But applying $top_r > 1$ solved this issue positively.
- In terms of accuracy, the final system achieved an accuracy of 68.30% on the test set. This means the proposed KGSQA produced answer sets (top_a answers for each sample) in the test set which 68.30% (2671 out of 3929 samples) of samples contained answers (gold answers exist in answer sets). Regarding this, the presented model disables producing a correct answer (in the answer set) for 1258 samples in the test set.
- We obtained the optimal value of $top_a = 5$ for the number of output answers. Because most of the questions contained only one or two answers, the number of correct answers for each question may be ended up with 1 or 2 true answers, which results in low precision. One way of solving this issue is decreasing top_a or considering a separate ranker from EL for top_a answer selections.
- The high recall alarms the number of outputs that are well intersected with gold answers. So, answers are mostly among the top_a answers.

8 Conclusion

This paper introduced ParsSimpleQA, the first KGSQA dataset for the Persian language that contains questions with corresponding entities, entity links, relation types, and answers. The machine-generated questions using human-generated templates are preprocessed and divided into train, validation, and test sets for training and analyzing machine learning techniques. Next, we introduced the first Persian KGSQA to perform EL, RP, and EI. Our experimental results on the ParsSimpleQA dataset show that our proposed framework is robust and generalized well. This framework will play a baseline model that opens many works in Persian KGSQA. Moreover, our generated ParsSimpleQA dataset is available to the research community at the GitHub[1] repository.

Acknowledgements

The authors would like to give big thanks to Part AI Research Center[2] (the biggest AI company in Iran) for supporting and funding this research for digital humanities.

References

Majid Asgari-Bidhendi, Farzane Fakhrian, and Behrouz Minaei-Bidgoli. A graph-based approach for persian entity linking.

Majid Asgari-Bidhendi, Farzane Fakhrian, and Behrouz Minaei-Bidgoli. 2020. Parsel 1.0: Unsupervised entity linking in persian social media texts. In *2020 11th International Conference on Information and Knowledge Technology (IKT)*, pages 148–153. IEEE.

Majid Asgari-Bidhendi, Ali Hadian, and Behrouz Minaei-Bidgoli. 2019. Farsbase: The persian knowledge graph. *Semantic Web*, 10(6):1169–1196.

Majid Asgari-Bidhendi, Behrooz Janfada, Amir Havangi, Sayyed Ali Hossayni, and Behrouz Minaei-Bidgoli. 2021. An unsupervised language-independent entity disambiguation method and its evaluation on the english and persian languages. *arXiv preprint arXiv:2102.00395*.

Antoine Bordes, Nicolas Usunier, Sumit Chopra, and Jason Weston. 2015. Large-scale simple question answering with memory networks. *arXiv preprint arXiv:1506.02075*.

Happy Buzaaba and Toshiyuki Amagasa. 2021. Question answering over knowledge base: A scheme for integrating subject and the identified relation to answer simple questions. *SN Comput. Sci.*, 2:25.

Jacob Devlin, Ming-Wei Chang, Kenton Lee, and Kristina Toutanova. 2019. Bert: Pre-training of deep bidirectional transformers for language understanding. In *Proceedings of the 2019 Conference of the North American Chapter of the Association for Computational Linguistics: Human Language Technologies, Volume 1 (Long and Short Papers)*, pages 4171–4186.

Dennis Diefenbach, Vanessa Lopez, Kamal Singh, and Pierre Maret. 2018. Core techniques of question answering systems over knowledge bases: a survey. *Knowledge and Information systems*, 55(3):529–569.

Romina Etezadi and Mehrnoush Shamsfard. 2020. PeCoQ: A dataset for persian complex question answering over knowledge graph. In *2020 11th International Conference on Information and Knowledge Technology (IKT)*. IEEE.

Mehrdad Farahani, Mohammad Gharachorloo, Marzieh Farahani, and Mohammad Manthouri. 2021. Parsbert: Transformer-based model for persian language understanding. *Neural Processing Letters*, 53(6):3831–3847.

Nadime Francis, Alastair Green, Paolo Guagliardo, Leonid Libkin, Tobias Lindaaker, Victor Marsault, Stefan Plantikow, Mats Rydberg, Petra Selmer, and Andrés Taylor. 2018. Cypher: An evolving query language for property graphs. In *Proceedings of the 2018 International Conference on Management of Data*, SIGMOD '18, page 1433–1445, New York, NY, USA. Association for Computing Machinery.

Xingyu Fu, Weijia Shi, Xiaodong Yu, Zian Zhao, and Dan Roth. 2020. Design Challenges in Low-resource Cross-lingual Entity Linking. In *Proc. of the Conference on Empirical Methods in Natural Language Processing (EMNLP)*.

Bernhard Haslhofer, Antoine Isaac, and Rainer Simon. 2018. *Knowledge Graphs in the Libraries and Digital Humanities Domain*, pages 1–8. Springer International Publishing, Cham.

Lin Li, Mengjing Zhang, Zhaohui Chao, and Jianwen Xiang. 2021. Using context information to enhance simple question answering. *World Wide Web*, 24(1):249–277.

Tsung-Yi Lin, Priya Goyal, Ross Girshick, Kaiming He, and Piotr Dollár. 2017. Focal loss for dense object detection. pages 2980–2988.

Denis Lukovnikov, Asja Fischer, and Jens Lehmann. 2019. Pretrained transformers for simple question answering over knowledge graphs. In *International Semantic Web Conference*, pages 470–486. Springer.

Dhruv Mahajan, Ross Girshick, Vignesh Ramanathan, Kaiming He, Manohar Paluri, Yixuan Li, Ashwin Bharambe, and Laurens Van Der Maaten. 2018. Exploring the limits of weakly supervised pretraining. In *Proceedings of the European conference on computer vision (ECCV)*, pages 181–196.

Tomas Mikolov, Kai Chen, Greg Corrado, and Jeffrey Dean. 2013. Efficient estimation of word representations in vector space. *arXiv preprint arXiv:1301.3781*.

[1]https://github.com/partdpai/ParsSimpleQA

[2]https://www.partdp.ai

Bonan Min, Hayley Ross, Elior Sulem, Amir Pouran Ben Veyseh, Thien Huu Nguyen, Oscar Sainz, Eneko Agirre, Ilana Heinz, and Dan Roth. 2021. Recent advances in natural language processing via large pre-trained language models: A survey.

Salman Mohammed, Peng Shi, and Jimmy Lin. 2018. Strong baselines for simple question answering over knowledge graphs with and without neural networks. In *Proceedings of the 2018 Conference of the North American Chapter of the Association for Computational Linguistics: Human Language Technologies, Volume 2 (Short Papers)*, pages 291–296.

Michael Petrochuk and Luke Zettlemoyer. 2018. Simplequestions nearly solved: A new upperbound and baseline approach. *arXiv preprint arXiv:1804.08798*.

Stephen Robertson and Hugo Zaragoza. 2009. *The probabilistic relevance framework: BM25 and beyond*. Now Publishers Inc.

Georgios Sidiropoulos, Nikos Voskarides, and Evangelos Kanoulas. 2020. Knowledge graph simple question answering for unseen domains. In *Automated Knowledge Base Construction*.

Eylon Stroh and Priyank Mathur. 2016. Question answering using deep learning. *SCPD*, pages 1–2.

Mohammad Yani and Adila Alfa Krisnadhi. 2021. Challenges, techniques, and trends of simple knowledge graph question answering: A survey. *Information*, 12(7):271.

Enhancing Digital History – Event Discovery via Topic Modeling and Change Detection

King-Ip Lin, Sabrina Peng
Department of Computer Science
Lyle School of Engineering
Southern Methodist University
Dallas, TX 75205, USA
{kdlin, shpeng}@smu.edu

Abstract

Digital history is the application of computer science techniques to historical data in order to uncover insights into events occurring during specific time periods from the past. This relatively new interdisciplinary field can help identify and record latent information about political, cultural, and economic trends that are not otherwise apparent from traditional historical analysis. This paper presents a method that uses topic modeling and breakpoint detection to observe how extracted topics come in and out of prominence over various time periods. We apply our techniques on British parliamentary speech data from the 19th century. Findings show that some of the events produced are cohesive in topic content (religion, transportation, economics, etc.) and time period (events are focused in the same year or month). Topic content identified should be further analyzed for specific events and undergo external validation to determine the quality and value of the findings to historians specializing in 19th century Britain.

1 Introduction

The field of digital history involves the application of computer science techniques to historical data. Research in this field is aimed at uncovering both obvious and latent information about specific time periods from the past, allowing for a deeper understanding of historical events.

Specifically, using natural language processing techniques on historic text data can be valuable in determining what factors are catalysts for change. Issues, ideas, and sentiments can suddenly become viral and become triggers for influential events.

In this paper, we present our work on detecting these factors by pinpointing which topics gain or lose prominence over certain time periods in history. We test our methods by applying them to a dataset of 19th century British parliamentary debates from the House of Commons. We define our task as one that discovers when political, cultural, and economic trends grow and/or shrink with respect to significant increased or decreased discussion of certain topics in parliamentary discourse.

We model the ideas by turning to standard (generative) topic models, such as LDA (Biel, Ng, & Jordan, 2013). These models are well studied and have been applied in a variety of fields, including the humanities (Günther & Quandt, 2016; Ramage, Rosen, Chuang, Manning, & McFarland, 2009; Thomas & Droge, 2022; Guldi, 2019). In many such models, there is an intuitive description for topics that makes it feasible for users to detect what ideas are being represented in their data.

The next thing we need to model is the change in prominence of topics. There is a class of topic models known as Dynamic Topic Models (Biel & Lafferty, 2006) that attempts to determine the evolution of the most prominent topics over time. While this is useful in a lot of applications, this information does not necessarily show us the scope of the change in each topic's prominence. For instance, while a topic that is generated in time t does not appear in time t-1, it is not easy to determine whether its prominence suffers just

The 2nd International Workshop on Natural Language Processing for Digital Humanities (NLP4DH), pages 69–78
November 20, 2022.

a small drop or falls off a cliff. Thus, in this work, we took the approach of developing a single topic model for all documents across all time slots. We intentionally generate a larger number of topics and use measures to quantitively measure the importance of each topic for each time slot. Thus, we can generate a time series of importance for each topic. We then apply a changepoint/breakpoint detection algorithm on the time series to detect major changes in the time series and capture where certain topics enter/leave parliamentary debate.

Another issue we look at is the robustness of the results. Topic model algorithms generate different results for each run, an undesirable characteristic (Yong, Pan, Lu, Topkara, & Song, 2016). Methods have been proposed for combating this instability (Montyla, Claes, & Faroaq, 2018; Miller & McCoy, 2017) (Rieger, 2020). In our work, we incorporate methods to overcome the instability by running the model multiple times and using clustering techniques to combine the results and enhance stability.

2 Background

2.1 Topic Modeling and Latent Dirichlet Allocation

Topic modeling is a language modeling technique that represents a large corpus of documents via topics. In such models, like Probabilistic Latent Semantic Indexing (PLSI) (Hoffmann, 1999) and Latent Dirichlet Allocation (LDA) (Biel, Ng, & Jordan, 2013), a topic is represented by a probability distribution over the vocabulary of the corpus. Intuitively, a topic is defined by the words that are heavily associated with it.

We use the following notation for the rest of the paper:

- We have a corpus C of n documents, denoted by $C_1, \dots C_n$
- The set of all distinct words that makes up all documents is denoted by the set W $(w_1, \dots w_m)$
- Let k be the number of topics describing the corpus (provided by the user)

Given the above, the topic model is described by two sets of probability distributions, each represented by a set of vectors.

- Topic-word vector $(t_1, \dots, t_k)$: each vector corresponds to a topic, which is a probability distribution on W.
- Document-topic vector $(d_1, \dots, d_n)$: each vector corresponds to a probability distribution of topics 1..k. This represents the association of each topic to a given document.

The goal of the topic modeling is to find the set of vectors/distributions that maximizes the probability that the corpus is actually being represented by the corresponding model.

Among the most widely used topic models today is Latent Dirichlet Allocation (LDA). It assumes there is an underlying Dirichlet distribution governing the choice of the vectors. Two parameters that are associated with the Dirichlet distribution, α and β, are used to affect the likelihood of a certain probability distribution being picked.

Typically, users of LDA can examine the topics, and for each topic, extract the words that have high probability to describe them. Also, they can look at the document-topic vectors to cluster documents along the topics.

2.2 Dynamic Topic Model

While the basic topic model does not have a time dimension, there has been work done to incorporate the time dimension. Dynamic Topic Model (Biel & Lafferty, 2006; Wang, Biel, & Heckerman, 2008) is one such approach. For the discrete case (Biel & Lafferty, 2006), it assumes the topic-word vector at time t is conditional on the topic-word vector at time t-1. The method generates a set of topics for each time t, enabling the user to see the most prevalent topics at certain times. Other dynamic topic models have been proposed, many of which are being applied in a large variety of applications (Xu, Chen, Dai, & Chen, 2017; Hida, Takeishi, & Hori, 2018; Rieger, Jentsch, & Rahnenführer, 2021). While these models incorporate the notion of topic changes over time, they mostly focus on the generation of topics at different time points, meaning extra efforts are needed to obtain what we are looking for – the gain or loss of topic prominence.

The work by Wang and Goutte (Yunli & Cyril, 2018) is similar to this work in the sense that they also generate time series and apply change point detection. However, they are still generating topics on a per time slot basis and calculate the "dissimilarity" of topics from 1 slot to the next. The topic-CD model proposed in (Lu, Guo, & Chen, 2022) is also similar, with the caveat that the model builds in a fixed number of change points.

2.3 Changepoint/Breakpoint Detection Algorithms for Time Series

Changepoint / breakpoint detection in time series (Troung, Oudre, & Vayatis , 2020) has been applied to many problems involving climate data (Reeves, Chen, Wang, Lund, & Lu, 2007) and bioinformatics (Vito M. R. Muggeo, 2011). In this paper, we utilize the "ruptures" package (Truong, 2018), which contains a variety of change point detection algorithms. After some research, we selected the Pelt ("Pruned Exact Linear Time") algorithm, which computes the segmentation of the time series that minimizes the constrained sum of approximation errors. The Pelt algorithm does not require a fixed number of change points to be detected, which is ideal in our case, as we are conducting unsupervised learning and do not know the number of true breakpoints. The algorithm uses pruning rules to keep or discard samples from the set of potential change points, resulting in a considerable speedup when compared to other algorithms and a computational complexity that is linear on average.

3 Our Approach

3.1 Problem Specification and Basic Algorithm

Our goal for this work is to, given a set of historic documents spanning a time period, determine when and how certain ideas rise to prominence or fade into non-existence over that period.

We assume there is a corpus C of documents (C_1, …, C_n). Each document has a time point (chosen from a set of time points $t_1 \leq \ldots \leq t_m$) associated with it. We assume m is much smaller than n. Notice that a timepoint can be a single instance in time (e.g. 1/1/2001, 12:00 am), or a period of time (e.g. March 1854 – June 1855). Our approach allows the user to choose any way of grouping the documents by time periods as they see fit.

We capture the notion of ideas by using topic models to represent them. Each topic can be represented by the words associated with it that have the highest probabilities. This provides a reasonable starting point for users to infer the ideas based on the words that are used to describe it.

Our approach consists of the following steps (for the rest of the paper, we use LDA as our topic model, but any topic model that generates topic-word and document-topic vectors can be used):

1. Run LDA on C, with k topics.
2. For each timepoint t_i, calculate and aggregate the document-topic vectors for all documents to form a vector denoting the importance of each topic at each timepoint.
3. For each topic, generate a time series based on the aggregated vector's value over the timepoints.
4. Apply breakpoint detection algorithms on the time series to detect when there is a sudden increase/decrease of weight of each topic.

Here we provide some additional details about each step:

- We want the number of topics k to cover the possible topics over all timepoints. Thus, we suggest setting k to a larger number than normal – i.e. larger than what one expects the number of topics to be over the timepoints.

- In step 2, we leave the option of how to aggregate the document-topic vector open. In this paper, we choose to simply add the document-topic vectors for all documents – essentially treating probabilities as "weights". We also choose not to normalize the results to get back to a probability distribution. One reason we take the raw sum is that we want to model not just the relative importance of the topics amongst themselves, but also the quantitative strength of the topic being mentioned. Other aggregation functions can be chosen if they can be justified.

- As mentioned in section 2, we use Pelt as our breakpoint detection algorithm.

3.2 Data used and simple example

To illustrate our methods, we use a data set of British parliamentary debates from 1803-1910. The dataset contains raw text and metadata for 10,979,009 sentences in speeches made by the legislators during parliamentary debates. In addition to the raw text of each sentence spoken, important metadata fields used in the event detection process include the date the sentence was spoken and the speech the sentence belongs to. As the dataset is large and analysis requires extensive computational resources, a subset of the dataset is created by performing stratified random sampling by speech month. For data cleaning and preparation, the raw text from each sentence is tokenized into words. We lowercase all words, strip out all punctuation, and filter out words that are less than 3 letters long. Then, all common English and dataset-specific (government-related) stop words are removed to retain more interesting terms. Finally, lemmatization is conducted to remove inflectional endings and retain the base form of each word.

In terms of segmenting the speech into documents, we consider each time a legislator speaks as a document to be fed into LDA.

Figures 1 and 2 show sample results from various steps of our methodology – LDA document-topic vector aggregation, time series generation, and breakpoint detection.

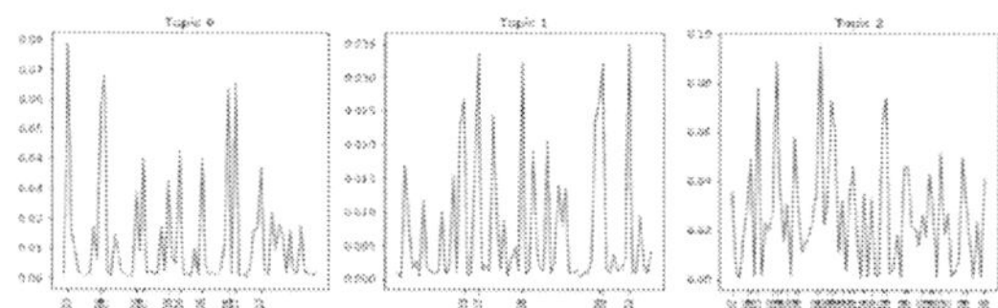

Figure 1. Examples of time series generated from aggregated LDA document-topic vectors.

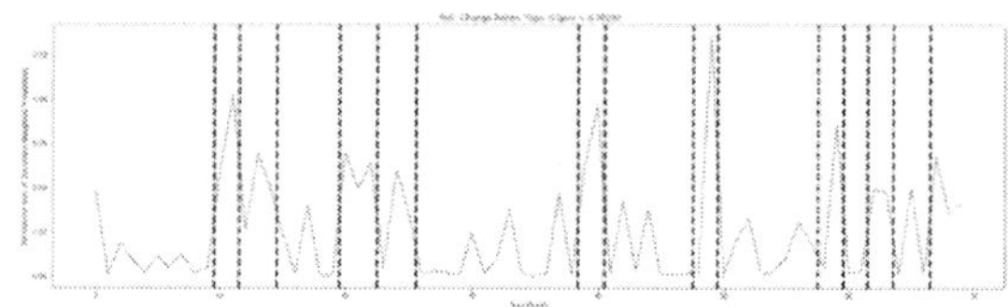

Figure 2. Example of breakpoints detected by the Pelt change point algorithm.

3.3 Enhancing robustness

Using LDA introduces the problem of instability. LDA is a non-deterministic algorithm that uses a stochastic process to update internal weights. Therefore, the results generated by LDA are not reproducible between different runs of the algorithm on the same dataset.

As stated in the introduction, there has been work on enhancing the stability of the method. Most methods try to run LDA on the same data set multiple times, and then aggregate the results. We follow a similar technique here. In our experiments below, we run our algorithms 10 times and aggregate the results for analysis.

However, compared to other methods, we have options on how we aggregate the topics generated over multiple runs. In our case, each topic is associated with two items: the topic-word vector describing it, and the time series that is generated from that topic. Thus, we can aggregate the topics in one of two ways.

The first way is to cluster the topics based on the topic-word vector with agglomerative hierarchical clustering. Once the documents are clustered, the previously calculated changepoints of each time series for each topic are examined. Those points that appear with high frequency in the cluster will be returned as the breakpoints.

For clustering purposes, we need a similarity/distance metric between pairwise topic-word vectors. Our approaches rely on using selective terms from each topic. With a decent vocabulary size, each topic-word vector will have a lot of terms that have small (but non-zero) values. Since those terms are usually ignored by humans anyway, it makes some sense to ignore those terms when calculating similarity between topics. Thus, each topic is now represented by a subset of the vocabulary that is deemed "important" – for example, the set of words having high probabilities of belonging to the topic. After that, we apply Jaccard coefficient and Jensen-Shannon distance to calculate the similarity between topics. We apply two versions of the Jaccard coefficient, by considering only the top k words of each topic (denoted by Jaccard), or by considering all words in a topic that have a probability greater than a threshold p (denoted by Jaccard-p). We also apply Jensen-Shannon distance, which is the square root of Jensen-Shannon divergence. It measures the similarity between two probability distributions and is the symmetric version of Kullback-Leibler divergence.

The advantage of this method is that since the topic-word vector is the defining feature of the topic, it theoretically makes sense to cluster the topics in this way (as opposed to other stability methods). However, there is no guarantee that they share the same breakpoints, which may render some clusters useless.

Alternatively, we can cluster the topics based on the time series that are associated with each topic. We use both Euclidean and Manhattan distance as distance measures. Once the topics have been clustered, we examine the topics within a cluster and find words that have high probability among most of the topics and use them to represent the clusters.

We will then apply the changepoint detection algorithms to the sequences of the clusters to denote the breakpoints. For this method, the clustering usually places sequences with similar breakpoints together. The challenge is to find frequent words that are shared among the topics. Space limitations means that we will only discuss the result of our first approach.

4 Experimental Results

We create a subset of the data for use in our experiments by selecting 500 samples from each month of the dataset's representative time period using stratified random sampling. We set the number of clusters detected by agglomerative clustering to $N = 10$. We evaluate results for the distance metrics used in both methods on the basis of both cluster cohesion and topic distinctiveness. For each approach-metric combination, we analyze cluster tendency plots and the spread of topics across clusters. Cluster tendency plots used include VAT and iVAT, which reveals hidden cluster structures as dark blocks along the diagonal of the image representation. We also analyze topic annotations created by extracting the top documents from each cluster based on the aggregated probability of a document belonging to the cluster topics.

As mentioned in the previous section, we utilize the Jaccard coefficient, Jaccard-p coefficient, and Jensen-Shannon distance as distance metrics for agglomerative clustering. For the Jaccard approach, the sets of terms used to calculate the coefficient include the top terms from each topic with a topic-word probability 100x greater than the overall probability the term would appear in a random document. We further add rare words (those occurring less than 10 times across all topics) and unique words (those that were completely unique to the given topic). For the Jaccard-p approach, the sets of terms used to calculate the coefficient include the top terms from a topic that have a topic-word probability of greater than 0.25%. For the Jensen-Shannon approach, the topic-word vectors used to calculate the distance include the top 1000 terms from each topic with the highest probabilities.

The Jaccard approach resulted in a less effective extraction and clustering of topics. Over 70% of the total topics were contained within one cluster, indicating one large generic cluster and many small specific ones. The topic annotations corroborate this finding – the top documents from the large cluster have a variety of topics, and the number of topics in the other clusters are too small.

The Jaccard-p approach seems to mitigate the original issues of using Jaccard due to its different word set composition and probability threshold. One larger cluster still exists, but the topics are more evenly spread across the identified cluster, as shown in Figure 3. Moreover, the VAT diagram (Figure 4) shows greater cluster distinctiveness.

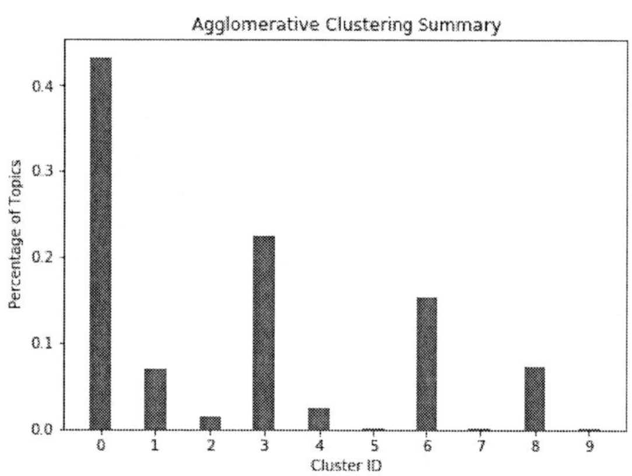

Figure 3. LDA topic distribution over Jaccard-p agglomerative clustering.

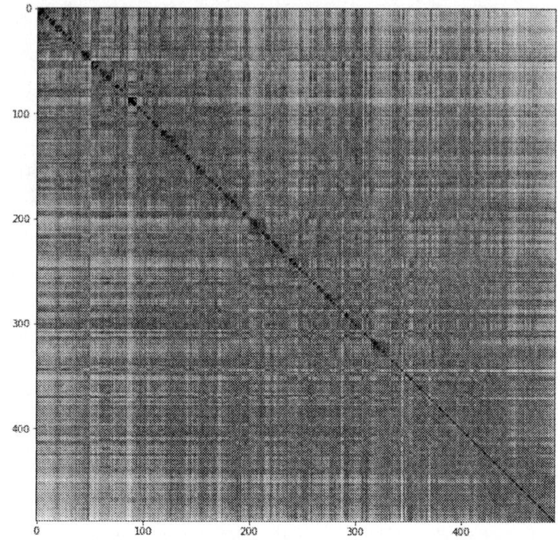

Figure 4. VAT diagram for Jaccard-p agglomerative clustering.

The topic annotations generated from the Jaccard-p approach indicate that certain clusters do exhibit topic cohesion. Relevant speeches for the clusters show thematic similarities, and topic-generated time series show similar trends in rise and fall across time intervals.

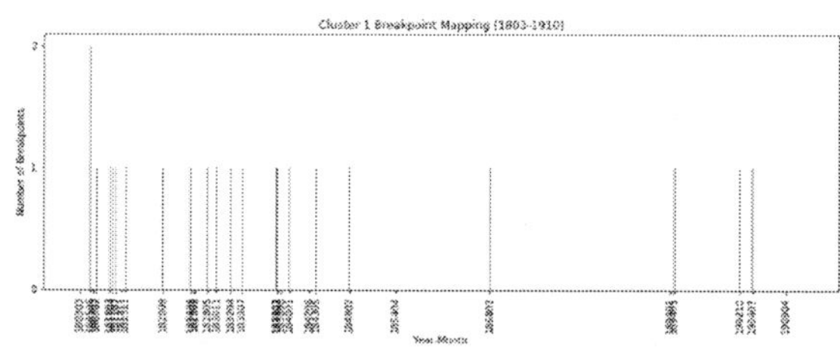

Figure 5. Breakpoints associated with topics in Jaccard-p cluster, mapped against time.

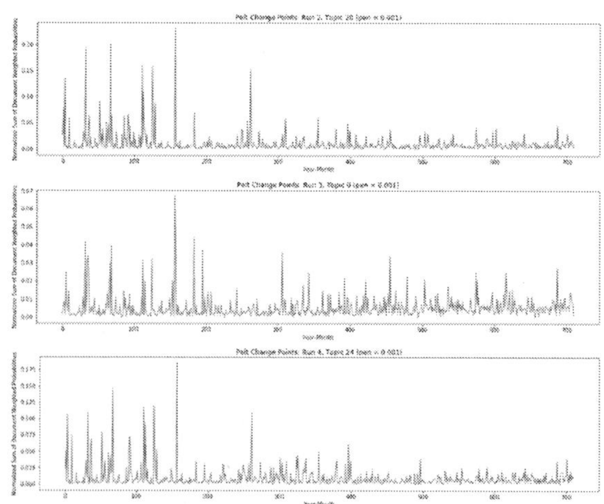

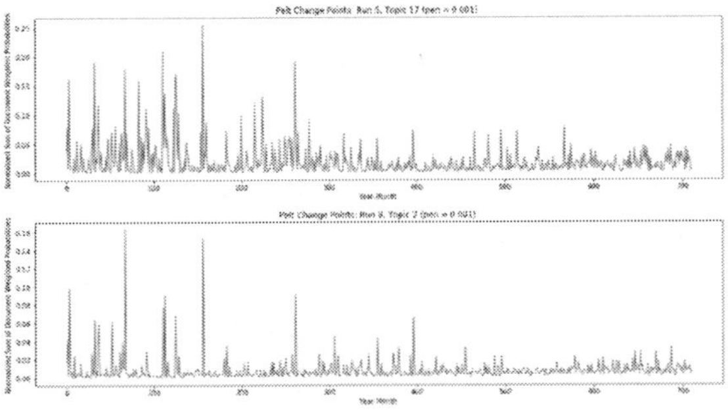

Figure 6. Subset of topic time series associated with a Jaccard-p cluster, indicating corresponding movement across many timepoints.

Figures 5 and 6 shows the information of one such cluster. The breakpoint mapping over time in Figure 5 shows that there are identifiable periods of time (spanning months or years) for the events or trends associated with this cluster. Figure 6 shows a selected subset of the time series of the LDA topics from this cluster. There are similarities in time series across multiple runs, showing that there are corresponding rises and falls in topic prominence over time. The similarities also show that the agglomerative clustering was effective in combating LDA instability.

The examined Jaccard-p cluster's topic annotations indicate topic cohesion. The top documents of this cluster cover discussions on treasury legal tender, the value of money used international trade, and the interest rates established by the Bank of England. These points of discussion are related in the areas of economics, finance, and trade. Common important terms extracted from the documents include "gold," "payment," "price," and "bank." One note is that clusters, including the one being examined, can include certain documents that are not as related to the common theme. For example, this cluster's fifth most important document relates to education, instead of economics. This indicates that we can continue to improve upon our approach to filter out unrelated documents.

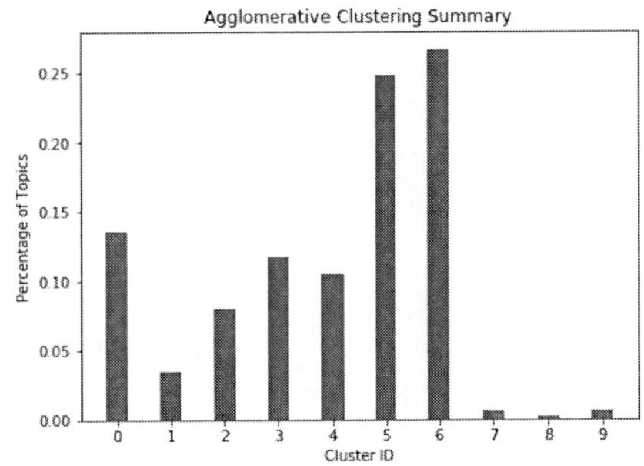

Figure 7. LDA topic distribution over Jensen-Shannon agglomerative clustering.

The Jensen-Shannon approach behaves somewhat better than the Jaccard-p approach in terms of topic distribution across clusters (Figure 7). The VAT diagram (Figure 8) shows internal cluster cohesion, and the topic cohesion is present for many clusters. In addition, we discovered a Jensen-Shannon cluster about finance and economics, containing similar content, documents, and breakpoints to the Jaccard-p cluster discussed earlier. This observation indicates that we can compare clusters across approaches.

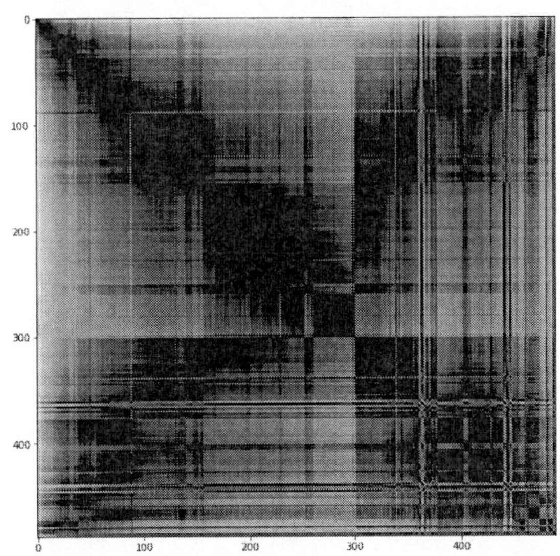

Figure 8. VAT diagram for Jensen-Shannon agglomerative clustering.

The Jensen-Shannon cluster chosen for examination here (Figures 9 and 10) highlights ideas that reoccur frequently across the century. The selected subset of LDA topic time series from this cluster again show similarities between time series and robustness across runs of LDA.

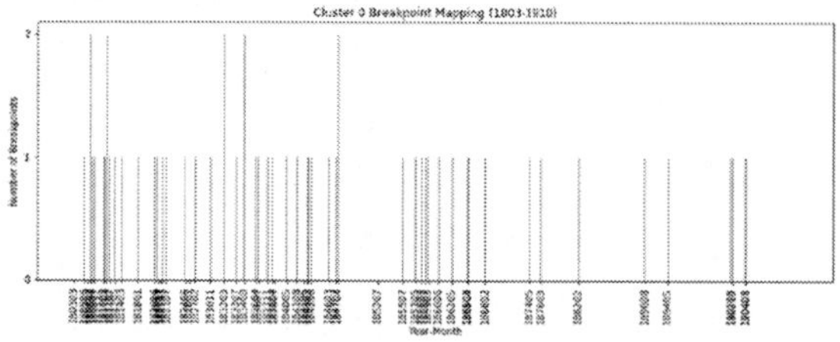

Figure 9. Breakpoints associated with topics in Jensen-Shannon cluster, mapped against time.

The topic annotations of the Jensen-Shannon cluster also indicate topic cohesion. The top documents of this cluster have a focus on educational systems, with additional commentary on government and political systems. Common important terms extracted from the documents include "school," "teacher," "election," and "representative." Future work can focus on distinguishing between these somewhat discrete topics – breaking down larger clusters into smaller ones on other criteria can yield more specific identifications of events and trends.

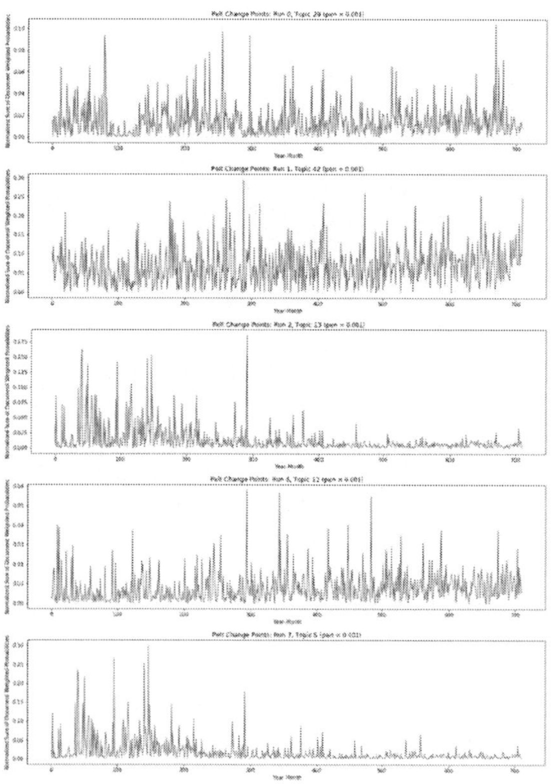

Figure 10. Subset of topic time series associated with a Jensen-Shannon cluster, indicating corresponding movement across many timepoints.

The difference in the word sets used for each approach contributed to the differences seen in the results. With the Jaccard approach, we saw less success with clustering and identification of topics, indicating that we can modify the Jaccard word set composition to be similar to those used in the Jaccard-p and Jensen-Shannon approaches for future experiments.

5 Conclusions and Future Work

The problem of event discovery using topic modeling and change detection is a challenging one. The two experimental methods we define in this paper yielded results with varying degrees of success. Our most reliable results came from the Jaccard-p and Jensen-Shannon approaches from Method 1, where generated LDA topics were clustered based on their document content. We were able to create clusters with distinct areas of discussion, such as finance or education, which we can continue to do analysis on to identify specific historical events.

Our first approach can be improved by increasing the number of samples analyzed per time interval or increasing the granularity of the time interval used. We plan to break down each cluster into smaller sub-clusters to examine more specific topic content – for example, our Jaccard-p cluster could be dissected to explore historical discussions on specific components of the British economic system.

We would also like to explore dynamic time warping technique to measure time series similarity. The simple distance metrics used in our approach suffer from a misalignment problem, where computations rely on a one-to-one mapping of corresponding observations in time series. Dynamic time warping solves the misalignment issue by exploring different warping paths and finding the optimal one that allows for matching of similar time series with different phases.

Finally, we aim to consult with historical experts specializing in the analyzed time period. These experts can provide external validation of the topics generated and insight into what potential changes can be made to our approaches to benefit future historical work.

Acknowledgments

The authors would like to thank the SMU Computer Science and History departments, with particular thanks to Dr. Jo Guldi, Dr. Eric Larson, and Steph Buongiorno.

References

David M. Biel and John D. Lafferty, Dynamic topic models, in *Proceedings of the 23rd international conference on Machine learning*, New York, NY, 2006.

David M. Biel, Andrew Y. Ng and Michael I. Jordan, Latent dirichlet allocation, *Journal of machine Learning research,* vol. 3, pp. 993-1022, 2013.

Jo Guldi, Parliament's debates about infrastructure: an exercise in using dynamic topic models to synthesize historical change., *Technology and Culture,* vol. 60, no. 1, pp. 1-33, 2019.

Elisabeth Günther and Thorsten Quandt, Word Counts and Topic Models, Automated text analysis methods for digital journalism research, *Digital Journalism,* vol. 4, no. 1, pp. 75-88, 2016.

Rem Hida, Naoya Takeishi, Takehisa Yairi and Koichi Hori, Dynamic and Static Topic Model for Analyzing Time-Series Document Collections, in *Proceedings of the 56th Annual Meeting of the Association for Computational Linguistics (Volume 2: Short Papers)*, Melbourne, Australia, 2018.

Thomas Hoffmann, Probabilistic latent semantic indexing, in *Proceedings of the 22nd annual international ACM SIGIR conference on Research and development in information retrieval*, Berkeley, CA, 1999.

Xiaoling Lu, Yuxuan Guo, Jiayi Chen and Feifei Wang, Topic change point detection using a mixed Bayesian model, *Data Mining and Knowledge Discovery,* vol. 36, pp. 146-173, 2022.

John Miller and Kathleen McCoy, Topic Model Stability for Hierarchical Summarization, in *Proceedings of the Workshop on New Frontiers in Summarization*, 2017.

Mika V. Montyla, Maelick Claes and Umar Faroaq, Measuring LDA topic stability from clusters of replicated runs, *In Proceedings of the 12th ACM/IEEE International Symposium on Empirical Software Engineering and Measurement (ESEM '18)*, 2018.

Vito M. R. Muggeo and Giada Adelifio, Efficient change point detection for genomic sequences of continuous measurements, *Bioinformatics,* vol. 27, no. 2, pp. 161-166, 2011

Daniel Ramage, Evan Rosen, Jason Chuang, Christopher D. Manning and Daniel A. McFarland, Topic Modeling for the Social Sciences, in *NIPS*, 2009.

Jaxk Reeves, Jien Chen, Xiaolan L. Wang, Robert Lund and Qi Qi Lu, A Review and Comparison of Changepoint Detection Techniques for Climate Data, *Journal of Applied Meteorology and Climatology,* vol. 46, no. 6, pp. 900-915, 2007.

Jonas Rieger, ldaPrototype: A method in R to get a Prototype of multiple Latent Dirichlet Allocations, *The Journal of Open Source Software,* vol. 5, no. 51, 2020.

Jonas Rieger, Carsten Jentsch and Jorg Rahnenführer, RollingLDA: An Update Algorithm of Latent Dirichlet Allocation to Construct Consistent Time Series from Textual Data, in *EMNLP*, Punta Cana, Dominican Republic, 2021.

Charles Truong, Laurent Oudre, Nicolas Vayatis, ruptures: change point detection in Python, arvix preprint, 2018. [Online]. Available: https://arxiv.org/abs/1801.00826.

Charles Troung, Laurent Oudre and Nicolas Vayatis, Selective review of offline change point detection methods, *Signal Processing,* vol. 167, 2020.

Chong Wang, David M. Biel and David Heckerman, Continuous time dynamic topic models, in *Proceedings of the 24th Conference on Uncertainty in Artificial Intelligence (UAI)*, Helsinki, Finland, 2008.

Yunli Wang and Cyril Goutte, Real-time Change Point Detection using On-line Topic Models, in *Proceedings of the 27th International Conference on Computational Linguistics*, Santa Fe, New Mexico, USA. 2018

Zhengxing Xu, Ling Chen, Yimeng Dai and Gencai Chen, A Dynamic Topic Model and Matrix Factorization-Based Travel Recommendation Method Exploiting Ubiquitous Data, *IEEE Transactions on Multimedia,,* vol. 19, no. 8, pp. 1933-1945, August 2017.

Yi Yong, Shimei Pan, Jie Lu, Mercan Topkara and Yangqiu Song, The stability and usability of statistical topic models, *ACM Trans. Interact. Intell. Syst,* vol. 6, no. 2, 2016.

A Parallel Corpus and Dictionary for Amis-Mandarin Translation

Francis Zheng, Edison Marrese-Taylor, Yutaka Matsuo
Graduate School of Engineering
The University of Tokyo
{francis, emarrese, matsuo}@weblab.t.u-tokyo.ac.jp

Abstract

Amis is an endangered language indigenous to Taiwan with limited data available for computational processing. We thus present an Amis-Mandarin dataset containing a parallel corpus of 5,751 Amis and Mandarin sentences and a dictionary of 7,800 Amis words and phrases with their definitions in Mandarin. Using our dataset, we also established a baseline for machine translation between Amis and Mandarin in both directions. Our dataset can be found at https://github.com/francisdzheng/amis-mandarin.

1 Introduction

Amis is a minority language spoken on the east coast of Taiwan and has been described as a vulnerable or endangered language (Moseley, 2010; Edmondson et al., 2005; Kuo, 2015; Liu, 2011). Though there have been some efforts to preserve the language through education and linguistic research (Wu and Lau, 2019; Kuo, 2015; Liu, 2011), Amis and its preservation have not yet benefited from (to the best of our knowledge) data-based methods used in machine learning and natural language processing.

Low-resource machine translation has recently attracted more attention in the field of natural language processing for languages such as Amis that have a relatively low amount of data due to a small population of speakers. Because neural machine translation (NMT) systems typically do not perform well for low-resource languages, which lack parallel data (Koehn and Knowles, 2017), approaches such as collaborating with language communities to increase parallel data, transfer learning from other machine translation systems, and using multilingual models, among others are being explored (Haddow et al., 2022). However, despite all these new approaches to low-resource machine translation, it is clear that parallel data is still essential for training state-of-the-art machine translation systems (Haddow et al., 2022), as high-resourced language pairs still require large amounts of data to achieve state-of-the-art translation quality (Akhbardeh et al., 2021).

Due to the lack of Amis resources available for use in machine translation, we developed an Amis-Mandarin parallel corpus and dictionary. Our contributions can be summarized as follows:

- We present an Amis-Mandarin dataset, which consists of an Amis-Mandarin parallel corpus containing 5,751 sentences and a dictionary containing 7,800 unique words and phrases in Amis with definitions in Mandarin.
- We trained neural machine translation models on the Amis-Mandarin dataset and produced baselines for future studies.

2 Amis

Amis (ISO 639-3 language code *ami*) is an East Formosan language (Blust, 1999; Ross et al., 2009) spoken on the east coast of Taiwan between Hualien and Taitung (Liu, 2011; Kuo, 2015) by the Amis, one of Taiwan's several indigenous ethnic groups. Formosan languages are spoken by the indigenous peoples of Taiwan (Liu, 2011) and are part of the Austronesian language family. They are believed to be the most diverse of the Austronesian languages (Li, 2008), and because high diversity in a group of genetically-languages found in a geographical area implies earlier settlement in that area (Sapir, 1916), Taiwan is considered to be the homeland of Austronesian languages (Li, 2008; Blust, 1999). Figure 1 shows the distribution of these languages in Taiwan with the region where Amis is spoken being shaded in gray.

Though the vast majority of Taiwan's population is Han Chinese, Taiwan is home to several groups of indigenous peoples who are Austronesian (Trejaut et al., 2014). According to official

The 2nd International Workshop on Natural Language Processing for Digital Humanities (NLP4DH), pages 79–84
November 20, 2022.

Figure 1: Distribution of Taiwan's Indigenous Languages (Li, 2004, as cited in Liu, 2011).

government statistics[1], Taiwan's indigenous population is 582,008, which is approximately 2.4% of Taiwan's total population. The Amis people have a population of 217,216, making up approximately 37.3% of Taiwan's indigenous population. Mandarin Chinese is the language of education (Scott and Tiun) and is spoken along with other Chinese languages (e.g. Hokkien) by the majority of the population, whether indigenous or not. Despite the Amis population being over 200,000, the Amis language has just roughly 30,000 speakers (Kuo, 2015).

These roughly 30,000 speakers, however, do not all speak the same dialect of Amis. According to Tsuchida (1982, 1988, as cited in Kuo, 2015), Amis has five major dialects: (i) Sakizaya (撒奇萊雅群), (ii) Northern/Nanshi Amis (北部/南勢阿美群), (iii) Tavalong-Vata'an (太巴塱-馬太鞍群), (iv) Central/Haian Amis (中部/海岸阿美群), and (v) Southern/Peinan and Hengchun Amis (南部/卑南恆春阿美群). The dataset described in Section 3 in this paper uses data from Central Amis. The existence of several dialects of Amis means that any one dialect has a relatively low number of speakers.

Amis is classified as a vulnerable language by UNESCO (Moseley, 2010), meaning that most, but not all, children and families of the Amis, an indigenous Austronesian ethnic group native to Taiwan, speak Amis as a first language but that their use of Amis may be limited to specific social settings (such as the home, where it is used amongst family) (Moseley, 2010). However, Amis has also been described as an endangered language by several linguists (Edmondson et al., 2005; Kuo, 2015; Liu, 2011). Liu (2011), who researched the Amis language in Taiwan since 1995, performing extensive fieldwork and data gathering with native Amis speakers, notes that only those over 50 are proficient in Amis. Whether Amis is "vulnerable" or "endangered," it is clear that the language is at risk and would benefit from more attention from linguists and natural language processing technologies to help preserve the language digitally and enable its use in modern technologies.

3 Amis-Mandarin Dataset

We compiled Amis-Mandarin parallel data from an Amis-Mandarin online dictionary (原住民族語言線上辭典)[2] published by the Indigenous Languages Research and Development Foundation (原住民族語言研究發展基金會). This dictionary consists of words, phrases, and example sentences of these words and phrases in Central Amis with their Mandarin translations. It was compiled in 2012 by National Taiwan Normal University.

Though these data have been made searchable in the format of an online dictionary, they are not designed for computational use. The website allows one to download the dictionary in parts or in whole as a PDF or ODT file. However, due to some inconsistencies in how words, translations, and example sentences are laid out in these files, neither is easy to use for computational tasks. Thus, we downloaded PDFs of the dictionary made available by this online dictionary, converted them to HTML using PDFMiner[3], and extracted data using Beautiful Soup[4] indepen-

[1] July 2022 statistics from Taiwan's Council of Indigenous Peoples (原住民族委員會) https://www.cip.gov.tw/zh-tw/news/data-list/940F9579765AC6A0/C89C009B11A070EC725C4C571E9FFD7B-info.html

[2] https://e-dictionary.ilrdf.org.tw/ami/search.htm

[3] https://github.com/pdfminer/pdfminer.six

[4] https://www.crummy.com/software/

Table 1: Summary of the Amis-Mandarin Parallel Corpus

	Total	Train	Dev	Test
Number of sentences	5,751	4,600	576	575
Number of Amis words	38,946	31,136	3,947	3,863
Number of Chinese characters	69,864	55,672	7,289	6,903

dently from the authors of this dictionary. Each Amis word/phrase and its Mandarin dictionary entry were extracted, and when available, example sentences in Amis along with their Mandarin translations were also taken. Dictionary entries and their Mandarin definitions were put into one pickle file, while example sentences and their Mandarin translations were put into another pickle file. These files can be opened using pandas[5]. The dictionary is also available as a tab-delimited text file, and the parallel sentence data are also available as text files split into train, dev, and test sets. The parallel data were shuffled before being split into the train, dev, and test sets, which were taken from 80%, 10%, and 10% respectively from the shuffled data. The dataset we compiled can be found at `https://github.com/francisdzheng/amis-mandarin`.

Our dictionary dataset contains 7,800 unique entries in Amis along with their Mandarin equivalents. Amis dictionary entries that had more than one definition in Mandarin were added to our dictionary dataset as separate entries for each additional definition. Thus, there are a total of 7,926 pairs of Amis and Mandarin words/phrases in our dictionary dataset. Our parallel corpus dataset contains 5,751 Amis sentences and their Mandarin translations. This parallel corpus dataset is summarized in Table 1. Due to the concept of a word being different in Amis and Mandarin, Table 1 describes the Mandarin data in terms of characters and the Amis data in terms of words, which are typically separated by spaces unlike in Mandarin, which does not use spaces in writing.

4 Amis-Mandarin Machine Translation

Using our Amis-Mandarin dataset, we trained models for machine translation between Amis and Mandarin in both directions.

4.1 Methods

4.1.1 Preprocessing

Data were tokenized using a unigram (Kudo, 2018) implementation of SentencePiece (Kudo and Richardson, 2018). A vocabulary size of 4,000 and a character coverage rate of 0.9995 were used. Using our SentencePiece (Kudo and Richardson, 2018) model and vocabulary, we used FAIRSEQ[6] (Ott et al., 2019) to build vocabularies and binarize our training data in preparation for training our model.

4.1.2 Training

We trained a Transformer (Vaswani et al., 2017) model using an mBART (Liu et al., 2020) implementation of FAIRSEQ (Ott et al., 2019) for translation between Amis and Mandarin in both directions. Our Transformer (Vaswani et al., 2017) model used six encoder and decoder layers with eight attention heads each, a hidden dimension of 512, and a feed-forward size of 2048, and a learning rate of 0.0003. Our model was optimized using Adam (Kingma and Ba, 2015) with hyperparameters $\beta = (0.9, 0.98)$ and $\epsilon = 10^{-6}$. A dropout rate of 0.1 and a weight decay of 0.01 were used for regularization.

We conducted two experiments, one in which training involved only the training set from our parallel Amis-Mandarin corpus (consisting of sentences) and one which included the dictionary dataset as part of the training data. The dictionary data were treated as additional parallel data (though they're not full sentences) and simply added on to the parallel sentence training data. This was done to see the effect of exposing models to the dictionary dataset and to establish two baselines for translation as a dictionary may not always be available when training models.

4.1.3 Evaluation

Translations outputted by our model were evaluated with detokenized BLEU (Papineni et al.,

BeautifulSoup/

[5]https://pandas.pydata.org

[6]https://github.com/facebookresearch/fairseq

Table 2: Results

	Without Dictionary		With Dictionary	
	BLEU	CHRF	BLEU	CHRF
Amis to Mandarin	5.33	0.1596	**7.07**	**0.2198**
Mandarin to Amis	15.36	0.4018	**18.94**	**0.4618**

2002; Post, 2018) using the SacreBLEU library[7] (Post, 2018) on the test data from our parallel corpus. We also used CHRF (Popović, 2015) to measure performance at the character level.

4.2 Results

Our results are presented in Table 2. Models trained using only the parallel corpus dataset performed worse than the models trained using both our parallel corpus dataset and dictionary dataset. This is expected as these models were able to learn direct translations of individual words and phrases that are used in the parallel sentence data in addition to translations of whole sentences. Though dictionaries are not as useful as parallel data in that dictionaries do not reveal much about how a word or phrase should be used in a sentence, using dictionary data in the training process proved to significantly improve translation quality.

The improvement in translation quality after adding the dictionary dataset can be seen in both the Amis → Mandarin and Mandarin → Amis directions and is reflected in both the BLEU and CHRF scores. Notably, the improvement in translation quality as measured by BLEU for the Mandarin → Amis direction was greater than that for the Amis → Mandarin direction. One possible explanation for this is the fact that some Amis words in the dictionary dataset are paired with multiple Mandarin equivalents or longer Mandarin explanations, exposing the model to relatively more Mandarin words for a single given word or phrase in Amis. Thus, the model may map multiple words in Mandarin to single words or phrases in Amis, which are almost sure to appear in the parallel sentence data (as mentioned in Section 3, the parallel sentence data come from example sentences for the Amis words in the dictionary). On the other hand, the Mandarin definitions for each Amis entry in the dictionary dataset do not necessarily appear in the parallel sentence data. More research is needed to see whether the model trained on both the parallel corpus dataset and dictionary dataset still performs better in the Mandarin → Amis direction on other parallel data.

5 Conclusion

We presented an Amis-Mandarin parallel corpus and dictionary, which is the first, to the best of our knowledge, Amis-Mandarin dataset documented in English for the natural language processing community. Though the online dictionary from which we obtained the data is available to anyone, the dictionary interface is only available in Mandarin, and the data is not in a form that NLP researchers can easily use. Other Amis-Mandarin data we found on the web were also not in an easily usable format and not friendly for English-speaking researchers. The dataset we compiled consists of 5,751 parallel sentences and 7,800 Amis words and phrases paired with their definitions in Mandarin. Using this dataset, we experimented with Amis-Mandarin machine translation and established baseline BLEU and CHRF scores. Using both the parallel corpus and dictionary during training produced models that performed the best on our test data from our parallel corpus.

Aside from sentence translation, we also envision that the dataset we compiled can be used for exploring how dictionary entries can be predicted using parallel data (instead of using dictionary entries to aid in the translation of sentences). Defining words is also an important part of language documentation, and it would be interesting to see how machines can draw meaning for individual words or short phrases given parallel sentence data.

In the future, we would like to take a closer look at how tokenization can be optimized for the two languages and try using other existing tokenizers that have been trained more specifically for Mandarin. We also want to try to incorporate more external knowledge and perhaps acknowledge that parallel data may never be enough. Our dataset is small, and we hope to explore how knowledge

[7] https://github.com/mjpost/sacrebleu

from grammars and other literature written on Amis can be incorporated into our model or into the creation of synthetic parallel data. As Amis is an Austronesian language like Indonesian, which is widely spoken and has much more literature available, it is possible that knowledge from Indonesian can be helpful in NLP tasks involving Amis. We hope that our dataset can spark more interest from the machine learning community in not only Amis, but other Formosan languages as well.

References

Farhad Akhbardeh, Arkady Arkhangorodsky, Magdalena Biesialska, Ondřej Bojar, Rajen Chatterjee, Vishrav Chaudhary, Marta R. Costa-jussa, Cristina España-Bonet, Angela Fan, Christian Federmann, Markus Freitag, Yvette Graham, Roman Grundkiewicz, Barry Haddow, Leonie Harter, Kenneth Heafield, Christopher Homan, Matthias Huck, Kwabena Amponsah-Kaakyire, Jungo Kasai, Daniel Khashabi, Kevin Knight, Tom Kocmi, Philipp Koehn, Nicholas Lourie, Christof Monz, Makoto Morishita, Masaaki Nagata, Ajay Nagesh, Toshiaki Nakazawa, Matteo Negri, Santanu Pal, Allahsera Auguste Tapo, Marco Turchi, Valentin Vydrin, and Marcos Zampieri. 2021. Findings of the 2021 conference on machine translation (WMT21). In *Proceedings of the Sixth Conference on Machine Translation*, pages 1–88, Online. Association for Computational Linguistics.

Robert Blust. 1999. Subgrouping, circularity and extinction: Some issues in Austronesian comparative linguistics. In E. Zeitoun and Paul Jen-Kuei Li, editors, *Selected Papers from Eighth International Conference on Austronesian Linguistics*, pages 31–94. Academica Sinica, Taipei.

Jerold Edmondson, John Esling, Jimmy Harris, and Tung-Chiou Huang. 2005. A laryngoscopic study of glottal and epiglottal/pharyngeal stop and continuant articulations in Amis– an Austronesian language of Taiwan. *Language and Linguistics*, 3:381–396.

Barry Haddow, Rachel Bawden, Antonio Valerio Miceli Barone, Jindich Helcl, and Alexandra Birch. 2022. Survey of low-resource machine translation. pages 1–60.

Diederik P. Kingma and Jimmy Ba. 2015. Adam: A method for stochastic optimization. In *3rd International Conference on Learning Representations, ICLR 2015, San Diego, CA, USA, May 7-9, 2015, Conference Track Proceedings*.

Philipp Koehn and Rebecca Knowles. 2017. Six challenges for neural machine translation. In *Proceedings of the First Workshop on Neural Machine Translation*, pages 28–39, Vancouver. Association for Computational Linguistics.

Taku Kudo. 2018. Subword regularization: Improving neural network translation models with multiple subword candidates. In *Proceedings of the 56th Annual Meeting of the Association for Computational Linguistics (Volume 1: Long Papers)*, pages 66–75, Melbourne, Australia. Association for Computational Linguistics.

Taku Kudo and John Richardson. 2018. SentencePiece: A simple and language independent subword tokenizer and detokenizer for neural text processing. In *Proceedings of the 2018 Conference on Empirical Methods in Natural Language Processing: System Demonstrations*, pages 66–71, Brussels, Belgium. Association for Computational Linguistics.

Jonathan Cheng-Chuen Kuo. 2015. *Argument alternation and argument structure in symmetrical voice languages: A case study of transfer verbs in Amis, Puyuma, and Seediq*. Ph.D. thesis, University of Hawai'i at Manoa.

Paul Jen-kuei Li. 2008. The great diversity of Formosan languages. *Language and Linguistics*, 9(3):523–546.

Chunxi Liu, Qiaochu Zhang, Xiaohui Zhang, Kritika Singh, Yatharth Saraf, and Geoffrey Zweig. 2020. Multilingual graphemic hybrid ASR with massive data augmentation. In *Proceedings of the 1st Joint Workshop on Spoken Language Technologies for Under-resourced languages (SLTU) and Collaboration and Computing for Under-Resourced Languages (CCURL)*, pages 46–52, Marseille, France. European Language Resources association.

Tsai-hsiu Liu. 2011. *Complementation in three Formosan languages: Amis, Mayrinax Atayal and Tsou*. Ph.D. thesis, University of Hawai'i at Mnoa, Honolulu, HI.

Christopher Moseley. 2010. *Atlas of the World's Languages in Danger*. UNESCO.

Myle Ott, Sergey Edunov, Alexei Baevski, Angela Fan, Sam Gross, Nathan Ng, David Grangier, and Michael Auli. 2019. fairseq: A fast, extensible toolkit for sequence modeling. In *Proceedings of the 2019 Conference of the North American Chapter of the Association for Computational Linguistics (Demonstrations)*, pages 48–53, Minneapolis, Minnesota. Association for Computational Linguistics.

Kishore Papineni, Salim Roukos, Todd Ward, and Wei-Jing Zhu. 2002. Bleu: a method for automatic evaluation of machine translation. In *Proceedings of the 40th Annual Meeting of the Association for Computational Linguistics*, pages 311–318, Philadelphia, Pennsylvania, USA. Association for Computational Linguistics.

Maja Popović. 2015. chrF: character n-gram F-score for automatic MT evaluation. In *Proceedings of the Tenth Workshop on Statistical Machine Translation*, pages 392–395, Lisbon, Portugal. Association for Computational Linguistics.

Matt Post. 2018. A call for clarity in reporting BLEU scores. In *Proceedings of the Third Conference on Machine Translation: Research Papers*, pages 186–191, Brussels, Belgium. Association for Computational Linguistics.

Malcolm Ross et al. 2009. Proto Austronesian verbal morphology: A reappraisal. In *Austronesian historical linguistics and culture history: A festschrift for Robert Blust*. Asia-Pacific Linguistics, College of Asia and the Pacific, The Australian ⋯.

Edward Sapir. 1916. *Time perspective in aboriginal American culture: A study in method*. 13. Government Printing Bureau.

Mandy Scott and Hak-khiam Tiun. Mandarin-only to Mandarin-plus: Taiwan. 6(1):53–72.

Jean A. Trejaut, Estella S. Poloni, Ju-Chen Yen, Ying-Hui Lai, Jun Hun Loo, Chien liang Lee, Chunfen He, and Marie Lin. 2014. Taiwan Y-chromosomal DNA variation and its relationship with Island Southeast Asia. *BMC Genetics*, 15:77 – 77.

Ashish Vaswani, Noam Shazeer, Niki Parmar, Jakob Uszkoreit, Llion Jones, Aidan N Gomez, Ł ukasz Kaiser, and Illia Polosukhin. 2017. Attention is all you need. In *Advances in Neural Information Processing Systems*, volume 30. Curran Associates, Inc.

Li-ying Wu and Ken Lau. 2019. Language education policy in Taiwan. In *The Routledge international handbook of language education policy in Asia*, pages 151–161. Routledge.

Machines in the media: semantic change in the lexicon of mechanization in 19th-century British newspapers

Nilo Pedrazzini
The Alan Turing Institute (UK)
npedrazzini@turing.ac.uk

Barbara McGillivray
King's College London (UK)
The Alan Turing Institute (UK)
barbara.mcgillivray@kcl.ac.uk

Abstract

The industrialization process associated with the so-called Industrial Revolution in 19th-century Great Britain was a time of profound changes, including in the English lexicon. An important yet understudied phenomenon is the semantic shift in the lexicon of mechanisation. In this paper we present the first large-scale analysis of terms related to mechanization over the course of the 19th century in English. We draw on a corpus of historical British newspapers comprising 4.6 billion tokens and train historical word embedding models. We test existing semantic change detection techniques and analyse the results in light of previous historical linguistic scholarship.

1 Introduction

Started in the 18th century in Great Britain, the industrial mechanization saw a dramatic acceleration in the 19th century. New machines were introduced in different industries at a rapid pace and the ever more pervasive automation of manufacture meant large-scale reorganization and movement of the workforce throughout the territory. This had profound repercussions on many aspects of daily life from a cultural, political, and social perspective.

The English language, particularly its lexicon, used by 19th-century sources to describe these changes reflected the same rapid pace at which the objects and the societal landscape had been shifting, making it an important, and yet understudied, research topic. Previous studies on the English language in the 19th century have focussed on how the changes observed in the lexicon of the period often reflect 'new interpretations given to older words in a time of changing societal values' in Victorian Britain (Görlach, 1999, 132), as in the shift in the usage of words describing men and women (Bäcklund, 2006), or have highlighted the plethora of neologism and new loanwords introduced as a result of the Industrial Revolution (Kay and Allan, 2015, 20; Bergs and Brinton, 2012). As Görlach (1999, 133) also notes, meaning change (besides mere new word formations) 'is best illustrated from semantic fields relating to the new technologies that rapidly became part of everyday experience, such as the field of vehicles/transport/traffic'.

In this paper we investigate the issue of tracing these subtle shifts at scale using computational methods. Drawing from examples of lexical semantic change in 19th-century English from previous literature, we train diachronic word embedding models on a very large collection (4.6 billion tokens) of digitized 19th-century British newspaper articles. We then compare these data-driven analyses with previous qualitative studies, to verify the extent to which historical language models reflect expert knowledge. In addition to validating the computational models, we assess how these methods can be employed to answer new complex questions on the linguistic effects of mechanization and other historical events.

Using historical newspapers as a data source presents specific methodological challenges, and in particular historical (issues of representativeness, Beelen et al. 2022) and computational (processing OCR'd collections, van Strien et al. 2020) complexities. However, given the size of newspaper archives and the possibility to sample them by variables of interest (e.g. time period, political leaning, place of circulation or publication), these sources are a very good fit for large-scale analyses of lexical change in periods of on-going deep societal changes. This is also shown by the growing number of projects which use historical newspapers as sources for large-scale semantic processing and data-driven historical analysis, including News-

The 2nd International Workshop on Natural Language Processing for Digital Humanities (NLP4DH), pages 85–95
November 20, 2022. ©2022 Association for Computational Linguistics

Eye,[1] Translantis,[2] Impresso,[3] and Living with Machines.[4]

This work is the first to provide a large-scale analysis of the English lexicon of mechanisation in the 19th century. From a methodological point of view, our dataset presents challenges that are shared by other historical newspaper archives and thus our research can inform similar studies on other languages. From the point of view of historical linguistics and historical research, we present the first study of the English lexicon of mechanisation that employs computational techniques, which allows us to compare automatically detected semantic changes with those identified by close-reading methods in previous literature.

2 Previous work

According to Görlach (1999) and Mugglestone (2008), the 19th century was a pivotal period in the history of English, when its lexicon underwent a significant transformation in both spoken and written sources, although the academic literature has paid less attention to Late Modern English (1700-1950) compared to other periods in the history of the English language (Kytö et al., 2006). In recent years a number of NLP studies have proposed algorithms for the automatic detection of lexical semantic change from historical texts using word type and token embeddings (Hamilton et al., 2016; Tsakalidis et al., 2019). Algorithms based on type embeddings have been shown to perform best in the 2020 SemEval shared task (Schlechtweg et al., 2020) and they typically consist of the following steps: the corpus of interest is divided into time-dependent slices; then word embedding models are trained from each subcorpus and their spaces aligned. Finally, the cosine similarity between a word's embedding in the first (or last) space and its embedding in each of the spaces is computed. If the similarity is below a predefined threshold (i.e. the two embeddings are sufficiently different), the word is marked as a potential candidate for semantic change. In few cases these algorithms have been applied in real-world digital humanities research: Wevers and Koolen (2020), for instance, present a study on word embeddings trained on a 500,000 digitized Dutch newspaper corpus for the purpose of studying the evolution of concepts.

3 Data and methods

Two newspaper collections were used for this experiment. A selection of titles from the British Library's *Heritage Made Digital* digitization project,[5] comprising 12 titles and around 2.3 billion tokens, and a collection specifically digitized for the Living with Machines project, comprising 107 titles and also around 2.3 billion tokens. Jointly, the collections span the period between 1801 and 1920. To prepare the corpora for training diachronic word embeddings, we first split them into time slices of 10 years each. We preprocessed the articles for each decade by removing word breaks resulting from OCR, newlines, and punctuation, by lowercasing the text and removing the stop words provided by the NLTK library for English.[6]

We trained Word2Vec (Mikolov et al., 2013) models as implemented in the Gensim library (Řehůřek and Sojka, 2010). To choose the optimal hyperparameters for training, we performed a grid search comparing the skip-gram and the continuous-bag-of-words architectures, as well as different number of epochs ({5,10}), vector dimensions ({200,300}), context windows ({3,5,10}) and minimum word counts ({1,5,10}). We evaluated the quality of the models resulting from all combinations of these parameters on one decade (all articles published between 1821 and 1830) calculating the cosine similarity between pairs of synonyms[7] in each model and choosing the model that returned the highest average score for all pairs. The final models were trained using the skip-gram architecture, 5 epochs, 200 dimensions, a context window of 3 and a minimum count of 1. Since the models for each decade are trained independently, the resulting word vectors in different decades are not aligned along the same coordinate axes. To allow for comparison between the representation of the same word across different decades, we aligned the semantic spaces on the basis of the Or-

[1] https://www.newseye.eu/

[2] https://translantis.wp.hum.uu.nl/

[3] https://impresso-project.ch/

[4] livingwithmachines.ac.uk

[5] https://www.bl.uk/projects/heritage-made-digital

[6] https://www.nltk.org/search.html?q=stopwords

[7] The list the synonyms considered is the following: *superfluous/unnecessary, display/exhibit, mimetic/imitative, disappear/vanish, alike/identical.*

The pairs were chosen so that at least one sense of one word is linked to a sense of the paired word via the linking between the Oxford English Dictionary and the Historical Thesaurus of English and the linked senses have quotations that include the range 1800-1920 or a portion of it.

thogonal Procrustes problem (Schönemann, 1966). Given $W^{(d)} \in \mathbb{R}^{n \times m}$, denoting the matrix of the vectors in decade d, the Orthogonal Procrustes problem consists in finding the orthogonal matrix $Q \in \mathbb{R}^{m \times m}$ that most closely maps the matrices $W^{(d)}$ and $W^{(d+1)}$. This is done by:

$$\min_{Q} ||W^{(d)}Q - W^{(d+1)}||_F, \quad \text{subject to } Q^T Q = I \tag{1}$$

where I is the $n \times m$ identity matrix and $||\ldots||_F$ the Frobenius norm. The problem in (1) is solved via singular value decomposition: $U\Sigma V^T$, in this case $W^{(d)}(W^{(d+1)})^T$ (Tsakalidis et al., 2019, 2021). After all embedding spaces are aligned, we can use the cosine similarity between vectors across different decades to assess their semantic shift.

We compiled a list of words drawing from those indicated by Görlach (1999) as having undergone semantic change at some point during the 19th century.[8] For each word we calculated the cosine similarity between its vector in the semantic space for the most recent decade (the 1910s) and its vector in each of the previous decades. We followed Shoemark et al. (2019), who found that comparing the embeddings to the last time period leads to better results in semantic change detection. We then analysed the resulting scores in the following way. Any time point t with a cosine similarity significantly higher than the one in the time point $t-1$ was considered a potential changepoint in the meaning of a word. Significant changepoints were detected using the pruned exact linear time (PELT) algorithm (Killick et al., 2012), a penalized-cost method for detecting multiple changepoints in time-series data. We ran the algorithm with a jump parameter of 1 and comparing results with penalty set to 0.25 and 0.5.[9] We then extracted the nearest neighbours of each word for each decade to establish what type of semantic change might have occurred at each potential changepoint. We evaluated the accuracy of the models at detecting semantic change for a word against its entry in the Oxford English Dictionary (OED).[10] Using the OED API,[11] for each word we extracted the list of its senses, their definition and first record in writing, and selected all senses that had a first recorded year later than 1800 and earlier than 1920. To identify whether the detected potential changepoint for a word corresponded to one (or several) of its selected senses from the OED, we extracted the nearest neighbours of the word in each time period and compared those from the relevant decade(s) with the OED senses.

4 Qualitative analysis

word	changepoint
coach	1830
gear	1830
traffic	1830
train	1830
stamp	1840
fellow	1860
railway	1860
matches	1880

Table 1: Words with a changepoint detected by the PELT algorithm by setting the penalty to 0.5.

word	changepoint
wheel	1810, 1880
coach	1830
gear	1830
traffic	1830, 1860
train	1830
stamp	1840
fellow	1860
railway	1860
matches	1880

Table 2: Words with a changepoint detected by the PELT algorithm by setting the penalty to 0.25.

Table 1 contains the 8 words for which a semantic changepoint was detected by setting penalty to 0.5. As Table 2 shows, setting penalty to 0.25 resulted in detecting changepoints for one extra word.

[8]The complete list includes: *traffic, trade, train, coach, wheel, railway, matches, bulb, gear, stamp*. *Fellow* was also included as an example of semantically stable word made by Görlach (1999). For the purpose of this paper, words are considered only in their singular form for simplicity, even though considering both singulars and plurals may give a more complete picture. The only exception is the lemma *match*, which was considered only in its plural form, due to the intuitively more likely usage of this word in the plural (*matches*) in its new, phosphorous sense. Future studies may wish to consider both numbers for all the words and attempt reconciling, if needed, any different observations made on them.

[9]For this experiment we used the implementation of the PELT method by the `ruptures` library: `https://pypi.org/project/ruptures/`.

[10]`https://www.oed.com`

[11]`https://languages.oup.com/research/oed-researcher-api/`

We can immediately see that *fellow*, indicated by Görlach (1999, 131) as having a stable semantics in the 19th century, is included among the words in both tables. Two changepoints were also detected by the model trained with the lower penalty for *wheel*, another word cited by Görlach (1999, 131) as semantically stable. If we compare the trajectories of *wheel* and *train* (Figure 1), for example, it is not surprising to see that a changepoint detection model trained with stricter parameters may detect a change for the latter but not for the former, even though the plot suggests that a change in usage, albeit more gradual, occurred for *wheel* as well.

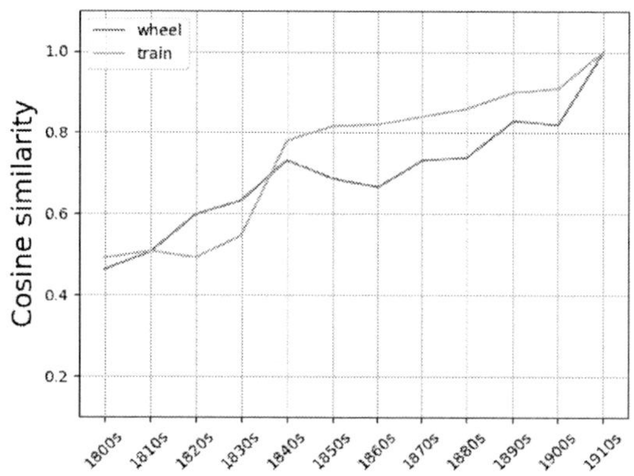

Figure 1: Time series for the cosine similarity between *wheel*, *train* in each decade and their respective vector in the time reference (the last decade, i.e. the 1910s).

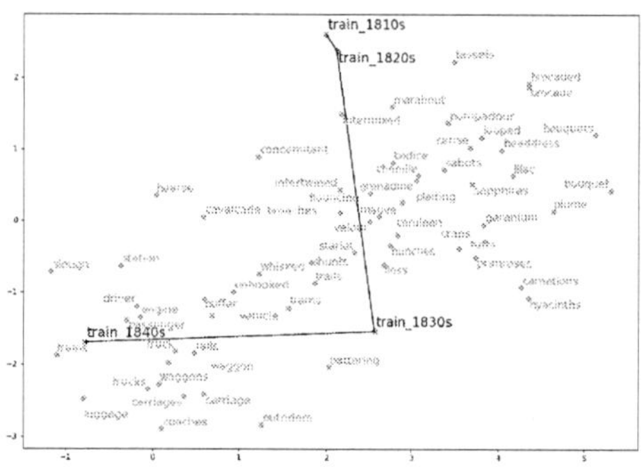

Figure 2: Semantic change trajectory of *train*.

4.1 *Train*

In Figure 2, we can see that *train* moved considerably in the semantic space between the 1810s and 1830s, to the extent that its 50-nearest neighbours in the 1810s and the 1840s have no words in

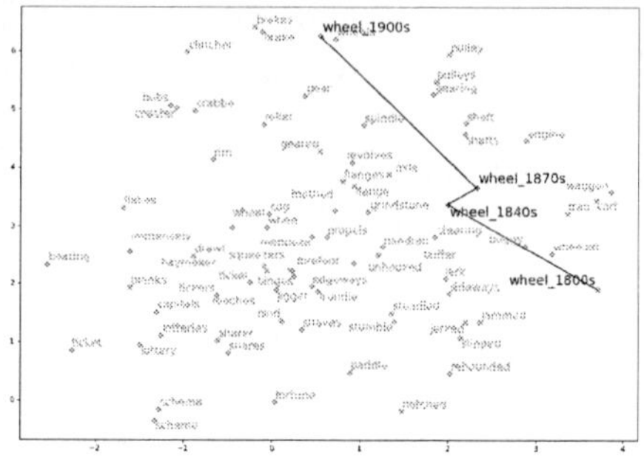

Figure 3: Semantic change trajectory of *wheel*.

common (see a selection of these in Table 3), with a decade in between, the 1820s, in which the words related to the older, more common sense ('an elongated back of a robe or skirt') are found together with those related to the newer one ('a series of connected railway carriages').[12] The semantics of this word appears to have changed steadily for at least two decades: our changepoint detection model was trained with a jump parameter of 1 (i.e. in our case, a change spanning at least one decade), so that a jump of 2 time units made it an even more likely candidate.

4.2 *Wheel*

On the other hand, the semantic change of *wheel*, as suggested by our models, is less abrupt and may rather reflect an increased usage in specific senses related to technological innovations (or collocations describing these) throughout the century than the introduction of a new sense altogether, as was the case for *train*. If we compare the nearest neighbours of this word around the first changepoint (Table 3), we can see that words related to *wheel* in its figurative use referring to 'the course or sequence of events, procedure, the passage of time' prevail in the 1810s and 1820s, whereas words related to its sense 'various mechanical contrivances' are already the majority in the 1830s and 1840s. Terms related to the latter sense, however, are not exclusive of the period following the detected changepoint, as *carriage*, *cart*, *vehicle*, and *wagon* in the 1810s and 1820s all indicate. The OED lists the introduction of different specific usages of *wheel* in this

[12]Throughout the paper, the definition of the senses are quoted directly from the OED and reported in single quotation marks.

Word	Moving away from or adding new meanings to	Moving towards
wheel	*shafts, dray, stumble, draws, revolve, carriage, lottery, cart* (1810s); *drawn, dray, prizes, cart, prizes, shafts, capitals, vehicle, wagon* (1820s)	*axle, shaft, jerk, wheelers, flanges, jerked, axles, cart, paddle* (1830s); *axle, shaft, engine, buffer, flange, paddle, jammed* (1840s)
train	*chenille, intermixed, brocaded, lama, carnations* (1820s); *shunts, brocaded, mauve, hearse, carriages* (1830s)	*luggage, engine, carriages, waggons, trucks* (1840s)
fellow	*college, scholar, countrymen, bursar, tutor* (1850s)	*creatures, townsmen, countrymen, man, citizens* (1860s)
railway	*tunnel, turnpike, aqueducts, canals, navigation, drainage, waterworks* (1820s)	*railroad, junction, bridge, station, lines, tramway* (1830s); beltway, companies, colliery, stakeholders, passengers, trains (1860s)
traffic	*trafficking, slave, nefarious, kidnapping, illicit, contraband, smuggling, piracy* (1820s)	*railways, railroads, conveyance, transit, line* (1830s); *passengers, trains, coaches, milage* (1860s)
coach	*saddle, harness, horses, post, telegraph* (1810s)	*wagon, carriage, driver, carriage, truck* (1830s)

Table 3: Nearest neighbours of *wheel, train, fellow, railway, traffic*, and *coach* in the decades around the detected changepoints.

sense at different points in time since at least the 14th century, with *steering wheel* (1743) already in use in the nautical field and then extended to 'the steering-wheel of a motor vehicle'. A new usage of *wheel* recorded by the OED is that of *paddle wheel*, which appears among the nearest neighbours for the 1830s and 1840s (see Table 3), despite the OED reporting 1842 as its first written record. The clearest change between the 1820s and the 1830s is given by *train*-related words, such as *wagon* in the 1820s and *axle*, the closest neighbour of *wheel* in both the 1830s and 1840s.

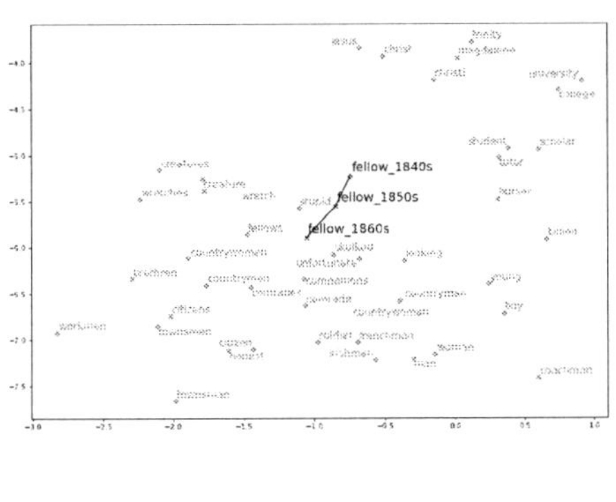

Figure 4: Semantic change trajectory of *fellow*.

4.3 *Fellow*

The case of *fellow* is also rather complex. By once again visualising the nearest neighbours for the detected changepoint and the preceding decades in a two-dimensional space, the neighbours are overall clearly divided between those related to *fellow* used in academic context (e.g. *tutor, scholar, college, bursar*, as names of specific colleges–*Magdalene, Trinity, Christi*), attested since the 15th century according to the OED, and those related to the sense of *fellow* broadly defined by the OED as 'a person who or thing which shares an attribute with another specified person or thing; a person or thing belonging to the same class or category as another' (e.g. *brethren, citizens, comrade, countrymen/countrywomen*), attested since the 13th century according to the OED. The OED however also records one new usage for the latter sense from 1844 ('a person's contemporary, esp. in a particular profession, art form, field of study, etc. chiefly in plural'), in addition to the similar, albeit more generic, pre-existing usage 'something that resembles another specified thing; a match; the like' for the same sense. Our models appear to reflect the new 1844 usage particularly in politically loaded words such as *citizens, brethren* and *comrade*, whose similarity with *fellow* may be due to the political leanings of the newspapers in which this term appears the most. A new usage also recorded from 1816 by the OED is 'an animal or thing. Often affectionate, humorous, or ironic', which may be reflected in words such as *creatures*, the closest neighbour of *fellow* in the 1860s, as well as *unfortunate* and *wretch.*

4.4 *Railway* and *traffic*

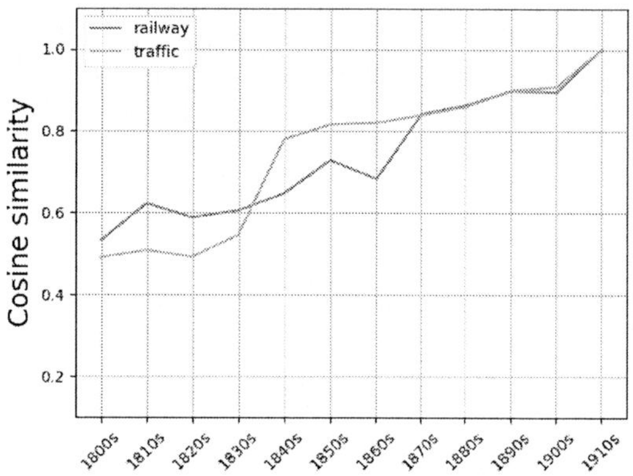

Figure 5: Time series for the cosine similarity between *railway* and *traffic* in each decade and their respective vector in the time reference (the last decade, i.e. the 1910s).

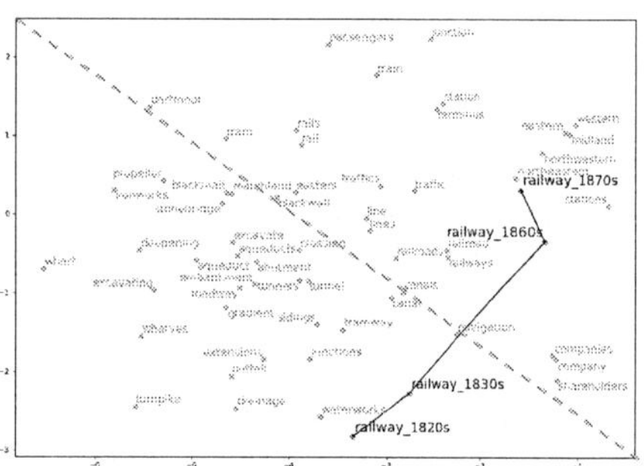

Figure 6: Semantic change trajectory of *railway*.

Other words from Tables 1 and 2 that pertain to the language of mechanization and that were mentioned by Görlach (1999) as examples of semantic change are *railway* and *traffic*. Two changepoints, the 1830s and the 1860s, were detected for *traffic* by the model trained with a lower penalty and both of these can be clearly seen in Figure 5. Only one changepoint, the 1860s, was instead detected for *railway*, as we can also gather from the steeper change in cosine similarity in the plot in Figure 5. However, it is quite evident that, besides the steep increase in cosine similarity between the 1860s and the 1870s, considerable change, though perhaps more gradual, occurred between the 1820s and the 1850s. This is in fact what we also observe if we compare the neighbours of *railway* before 1820 and after 1830 (Figure 6). A possible reason why no changepoint was detected pre-1860s is that its semantics up until the 1850s is not significantly dissimilar yet from the usage of the word in the previous two decades, when it may have been still widely used in the sense of 'a roadway laid with rails (originally of wood, later also of iron or steel) along which the wheels of wagons or trucks may run, in order to facilitate the transport of heavy loads'. A neater departure from the latter is observed by the 1860s, when it was probably already used predominantly in the sense of 'a line or track typically consisting of a pair of iron or steel rails, along which carriages, wagons, or trucks conveying passengers or goods are moved by a locomotive engine or other powered unit', first attested, according to the OED, in the 1820s. Between the 1830s and the 1860s, the key change in the meaning of *railway*, which can be inferred from the semantic space in Figure 6, is two-fold. First, there is a definite departure from railways as only a means for the transport of goods to railways as a means of transportation for passengers. This is evident from the distance of *railway* in the 1860s from the words in Figure 6 concerning precisely this semantic field, such as *canals, tunnel, navigation, waterworks, excavating, wharf, embankment, roadway, turnpike* or *aqueducts*, and the greater proximity to words such as *train, station, passengers* and *tram*. The proximity to these latter words is particularly clear by focussing on the axis highlighted with a red dashed line in Figure 6, across which the semantic change seems to have occurred. Second, we observe a shift towards the usage of *railway* in the meaning of 'a network or organization of such lines [as defined by the new sense defined of railway above]; a company which owns, manages, or operates such a line or network; this form of transportation'. This is clear from neighbours such as *company* and *shareholders*, and modifiers that were likely to identify clearly defined regional railway networks, such as *northernwestern*, *midland*, and *western*.

Both changepoints for the word *traffic* are supported by our neighbour analysis. Between the 1820s and the 1830s the main meaning of

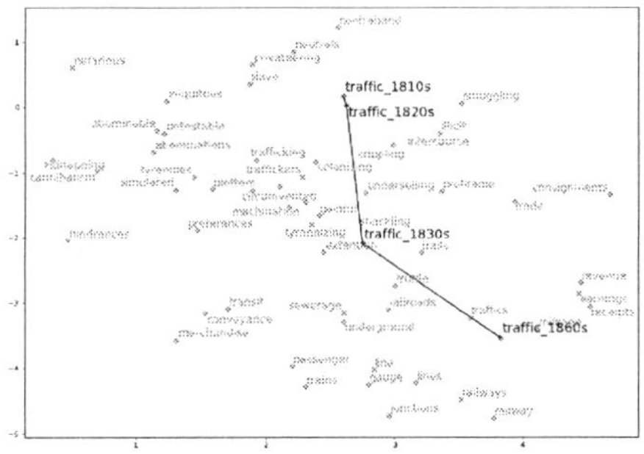

Figure 7: Semantic change trajectory of *traffic*.

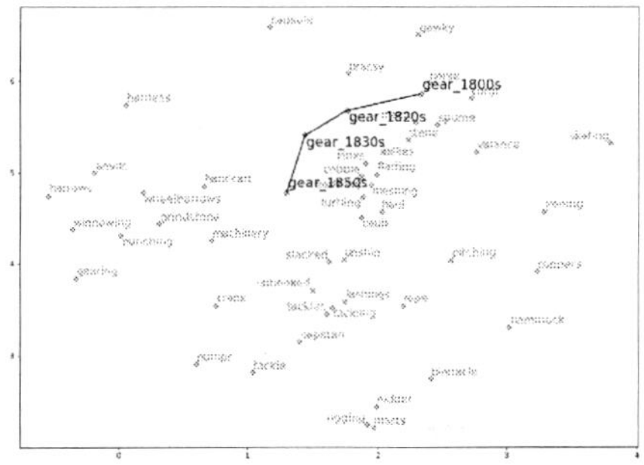

Figure 8: Semantic change trajectory of *gear*.

traffic drifted away from the sense defined by the OED as 'the activity or business of acquiring, transporting, and selling something which, for legal or moral reasons, should not be treated as a mere commodity; trade of an illegal, immoral, or otherwise objectionable nature', exemplified by 1810s-1820s nearest-neighbours such as *slave, contraband, detestable, infamous, inhuman, abominable, execrable, disgraceful, trafficking*[13], *piracy, illicit,* and so on. Its main usage by the 1830s, as suggested by its neighbours, is in the sense of 'passage of vehicles, vessels, etc., to and fro along a route', and by the 1860s several neighbours are related to its usage (first recorded, according to the OED, in the 1830s) as 'the quantity of goods, or number of passengers, carried by a transportation service over a particular period; the business or revenue generated from this', as exemplified by words such as *passengers, coaches, railways, trains* and *milage*.

4.5 *Gear*

The trajectory of *gear* (Figure 8) is exemplary of a general trend towards specific senses related to new mechanical advances throughout the 19th century, reflecting the several new usages related to 'machinery' recorded by the OED as first being attested at different points between the 1810s and the 1870s.

4.6 *Matches* and *stamp*

The words *matches* and *stamp*, for both of which a potential changepoint was detected by the model trained with a lower penalty, were mentioned by Görlach (1999, 128) when noting that Soule (1871) in his *A Dictionary of English Synonymes* failed to include the 'phosphorous sense of match [and] the philatelic sense of stamp', which Görlach explains as possibly due to the fact the new senses had not become dominant in the 19th century yet.

Our results for *stamp* (Figure 9), however, suggests that by the 1860s the philatelic sense (first attested according to the OED in 1837) was already prominent, as we can see from words such as *envelope, postage*, and *penny* (possibly referring to the price of a stamp), unlike the nearest neighbours of the word in the 1840s, such as *affixing, engrave, government*, or *grave*, which are related to the main older sense of *stamp* as 'the mark, impression, or imprint made with an engraved block or die'.

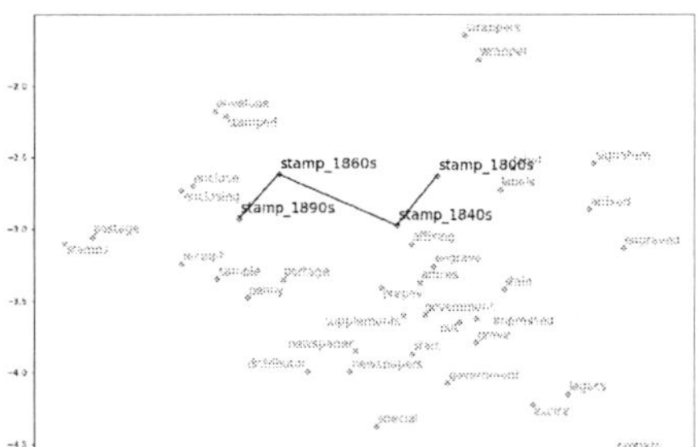

Figure 9: Semantic change trajectory of *stamp*.

Unlike *stamp*, the results of our changepoint detection method for *matches* are likely to be misleading and could be heavily biassed by a particular event (possibly sports-related) being heavily covered by the news between the 1880s and 1890s. In Figure 10 we can see that, although the new 'phosphorous sense' of the word is among the nearest

[13]This word specifically is indicated by the OED as an example of traffic in this sense.

neighbours in the plot (e.g. *phosphorus* and *ignite*), their cosine similarity with *match* is likely not as high between the 1860s and the 1880s (the period within which a potential changepoint was detected) as that with words related to the pre-existing sense 'a contest or competitive trial of skill in a particular sport, game, or other activity'.

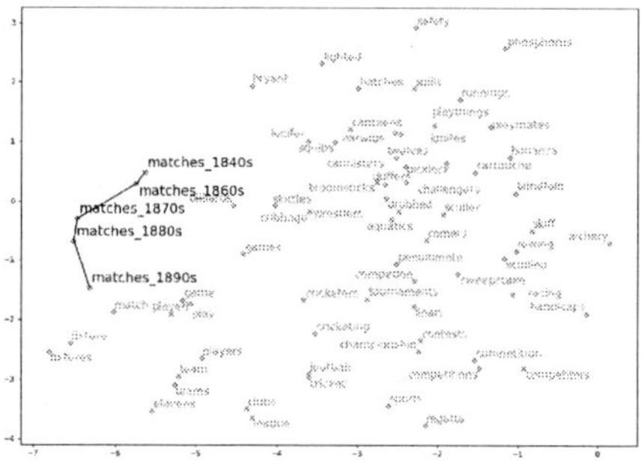

Figure 10: Semantic change trajectory of *matches*.

4.7 *Coach*

Coach is discussed by Görlach (1999, 128) as having undergone semantic extension from its meaning as a 'large horse-drawn carriage', attested since the 16th century, to the sense, recorded in the OED, 'a railway carriage', an extension which is also visible from the semantic space of this word and its neighbours from our diachronic models (Figure 11). This is an especially encouraging result, since our models captured this semantic extension as early as the decade recorded by the OED as the first written attestation, while also showing that its usage in the first half of the 19th century was not exclusively American English as defined in the OED and reported by Görlach (1999, 128).

A possible explanation as to why for words like *bulb* no definite changepoint was detected is that the semantic change trajectory of such words may be much more complex than a mere addition of a sense and a significant spread in use of the latter around a specific decade. Specifically in the case of *bulb*, according to the OED, at least three main senses were already in use at the beginning of the 19th century from different semantic fields (anatomy, botany, and, broadly, electricity). New specific uses of the word are then attested from the mid-19th century, but these are classified by the OED as specialisations of two of the previously existing senses, sometimes specifically when the

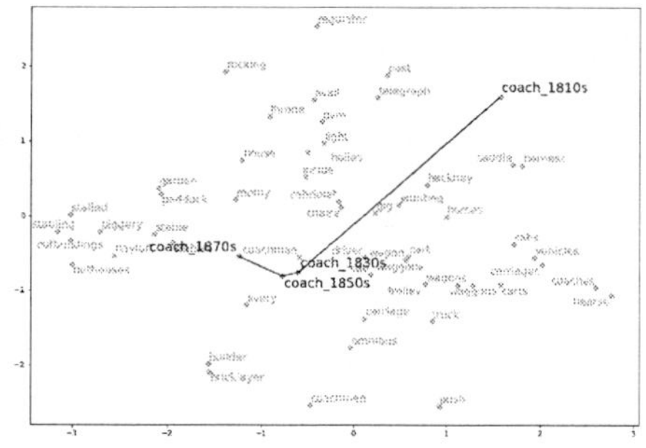

Figure 11: Semantic change trajectory of *coach*.

words are found within certain collocations (as in *electric light bulb*, first recorded in 1856 according to the OED). Görlach (1999, 134) mentions *bulb*, together with *gear* and *stamp*, as examples of words that underwent 'conspicuous semantic changes caused by technological progress', comparing the expansion of meaning of these words to that of *circuit* and *current* towards their electricity-related sense in the previous century. It is useful to note that overall trajectory of *bulb*, *gear* and *stamp* appears to be quite similar (Figure 12).

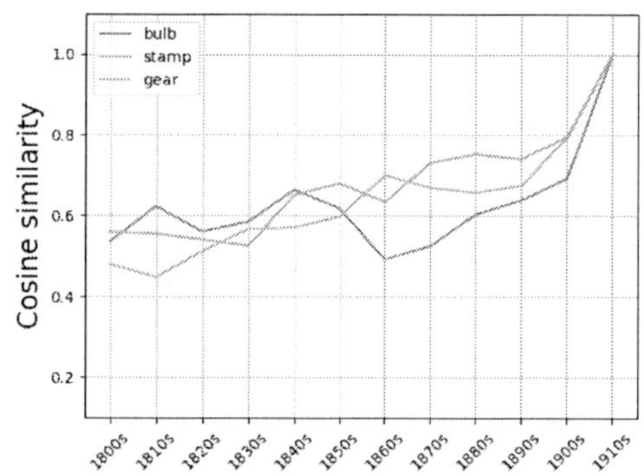

Figure 12: Time series for the cosine similarity between *bulb*, *gear*, *stamp* in each decade and their respective vector in the time reference (the last decade, i.e. the 1910s).

Although the general trajectory is slightly upward (i.e. there is likely an overall change in meaning) for all three words, *stamp* and *gear* show a more gradual but somewhat steadier change in cosine similarity with the vector of the reference time period (1910s), starting from a cosine similarity below 0.6 and reaching 0.8, a very high score, towards the beginning of the 20th century. *Bulb*, on the other hand, has a less regular trajectory and hardly reaches a cosine similarity with its 1900s representation of 0.7.

5 Quality control

Since large digitized newspaper collections are frequently not created with a specific criterion in mind, but rather following specific policies of the digitizing institution, we needed to be particularly wary that the likely biassed content of our data (cf. Beelen et al., 2022) would not significantly interfere with our research questions. The quality of our models and validity of our method were checked in several ways.

First, to make sure that potential detected changepoints were not simply the result of a biassed dataset, we ran our changepoint detection method individually on all the words in the list of synonym pairs which were also used to optimize the embedding hyperparameters, since they were indicated by the OED as semantically stable throughout our period of interest. With a jump parameter of 1 and a penalty of 0.5 (the safer, stricter option), no changepoint was detected for any of the words, with the exception of *identical*, suggesting an overall good reliability for our models.

Second, throughout the analysis we used two external sources to validate our results. *A history of the English Language in the Nineteenth Century* by Görlach (1999), specifically its chapter on lexical change, was used to draw examples from the language of mechanization that the scholar indicated as having undergone some type of semantic change. We also included words which he mentioned as seeming semantically stable throughout the century (namely *fellow* and *wheel*, the former not in the lexical field of mechanization) as a further form of comparison with non-digital scholarship on the subject. Finally, throughout the analysis we employed the OED as a benchmark to check whether a changepoint coincided with a newly recorded senses, as well as to identify definition of new senses and usages, especially in highly polysemous or ambiguous contexts.

6 Conclusions

In this paper we presented a first attempt at a large-scale computational study of semantic change of terms related to the lexical field of mechanisation in 19th-century English. Our main goal was to find out whether vector space models trained on very large (4.6B tokens) digitized, hence noisy, historical newspapers were able to stand the test of expert knowledge on the topic. We showed that using changepoint detection methods on the diachronic word embeddings that we trained gave results most often matching the observations made by traditional scholarship. Through a combination of changepoint detection and neighbour analysis it was possible to provide explanations for mismatches between previous literature and our findings, in some cases noticing that our results were able to capture features of semantic change not identified by the expert sources (see, for example, the analysis of *coach* above).

Our analysis provides the bases for new data-driven investigations on the lexical field of mechanization that do not rely so closely on external knowledge bases as in our study.

Acknowledgments

Work for this paper was carried out as part of *Living with Machines*. This project, funded by the UK Research and Innovation (UKRI) Strategic Priority Fund, is a multidisciplinary collaboration delivered by the Arts and Humanities Research Council (AHRC grant AH/S01179X/1), with The Alan Turing Institute, the British Library and King's College London, East Anglia, Exeter, and Queen Mary University of London.

References

Kaspar Beelen, Jon Lawrence, Daniel C. S. Wilson, and David Beavan. 2022. Bias and representativeness in digitized newspaper collections: Introducing the environmental scan. *Digital Scholarship in the Humanities*, pages 1–22.

Alexander Bergs and Laurel J. Brinton, editors. 2012. *English Historical Linguistics*. Handbücher zur Sprach- und Kommunikationswissenschaft / Handbooks of Linguistics and Communication Science 34.1. De Gruyter Mouton, Berlin, Boston.

Ingegerd Bäcklund. 2006. *Modifiers describing women and men in nineteenth-century English*, pages 17–55. Cambridge University Press, Cambridge.

Manfred Görlach. 1999. *English in Nineteenth-Century England: An Introduction*. Cambridge University Press, Cambridge.

William L. Hamilton, Jure Leskovec, and Dan Jurafsky. 2016. Diachronic word embeddings reveal statistical laws of semantic change. In *Proceedings of the 54th Annual Meeting of the Association for Computational Linguistics (Volume 1: Long Papers)*, pages

1489–1501, Berlin, Germany. Association for Computational Linguistics.

Christian Kay and Kathryn Allan. 2015. *English Historical Semantics*. Edinburgh University Press, Edinburgh.

Roberta Killick, Paul Fearnhead, and Idris A. Eckley. 2012. Optimal detection of changepoints with a linear computational cost. *Journal of the American Statistical Association*, 107(500):1590–1598.

M. Kytö, M. Rydén, and E. Smitterberg, editors. 2006. *Nineteenth-century English: Stability and change*. Cambridge University Press, Cambridge.

Tomas Mikolov, Kai Chen, Greg Corrado, and Jeffrey Dean. 2013. Efficient estimation of word representations in vector space.

Lynda Mugglestone. 2008. *The Oxford History of English*. Oxford University Press, Oxford.

Radim Řehůřek and Petr Sojka. 2010. Software Framework for Topic Modelling with Large Corpora. In *Proceedings of the LREC 2010 Workshop on New Challenges for NLP Frameworks*, pages 45–50, Valletta, Malta. ELRA. `http://is.muni.cz/publication/884893/en`.

Dominik Schlechtweg, Barbara McGillivray, Simon Hengchen, Haim Dubossarsky, and Nina Tahmasebi. 2020. SemEval-2020 task 1: Unsupervised lexical semantic change detection. In *Proceedings of the Fourteenth Workshop on Semantic Evaluation*, pages 1–23, Barcelona (online). International Committee for Computational Linguistics.

Peter H. Schönemann. 1966. A generalized solution of the orthogonal procrustes problem. *Psychometrika*, 31:1–10.

Philippa Shoemark, Farhana Ferdousi Liza, Dong Nguyen, Scott Hale, and Barbara McGillivray. 2019. Room to Glo: A systematic comparison of semantic change detection approaches with word embeddings. In *Proceedings of the 2019 Conference on Empirical Methods in Natural Language Processing and the 9th International Joint Conference on Natural Language Processing (EMNLP-IJCNLP)*, pages 66–76, Hong Kong, China. Association for Computational Linguistics.

Richard Soule. 1871. *A Dictionary of English Synonymes and Synonymous Or Parallel Expressions: Designed as a Practical Guide to Aptness and Variety of Phraseology*.

Adam Tsakalidis, Piero Basile, Marya Bazzi, Mihai Cucuringu, and Barbara McGillivray. 2021. DUKweb, diachronic word representations from the UK Web Archive corpus. *Scientific Data*, 8(269).

Adam Tsakalidis, Marya Bazzi, Mihai Cucuringu, Pierpaolo Basile, and Barbara McGillivray. 2019. Mining the UK web archive for semantic change detection. In *Proceedings of the International Conference on Recent Advances in Natural Language Processing (RANLP 2019)*, pages 1212–1221, Varna, Bulgaria. INCOMA Ltd.

Daniel van Strien, Kaspar Beelen, Mariona Ardanuy, Kasra Hosseini, Barbara McGillivray, and Giovanni Colavizza. 2020. Assessing the Impact of OCR Quality on Downstream NLP Tasks. In *Proceedings of the 12th International Conference on Agents and Artificial Intelligence - Volume 1: ARTIDIGH*, pages 484–496. INSTICC, SciTePress.

Melvin Wevers and Marijn Koolen. 2020. Digital begriffsgeschichte: Tracing semantic change using word embeddings. *Historical Methods: A Journal of Quantitative and Interdisciplinary History*, 53(4):226–243.

A Scripts and models

All the Python scripts used to train the diachronic word embeddings, as well as several Jupyter notebooks to replicate the methodology employed in this paper, can be found at `https://github.com/Living-with-machines/DiachronicEmb-BigHistData`.

The vectors used for the analysis in this paper can be found in the following repository in Zenodo: `https://doi.org/10.5281/zenodo.7181681`.

B Visualization method

Visualization of the semantic trajectories is carried out in the following steps:

1. Define three or four decades around which a semantic shift appears to have taken place for a word *w*. This is established through a combination of automatic changepoint detection and close reading of the neighbours of *w*. The selected decades should be adjusted across different runs to achieve the clearest visual rendition of a semantic shift (if any).

2. Extract the 20-nearest neighbours of *w* for the selected decades and remove any duplicate (i.e. neighbours of *w* appearing in more than one decade).

4. From the extracted neighbours, remove words that are clear misspellings (likely due to OCR errors).

5. From the model for the most recent decade (among the selected decades) extract the vector of each word in the list of neighbours. Discard words that are not in the vocabulary of the model.

6. Add the vectors for *w* from each of the selected decades to resulting list of vector and convert this list to a `numpy` array.
7. Reduce dimensionality using T-distributed Stochastic Neighbor Embedding (t-SNE)[14]
8. Visualize the resulting two-dimensional embedding space in a scatter plot, highlighting the label for *w* in the selected decades. For details on the latter, see the code repository.

[14]To do this, we used the implementation of t-SNE by the `sklearn` library, setting the number of dimensions to `2`, the maximum number of iterations to `1000`, and the initialization method to `random`.

Optimizing the weighted sequence alignment algorithm for large-scale text similarity computation

Maciej Janicki
Department of Digital Humanities
University of Helsinki
Unioninkatu 40, 00170 Helsinki, Finland
maciej.janicki@helsinki.fi

Abstract

We present an optimized implementation of the weighted sequence alignment algorithm (a.k.a. weighted edit distance) in a scenario where the items to align are numeric vectors and the substitution weights are determined by their cosine similarity. The optimization relies on using vector and matrix operations provided by numeric computation libraries (including GPU acceleration) instead of loops. The resulting algorithm provides an efficient way of aligning large sets of texts represented as sequences of continuous-space numeric vectors (embeddings). The optimization made it possible to compute alignment-based similarity for all pairs of texts in a large corpus of Finnic oral folk poetry for the purpose of studying intertextuality in the oral tradition.

1 Introduction

Sequence alignment algorithms have a long history of usage in both bioinformatics and natural language processing (NLP). The concept of 'edit distance' dates back to Levenshtein (1966), while a dynamic algorithm for its performant computation was presented independently at least by Needleman and Wunsch (1970) and Wagner and Fischer (1974).

With the popularization of the concept of embeddings in NLP, units of text (typically words) are often represented as vectors in a high-dimensional continuous space, with some similarity measure on such vectors (typically cosine similarity) capturing abstract similarity between those units (e.g. similarity of words in meaning).[1] This opens up the possibility of non-exact sequential comparison of texts using weighted alignment with cosine similarities of embedding vectors as weights.

A concrete example of such computation was recently presented by Janicki et al. (2022), who apply alignment to study intertextuality in *Old Poems of the Finnish People* (*Suomen Kansan Vanhat Runot*, SKVR) – a large collection of Finnic folk poetry recorded from oral tradition. In Janicki et al.'s article, texts are represented as sequences of lines and the similarity measure for lines is defined based on bag-of-bigrams vector representation. Although this is a very simple kind of embedding, it was proven useful in tackling the high linguistic variation that characterizes this corpus.

However, due to the size of the corpus (around 90,000 texts), the authors were only able to compute the alignment-based similarity between pairs of poems pre-selected based on certain criteria, which might miss some interesting cases.[2] In this paper, we are going to present an optimization of the alignment computation which allows one to deal with large amounts of texts. It can be used to compute an alignment between every single pair of poems in SKVR using Janicki et al.'s embedding method. More generally, it can be applied to find similar passages in any large collection of texts using an embedding representation of smaller text units (e.g. words or lines) as basis for similarity.

As the present short paper is incremental work focused on optimizing a particular well-known, general-purpose algorithm, we limit the discussion on its application in the study of Finnic folk poetry to a short example in section 4 showing the benefit of the current improvements. For a broader Digital Humanities context and a more thorough discussion of using text similarity in the study of oral tradition, the reader may be referred to Janicki et al. (2022).

Existing approaches. Most available Python packages for sequence alignment are either de-

[1]For a thorough introduction to the subject, see e.g. Pilehvar and Camacho-Collados (2020).

[2]Janicki et al. (2022) first apply a clustering algorithm on individual lines, and then find pairs of poems sharing lines from same clusters as candidates for alignment. However, the clustering is meant to group 'equivalent lines' with exactly the same content, so it misses similarities of smaller degree.

The 2nd International Workshop on Natural Language Processing for Digital Humanities (NLP4DH), pages 96–100
November 20, 2022.

signed specifically for biological sequences (like e.g. `Bio.Align`[3]) or very simple pure-Python implementations of the base algorithm (like e.g. `alignment`[4], `edit-distance`[5]). A notable example of a library allowing for alignment of sequences of numeric vectors using a custom similarity measure, as well as providing a fast C++ implementation, is `pyalign`[6]. However, as we will see in sec. 3, it does not provide sufficient performance to solve the problems addressed here.

Optimizations to the base algorithm are typically based on restricting the allowed edit distance to a small number and pre-selecting or filtering candidate pairs (e.g. Bocek et al., 2007; Soru and Ngonga Ngomo, 2013). For handling large numbers of strings, also finite state automata have been used (Schulz and Mihov, 2002). However, these methods are only applicable to sequences of symbols from a finite alphabet.

2 The Algorithm

2.1 The basic algorithm

We consider the case in which the weight of substitution of a single unit of text is defined by the similarity of units being substituted, with 1 meaning complete similarity (identity) and 0 none. Also the weight of insertions and deletions is 0. In this formulation, we are looking for the maximum-weight alignment, which detects as much overlap between the two sequences as possible.

Let S denote the matrix of similarities between individual units of both sequences. The alignment matrix D can be computed using the following recursive formula (cf. Wagner and Fischer, 1974):

$$d_{i,j} = \max \left\{ \begin{array}{c} d_{i-1,j} \\ d_{i,j-1} \\ d_{i-1,j-1} + s_{i,j} \end{array} \right\} \quad (1)$$

where the considered values amount to the edit operations of deletion, insertion and substitution, respectively. After computing the matrix D, the optimal alignment can be found by backtracing, from which direction the optimal value was chosen at each step.

[3] `https://biopython.org/docs/1.75/api/Bio.Align.html`

[4] `https://pypi.org/project/alignment/`

[5] `https://pypi.org/project/edit-distance/`

[6] `https://pypi.org/project/pyalign/`

Because in the application we are concerned with computing the alignment-based similarity between sequences, i.e. the weight of the optimal alignment (possibly with some further normalization), rather than the alignment itself, we will skip the part of alignment extraction and concentrate on computing the matrix D efficiently.

2.2 Optimization

Our optimization is based on the idea that computation on vectors and matrices is faster than computing individual numbers iteratively, especially when using a GPU. We will thus group the computations in two ways:

1. Use vector operations to compute entire rows of the alignment matrix.

2. Use matrix operations to compute the next row of alignment matrices between one document and all other documents at once.

Optimization 1. Because in the formula (1) every cell of the matrix D depends on the cell to the left, we cannot use it directly to compute entire rows. However, we can break down this computation into two stages:

$$d^*_{i,j} = \max \{ d_{i-1,j} \; ; \; d_{i-1,j-1} + s_{i,j} \} \quad (2)$$

$$d_{i,j} = \max \{ d^*_{i,j} \; ; \; d_{i,j-1} \} = \max_{k \leq j} d^*_{i,k} \quad (3)$$

Now (2) depends only on the previous row, so it can be computed row-wise, whereas (3) is a cumulative maximum operation. Let $\text{fmax}(\cdot;\cdot)$ denote the element-wise maximum of two vectors or matrices and $\text{cummax}(\cdot)$ the cumulative maximum (row-wise in case of matrices). Then we can rewrite (2, 3) in vector notation as:

$$d^*_{i,1:n} = \text{fmax} \left(\begin{array}{c} d_{(i-1),1:n} \\ d_{(i-1),0:(n-1)} + s_{i,1:n} \end{array} \right) \quad (4)$$

$$d_{i,0:n} = \text{cummax} \left(d^*_{i,0:n} \right) \quad (5)$$

Note that the latter step (cummax) relies on the fact that the insertion weight is 0, and the optimization could not be applied otherwise.

Optimization 2. Assuming that we are computing the alignment between a single *target* document and multiple *source* documents, the next row for each source document can be computed at once. We will stack the matrices S and D vertically, so that the columns correspond to the items of the target sequence and the rows to the items of all source sequences concatenated.[7] Let B denote a set of sequence boundaries, i.e. row indices in the stacked matrices, at which a new sequence begins. Further, let m, n denote the (zero-based) indices of the last row and column of the D and S matrices.

Algorithm 1 Alignment of a single document against multiple others.

1: $D_{B,0:n} \leftarrow \text{cummax}(S_{B,0:n})$
2: $I \leftarrow (B+1) \setminus B$
3: **while** $I \neq \emptyset$ **do**
4: $\quad D_{I,0} \leftarrow \text{fmax}\left(D_{I-1,0}, S_{I,0}\right)$
5: $\quad D_{I,1:n} \leftarrow \text{fmax}\begin{pmatrix} D_{I-1,1:n} \\ D_{I-1,0:n-1} + S_{I,1:n} \end{pmatrix}$
6: $\quad D_{I,0:n} \leftarrow \text{cummax}(D_{I,0:n})$
7: $\quad I \leftarrow (I+1) \setminus B \setminus \{m+1\}$
8: **end while**

Algorithm 1 computes the stacked alignment matrix D. Each iteration computes the next row of the alignment matrix for each source sequence simultaneously. The set I contains the indices of currently computed rows. The notation like $I+1$ for a set of indices is a shorthand for $\{i+1 : i \in I\}$. Once an index reaches the start of a new sequence or the end of the corpus, it is removed from the set (line 7). The first row for each sequence (line 1) and the first column (line 4) are processed separately as they cannot refer to the previous row or column, respectively.

3 Benchmarks

In order to test the optimizations, we compute pairwise maximum-weight alignment matrices for poems from the SKVR collection, using the vectorization of verses as bags of character bigrams (following Janicki et al. 2022). We conduct the experiments on subsets of the collection with different sizes, comparing the following algorithm variants:

0 No optimizations – the alignment matrix is computed for each pair of documents separately using the standard dynamic programming algorithm implemented as a Python loop.

0-PA Using the `pyalign` library for computing alignment scores pair by pair. (The matrix S is precomputed as a single dot product per target document.)

1 Only optimization 1 – the alignment matrix is computed for each pair of documents separately, but using vectorized row-wise operations (NumPy library).

2-NP Optimizations 1 and 2, using the NumPy library.

2-T-CPU Like above, but using the PyTorch library on a CPU.

2-T-GPU Like above, but using the PyTorch library on a GPU.[8]

In all the variants, we applied a threshold of 0.5 on the similarity of individual items and then rescaled the values to the interval $[0, 1]$. This was done to avoid false positives, but it should not influence the runtime of the algorithm. The benchmarks were run on a mid-range desktop PC with an 8-threaded Intel Core i7-6700 3.4 GHz CPU and a GeForce GTX 1060 GPU.

The results are shown in Table 1. They indicate a dramatic reduction in runtimes when using both optimizations. For larger dataset sizes, the GPU version is the most efficient, providing around 3x speedup over the CPU. It can be projected from the growth that the non-optimized variants (including the one using `pyalign`)[9] would take weeks to compute the similarities for the entire SKVR, while the GPU version does it in less than 9 hours, and thus can be scaled up to even larger corpora.

4 Application

Using the optimized algorithm, we are able to compute alignment-based similarity between every single poem pair in the SKVR collection, and thus get rid of the pre-selection criteria employed by Janicki et al. (2022) (which required the poems to

[7] Because the alignment is symmetric, assuming that the goal is to compute alignment between all document pairs and thus we will take every document in turn to be a target document, it suffices if the source sequences are all documents *following* the target document in the corpus (rather than the entire rest of the corpus).

[8] For memory-saving reasons, the GPU version uses 16-bit floating point numbers, while the CPU versions use the default 64-bit float. It might be that the difference in speed is partly due to the different data type used. PyTorch on CPU currently does not implement 16-bit floating point arithmetic, but seems to be faster for 32-bit than 64-bit. This could be studied in more detail if needed, but the purpose of the current comparison is to show the benefit from the optimizations.

[9] It should be noted that `pyalign` is a very generic and flexible library, providing much more functionality than what is tested here. This comparison is intended to prove the need for the optimizations in our case, but by no means to cast doubt at the usefulness of `pyalign` in general.

#docs	variant					
	0	0-PA	1	2-NP	2-T-CPU	2-T-GPU
100	85.8	18.4	6.7	5.5	5.8	13.4
200	282	53.2	20.3	10.5	9.9	19.8
500	1,109	186	88.6	32.3	27.1	48.3
1,000	3,261	525	283	86.0	69.6	113
2,000	10,400	1,897	1,168	266	204	247
5,000	–	6,287	4,543	888	668	781
10,000	–	24,232	21,963	3,340	2,319	1,800
20,000	–	–	–	10,623	7,047	3,341
50,000	–	–	–	33,165	26,291	9,387
88,078	–	–	–	78,720	92,850	32,036

Table 1: Execution times (in seconds) for the different algorithm variants and different dataset sizes (the last row is entire SKVR). The experiments marked with '–' were skipped because of long expected computation times and when the lower performance of the respective variant has already been sufficiently demonstrated.

Ingrian-Finnish	Estonian	translation	sim.
Lilla istu kamperissa,	Lilla istus kammeris,	The girl was sitting in a chamber,	**.79**
Aik' oli ikäv uottaa,	Tal aeg oli igav oota.	It was a sad time waiting.	.46
Näki vennan reissivanna	Ta nägi venda sõudema	She saw a brother [travelling / rowing]	.20
Pitkin mere rantaa.	Seal üle mereranna.	Along the sea coast.	.45
"Rikas venna, rakas venna,	"Kulla venda, rikas venda	'Rich brother, [dear / golden] brother	**.64**
Lunast minnuu täältä vällää!"	Lunasta mu südant!"	Ransom [me from here / my heart]!'	.31
"Millä mie lunassan,	"Kellega ma lunastan,	'With what do I ransom you,	.41
Kui miull' ei ole varraa?"	Kui mul ei ole raha."	When I don't have money?'	**.73**
"On siull' koton kolme miekkaa,	"Sul on kodu kolmi mõeka,	'You've got three swords at home,	**.66**
Pane niist' yksi pantiks!"	Pane üks neist pandiks."	Pawn one of them!'	**.74**
"Enne mie luovun siusta	"Ennem mina lahkun õekesest,	'I'd rather give up [you / a sister],	.36
Kui omast' kolmest' miekast'."	Kui oma sõjamõegast."	Than my own [three / war] sword[s].'	.44

Table 2: Fragment of an Ingrian-Finnish and Estonian version of the song *The maid to be ransomed*, showing the possibility of cross-lingual alignment.

have a couple of highly similar verses in common to be considered for alignment).

The algorithm is scalable enough to be practically usable even if the SKVR collection is combined with further corpora of similar size. In our current research, we combine SKVR with the Estonian Runosongs Database[10] (*Eesti Regilaulude Andmebaas*, ERAB), which contains around 100,000 documents. This allows us to search for cross-dataset and cross-lingual similarities.

An example for this is given in Table 2. It shows a fragment of a song *The maid to be ransomed* in an Ingrian-Finnish and Estonian version (from SKVR and ERAB, respectively). Cosine similarities of verses (in a bag-of-character-bigrams representation) are given on the right. While the texts are built in a very similar way, the string-level similarity is low due to considerable linguistic differences.

The threshold used by the current method is 0.5, which allows us to align the verse pairs with similarity scores marked in bold. Because there are quite many alignable pairs, the poems will be easily recognized as similar. On the other hand, the method described by Janicki et al. (2022) required the poems to share verse pairs with similarity of at least 0.8 in order to be considered for alignment. Such pairs do not occur here, and thus this poem pair would go unrecognized.

Furthermore, the runtime of the current method does not depend on the threshold (unlike the former), so it could be adjusted to any lower value if needed. The only limitation for that is that values below 0.5 are increasingly common for completely unrelated lines, so lowering the threshold increases the number of false positives.

5 Conclusion

We have presented an optimized version of the maximum-weight sequence alignment algorithm

[10]https://www.folklore.ee/regilaul/andmebaas/

(a variant of the weighted edit distance algorithm, a.k.a. Needleman-Wunsch or Wagner-Fisher algorithm). The optimization utilizes matrix operations for efficient computation on a large number of sequences. The weighted alignment can be used for non-exact comparison of texts, in which individual text units (like words or poetry lines) are represented with embeddings. The presented optimization made it possible to compute alignment-based similarity scores for all pairs of poems within a large collection of Finnic oral folk poetry, opening possibilities for a large-scale quantitative study of intertextuality in the Finnic oral tradition.

Funding

This work was funded by the Academy of Finland research project no. 333138 'Formulaic intertextuality, thematic networks and poetic variation across regional cultures of Finnic oral poetry'.

References

Thomas Bocek, Ela Hunt, and Burkhard Stiller. 2007. Fast similarity search in large dictionaries. Technical report, University of Zurich.

Maciej Janicki, Kati Kallio, and Mari Sarv. 2022. Exploring Finnic oral folk poetry through string similarity. *Digital Scholarship in the Humanities.*

Vladimir I. Levenshtein. 1966. Binary codes capable of correcting deletions, insertions, and reversals. *Soviet Physics Doklady*, 10(8):707–710.

Saul B. Needleman and Christian D. Wunsch. 1970. A general method applicable to the search for similarities in the amino acid sequence of two proteins. *Journal of Molecular Biology*, 48:443–453.

Mohammad Taher Pilehvar and Jose Camacho-Collados. 2020. Embeddings in natural language processing: Theory and advances in vector representations of meaning. *Synthesis Lectures on Human Language Technologies*, 13(4):1–175.

Klaus Schulz and Stoyan Mihov. 2002. Fast string correction with levenshtein-automata. *International Journal of Document Analysis and Recognition*, 5:67–85.

Tommaso Soru and Axel-Cyrille Ngonga Ngomo. 2013. Rapid execution of weighted edit distances. In *Proceedings of the 8th International Workshop on Ontology Matching.*

Robert A. Wagner and Michael J. Fischer. 1974. The string-to-string correction problem. *Journal of the ACM*, 21(I):168–173.

Domain-Specific Evaluation of Word Embeddings for Philosophical Text using Direct Intrinsic Evaluation

Goya van Boven
Utrecht University
j.g.vanboven@students.uu.nl

Jelke Bloem
University of Amsterdam
j.bloem@uva.nl

Abstract

We perform a direct intrinsic evaluation of word embeddings trained on the works of a single philosopher. Six models are compared to human judgements elicited using two tasks: a synonym detection task and a coherence task. We apply a method that elicits judgements based on explicit knowledge from experts, as the linguistic intuition of non-expert participants might differ from that of the philosopher. We find that an in-domain SVD model has the best 1-nearest neighbours for target terms, while transfer learning-based Nonce2Vec performs better for low frequency target terms.

1 Introduction

Many applications of Artificial Intelligence methods to textual data rely on language models pretrained on large amounts of web text. However, this does not necessarily yield models suited to the analysis of texts in the humanities, as such texts may deviate in style, vocabulary, register and other regards. On the other hand, models trained on texts from a specific humanities domain have far less data available to learn from. As a trade-off, transfer learning can be applied, where a model is first trained on a large, general-domain dataset and then tuned on a smaller, domain-specific dataset. We compare several tuning approaches based on Word2Vec (Mikolov et al., 2013a) to a baseline of a SVD model trained only on domain-specific data, for the purpose of learning meaning representations of the terminology of a specific philosopher.

In philosophy, there is interest in supporting the close reading of texts with the use of information retrieval methods (Ginammi et al., 2021) based on distributional semantic (DS) models (Turney and Pantel, 2010; Erk, 2012; Mikolov et al., 2013a) to provide a different perspective on texts (Herbelot et al., 2012). Philosophical terms have domain-specific meanings: for example an *accident* is a non-essential property of an entity, rather than an unfortunate incident. Thus, domain-specific models and methods of evaluation are necessary.

DS models are often evaluated by comparing their performance to a *gold standard*, such as the SimLex-999 dataset (Hill et al., 2015). However, these similarity rankings concern general language terms and their typical senses, rather than domain-specific philosophical terms. Meanings of terms may differ between philosophers or even within the works of a single philosopher. Rather than modeling a standard jargon that a group of people uses, we aim to model the semantics of some particular philosopher, with no 'native speaker' besides that philosopher. Any evaluation of the quality of the semantic representations in this kind of model would require expert knowledge. For this reason we apply the direct intrinsic evaluation methods proposed by van Boven and Bloem (2021) with expert participants. We evaluate six models: we use Wikipedia data as a general-domain text corpus for training, and we use a domain-specific corpus of the works of Willard V. O. Quine for tuning. Quine was a 20th century American philosopher, whose works are still of great interest to philosophers, logicians and linguists. This evaluation will show us which tuning approach, if any, performs best for creating meaning representations of philosophical terms, and for digital humanities applications more broadly.

2 Related work

Suissa et al. (2022) present an overview of AI-based text analysis in digital humanities, arguing that lack of data availability characterizes the field and that domain adaptation is essential. Sommerauer and Fokkens (2019) discuss the difficulties of applying distributional semantic models to study conceptual change in digital humanities, drawing attention to frequency effects and effects of random initialization, and the importance of studying domain-relevant exemplar terms.

The 2nd International Workshop on Natural Language Processing for Digital Humanities (NLP4DH), pages 101–107
November 20, 2022.

Various digital humanities studies using word embeddings have been published, but they rarely include in-domain evaluations of those embeddings. Bjerva and Praet (2015) apply word embeddings to study relationships between persons in 6th century Latin text, but do not evaluate their model. Nelson (2021) train domain-specific word embeddings on an 18M word corpus of narratives on slavery in the American South, but do not evaluate them. Meinecke et al. (2019) use domain-specific vectors for aligning medieval text versions, extrinsically evaluating by having an expert manually inspect the resulting alignments, but without intrinsically evaluating the embeddings.

Kenter et al. (2015) use word embeddings to study vocabulary shifts and have human annotators associate words to topics and time periods for evaluation. They do not use any pre-trained models. Wohlgenannt et al. (2019) do perform in-domain evaluation, evaluating word embedding models trained on two fantasy novel book series of about 1M tokens each, manually constructing test datasets with domain experts. They compare domain-specific models including Word2Vec to a transfer learning setup where a pretrained Word2Vec model is tuned on the fantasy novel corpus. They find that an in-domain Word2Vec model outperforms the other approaches in an analogy task and a word intrusion task. Todorov and Colavizza (2020) find that fine-tuning pre-trained BERT embeddings does not help for named entity recognition in historical corpora, though this is in addition to the use of in-domain FastText embeddings.

In the philosophical domain, several domain-specific evaluation methods have been proposed, but none have directly evaluated model output. Evaluated models include the widely used *Word2Vec* (W2V; Mikolov et al., 2013a,b) predictive model, *Nonce2Vec* (N2V; Herbelot and Baroni, 2017) which is an adaptation of the skip-gram W2V model designed for learning from few training examples in *tiny* text corpora, and count-based *SVD* models in the Levy et al. (2015) implementation.

Avoiding the issue of obtaining expert knowledge, Bloem et al. (2019) evaluate these models using a metric of model consistency, which rewards models that yield similar vectors when trained on different samples of the same target term within the same domain. They found that N2V outperforms a SVD baseline by this metric.

What word is most related to 'Information' ?	
a) *Learning*	b) *Reductions*
c) *Collateral*	d) *Application*
e) *Ordered Pair*	f) *None of these words is even remotely related*

Table 1: Synonym detection task example question. Here, the options are the k-nearest neighbours of target word 'information' of the various evaluated models.

What word does not belong to the group?	
a) *Numbers*	b) *Pronouns*
c) *Subtraction*	d) *Actually*

Table 2: Coherence task example question, with target word a), nearest neighbours b) and c), and outlier d).

Oortwijn et al. (2021) evaluated these models based on a conceptual network they constructed, comparing the similarity of learned embeddings for specific philosophical target terms to their position in this network. They found that domain-specific N2V and the count-based baseline models outperformed a domain-general W2V model. As the network was pre-defined, only a limited set of terms could be considered. Betti et al. (2020) propose the use of a more elaborate ground truth in evaluation that includes many relevant as well as irrelevant terms, centered around a specific concept as defined by a specific philosopher. This still would not account for creative model output.

Lastly, van Boven and Bloem (2021) proposed the use of direct intrinsic evaluation to provide more comprehensive coverage of anything the models might output. Methods from Schnabel et al. (2015) are adapted to the scenario of eliciting expert knowledge where experts respond to nearest neighbour words that the model generates. Van Boven and Bloem (2021) report competitive inter-rater agreement scores between experts for this method. We adopt this approach for philosophical domain model evaluation.

3 Methods and data

The direct intrinsic evaluation method consists of a *synonym detection task* and a *coherence task*, adapted from Schnabel et al. (2015). Synonym detection entails selecting the most related word to target word *t* from a set of words, which are the k-nearest neighbours of *t* in each included model. In this task, participants thus indicate their preference between the outputs of all evaluated models. Table 1 illustrates the set-up of this task. In the coherence task, which is illustrated in Table 2, expert participants are asked to identify a semantic outlier in a set of words, which is less close to t in the model than the other options. The aim of this task is to assess whether groups of words are mutually related in a small neighbourhood in the embedding, evaluating model coherence. Here, each model is evaluated individually. The combination of the two tasks provides insight into the absolute as well as the relative performance of the models. We refer to van Boven and Bloem (2021) for further details on the tasks, and an evaluation of the method. The evaluation tasks were conducted through online surveys on the platform *Qualtrics*[1].

Following Schnabel et al. (2015), we analyse the results of both tasks through a random permutation test, with the number of permutations $n = 100,000$. We use the difference in mean scores (i.e. the percentage of votes) between models as our test statistic for the synonym detection task, and for the coherence task we use the precision scores (i.e. the proportion of correctly identified outliers per model). As each model has its own qualities and the tasks evaluate different aspects, it is possible for the two tasks to yield different 'winners'.

3.1 Data

As training data we use a 140M token domain-general Wikipedia corpus and the 2.15M token QUINE corpus (v0.5, Betti et al., 2020), which includes 228 philosophical articles, books and bundles written by Quine. Following van Boven and Bloem (2021) we use the test set for the influential book *Word & Object* (Quine, 1960) by Bloem et al. (2019) as target terms for evaluation. This test set contains 55 terms selected from the index of the book, of which we use 25 in Experiment 1, 14 in Experiment 2 and 6 in both of the experiments.[2] For models that processed both datasets, the target terms were marked in the QUINE corpus so that embeddings for target terms in both corpora were learned independently of each other.

3.2 Models

We compare a $W2V$ model, two instances of a count-based SVD and three instances of the $N2V$ model, which we chose for comparability to Oortwijn et al.'s (2021) evaluation on this data. Nonce2Vec works by training target terms and their in-domain context sentences into a general-domain background model (trained on Wikipedia). We apply Word2Vec in a similar setup where we continue training the Wikipedia model only on a target term's context sentences from the QUINE corpus. This is done for comparability with N2V. Therefore, our $W2V$ and $N2V$ models are all trained on the Quine dataset with the Wikipedia corpus as a background model in a transfer learning setup, and we test different forms of transfer learning. We did not include a GloVe model as it is trained similarly to SVD and typically performs similarly to Word2Vec, and additional models would make the annotation task too lengthy for the domain experts. Rather than including BERT, we use only type-based embeddings because we consider them more transparent to the domain experts; each type only has one representation which is somewhat interpretable. We refer to Ehrmanntraut et al. (2021) for further arguments in support of their use in digital humanities applications, such as better performance on small datasets.

The first variant of the $N2V$ model, $N2V_{Add}$ is N2V's additive baseline model used for its initialization, which simply sums Wikipedia background vectors of a target term's context words (Lazaridou et al., 2017). $N2V_{Def}$ uses the default hyperparameters of Herbelot and Baroni (2017), tuned for very small datasets. $N2V_{Con}$ is tuned on Bloem et al.'s (2019) consistency metric. Learning rates and decays are lower in $N2V_{Con}$ than in the $N2V_{Def}$ model, so the tuning is less strong. The $W2V$ model is trained over 5 epochs, with start $\alpha = 1.0$ and end $\alpha = 0.1$.

For the count-based models, the *Hyperword* SVD-PPMI implementation of Levy et al. (2015) is used with a window size of 5. We have a transfer setup trained on both the in-domain and general domain corpus (SVD_{Q+W}), and lastly we have a baseline without transfer learning trained only on the in-domain corpus (SVD_Q).

Based on previous philosophy domain evaluations and other work indicating relatively poor W2V performance on smaller datasets (Asr et al., 2016) and rare words (Luong et al., 2013; Herbelot and Baroni, 2017), we expect N2V and SVD to outperform W2V. Furthermore, we expect N2V to outperform SVD, as this was the outcome of previous

[1] www.qualtrics.com

[2] The terms and their frequencies are those available in van Boven and Bloem's (2021) supplementary materials at https://github.com/gvanboven/direct-intrinsic-evaluation

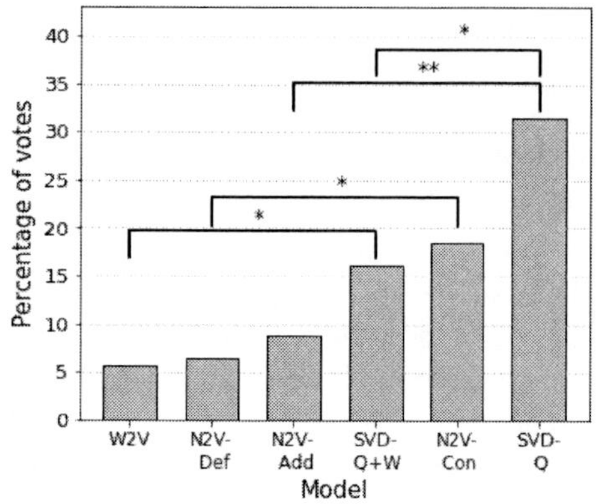

Figure 1: Results of the synonym detection task. $*$ indicates $p < 0.05$, $**$ indicates a significant p-value after Bonferroni-correction (Bonferroni, 1936).

evaluations by other metrics. Nevertheless, N2V is designed for tiny rather than small data. For this data size, count-based models have been shown to perform well (Sahlgren and Lenci, 2016).

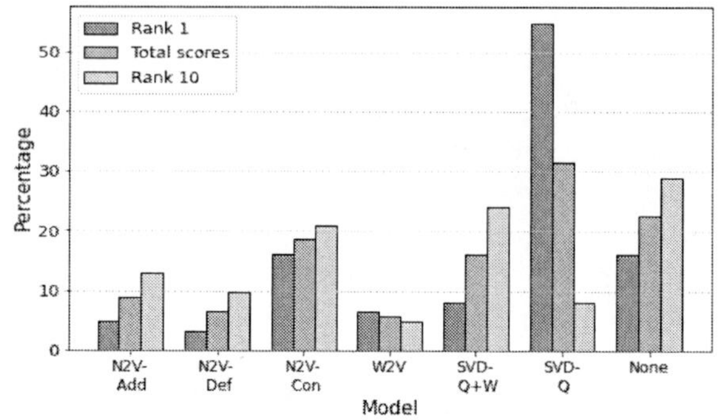

Figure 2: Synonym detection task: scores by nearest neighbour rank of the test items.

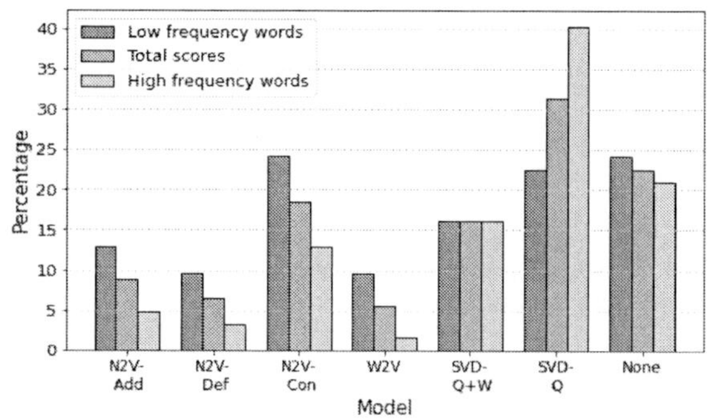

Figure 3: Synonym detection task: scores split by term frequency n. For high frequency terms, $n > 275$ and for low frequency terms $n < 84$.

4 Results

4.1 Experiment 1: Synonym detection task

Three experts on the work of Quine, who all hold a Master's degree in philosophy and have studied his work extensively, participated in this experiment. They evaluated 31 target words on two nearest neighbour ranks k, with $k \in \{1, 10\}$. We compare the mean scores of all model combinations, resulting in 15 comparisons. The total number of cast votes for best synonym is 136.[3] The data from one of the participants was excluded, as the participant indicated that the task was too difficult.

The overall scores, including the comparisons that were found to be significant, are shown in Figure 1. Figure 2 displays the scores by rank. SVD_Q receives most (31.5%) of the votes, but performs by far best on the rank 1 nearest neighbours. SVD_{Q+W} performs best on rank 10 nearest neighbours. Significant differences are found between SVD_Q and $N2V_{Add}$ ($p = 0.00079$), $N2V_{Def}$ ($p = 0.00014$) and $W2V$ ($p = 0.00009$). Inter-rater agreement is $\kappa = 0.492$. Figure 3 displays the scores split by term frequency, where $N2V_{Con}$ scores best for low frequency words and SVD_Q on high frequency words.

Surprisingly, the $N2V_{Def}$ model performs poorly even compared to $N2V_{Add}$, the Nonce2Vec baseline. This could be because $N2V_{Def}$ is designed for learning from only a few occurrences. Conversely, as the learning rate and its decay are lower in the $N2V_{Con}$ model, it may be better for representing small but not tiny datasets.

4.2 Experiment 2: Coherence task

In this task, we include the two best performing models (SVD_Q and $N2V_{Con}$) and the model that obtains the lowest score ($W2V$) in Experiment 1. Only three models were selected because they have to be evaluated one-by-one in this task. All models are tested on 20 target words and evaluated by the two expert participants. The total amount of ratings is 40 for each model. Figure 4 shows that $W2V$ performs significantly worse than both $N2V_{Con}$ and SVD_Q, while the difference between the two latter models is not significant. Inter-rater agreement is $\kappa = 0.345$.[4] Figure 5 and 6 display the scores split by term frequency, where we find

[3] 124 ratings + 12 votes that counted double as the selected option word is returned by multiple models

[4] As van Boven and Bloem (2021) discuss, the observed inter-rater agreement rates are similar to those of traditional semantic annotation tasks involving implicit knowledge.

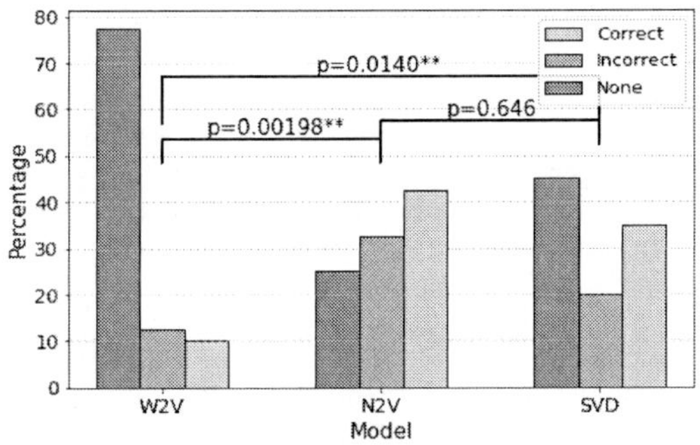

Figure 4: Results of the coherence task. *Correct* indicates the outlier was correctly identified, *Incorrect* means another words was chosen as the outlier, and *None* indicates that the option *"No coherent group can be formed from these words"* was selected.

that the best scoring $N2V_{Con}$ also performs best for high frequency words, while for low frequency words $N2V_{Con}$ and SVD_Q obtain the same score.

5 Discussion

The models that perform best are SVD_Q (the non-transfer learning baseline) and $N2V_{Con}$. SVD_Q received the most votes in the synonym detection task, and performed especially well at producing rank 1 nearest neighbours related to the target term. $N2V_{Con}$ scored higher in the coherence task, producing better clusters of related top neighbours, and producing better rank 10 neighbours in Experiment 1. This suggests SVD_Q would be more suitable for applications where top 1 precision is important, while $N2V_{Con}$ would do better in exploratory applications where a larger range of related terms is examined. The poor performance of the popular $W2V$ model for this domain and corpus size is in line with the findings of Oortwijn et al. (2021).

Both the count-based approach and the predictive approach produced a well-performing model. The hyperparameters and the transfer learning setup seemed to affect the scores more than the chosen approach. This matches Levy et al.'s (2015) claim that design choices and parameter settings influence embedding quality more than the model.

For philosophical inquiry it is important that representations of low frequency words are good, as few resources are available and low frequency terms can be crucial to understanding a concept. In the synonym detection task, $N2V_{Con}$ does better on low frequency words while SVD_Q does better on high frequency words. Conversely, in the

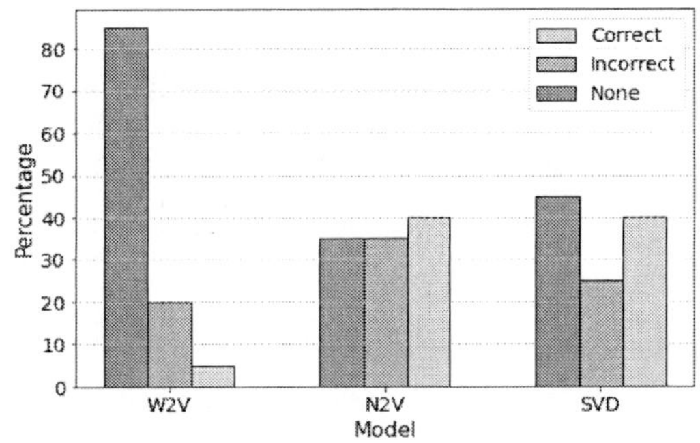

Figure 5: Scores for all models in the coherence task for low frequency terms ($n < 142$) only.

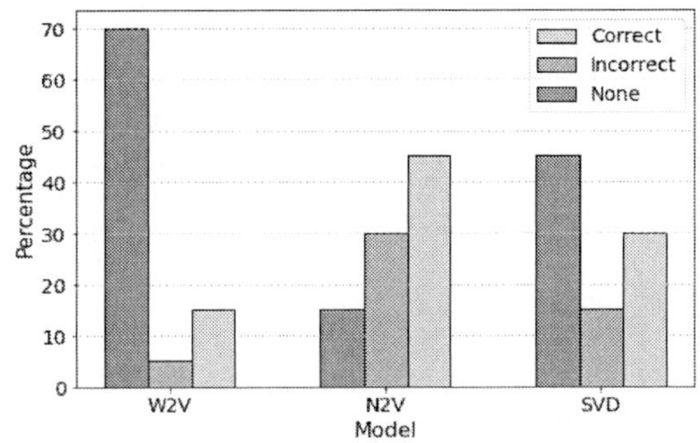

Figure 6: Scores for all models in the coherence task for high frequency terms ($n > 187$) only.

coherence task, $N2V_{Con}$ does better on high frequency words, though its low frequency performance is still equal to SVD_Q. As $N2V_{Con}$ scored well overall on our low frequency target terms and in Bloem et al.'s (2019) consistency evaluation, it appears the most promising for modeling philosophical terms. However, it is remarkable that a simple SVD baseline performs so well compared to W2V-based transfer learning approaches. Together with results from other work (Wohlgenannt et al., 2019), this suggests that in digital humanities applications, in-domain data should be favoured over transfer learning approaches at least when 1M tokens of training data (or more)[5] are available.

Acknowledgements

We are grateful to Yvette Oortwijn, Thijs Ossenkoppele and Arianna Betti for their input as Quine domain experts. This research was supported by VICI grant *e-Ideas* (277-20-007), financed by the Dutch Research Council (NWO).

[5]Value based on our and Wohlgenannt et al.'s (2019) in-domain corpus size, as well as the dataset sizes used in Sahlgren and Lenci's (2016) ablation study.

References

Fatemeh Torabi Asr, Jon Willits, and Michael Jones. 2016. Comparing Predictive and Co-occurrence Based Models of Lexical Semantics Trained on Child-directed Speech. In *Annual Conference of the Cognitive Science Society*.

Arianna Betti, Martin Reynaert, Thijs Ossenkoppele, Yvette Oortwijn, Andrew Salway, and Jelke Bloem. 2020. Expert Concept-Modeling Ground Truth Construction for Word Embeddings Evaluation in Concept-Focused Domains. In *Proceedings of the 28th International Conference on Computational Linguistics*, pages 6690–6702, Barcelona, Spain (Online). International Committee on Computational Linguistics.

Johannes Bjerva and Raf Praet. 2015. Word Embeddings Pointing the Way for Late Antiquity. In *Proceedings of the 9th SIGHUM Workshop on Language Technology for Cultural Heritage, Social Sciences, and Humanities (LaTeCH)*, pages 53–57, Beijing, China. Association for Computational Linguistics.

Jelke Bloem, Antske Fokkens, and Aurélie Herbelot. 2019. Evaluating the Consistency of Word Embeddings from Small Data. In *Proceedings of the International Conference on Recent Advances in Natural Language Processing (RANLP 2019)*, pages 132–141, Varna, Bulgaria. INCOMA Ltd.

Carlo Bonferroni. 1936. Teoria statistica delle classi e calcolo delle probabilita. *Pubblicazioni del R Istituto Superiore di Scienze Economiche e Commericiali di Firenze*, 8:3–62.

Anton Ehrmanntraut, Thora Hagen, Leonard Konle, and Fotis Jannidis. 2021. Type-and Token-based Word Embeddings in the Digital Humanities. In *Proceedings of the Conference on Computational Humanities Research*, pages 16–38, Amsterdam, The Netherlands.

Katrin Erk. 2012. Vector space models of word meaning and phrase meaning: A survey. *Language and Linguistics Compass*, 6(10):635–653.

Annapaola Ginammi, Jelke Bloem, Rob Koopman, Shenghui Wang, and Arianna Betti. 2021. Bolzano, Kant and the Traditional Theory of Concepts - A Computational Investigation [final author version after R&R submitted 12 Sep, 2020]. In Andreas de Block and Grant Ramsey, editors, *The Dynamics of Science: Computational Frontiers in History and Philosophy of Science*. Pittsburgh University Press, Pittsburgh.

Aurélie Herbelot and Marco Baroni. 2017. High-risk learning: acquiring new word vectors from tiny data. In *Proceedings of the 2017 Conference on Empirical Methods in Natural Language Processing*, pages 304–309, Copenhagen, Denmark. Association for Computational Linguistics.

Aurélie Herbelot, Eva von Redecker, and Johanna Müller. 2012. Distributional techniques for philosophical enquiry. In *Proceedings of the 6th Workshop on Language Technology for Cultural Heritage, Social Sciences, and Humanities*, pages 45–54, Avignon, France. Association for Computational Linguistics.

Felix Hill, Roi Reichart, and Anna Korhonen. 2015. SimLex-999: Evaluating Semantic Models With (Genuine) Similarity Estimation. *Computational Linguistics*, 41(4):665–695.

Tom Kenter, Melvin Wevers, Pim Huijnen, and Maarten De Rijke. 2015. Ad hoc monitoring of vocabulary shifts over time. In *Proceedings of the 24th ACM international on conference on information and knowledge management*, pages 1191–1200.

Angeliki Lazaridou, Marco Marelli, and Marco Baroni. 2017. Multimodal word meaning induction from minimal exposure to natural text. *Cognitive science*, 41:677–705.

Omer Levy, Yoav Goldberg, and Ido Dagan. 2015. Improving Distributional Similarity with Lessons Learned from Word Embeddings. *Transactions of the Association for Computational Linguistics*, 3:211–225.

Thang Luong, Richard Socher, and Christopher Manning. 2013. Better Word Representations with Recursive Neural Networks for Morphology. In *Proceedings of the Seventeenth Conference on Computational Natural Language Learning*, pages 104–113, Sofia, Bulgaria. Association for Computational Linguistics.

Christofer Meinecke, David Joseph Wrisley, and Stefan Jänicke. 2019. Automated Alignment of Medieval Text Versions based on Word Embeddings. In *LEVIA'19: Leipzig Symposium on Visualization in Applications 2019*.

Tomas Mikolov, Kai Chen, Greg Corrado, and Jeffrey Dean. 2013a. Efficient Estimation of Word Representations in Vector Space. *arXiv preprint arXiv:1301.3781*.

Tomas Mikolov, Ilya Sutskever, Kai Chen, Greg S Corrado, and Jeff Dean. 2013b. Distributed Representations of Words and Phrases and their compositionality. In *Advances in neural information processing systems*, pages 3111–3119.

Laura K Nelson. 2021. Leveraging the alignment between machine learning and intersectionality: Using word embeddings to measure intersectional experiences of the nineteenth century US South. *Poetics*, 88:101539.

Yvette Oortwijn, Jelke Bloem, Pia Sommerauer, Francois Meyer, Wei Zhou, and Antske Fokkens. 2021. Challenging distributional models with a conceptual network of philosophical terms. In *Proceedings of the 2021 Conference of the North American Chapter of the Association for Computational Linguistics: Human Language Technologies*, pages 2511–2522, Online. Association for Computational Linguistics.

Willard Van Orman Quine. 1960. Word and Object. *MIT Press*.

Magnus Sahlgren and Alessandro Lenci. 2016. The Effects of Data Size and Frequency Range on Distributional Semantic Models. In *Proceedings of the 2016 Conference on Empirical Methods in Natural Language Processing*, pages 975–980, Austin, Texas. Association for Computational Linguistics.

Tobias Schnabel, Igor Labutov, David Mimno, and Thorsten Joachims. 2015. Evaluation methods for unsupervised word embeddings. In *Proceedings of the 2015 Conference on Empirical Methods in Natural Language Processing*, pages 298–307, Lisbon, Portugal. Association for Computational Linguistics.

Pia Sommerauer and Antske Fokkens. 2019. Conceptual Change and Distributional Semantic Models: an Exploratory Study on Pitfalls and Possibilities. In *Proceedings of the 1st International Workshop on Computational Approaches to Historical Language Change*, pages 223–233, Florence, Italy. Association for Computational Linguistics.

Omri Suissa, Avshalom Elmalech, and Maayan Zhitomirsky-Geffet. 2022. Text analysis using deep neural networks in digital humanities and information science. *Journal of the Association for Information Science and Technology*, 73(2):268–287.

Konstantin Todorov and Giovanni Colavizza. 2020. Transfer learning for named entity recognition in historical corpora. In *CLEF (Working Notes)*.

Peter D Turney and Patrick Pantel. 2010. From frequency to meaning: Vector space models of semantics. *Journal of artificial intelligence research*, 37:141–188.

Goya van Boven and Jelke Bloem. 2021. Eliciting Explicit Knowledge From Domain Experts in Direct Intrinsic Evaluation of Word Embeddings for Specialized Domains. In *Proceedings of the Workshop on Human Evaluation of NLP Systems (HumEval)*, pages 107–113, Online. Association for Computational Linguistics.

Gerhard Wohlgenannt, Ariadna Barinova, Dmitry Ilvovsky, and Ekaterina Chernyak. 2019. Creation and evaluation of datasets for distributional semantics tasks in the digital humanities domain. *arXiv preprint arXiv:1903.02671*.

Towards Bootstrapping a Chatbot on Industrial Heritage through Term and Relation Extraction

Mihael Arcan, Rory O'Halloran, Cécile Robin and Paul Buitelaar
Insight SFI Research Centre for Data Analytics,
Data Science Institute, University of Galway
firstname.lastname@insight-centre.org

Abstract

We describe initial work in developing a methodology for the automatic generation of a conversational agent or 'chatbot' through term and relation extraction from a relevant corpus of language data. We develop our approach in the domain of industrial heritage in the 18th and 19th centuries, and more specifically on the industrial history of canals and mills in Ireland. We collected a corpus of relevant newspaper reports and Wikipedia articles, which we deemed representative of a layman's understanding of this topic. We used the Saffron toolkit to extract relevant terms and relations between the terms from the corpus and leveraged the extracted knowledge to query the British Library Digital Collection and the Project Gutenberg library. We leveraged the extracted terms and relations in identifying possible answers for a constructed set of questions based on the extracted terms, by matching them with sentences in the British Library Digital Collection and the Project Gutenberg library. In a final step, we then took this data set of question-answer pairs to train a chatbot. We evaluate our approach by manually assessing the appropriateness of the generated answers for a random sample, each of which is judged by four annotators.

1 Introduction

Conversational agents or 'chatbots' are a convenient way of making information available, as can be witnessed from the significant growth of chatbots used in all kinds of settings, from banks to public services.[1] Also in cultural heritage settings, chatbots are now being employed more and more to interact with visitors to websites and virtual exhibitions.[2] Although frameworks such as Rasa (Bocklisch et al., 2017) enable the development of sophisticated chatbots that allow for fluent dialogue, an important bottleneck is in collecting and defining the training data for such systems. Training data comes in the form of 'intent-question' pairs, for example: `order` - *Are you open*?; *Can I order*?; *Will you deliver*. The definition and collection of such training data for any given application domain are challenging and costly, in particular for more specific and content-rich topics such as in cultural heritage settings. The range of possible intents will be significantly larger and more varied than in typical commercial settings such as ordering products or services. We, therefore, explore the use of term and relation extraction from a relevant corpus of language data as a bootstrapping step in identifying relevant concepts that can serve as intents.

Figure 1: Example of a "mill race" or "mill run" that was used to provide continuous water power to mills (image: author).

In this paper, we describe our work towards developing a methodology where we focus on term and relation extraction for end-to-end text gener-

[1] https://www.marketsandmarkets.com/Market-Reports/smart-advisor-market-72302363.html

[2] https://pro.europeana.eu/page/culture-chatbot

The 2nd International Workshop on Natural Language Processing for Digital Humanities (NLP4DH), pages 108–122
November 20, 2022.

Galway Advertiser	The Journal	Buildings of Ireland	History of Ireland
Galway Educate Together	The Irish Times	Stormontfield Heritage	Galway Library
Irish Waterway History	Clifden Heritage	This is Galway	Galway.net
National Archives	Galway Museum	Wikipedia	

Table 1: Identified online resources related to the city of Galway.

ation. This allows us to be independent of the existing resources needed to train a conversational agent. We develop our approach in the domain of industrial heritage, and more specifically on the industrial history of canals and mills in Ireland.

2 Related Work

Term extraction for conversational agents was presented by Pereira et al. (2019) and applied for customer service dialogue in the FinTech domain. The authors provide insights on term extraction for automatic generation of taxonomies from customer service dialogue data, which can contribute to the conversational agent use case by taking advantage of existing dialogues between customers and agents as learning data about the domain. Similarly, Atzori et al. (2017) create a recommender system within the travel domain, leveraging lightweight access through chatbots to support travellers during their holiday stay.

Huang et al. (2007) presents an approach for extracting question-answer pairs as chat knowledge from online discussion forums to train a chatbot for a certain domain. The authors use an SVM classifier to identify and rank relevant question-answer pairs based on content similarity. Domain-specific terms have been identified as a key part of understanding user requests in chatbot interaction (Mohapatra et al., 2018).

Chao et al. (2021) study chatbot development using a systematic patent analytic approach. They apply text-mining techniques, including document term frequency analysis for key terminology extractions, a clustering method for identifying the subdomains, and Latent Dirichlet Allocation (LDA) for finding the key topics of a patent set.

Abu-Shawar and Atwell (2016) focus on transforming corpora to a specific chatbot format, which is used to retrain a chatbot system. For this task, the authors use different dialogue corpora, i.e., such as the British National Corpus of English (BNC) and the Quran, which is a monologue corpus where verse and following verse are turns. The main goal of this automation process is the ability to generate different chatbot prototypes that communicate in different languages based on the corpus.

In contrast to previous work, our approach does not leverage classification methods to align a question to a predefined intent or answer, respectively. Additionally, leveraging term and relation extraction on a relevant corpus of language data, our approach is not limited to existing resources, such as the Ubuntu Dialogue Corpus (Lowe et al., 2015), data sets drawn from Twitter (Ritter et al., 2010) or Reddit (Roller et al., 2021), needed to train a conversational agent.

3 Data

This section provides insights on the resources used to build a chatbot in the domain of industrial heritage in the 18th and 19th centuries, i.e. the Galway Data Set, British Library Digital Collection and the Project Gutenberg library.

3.1 Galway Data Set

For our work, we initially leveraged 14 online resources to extract the required data for term and relation extraction in the domain of industrial heritage (see Table 1). In addition to online resources, we also leverage Wikipedia,[3] a freely available encyclopaedia that is built by a collaborative effort of voluntary contributors, to further increase the data set for term and relation extraction.

3.2 British Library Digital Collection

The British Library Digital Collection (BLDC) includes a collection of digitised books created by the British Library. This is a collection of books that have been digitised and processed using Optical Character Recognition (OCR) software to make the text machine-readable. We used the Curatr online platform (cf. Section 5.2) to access BLDC to retrieve a corpus in the domain of industrial heritage.[4]

[3] https://en.wikipedia.org/

[4] See Appendix A.1 for the list of digitised books used in this work.

3.3 Project Gutenberg library

Project Gutenberg[5] is the oldest digital library founded in 1971 and aims to digitise and archive cultural works. Most of the items in its collection are the full texts of books or individual stories in the public domain. All files can be accessed for free under an open format layout, which stores more than 50,000 items in its collection. Most items are in the English language, but many non-English works are also available. There are multiple affiliated projects that provide additional content, including region- and language-specific works. We selected 100 items from the Project Gutenberg library that represent the 18th and the 19th century.[6]

4 Methodology

Within our work, we first leverage the Galway data set to extract most relevant terms and relations between them in the domain of industrial heritage. We use these terms and relations in the next step to extract sentences from the BLDC and the Project Gutenberg corpus containing these terms and relations.

4.1 Term Extraction

For our initial step in extracting the most relevant terms within the targeted domain, we leveraged the identified online resources and collected documents relating to the city of Galway. Once the documents were collected, we employ the Saffron framework[7] (see Section 5.1) to extract the 100 most relevant terms from the collected documents, with a maximum term length of four words. Candidate term retrieval is the first step in the term extraction process. Saffron extracts potential candidate terms using noun phrase extraction, which are filtered based on term length, as specified in the configuration.

After selecting candidate terms, Saffron evaluates their relevance to the domain and ranks them accordingly from the most relevant to the least relevant. Saffron uses a combination of scoring functions calculated for each of the candidate terms. It combines functions, such as `comboBasic`, `totalTfIdf`, `cValue` and `residualIdf` (Astrakhantsev, 2018), which are based on occurrence frequencies. More in detail, we leverage frequencies of candidate terms across the documents or occurrences as part of other candidate terms, and that are based on reference corpora, i.e., comparing occurrences in the data set versus a generic reference data set ("weirdness" function, with Wikipedia being used as reference corpus). Finally, a voting algorithm (Zhang et al., 2008) is then used to combine the functions.

The final set of terms is selected from the original list of candidate terms after ranking, by filtering the top 100 terms of the list.

4.2 Relation Extraction

In the next step, we first parsed the initial data set and extracted the dependencies between tokens by the usage of the Stanza[8] dependency parser (Qi et al., 2020). We retrieved the dependencies where the extracted terms were identified with their relation, e.g. `subj(flow, water)`. Finally, we identified triples, where two terms are linked through a relation. As an example, from the extracted dependencies `subj(leave, canal)` and `obj(leave, river)` we construct the triple `subj_obj(canal, leave, river)`.

4.3 Conversational Data Set Creation

In the final step, the extracted terms and the relations were used to query the BLDC corpus and the Project Gutenberg library to obtain a more relevant data to train the chatbot system. With this, we obtained four different data sets, i.e.:

- subject or object term data set: A subject or object term has to be present in the sentence from the BLDC and the Project Gutenberg corpus.
- subject and object term data set: The subject and the object term of the same triple have to be present in the sentence from the BLDC and the Project Gutenberg corpus.
- subject or object term and relation data set: The subject or object term with its relation within the same triple have to be present in the sentence from the BLDC Corpus or the Project Gutenberg corpus.
- concatenated corpus: A weighted corpus of the sub-corpora mentioned above is generated.

The final data set to train the chatbot is derived from the Galway data set, the BLDC and the

[5] https://www.gutenberg.org/

[6] See Appendix A.2 for the list of item used in this work.

[7] https://saffron.insight-centre.org/

[8] https://stanfordnlp.github.io/stanza/

	lines	Questions		Answers	
		tokens	types	tokens	types
subject or object term	659,433	3,062,197	120	29,964,660	123,381
subject and object term	70,584	570,689	114	4,088,592	41,944
subject or object term and relation	4,010	25,355	132	246,759	19,124
concatenated corpus	729,636	3,595,795	164	33,542,445	123,052

Table 2: Statistics on extracted question-sentence pairs based on the extracted terms and relations.

Question pattern	Term(s)	Relation	Term(s) embedded within a Question
What is a TERM?	canal	/	What is a canal?
Tell me about a TERM	staircase	/	Tell me about a staircase
I'm interested in TERM	steam engine	/	I'm interested in steam engine
Was TERM used in Galway?	gate used	/	Was lock gate used in Ireland?
What was TERM used for?	mill	/	What was mill used for?
What is the relation between SUBJECT-TERM and OBJECT-TERM?	chamber, gate	/	What is the relation between a chamber and a gate?
What does a SUBJECT-TERM PREDICATE?	bridge	cross	What does a bridge cross?

Table 3: Examples of question patterns and the extracted terms and relations embedded within a question.

Project Gutenberg corpus, which represents a broad overview of the industrial environment of late 18th and 19th century Ireland. As discussed, from the collected documents, key terms and relations between them were identified using the knowledge extraction framework Saffron and the dependency parser Stanza. The terms and relations serve as a means of extracting high-relevance sentences that inform the chatbot's proficiency. This resulted in 659,433 relevant sentences (Table 2), which contained at least one of the extracted terms. We used 90% of the sentences for training and 10% for validation (development set) purposes. We filter this corpus based on subject and object terms in combination with the relation that appeared in the sentence, resulting in four sub-corpora for chatbot generation. From the held-out evaluation set, 50 sentences were randomly selected for manual evaluation by the four annotators.

4.4 Question Generation

As end-to-end chatbots are trained based on question-answer pairs, we use the extracted terms and relations for the question part and embed them within manually defined questions. As an example, the extracted term *canal* would become *What is a canal?* Table 3 shows the patterns used to construct the questions needed to train the chatbot. Using the OpenNMT toolkit (Section 5.3), the chatbot learns to properly respond to a question through the identified sentences, which contains the relevant (extracted) terms and relations.

5 Experimental Setup

In this section, we give an overview of the Saffron framework used for term and relation extraction. We leverage these terms to query the BLDC corpus through the Curatr online platform. Furthermore, we provide information on OpenNMT and the architecture of the trained sequence-to-sequence neural network. Finally, we provide insights on the evaluation approach.

5.1 Term Extraction with Saffron

Term extraction was performed with the knowledge extraction framework Saffron. This open-source tool allows us to extract terms (i.e. multi-word expressions) of the domain of the corpus, i.e. here the industrial history of canals and mills. Several parameters can be specified, such as N, the number of terms extracted, which we set up to 100 in order to cover a range of various terms (Bordea et al., 2013). The minimum and the maximum length of the terms can be determined, which we set to one and four words, in order to obtain generic terms (e.g. *canal*) as well as more specific ones (e.g. *mill race*).

5.2 Curatr

Curatr[9] is an online platform providing access to the British Library Digital Collection. The platform hosts digitised versions of all English-language books from the British Library collection, corresponding to over thirty-five thousand unique titles, from 1700 to 1899. The data collection consists of over forty-six thousand unique volumes of text.

The system enables queries on the equivalent of over 12 million individual pages of text, which can be searched and sorted by author, title, year, and the actual full-text of the volumes themselves. This allows us to identify content relating to specific themes within little known or very long, unwieldy texts.

As Curatr supports the creation and export of smaller sub-corpora, we used it to filter the entire collection to produce a much smaller set of texts for closer inspection. We used the terms `mills` and `canals` to retrieve a corpus in the domain of industrial heritage in the 18th and 19th centuries.

5.3 Text Generation

The neural models for text generation were performed with the OpenNMT toolkit (Klein et al., 2017). We used the transform-based network with its default setting. The network used a six-layer encoder-decoder model with the attention mechanism enabled (Vaswani et al., 2017). To cover the entire vocabulary of the training set, we use sentencepiece to split the words into subword units. The training approach uses a batch size of 4,096, leveraging the ADAM optimiser (Kingma and Ba, 2015). We set the word embeddings' size to 500, and hidden layers to size 500, dropout = 0.1, respectively. We used a maximum sentence length of 50.

5.4 Evaluation Approach

The evaluation of responses of open-domain conversational agents, such as chatbots, is still an open question (Liu et al., 2016) since a variety of answers can be considered as correct. Therefore, we randomly selected 50 question-term pairs (out of the 100 pairs of the evaluation set) and evaluated manually the generated answers. Following the error classes by (Coughlin, 2003), four volunteers were assessing the chatbot's responses to the questions into three classes:

- Unacceptable = 1. Absolutely not comprehensible and/or little or no information generated accurately.
- Possibly Acceptable = 2. Possibly comprehensible (given enough context and/or time to work it out); some information generated accurately.
- Acceptable = 3. Not perfect (stylistically or grammatically odd), but definitely comprehensible, AND with all important information generated accurately.

In addition to the manual evaluation, we analysed the Inter Annotation Agreement (IAA) between the four annotators. For this, the Fleiss' Kappa (Fleiss et al., 1971) was calculated (Equation 1). P (actual agreement) and P_e (expected agreement) measure the reliability of agreement between a fixed number of annotators when assigning categorical ratings to several items or classifying items.

$$\kappa = \frac{P - P_e}{1 - P_e} \quad (1)$$

6 Results and Discussion

In this section, we present the evaluation results of generated answers and provide some further insights into the challenges of generating accurate responses.

6.1 Evaluation Results

Table 4 illustrates the manual evaluation of the 50 automatically generated answers. All annotators marked each answer either as *unacceptable* (1), *possible acceptable* (2) or *acceptable* (3). The scores from the annotation campaign range from 1.30 to 2.54. As seen from the table, the annotators evaluated the responses generated from the `subject and object term` training set with the highest score, an average of 2.40. The answers generated from the training set `concatenated corpus` were annotated with the lowest scores. The chatbot trained on `subject and object term` benefits from various generated questions containing two relevant terms, while all other corpora contain more

[9] `http://erdos.ucd.ie/curatr/about`

	Annotator 1	Annotator 2	Annotator 3	Annotator 4	Average
`subject or object term`	2.20	2.00	1.92	1.64	1.94
`subject and object term`	2.54	2.46	2.24	2.34	2.40
`subject/object term and relation`	1.52	1.56	1.92	1.38	1.60
`concatenated corpus`	1.34	1.54	1.64	1.30	1.46

Table 4: The evaluation scores of each annotator, based on the 50 automatically generated answers with its average score.

	κ
`subject or object term`	0.21
`subject and object term`	0.33
`subject/object term and relation`	0.36
`concatenated corpus`	0.41

Table 5: Annotator agreement scores based on the quality of the generated answers.

general questions with only one term or the combination of a term and its relation, depending on if terms and relations were used to extract the sentences.

Inter Annotator Agreement Due to the annotation approach with four annotators, we calculated the Fleiss' κ score based on the evaluation of the quality of the generated answers. Table 5 shows the different scores for each of the different corpora the chatbot was trained on. The annotators achieved a fair agreement[10] evaluating the first three corpora, and moderate agreement[11] (Fleiss et al., 1971) evaluating the chatbot's answers trained on the `concatenated corpus`.

6.2 Discussion

As mentioned before, the evaluation of an open-domain chatbot is still an open challenge, as various answers can be considered as correct. In a manual analysis of the chatbot's responses, we observed meaningful answers across all different data sets. Nevertheless, the first two examples in Table 6, *Tell me about a cotton and a sawmill*) and *What is the relation between a gate and a river*, illustrate examples, where the system did not provide a meaningful answers. While the first example only gives answer related to one term, i.e., *sawmill*. Although both terms are present in the generated answer, the second example demonstrates an incomprehensible answer where additional information is missing in the sentence. The third example illustrates the lexical ambiguity of the word *lock*.[12] Whereas the desired answer relating to the *enclosure consisting of a section of canal*, the chatbot generates an answer with the meaning of *a fastener fitted to a door*.

Analysing the remaining examples in Table 6, i.e., *What is the relation between a log and water?* or *What is the relation between a lumber and a mill*, the chatbot provided acceptable responses. For the former example, the chatbot provides the information on switching the transport of *logs* from *water* to railroads, while for the latter, the system generates a meaningful explanation that *logs* were cut into *lumber* by a *mill*.

7 Conclusion and Future Work

We described an approach towards the bootstrapping of a chatbot in the cultural domain through the application of readily available tools for term and relation extraction and natural language generation. The evaluation shows that the end-to-end neural model produces acceptable results when asking questions about the industrial heritage of the 18th and 19th centuries. Nevertheless, the approach does require more extension and refinement to be useful for automatic chatbot development. The current limitations of the approach are in data collection, term and relation extraction and eval-

[10] fair agreement = 0.21 – 0.40

[11] moderate agreement = 0.41 – 0.60

[12] from Princeton WordNet, 1: a fastener fitted to a door or drawer to keep it firmly closed, 2: enclosure consisting of a section of canal that can be closed to control the water level; used to raise or lower vessels that pass through it. `http://wordnetweb.princeton.edu/perl/webwn?s=lock`

Question #1	Tell me about a cotton and a sawmill
Generated Answer	A sawmill or lumber mill is a facility where logs are cut into lumber.
Question #2	What is the relation between a gate and a river?
Generated Answer	On the clare side of the river, at the foot of thomond gate 587 limerick.
Question #3	Tell me about a city and a lock
Generated Answer	287 the gates of the city to be put in repair with locks and keys
Question #4	What is the relation between a log and water?
Generated Answer	Availability of railroad transportation for logs and lumber encouraged building of rail mills away from navigable water.
Question #5	What is the relation between a lumber and a paper?
Generated Answer	The larger pieces of wood that wo n't make lumber are chipped into wood chips and provide a source of supply for paper mills.
Question #6	What is the relation between a lumber and a mill?
Generated Answer	A sawmill or lumber mill is a facility where logs are cut into lumber.
Question #7	What is the relation between a boat and a wheel?
Generated Answer	[25] these floating mills had a wheel that was attached to a boat moored in a fast flowing river.
Question #8	Tell me about a machine and water
Generated Answer	The water power could be used for driving the splint and box-making machines.
Question #9	Tell me about a lock and water
Generated Answer	The lock is filled with water from upstream.

Table 6: Examples of questions and the generated answers from the best performing model.

uation. In particular, our current data set consists only of a small number of contemporary documents of general but not of specific relevance to the application under consideration, i.e. industrial heritage of Ireland in the 18th and 19th centuries. Instead, in future work, we want to focus on data collection in digital libraries on contemporary as well as historical documents specifically on topics that are of direct relevance to this application context. While we extracted relevant terms and relations in the targeted domain, these terms are mostly single-word terms. Therefore, we are planning to focus on extracting more multi-word terms, which will help us to identify relevant sentences for training the chatbot system. Further, the generation of questions based on the extracted terms and relations is currently limited to a template-based approach. We envision that the inclusion of neural models, such as `Text-To-Text Transfer Transformer` (T5) (Raffel et al., 2020) will generate better natural language questions. Furthermore, we plan to incorporate multi-modal approaches, i.e. incorporating images within the chatbot, for visual representation as well as for disambiguation approaches. Finally, we would like to include relevant historical expertise to better inform our approach from the use case perspective.

Acknowledgements

This publication has emanated from research conducted with the financial support of Science Foundation Ireland under Grant number SFI/12/RC/2289_P2. For the purpose of Open Access, the author has applied a CC BY public copyright licence to any Author Accepted Manuscript version arising from this submission.

References

Bayan Abu-Shawar and Eric Atwell. 2016. Automatic extraction of chatbot training data from natural dialogue corpora. In *RE-WOCHAT: Workshop on Collecting and Generating Resources for Chatbots and Conversational Agents-Development and Evaluation, Portoroz, Slovenia.*

Nikita Astrakhantsev. 2018. Atr4s: toolkit with state-of-the-art automatic terms recognition methods in scala. *Language Resources and Evaluation*, 52(3):853–872.

Maurizio Atzori, Ludovico Boratto, and Lucio Davide Spano. 2017. Towards chatbots as recommendation interfaces. In *Proceedings of the Second Workshop on Engineering Computer-Human Interaction in Recommender Systems co-located with the 9th ACM SIGCHI Symposium on Engineering Interactive Computing Systems (EICS 2017), Lisbon, Portugal, June 26, 2017*, volume 1945 of *CEUR Workshop Proceedings*, pages 26–31. CEUR-WS.org.

Tom Bocklisch, Joey Faulkner, Nick Pawlowski, and Alan Nichol. 2017. Rasa: Open source language understanding and dialogue management.

Georgeta Bordea, Paul Buitelaar, and Tamara Polajnar. 2013. Domain-independent term extraction through domain modelling. In *Proceedings of the 10th International Conference on Terminology and Artificial Intelligence (TIA 2013)*.

Min-Hua Chao, Amy J. C. Trappey, Chun-Ting Wu, and Abd E.I.-Baset Hassanien. 2021. Emerging technologies of natural language-enabled chatbots: A review and trend forecast using intelligent ontology extraction and patent analytics. volume 2021, USA. John Wiley & Sons, Inc.

Deborah Coughlin. 2003. Correlating automated and human assessments of machine translation quality. In *In Proceedings of MT Summit IX*, pages 63–70.

J.L. Fleiss et al. 1971. Measuring nominal scale agreement among many raters. *Psychological Bulletin*, 76(5):378–382.

Jizhou Huang, Ming Zhou, and Dan Yang. 2007. Extracting chatbot knowledge from online discussion forums. In *IJCAI*, volume 7, pages 423–428.

Diederik P. Kingma and Jimmy Ba. 2015. Adam: A method for stochastic optimization. In *3rd International Conference on Learning Representations, ICLR 2015, San Diego, CA, USA, May 7-9, 2015, Conference Track Proceedings*.

Guillaume Klein, Yoon Kim, Yuntian Deng, Jean Senellart, and Alexander M. Rush. 2017. OpenNMT: Open-Source Toolkit for Neural Machine Translation. *Proceedings of the 55th Annual Meeting of the Association for Computational Linguistics*, System Demonstrations:67–72.

Chia-Wei Liu, Ryan Lowe, Iulian Serban, Mike Noseworthy, Laurent Charlin, and Joelle Pineau. 2016. How NOT to evaluate your dialogue system: An empirical study of unsupervised evaluation metrics for dialogue response generation. In *Proceedings of the 2016 Conference on Empirical Methods in Natural Language Processing*, pages 2122–2132, Austin, Texas. Association for Computational Linguistics.

Ryan Lowe, Nissan Pow, Iulian Serban, and Joelle Pineau. 2015. The Ubuntu dialogue corpus: A large dataset for research in unstructured multi-turn dialogue systems. In *Proceedings of the 16th Annual Meeting of the Special Interest Group on Discourse and Dialogue*, pages 285–294, Prague, Czech Republic. Association for Computational Linguistics.

Prateeti Mohapatra, Yu Deng, Abhirut Gupta, Gargi Dasgupta, Amit Paradkar, Ruchi Mahindru, Daniela Rosu, Shu Tao, and Pooja Aggarwal. 2018. Domain knowledge driven key term extraction for it services. In *International Conference on Service-Oriented Computing*, pages 489–504. Springer.

Bianca Pereira, Cecile Robin, Tobias Daudert, John P. McCrae, Pranab Mohanty, and Paul Buitelaar. 2019. Taxonomy extraction for customer service knowledge base construction. In *Semantic Systems. The Power of AI and Knowledge Graphs*, pages 175–190, Cham. Springer International Publishing.

Peng Qi, Yuhao Zhang, Yuhui Zhang, Jason Bolton, and Christopher D. Manning. 2020. Stanza: A Python natural language processing toolkit for many human languages. In *Proceedings of the 58th Annual Meeting of the Association for Computational Linguistics: System Demonstrations*.

Colin Raffel, Noam Shazeer, Adam Roberts, Katherine Lee, Sharan Narang, Michael Matena, Yanqi Zhou, Wei Li, and Peter J. Liu. 2020. Exploring the limits of transfer learning with a unified text-to-text transformer. *Journal of Machine Learning Research*, 21(140):1–67.

Alan Ritter, Colin Cherry, and Bill Dolan. 2010. Unsupervised modeling of Twitter conversations. In *Human Language Technologies: The 2010 Annual Conference of the North American Chapter of the Association for Computational Linguistics*, pages 172–180, Los Angeles, California. Association for Computational Linguistics.

Stephen Roller, Emily Dinan, Naman Goyal, Da Ju, Mary Williamson, Yinhan Liu, Jing Xu, Myle Ott, Eric Michael Smith, Y-Lan Boureau, and Jason Weston. 2021. Recipes for building an open-domain chatbot. In *Proceedings of the 16th Conference of the European Chapter of the Association for Computational Linguistics: Main Volume*, pages 300–325, Online. Association for Computational Linguistics.

Ashish Vaswani, Noam Shazeer, Niki Parmar, Jakob Uszkoreit, Llion Jones, Aidan N Gomez, Łukasz Kaiser, and Illia Polosukhin. 2017. Attention is all you need. In *Advances in Neural Information Processing Systems*, pages 5998–6008.

Ziqi Zhang, Jose Iria, Christopher Brewster, and Fabio Ciravegna. 2008. A comparative evaluation of term recognition algorithms. In *Proceedings of the Sixth International Conference on Language Resources and Evaluation (LREC'08)*, Marrakech, Morocco. European Language Resources Association (ELRA).

A Appendices

A.1 British National Library Collection

	Title	Author(s)	Published
1	Kilkenny City and County Guide and Directory, etc. With a map.	Bassett, George Henry	1884
2	County Down Guide and Directory, including the borough of Newry, etc. With a map.	Bassett, George Henry	1886
3	The Book of Antrim. A manual and directory, etc. With a map.	Bassett, George Henry	1888
4	The Book of County Armagh. A manual and directory, etc. With a map.	Bassett, George Henry	1888
5	The history and antiquities of Tallaght, County Dublin	Handcock, William Domville	1877
6	The Post Chaise Companion ... By R. Lewis or William Wilson. The 3d edition, corrected and enlarged, with an entire new set of plates	Lewis, R., Wilson, William	1803
7	The Old Bridge of Athlone	Joly, John Swift	1881
8	The Post Chaise Companion ... By R. Lewis? or W. Wilson. The 4th edition, corrected and enlarged, with an entire new set of plates	Lewis, R., Wilson, William	1820
9	Ancient Naas. Extracted from the "Journal of the County Kildare Archæological Society."	De Burgh, Thomas J.	1895
10	The Ancient and Modern History of the Maritime Ports of Ireland	Marmion, Anthony	1855
11	The Ancient and Modern History of the Maritime Ports of Ireland.	Marmion, Anthony	1860
12	History of the Rise and Progress of Belfast, and Annals of the County Antrim, etc	Pilson, James Adair	1846
13	A Short Topographical and statistical account of the Bandon Union; with some observations on the trade, agriculture, manufactures and tideways of the district. With a map.	Spillar, William A.	1844
14	The Book of County Tipperary. A manual and directory, etc. With a map.	Bassett, George Henry	1889
15	History of Sligo, county and town, from the earliest ages to the close of the reign of Queen Elizabeth (to the present time). With illustrations, etc	Martin, William Gregory Wood	1882
16	Sights and Scenes in our Fatherland	Lacy, Thomas	1863
17	The Irish Commercial and Railway Gazetteer, showing every town and railway station in Ireland, alphabetically arranged, with county, distance from Dublin, etc	Leggatt, John E.	1879
18	Rigby's Illustrated Guide to Belfast and the North of Ireland	Rigby, Thomas	1895
19	How to spend a month in Ireland, and what it will cost	Roney, Cusack Patrick	1861
20	The new Hand-Book of Ireland; an illustrated guide for tourists and travellers	Walker, John A., Godkin, James	1871
21	Corporation. The Council Book of the Corporation of Youghal ... Edited from the original, with annals and appendices ... by R. Caulfield. With plates, etc.	Caulfield, Richard	1878

22	The Council Book of the Corporation of Kinsale, from 1652 to 1800. Illustrated. ... Edited from the original, with annals and appendices compiled from public and private records, by R. Caulfield	Caulfield, Richard	1879
23	The History of the Two Ulster Manors of Finagh, in the County of Tyrone, and Coole, otherwise Manor Atkinson, in the County of Fermanagh, and of their owners	Corry, Somerset Richard Lowry	1881
24	Limerick: its history and antiquities, ecclesiastical, civil, and military, from the earliest ages, with copious historical, archæological, topographical, and genealogical notes and illustrations; maps, plates, and appendices, etc	Lenihan, Maurice	1866
25	Guide to the most picturesque tour in Western Europe. Embracing the ... Lakes ... of Killarney, Glengarriff, ... Blarney, etc	Unknown	1888
26	Descriptive particulars of portions of the estates of the late J. Sadlier, situate in the counties of Tipperary and Limerick, and comprising, amongst others, the ... the demesne of Kilcommon, Cahir Castle, etc	Sadleir, John	1857
27	The Irish Sketch-book ... Second edition. , The Irish Sketch-Book	Thackeray, William Makepeace	1857
28	The West of Ireland: its existing condition, and prospects. Letters originally published in "Saunders's News-Letter." With plates and maps.	Coulter, Henry	1862
29	The history of the County and City of Cork	Gibson, Charles Bernard	1861
30	History of Enniscorthy, etc	Flood, William Henry Grattan	1898
31	Limerick and its Sieges ... Illustrated	Dowd, James	1890
32	"Devia Hibernia." The road and route guide for Ireland of the Royal Irish Constabulary. Compiled and edited by G. A. de M. E. Dagg. With a map.	Dagg, George Amyrald De Montmorency Edwin	1893
33	Official Tourist Guide of the Dublin, Wicklow, and Wexford Railway. Illustrated. Compiled by A. T. Hennessy	Hennessy, A. T.	1895
34	The History of the Town of Belfast with ... a statistical survey of the parish of Belfast, etc. By George Benn. , Appendix	Benn, George	1823
35	The Irish Sketch-book ... Second edition. , The Irish Sketch-Book	Thackeray, William Makepeace	1886
36	Guy's South of Ireland Pictorial Guide, etc	Unknown	1890
37	A Narrative of an Excursion to Ireland, by the Deputy Governor, two members of the Court, and the Assistant Secretary, of the Honorable Irish Society, of London. 1825. By the Deputy Governor i.e. Gilpin Gorst , Appendix. II. Miscellaneous	Gorst, Gilpin	1825
38	Picturesque guide to the Lakes of Killarney	Unknown	1851
39	Ancient and modern Sketches of the County Westmeath: historical, traditional, and legendary	Woods, James	1890
40	Here and there through Ireland ... With illustrations ... Reprinted from the "Weekly Freeman."	Banim, Mary	1891
41	Irish Pictures drawn with pen and pencil, etc	Lovett, Richard	1888
42	The Handbook for Youghal, containing an account of St. Mary's Collegiate Church. With the Historical Annals of the Town. (Third Series.) By S. Hayman.	Unknown	1852

43	History of Sligo, county and town, from the earliest ages to the close of the reign of Queen Elizabeth (to the present time). With illustrations, etc	Martin, William Gregory Wood	1882
44	Ireland. Revised edition. With a map of Ireland.	Browning, Walter Westcott	1884
45	Reminiscences of my Irish Journey in 1849. With a preface by J. A. Froude. , Single Works. Reminiscences of my Irish Journey	Carlyle, Thomas	1882
46	A History of the City of Dublin	Gilbert, John Thomas	1854
47	Illustrated Handbook to Cork, the Lakes of Killarney, and the South of Ireland ... From the Irish Tourists' Handbook or rather "The Tourists' Illustrated Handbook for Ireland" , Appendix	Unknown	1859
48	The Irish Sketch-book ... Second edition, The Irish Sketch-Book	Thackeray, William Makepeace	1845
49	The history and antiquities of the county of the town of Carrickfergus, etc.	Macskimin, Samuel	1823
50	The County and City of Cork Remembrancer; or, Annals of the county and city of Cork, etc	Tuckey, Francis H.	1837
51	Historical Sketches of Monaghan, from the earliest records to the Fenian movement	Rushe, Denis Carolan	1895
52	The City of Cork, how it may be improved. Lecture, etc. With a view and plan.	Walker, Robert	1883
53	The Irish Tourist's illustrated handbook for visitors to Ireland in 1852. Second edition	Unknown	1852
54	Two trips to the Emerald Isle. By "Faed" ... Illustrated, etc	Unknown	1888
55	Guide to North of Ireland, Giant's Causeway and Belfast, with history of Belfast	Aickin, Robert	1890
56	Trim: its ecclesiastical ruins, its castle, etc. By Edward Evans.	Evans, Edward	1886
57	Guy's South of Ireland Pictorial Guide, etc	Guy	1891
58	An Improved Topographical and Historical Hibernian Gazetteer ... Scientifically arranged, with an appendix of ancient names. To which is added, an introduction to the ancient and modern History of Ireland	Hansbrow, G.	1835
59	Queenstown and the Places around Cork Harbour. A handy guide, etc	Unknown	1895
60	The new Hand-book for Youghal: containing notes and records of the ancient religious foundations, and the historical annals of the town. Fourth series	Hayman, Samuel	1858
61	A Tour in Ireland, in 1813 and 1814 ... By an Englishman i.e. J. G.?	Gough, John	1817
62	The Saxon in Ireland: or, the rambles of an Englishman in search of a settlement in the West of Ireland. By John Henry Ashworth.	Ashworth, John Hervey	1851
63	The Shannon and its Lakes; or, a short history of that noble stream from its source to Limerick	Harvey, R.	1896
64	Popular Traditions of Glasgow: historical, legendary and biographical	Wallace, Andrew	1889
65	Notes and Gleanings relating to the County of Wexford, in its past and present conditions	Doyle, Martin	1868

66	Mellifont Abbey, Co. Louth: its ruins and associations. A guide and popular history. With illustrations.	Unknown	1897
67	Guide to Ireland. With illustrations. , Appendix. II. Miscellaneous	Unknown	1898
68	The Irish Sketch-book ... Second edition, The Irish Sketch-Book	Thackeray, William Makepeace	1845
69	The History of Dundalk, and its environs; from the earliest period to the present time; with memoirs of its eminent men. With plates and maps.	O'flanagan, James Roderick, D'alton, John	1864
70	Ireland, as I saw it: the character, condition, and prospects of the people	Balch, William S.	1850
71	Here and there through Ireland ... With illustrations ... Reprinted from the "Weekly Freeman."	Banim, Mary	1891
72	Guide to Ireland. (Second edition.) With illustrations. , Appendix. II. Miscellaneous	Unknown	1899
73	Lough Corrib, its shores and islands: with notices of Lough Mask ... Illustrated, etc	Wilde, William Robert Wills	1867
74	Rambling Recollections of Old Glasgow. By "Nestor."	Unknown	1880
75	The Sunny Side of Ireland. How to see it by the Great Southern and Western Railway ... With seven maps and over 130 illustrations, etc	O'mahony, John	1898
76	John Bull and his Other Island	Bennett, Arthur	1890
77	Ierne; or, Anecdotes and incidents during a Life in Ireland, with notices of people and places. First series, Appendix. II. Miscellaneous	Unknown	1861
78	The History of Bandon, and the principal towns in the West Riding of County Cork. Enlarged edition, with ... illustrations and a portrait	Bennett, George	1869
79	Dignam's Dublin Guide. With a handy map, etc	Dignam, James	1891
80	Ireland: its health resorts and watering places. With maps, etc	Flinn, David Edgar	1888
81	Three Months' Tour in Ireland ... Translated and condensed by Mrs. Arthur Walter. With illustrations, Trois mois en Irlande	Walter, Arthur, Bovet, Marie Anne De	1891
82	Through the Green Isle; a gossiping guide to the districts traversed by the Waterford, Limerick and Western Railway system ... Illustrated, etc	Hurley, M. J.	1895
83	The Council Book of the Corporation of the City of Cork, from 1609 to 1643, and from 1690 to 1800. Edited ... with annals and appendices ... by Richard Caufield	Caulfield, Richard	1876
84	Picturesque Scenery in Ireland drawn by T. Creswick. ... With descriptive jottings by a Tourist	Creswick, Thomas	1873
85	Pococke's Tour in Ireland in 1752. Edited, with an introduction and notes, by G. T. Stokes	Stokes, George Thomas, Pococke, Richard	1891
86	The South Isles of Aran, County Galway	Burke, Oliver Joseph	1887
87	The Council Book of the Corporation of the City of Cork, from 1609 to 1643, and from 1690 to 1800. Edited ... with annals and appendices ... by Richard Caufield	Caulfield, Richard	1876
88	A Fortnight in Ireland. Second edition	Head, Francis Bond	1852
89	A Fortnight in Ireland	Head, Francis Bond	1852

90	The Land of Eire. The Irish Land League. Its origin, progress and consequences. Preceded by a concise history of the various movements which have culminated in the last great agitation ... With a descriptive and historical account of Ireland from the earliest period to the present day. Illustrated by numerous fine engravings, etc	Devoy, John	1882
91	Historical Gleanings in Antrim and neighbourhood	Smith, William Sunderland	1888
92	An Ulster Parish: being a history of Donaghcloney, Waringstown. With plates.	Atkinson, Edward Dupré	1898
93	Irish Tourist Development. "Visit Ireland:" a concise, descriptive, and illustrated guide to Ireland. Compiled by F. W. Crossley	Crossley, F. W.	1892
94	Ulster as it is; or, twenty-eight years' experience as an Irish Editor	Macknight, Thomas	1896
95	Miscellaneous Essays on Topography, Ethnology, Language, ... contributed to the Ulster Journal of Archæology. With maps. MS. letter by the author	Hume, Abraham	1859
96	Lough Erne, Enniskillen, Belleek, Ballyshannon, and Bundoran, with routes from Dublin to Enniskillen, etc	Wakeman, William Frederick	1870
97	The history of the County and City of Cork	Gibson, Charles Bernard	1861
98	A History of the City of Dublin	Gilbert, John Thomas	1854
99	Topographical Sketches of Armagh and Tyrone ... Second edition	Rogers, Edward	1874
100	History of Sligo, county and town, from the earliest ages to the close of the reign of Queen Elizabeth (to the present time). With illustrations, etc	Martin, William Gregory Wood	1882

A.2 Project Gutenberg

	Title	Author(s)	Year
1	A Child's Dream of a Star	Charles Dickens	2013 [EBook 42232]
2	A Child's History of England	Charles Dickens	1996 [eBook 699]
3	A Christmas Carol	Charles Dickens	1992 [eBook 46]
4	A Christmas Carol	Charles Dickens	2007 [EBook 24022]
5	A Tale of Two Cities	Charles Dickens	1994 [eBook 98]
6	Adventures of Huckleberry Finn	Mark Twain (Samuel Clemens)	1993 [eBook 76]
7	The Adventures of Tom Sawyer	Mark Twain	1993 [eBook 74]
8	Alice's Adventures in Wonderland	Lewis Carroll	1991 [eBook 11]
9	American Notes for General Circulation	Charles Dickens	2013 [eBook 675]
10	Anna Karenina	Leo Tolstoy	1998 [EBook 1399]
11	An Enemy of the People	Henrik Ibsen	2000 [EBook 2446]
12	Around the World in Eighty Days	Jules Verne	1994 [eBook 103]
13	Bardell v. Pickwick	Percy Fitzgerald	2008 [eBook 25985]
14	Barnaby Rudge	Charles Dickens	2006 [EBook 917]
15	The Importance of Being Earnest	Oscar Wilde	1997 [eBook 844]
16	Bleak House	Charles Dickens	1997 [eBook 1023]
17	Youth	Joseph Conrad	1996 [EBook 525]

18	The Confidence-Man	Herman Melville	2007 [eBook 21816]
19	A Connecticut Yankee in King Arthur's Court	Mark Twain	1993 [eBook 86]
20	The Count of Monte Cristo	Alexandre Dumas	1998 [eBook 1184]
21	David Copperfield	Charles Dickens	1996 [Etext 766]
22	De Profundis	Oscar Wilde	2007 [eBook 921]
23	A Doll's House	Henrik Ibsen	2001 [eBook 2542]
24	Dombey and Son	Charles Dickens	1997 [eBook 821]
25	The Picture of Dorian Gray	Oscar Wilde	1994 [eBook 174]
26	Dracula	Bram Stoker	1995 [eBook 345]
27	Dracula's Guest	Bram Stoker	2003 [EBook 10150]
28	Emma	Jane Austen	1994 [eBook 158]
29	Frankenstein	Mary Wollstonecraft (Godwin) Shelley	1993 [eBook 84]
30	Ghosts	Henrik Ibsen	2005 [EBook 8121]
31	Great Expectations	Charles Dickens	1998 [eBook 1400]
32	Grimms' Fairy Tales	Jacob Grimm and Wilhelm Grimm	2001 [eBook 2591]
33	The Happy Prince	Oscar Wilde	1997 [eBook 902]
34	Hard Times	Charles Dickens	2013 [eBook 786]
35	Heart of Darkness	Joseph Conrad	1995 [eBook 219]
36	Hedda Gabler	Henrik Ibsen	2003 [Etext 4093]
37	The Hound of the Baskervilles	Arthur Conan Doyle	2001 [eBook 2852]
38	Hunted Down	Charles Dickens	2014 [eBook 807]
39	An Ideal Husband	Oscar Wilde	1997 [eBook 885]
40	The Innocents Abroad	Mark Twain (Samuel Clemens)	2006 [EBook 3176]
41	John Gabriel Borkman	Henrik Ibsen,Translated William Archer	2006 [eBook 18792]
42	A Journey to the Centre of the Earth	Jules Verne	2006 [EBook 18857]
43	The Lady From The Sea	Henrik Ibsen	2008 [EBook 2765]
44	The Last Man	Mary Wollstonecraft Shelley	2006 [eBook 18247]
45	Life On The Mississippi	Complete MarkTwain (Samuel Clemens)	2006 [EBook 245]
46	Little Dorrit	Charles Dickens	2008 [EBook 963]
47	Through the Looking-Glass	Charles Dodgson, AKA Lewis Carroll	1991 [eBook 12]
48	Lord Jim	Joseph Conrad	2006 [EBook 5658]
49	The Man in the Iron Mask	Alexandre Dumas, Père	2001 [eBook 2759]
50	Master and Man	Leo Tolstoy	1997 [Etext 986]
51	The Master Builder	Henrik Ibsen	2003 [Etext 4070]
52	Metamorphosis	Franz Kafka	2002 [eBook 5200]
53	Moby-Dick; or The Whale	Herman Melville	2001 [eBook 2701]
54	Nostromo: A Tale of the Seaboard	Joseph Conrad	2006 [EBook 2021]
55	Oliver Twist, illustrated	Charles Dickens	2014 [eBook 46675]
56	Oliver Twist	Charles Dickens	1996 [eBook 730]
57	Our Mutual Friend	Charles Dickens	2006 [EBook 883]
58	Persuasion	Jane Austen	2008 [EBook 105]
59	Pictures from Italy	Charles Dickens, Illustrated Marcus Stone	2013 [eBook 650]
60	Pillars of Society	Henrik Ibsen	2010 [EBook 2296]

61	The Piazza Tales	Herman Melville	2005 [eBook 15859]
62	Pride and Prejudice	Jane Austen	1998 [eBook 1342]
63	The Prince and The Pauper	Mark Twain (Samuel Clemens)	2006 [EBook 1837]
64	Rosmerholm	Henrik Ibsen	2010 [EBook 2289]
65	Best Russian Short Stories	Various	2004 [EBook 13437]
66	Sevastopol	Lyof N. Tolstoï	2014 [EBook 47197]
67	The Adventures of Sherlock Holmes	Arthur Conan Doyle	2002 [eBook 1661]
68	Sketches by Boz	Charles Dickens	1997 [eBook 882]
69	Some Christmas Stories	Charles Dickens	2015 [eBook 1467]
70	Stories of Intellect	Various	2020 [EBook 61668]
71	Tales and Stories	Mary Wollstonecraft Shelley	2018 [EBook 56665]
72	Ten Years Later	Alexandre Dumas	2001 [eBook 2681]
73	The Footpath Way	Sidney Smith, William Hazlitt, Isaak Walton, Walter Scott, et al.	2019 [eBook 59813]
74	The Great English Short-Story Writers, Vol. 1	Various, et al	2003 [eBook 10135]
75	The Collected Works of Henrik Ibsen	Henrik Ibsen	2021 [eBook 66186]
76	The Letters of Charles Dickens	Charles Dickens	2008 [EBook 25852]
77	The Life And Adventures Of Nicholas Nickleby	Charles Dickens	2006 [EBook 967]
78	The Lock and Key Library	Hawthorne, Ed.	1999 [Etext 1831]
79	The Mystery of Edwin Drood	Charles Dickens	1996 [eBook 564]
80	The Old Curiosity Shop	Charles Dickens	1996 [eBook 700]
81	The Pickwick Papers	Charles Dickens	2009 [EBook 580]
82	The Posthumous Papers of the Pickwick Club,v. 2(of 2)	Charles Dickens	2014 [EBook 47535]
83	The Uncommercial Traveller	Charles Dickens	1997 [eBook 914]
84	Pierre; or The Ambiguities	Herman Melville	2011 [eBook 34970]
85	Bartleby The Scrivener	Herman Melville	2004 [eBook 11231]
86	The Secret Agent	Joseph Conrad	1997 [eBook 974]
87	The Secret Sharer	Joseph Conrad	1995 [EBook 220]
88	The Trial	Franz Kafka	2005 [EBook 7849]
89	Three Ghost Stories	Charles Dickens	2013 [eBook 1289]
90	The Three Musketeers	Alexandre Dumas, Père	1998 [eBook 1257]
91	Twenty Thousand Leagues under the Sea	Jules Verne	1994 [eBook 164]
92	Twenty Years After	Alexandre Dumas, Père	1998 [eBook 1259]
93	Typee	Herman Melville	1999 [eBook 1900]
94	Typhoon	Joseph Conrad	2006 [EBook 1142]
95	War and Peace	Leo Tolstoy	2001 [eBook 2600]
96	What Men Live By and Other Tales	Leo Tolstoy	2004 [EBook 6157]
97	When We Dead Awaken	Henrik Ibsen	2003 [EBook 4782]
98	White-Jacket	Herman Melville	2004 [eBook 10712]

Non-Parametric Word Sense Disambiguation for Historical Languages

Enrique Manjavacas
Leiden University
Leiden, The Netherlands
enrique.manjavacas@gmail.com

Lauren Fonteyn
Leiden University
Leiden, The Netherlands
l.fonteyn@hum.leidenuniv.nl

Abstract

Recent approaches to Word Sense Disambiguation (WSD) have profited from the enhanced contextualized word representations coming from contemporary Large Language Models (LLMs). This advancement is accompanied by a renewed interest in WSD applications in Humanities research, where the lack of suitable, specific WSD-annotated resources is a hurdle in developing ad-hoc WSD systems. Because they can exploit sentential context, LLMs are particularly suited for disambiguation tasks. Still, the application of LLMs is often limited to linear classifiers trained on top of the LLM architecture. In this paper, we follow recent developments in non-parametric learning and show how LLMs can be efficiently fine-tuned to achieve strong few-shot performance on WSD for historical languages (English and Dutch, date range: 1450-1950). We test our hypothesis using (i) a large, general evaluation set taken from large lexical databases, and (ii) a small real-world scenario involving an ad-hoc WSD task. Moreover, this paper marks the release of GysBERT, a LLM for historical Dutch.

1 Introduction & Related Work

A common task in Natural Language Processing (NLP) applications is the disambiguation of a particular target word in a given context. Due to a variety of reasons (see e.g. Blank, 1999), word forms may be semantically extended to a range of different meanings or word senses (e.g. *rat* 'animal' > 'informer, snitch'). Automated disambiguation—i.e. the mapping of an ambiguous word form to its intended underlying word sense—is a task that can help in many different types of information extraction and text mining tasks.

In recent years, WSD approaches have shifted towards contextualized embeddings extracted from Large Language Models (LLM) like BERT (Devlin et al., 2019). These token-based embeddings incorporate substantial semantic information from the target lexical item and the sentential context that surrounds it. For this reason, LLMs are particularly well suited to disambiguation tasks and have, in fact, already been shown to indirectly capture word senses and perform competitively (Reif et al., 2019; Hadiwinoto et al., 2019). More recently, LLMs also obtained state-of-the-art performance using semantic networks (Loureiro and Jorge, 2019) and gloss information (Luo et al., 2018; Huang et al., 2019; Blevins and Zettlemoyer, 2020).

These recent advancements in WSD by means of LLMs are also interesting for Humanities scholars, as large-scale corpus-based studies have steadily become more standard practice over the last decades. Traditionally, data annotation in Humanities research is done manually, but with ever-growing size of corpora, such manual WSD has become decreasingly feasible. At the same time, researchers are also increasingly interested in disambiguating word senses without relying on intuitive judgment, which is ultimately subjective. This desire for a more data-driven approach to WSD is particularly prominent in research involving historical language, for which researchers are unable to solicit native speaker interpretations and expert annotators are rare. There is, in short, a growing interest in and need for automated WSD in Humanities research, and researchers have turned to NLP techniques to meet their needs.

As examples, we find projects aiming to trace the history of concepts over time (e.g. Beelen et al., 2021), automatically detect (different types of) lexical-semantic (e.g. Sagi et al., 2011; Giulianelli et al., 2020) and grammatical change (e.g. Fonteyn, 2020) or to quantify the evolution of the senses of a word (e.g. Tahmasebi et al., 2018). Because of their temporal dimension, such projects require NLP architectures that can process word senses in settings which are complicated by an evolving grammar and lexicon (Fonteyn, 2020), shifting spelling conventions, and noise introduced by

The 2nd International Workshop on Natural Language Processing for Digital Humanities (NLP4DH), pages 123–134
November 20, 2022.

OCR errors (Piotrowski, 2012). Yet, applications of LLMs on historical corpora tend to be either limited to arithmetic operations on the vector space of frozen contextual embeddings, or restricted to fine-tuning a linear layer to perform disambiguation to a pre-determined number of senses (Hagen et al., 2020; Beelen et al., 2021; Manjavacas and Fonteyn, 2021).

In this paper, we explore the capabilities of Large Language Models (LLMs) á la BERT (Devlin et al., 2019) for WSD on historical text. In doing so, we investigate to what extent (i) fine-tuning can improve WSD over arithmetic operations on plain frozen embeddings, and (ii) how much annotated data is needed in order to obtain gains over a baseline. Our focus lies on examining the data efficiency of LLM-based approaches for WSD, because annotated resources for WSD are generally scarce and costly to generate – a problem that is exacerbated with historical languages, where rare expert historical knowledge is required to produce annotated resources. To attain these goals, we take inspiration from recent metric-based non-parametric approaches (Holla et al., 2020; Du et al., 2021; Chen et al., 2021). These aim to optimize a model on a set of learning tasks (e.g. the disambiguation of a given ambiguous word) so that the model can quickly adapt to perform well on similar future tasks (e.g. disambiguating sentences of an ambiguous new word on the basis of a small annotated set of word senses). More specifically, we deploy a non-parametric approach to WSD fine-tuning that does not rely on additional task-specific parameters and that achieves surprisingly strong performance on out-of-domain lemmas. We argue that these results are promising if we aim to extend the scope of applications of WSD models in the Humanities.

Main Contributions Our experiments show that a metric-based parameter-free approach to few-shot WSD can achieve promising performance on historical data, even on held-out lemmas that were not seen during training. To do so, they require only a small number of training lemmas and word sense examples.

Moreover, we show that historical pre-training can push performance even further. To this end, we rely on `MacBERTh` (Manjavacas and Fonteyn, 2021, 2022), a LLM pre-trained on historical English. Additionally, in order to back up the results across different languages, a new historically pre-trained LLM for Dutch named `GysBERT` was developed and tested. The release of `GysBERT` accompanies the publication of the present study.[1]

Outline In Section 2, we describe the architecture used in order to tackle WSD in a non-parametric way. Subsequently, in Section 3, we describe the resources, datasets and pre-trained models underlying the present study. In Section 4, we present a series of experiments in order to illustrate the main results achieved by the evaluated approaches, focusing on small training regimes in Section 4.2, as well as the effect of time in Section 4.3. Section 4.4 showcases a downstream application on a type ad-hoc WSD task in a specific semantic field (i.e. the concepts MASS and WEIGHT in scientific language) that is common in Humanities reseearch but often overlooked in favor of full-coverage WSD. The paper concludes with a discussion and pointers to future work in Section 5.

2 Method

2.1 Architecture

The present approach deploys a parameter-free architecture which is heavily inspired by both the Matching Networks (Vinyals et al., 2016) and the Prototypical Networks (Snell et al., 2017) frameworks.

In this non-parametric approach, we fine-tune a given LLM using episodic training. In this type of training, each batch constitutes a training episode which is designed in order to match the experimental conditions expected at inference time. In the case of WSD, each episode consists of a number of randomly sampled sentences—a 'support set'—, exemplifying different word senses of a given lemma, as well as a second set of randomly sampled sentences—a 'query set'—, for which a word sense prediction needs to be made.[2]

Sentences in the query set are used in order to obtain a contextualized word embedding for the target word (i.e. the word representing the lemma to be disambiguated). The support set is used in order to compute abstract word sense representations for each of the word senses a lemma may have.[3]

[1]Both models can be accessed through the original `huggingface` repository through the following links `https://huggingface.co/emanjavacas/MacBERTh` and `https://huggingface.co/emanjavacas/GysBERT`.

[2]See Table 3 in the Appendix for an illustration of the structure of the lexical databases and an example of the sentences that are being classified.

[3]Note that for this approach to work, the true word sense

These abstract sense embeddings can be computed in multiple ways, but for simplicity we have chosen a centroid approach. First, the contextualized embeddings of the target lemma in the support sentences are extracted, and, then, averaged in order to get a single representation per word sense.[4]

More formally, let $E(S_i)$ and $E(Q_j)$ denote the contextualized embeddings of the target lemma in the ith support sentence and the jth query sentence in the current training episode. And let $R(S_j)$ denote the word sense of the jth sentence in the support set. Then, the representation for the kth word sense r_k in a given training episode is computed as follows:

$$E(r_k) = \sum_{\{j|R(S_j)=k\}} \frac{E(S_j)}{|\{j|R(S_j) = k\}|} \quad (1)$$

The objective of the approach is to maximize the probability of the true word sense given by the following equation.

$$p(k|E(Q_j)) \propto \text{sim}(E(Q_j), E(r_k)) \quad (2)$$

where **sim** is a similarity function in the embedding space. The probability that a given query example belongs to a given word sense is proportional to the similarity between the embedding of the query sentence and the word sense representation. In order to obtain a valid probability distribution, the similarity scores are normalized using the soft-max function.[5]

We fine-tune the entire set of LLM parameters over a number of training episodes. For each episode, we sample lemmas from the training set uniformly—i.e. disregarding lemma frequency—, which has been found to be helpful in order to improve the classification efficacy for low frequency words (Chen et al., 2021). Moreover, we sample a maximum of 10 sentences for the support set and 20 sentences for the query set. Each model is trained for a maximum of 3,000 training steps, or less if convergence is reached, as indicated by development performance.

of all sentences in the query set needs to be represented in the support set.

[4]During all the present experiments, we take the output of the last hidden layer as the contextualized embedding. Moreover, if the target word was sub-tokenized into multiple subwords, we average over the embeddings of these sub-words.

[5]From this point of view, the present approach resembles metric-based methods in the context of few-shot classification. See also Chen et al. (2021) for an application to WSD.

2.2 Historical Pre-Training

As we target WSD in historical text, the NLP models we employ need to address a number of additional difficulties that are usually not present when dealing with present-day text. First, historical languages often have non-consolidated spelling, which leads to an increased amount of orthographic variation. This is further aggravated by the fact that historical text exists primarily in printed or handwritten form, and hence requires error-prone digitization techniques to be computationally processed. Finally, in many studies, the collection of historical text under scrutiny covers a large time span and, thus, the language used in these texts has been subject to grammatical and semantic change.

Following previous research (Hosseini et al., 2021; Manjavacas and Fonteyn, 2021, 2022), we resort to historically pre-trained LLMs in order as the basis for our WSD experiments. More specifically, we deploy LLMs that are pre-trained from scratch on historical data instead of adapted from present-day models, since the former strategy has been shown to yield stronger performance when applied to historical data (Manjavacas and Fonteyn, 2021, 2022). For English, we used `MacBERTh` (Manjavacas and Fonteyn, 2022), and for Dutch we use the newly introduced `GysBERT`, which will be described in more detail in Section 3.1.

3 Datasets

The datasets underlying the present study come from the Oxford English Dictionary (henceforth: OED Oxford University Press) and the "Woordenboek der Nederlandsche Taal" (Dictionary of the Dutch Language, henceforth: WNT Instituut voor de Nederlandse Taal). Both resources consist of large historical lexicons, where each lemma is categorized into a hierarchy of word senses. Each word sense is given a definition, and is exemplified by a set of sentences spanning a certain time window.

To construct a suitable corpus for testing our WSD approaches, we sampled 1,000 words according to frequency from each language [6] and searched for them in the corresponding resource. The collected data for each language is described in Table 1.

On this data set, we produced a 10% split of lemmas, which were used to evaluate models on

[6]More specifically, we made sure to sample equally from different frequency bands in order to obtain a representative sample of the vocabulary.

	Lemmas	Senses	Quotations
OED	846	22,004	121,684
WNT	755	22,547	137,131

Table 1: Summary statistics of the used datasets.

unseen lemmas. We refer to this as the "held-out set". Finally, for each lemma, we produced a 50% split of quotations, following the original distribution of word senses.

3.1 GysBERT: A Historically Pre-Trained LLM for Dutch

In order to process historical Dutch, we have developed `GysBERT`, a historically pre-trained model for Dutch. To our knowledge, `GysBERT` represents the first such model for Dutch. Architecturally, `GysBERT` closely follows BERT-base uncased. For pre-training purposes, we compiled a data set using two databases of historical Dutch texts.

The first data set is Delpher, a database of historical newspapers, books and journals that comprises more than 130 million scanned and digitized pages, spanning from 1618 to the end of the 20th century (Koninklijke Bibliotheek). The second set is the Digital Library of Dutch Literature (DBNL) (Koninklijke Bibliotheek et al.). The DBNL consists in a comprehensive digital library of Dutch literature that resulted from the joint effort of Dutch and Flemish libraries, and aims to represent the entire linguistic area.

While the Delpher database contains OCR'd text of varying quality, the DBNL is the result of a thorough digitization campaign and presents generally high quality transcriptions. In order to make sure that only text of sufficiently quality is used for pre-training, we developed the following filtering strategy. First, we trained statistical character-level 5-gram language models using `KenLM` (Heafield, 2011). Specifically, we trained a single model per century of text available from the clean DBNL data. Then, for each snippet of Delpher data, we obtain a quality estimate as the perplexity that the corresponding DBNL-based model assigns to it. Manual observation of random snippets suggested discarding texts with a perplexity of 20 or higher. Furthermore, we restricted ourselves to texts published between 1500 and 1950.

In total, the remaining data set consists of 5.8B tokens from Delpher and 1.3B tokens from DBNL—which amounts to ca. 7.1B tokens. We used this data set in order to train a WordPiece tokenizer with a vocabulary of 30,000 tokens, and pre-trained BERT with default parameters, for 1,000,000 training steps, keeping the maximum sequence length at 128 subtokens.[7]

4 Experiments

In order to test the efficiency of this non-parametric approach, as well as the impact of historical pre-training, we ran a series of experiments comparing historically pre-trained models and present-day models. For English, we compare `MacBERTh` to `BERT`—which corresponds to the official release of BERT-base uncased (Devlin et al., 2019). For Dutch, we compare `GysBERT` with the BERT-based `BERTje` (de Vries et al., 2019) and the RoBERTa-based (Liu et al., 2019) `RobBERT` (Delobelle et al., 2020).

Moreover, for each model, we compare results with respect to non fine-tuned versions of the models—we refer to these variants as frozen baselines. When applicable, we also report the results obtained by a most frequent sense (MFS) baseline. We focus on F1-scores averaged over the different lemmas. Since the distribution of word senses is often heavily skewed, we report both micro and macro F1-scores.

4.1 General Results

Figure 1 and Figure 2 show the average F1-scores over **in-domain lemmas**—i.e. these lemmas were present in the training data, even though the specific sentences on which these results are computed were absent—and **held-out lemmas** for the different models in the full training data regime. In these plots, we highlight the effect of using an increasing number of shots (shown on the x-axis). Note that the number of shots in this context refers to the number of available support examples for each word sense during inference.

Figure 1 and Figure 2 show that the proposed fine-tuning approach is very efficient with respect to the frozen baselines, as we observe an increase of 0.2 points or more. The effect is larger when considering macro F1-scores and an increase in the number of shots, indicating that the proposed fine-tuning yields more discriminative models ir-

[7] `GysBERT` will be released on the `huggingface` platform.

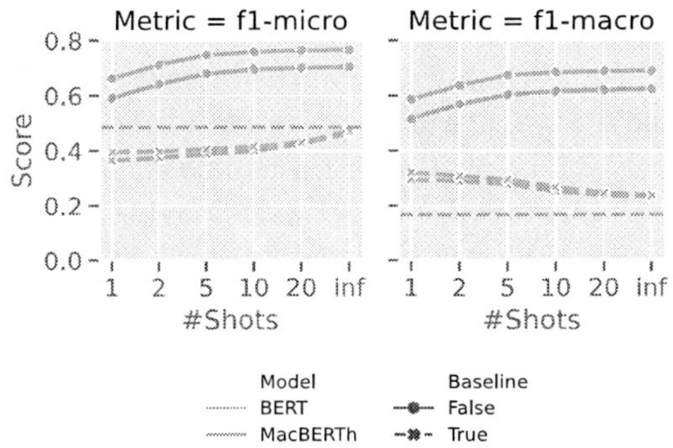

(a) In-domain

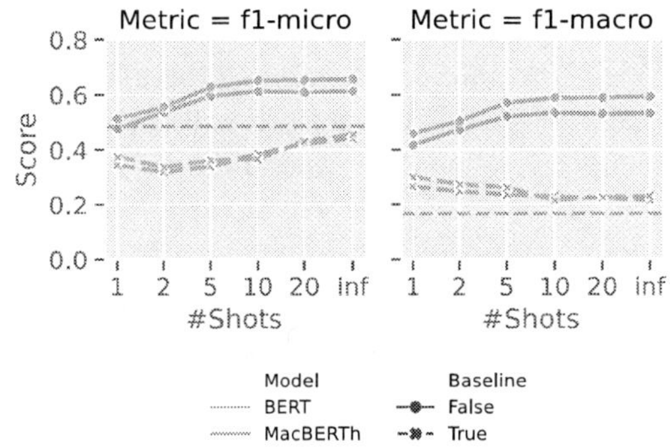

(b) Held-out

Figure 1: Results of WSD on the OED for in-domain lemmas (a) and held-out lemmas (b). Solid lines denote the proposed models trained on the full data sets. Dashed lines represent the corresponding frozen baselines. The MFS baseline is shown by a grey dashed line. The x-axis (number of shots) corresponds to the number of example sentences per sense shown during inference.

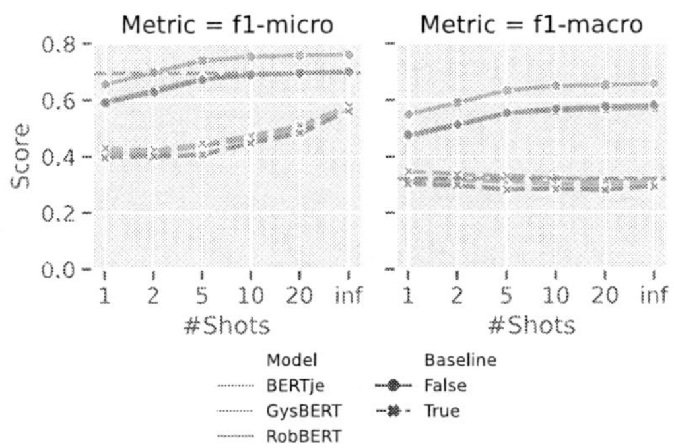

(a) In-domain

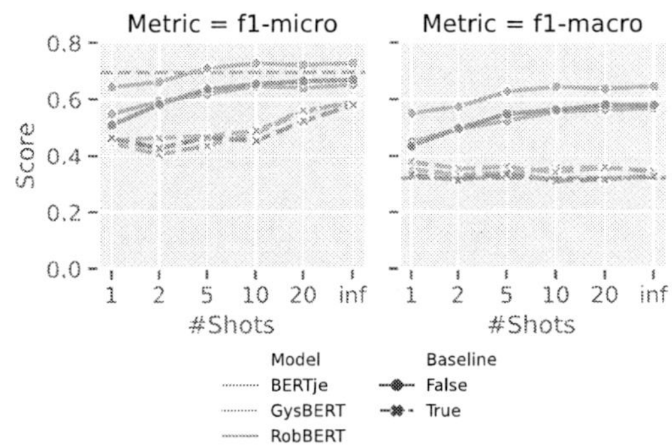

(b) Held-out

Figure 2: Results of WSD on the WNT for in-domain lemmas (a) and held-out lemmas (b). Solid lines denote the proposed models trained on the full data sets. Dashed lines represent the corresponding frozen baselines. The MFS baseline is shown by a grey dashed line. The x-axis (number of shots) corresponds to the number of example sentences per sense shown during inference.

respectively of the skewness of a given lemma's word senses. Interestingly, this happens under both in-domain and held-out conditions. Overall, frozen baselines underperform the MFS baseline in terms of micro F1. In terms of macro F1, frozen baselines do outperform the MFS baseline, albeit very slightly.

For held-out lemmas, there is just a mild decrease in performance, of less than 0.1 points in both data sets. This indicates encouraging generalization capabilities. Focusing on the x-axis, we observe that an increase in the number of shots results in a continuous increase in performance up until 5 shots, after which the improvement plateaus.

Overall, performance is slightly higher in the Dutch data set, which may be due to a larger skewness in the distribution of word senses. This skewness can, indeed, be inferred from the high micro F1-score obtained by the MFS baseline.

Finally, historically pre-trained models outperform present-day models with a safe margin. This result is particularly relevant in our case, since the superiority of historical pre-training cannot be concluded on the basis of the frozen baselines alone, but surfaces only after applying the non-parametric fine-tuning.

4.2 Small Training Regime

In order to assess the efficiency of the proposed approach on the low-data regime, we performed a series of experiments in which both the number of lemmas and the maximum number of examples per sense are limited **during training**. The results are shown in Figure 3 for the OED and in Figure 4 for the WNT. For inference, we keep the number of shots at 5. Note that the performance in these experiments refers to inference on held-out lemmas.

In Figure 3, we observe that the historically pre-trained models are consistently more effective than the present-day counterparts across training conditions. Furthermore, we observe that even a very small amount of training data (e.g. 50 training lemmas in total) yields consistent gains over the frozen baselines, regardless of the number of examples per sense.

Moreover, the effect of number of lemmas is small when using only 2 or 5 examples per sense. When using 10 or 50, an increase in the number of lemmas has a positive effect on performance up to 500 lemmas. Doubling this amount to 1,000 lemmas, however, yields little return. These experiments seem to indicate that strong generalization can be achieved with relatively small training data sets (e.g. 500 training lemmas and 10 example sentences per sense).

In the case of the Dutch data set from Figure 4, we observe similar patterns to those from the OED data set. Again, micro F1-scores are very high for the MFS baseline, and a larger number of training lemmas (i.e. 500) and number of examples per sense (i.e. 50) are needed in this data set for the models to outperform the MFS baseline.

4.3 Impact of Time

Since the example sentences of both the OED and WNT data sets display the publication year of the work in which they appear, we can inspect the performance of the different models over sentences in different time periods. From this angle, we expect to observe an improvement in performance for the earlier periods when the fine-tuned model was pre-trained historically. Figure 5 shows the time-aggregated results with the century on the x-axis.

The historically pre-trained models outperform the present-day models across the entire range. Moreover, these plots confirm that the relative improvement over present-day models is indeed larger in the earlier centuries, where the challenges presented by historical text are most acute.

4.4 Downstream Application

So far, we have examined the performance of the non-parametric fine-tuning on the basis of the lexical databases (OED and WNT), which offer large quantities of available training data and allow us to control the training conditions. In order to test the efficiency of non-parametric fine-tuning on smaller-scale scenarios, which can be considered more 'realistic' in the context of Humanities research, we ran an experiment on a classification task involving an ad-hoc WSD task around the word senses of the lemmas *mass* and *weight* in 18th and 19th century scientific writing.

This experiment is part of on-going research aimed at tracing the development of the concept of MASS when Newtonian physics forced a process of semantic differentiation between the terms *mass* and *weight*. To this end, all 56,813 instances of *mass* and *weight* in the Royal Society Corpus (RSC Fischer et al., 2020) will be analyzed with respect to a fine-grained classification of 6 word senses—see A for examples of these categories. With the goal of automating the annotation process, a sample of 1,500 instances—including 621 cases of *mass* and 879 of *weight*—was first manually annotated by a domain expert.

Subsequently, we set up a total of 4 competing fine-tuning approaches, including the non-parametric approach described in Section 2, and 3 additional ones to serve as baselines. The first one, `Standard`, consists in fine-tuning a classification layer on top of `MacBERTh`, as implemented in the `transformers` library (Wolf et al., 2020). The remaining two involve a K-Nearest Neighbours (`KNN`) and a Support Vector Machine classifier (`SVC`) on top of the token-embeddings produced by `MacBERTh`.[8] We optimize the models using a 10-fold Cross Validation procedure, where each fold respects the original word sense proportions.[9] For the non-parametric fine-tuning approach, we follow the hyper-parameterization from the main experiments reported in this paper.

We focus on micro and macro F1-scores, reporting means and standard deviations for each model. The results are shown in Table 2. The non-parametric approach outperforms the baselines in terms of both micro and macro F1-scores. However, taking into account the standard deviation from the Cross Validation, the advantage with respect to the best baseline in terms of macro F1-score does not hold.

[8]The latter two baselines were implemented with the `scikit-learn` library (Pedregosa et al., 2011).

[9]In the case of the `KNN` classifier, we hyper-optimize the number of nearest neighbors, as well as the distance metric. In the case of `SVC`, we hyper-optimize the C parameter.

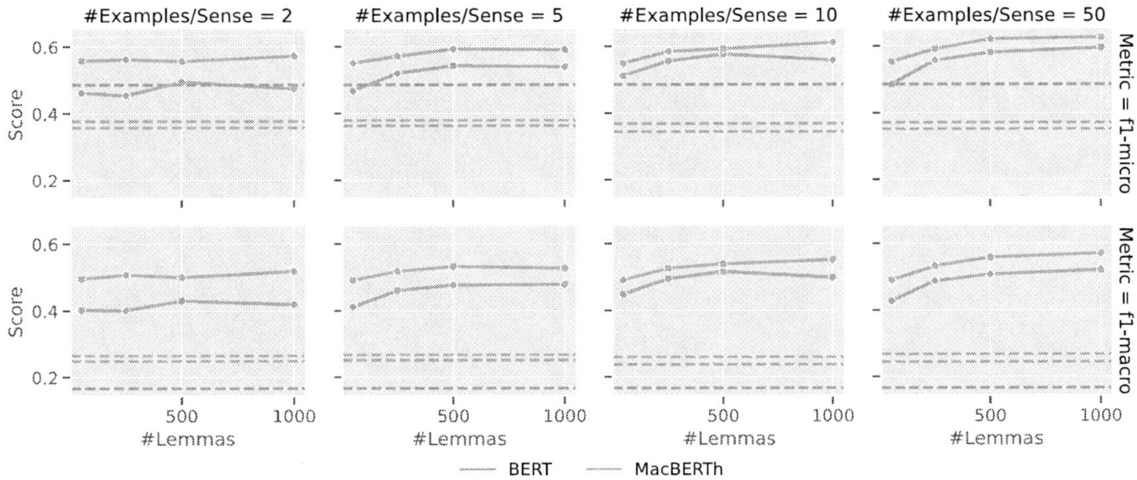

Figure 3: F1-scores for WSD on OED held-out lemmas for the proposed models trained on 50, 250, 500 and all lemmas (on the x-axis) and 2, 5, 10, and 50 example sentences per sense (on the columns).

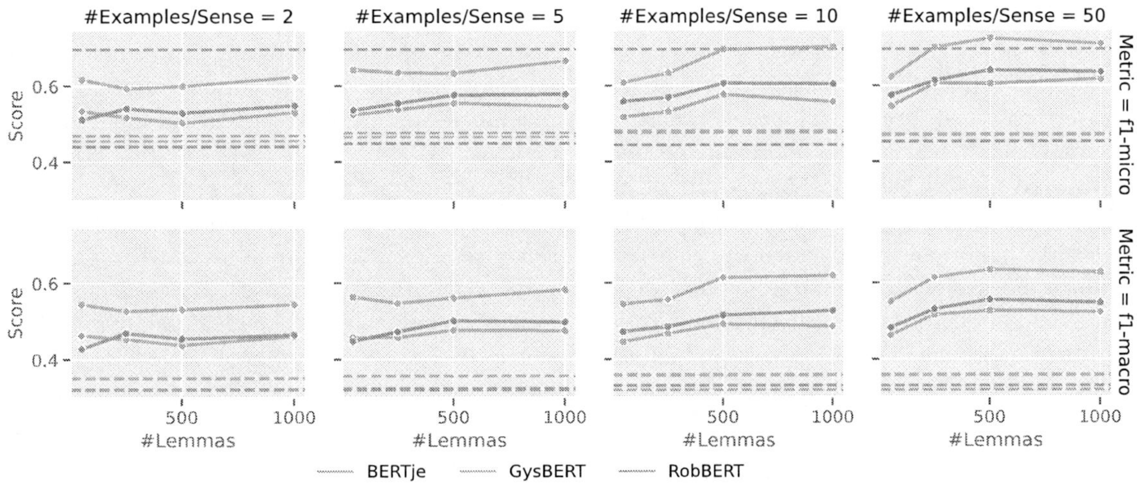

Figure 4: F1-scores for WSD on WNT held-out lemmas for the proposed models trained on 50, 250, 500 and all lemmas (on the x-axis) and 2, 5, 10, and 50 example sentences per sense (on the columns).

Surprisingly, the standard fine-tuning approach is not only less competitive than the baselines, but also suffers from strong variance across CV folds. This is probably due to the small number of training examples available for fine-tuning, and the large number of parameters that need to be tuned in this approach. In contrast, the non-parametric approach achieves not only the highest scores but also the lowest standard deviation of all competitors, indicating that this may be a much better suited approach for fine-tuning on small training data sets.

	Micro F1		Macro F1	
Model	Mean	StdDev	Mean	StdDev
KNN	0.830	0.007	0.695	0.032
SVC	0.819	0.007	0.601	0.035
Standard	0.827	0.029	0.520	0.066
Non-Parametric	**0.864**	0.006	**0.699**	0.025

Table 2: 10-fold cross-validated results of the classification experiments of "mass" and "weight" for 4 different fine-tuning methods. Best performing result in **bold**.

5 Discussion & Future Work

Our experiments highlight that Humanities researchers who seek to automatically disambiguate word senses over time may be able to do so with reasonable performance, even when they provide only a small amount of sentences exemplifying the target word senses and/or leverage general-purpose

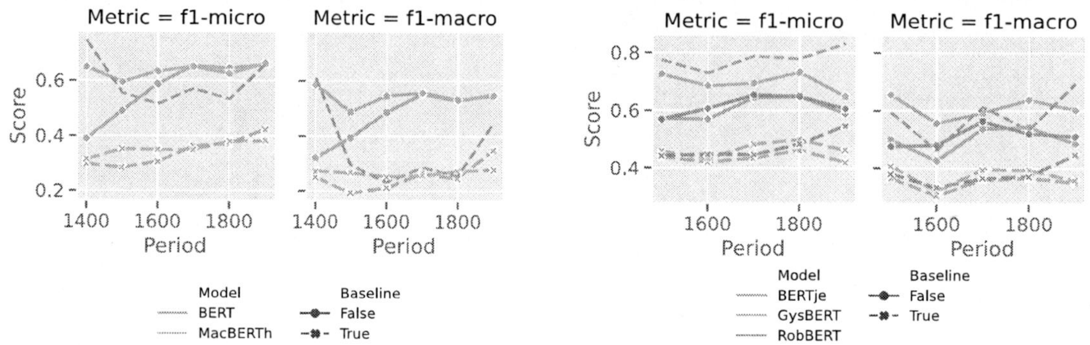

(a) OED

(b) WNT

Figure 5: Results of WSD over different periods of time (on the x-axis), using the fine-tuned models (solid lines) as well as the corresponding frozen baselines (dashed lines) and an MFS baseline (grey dashed line). Inference was done on held-out lemmas using 5 shots and the full-training regime.

lexical resources, such as the OED or the WNT. More specifically, in the full training data scenario, held-out lemmas could be classified with micro F1-scores of 0.627 for English and 0.71 for Dutch, using the historically pre-trained models. These results imply 40.3% and 34.22% improvements over the respective frozen baselines. Moreover, we observe that even a small number of training lemmas can lead to important improvements over frozen baselines. For example, when training on just 50 lemmas and only 2 instances per sense, micro F1-scores can be obtained of 0.557 for English and 0.617 for Dutch, which represent improvements of 32.8% and 24.4% over the frozen baselines.

In this sense, we go a step further than Chen et al. (2021), who—in contrast to our experiments—leveraged the training data in order to construct word sense representations at inference time. By doing so, they assumed that all lemmas in the test data are known from training data. What we found is that the fine-tuning approach is also effective on held-out lemmas, which means it can be applied in cases where practical constraints exist on the amount of available annotated data.

Our experiments also highlighted that historically pre-trained models are able to better handle the intricacies of historical data sets than present-day models when applying the discussed non-parametric fine-tuning approach. This result is particularly important in the present context, since the superiority of historical pre-training is not apparent on the basis of the frozen embeddings only. Using the frozen embeddings, the difference in performance between the historically pre-trained models and the present-day models is negligible. Moreover, we presented a case study which highlighted that non-parametric fine-tuning can be much more efficient than the more commonly used standard fine-tuning approaches, especially in small training regimes.

The main objective of the present fine-tuning approach is to push the embeddings of the query sentences closer to the non-parametric representations of the true word senses. By conjecture, the proposed approach works by learning to distill the semantic features in the input sentences that are most relevant to lexical semantics, stripping off irrelevant information for WSD. Thus, the fine-tuned model is allegedly able to achieve improved performance when classifying lemmas that have not been encountered during training.

Finally, we wish to note that we limited ourselves to normalized dot products as the measure of relatedness between representations in this study, and we deployed the transformer (Vaswani et al., 2017) architecture underlying BERT as is. Future work could, however, investigate what can be gained by experimenting with other similarity functions, and adding more complex layers such as an attention module over different word sense representations.

References

Kaspar Beelen, Federico Nanni, Mariona Coll Ardanuy, Kasra Hosseini, Giorgia Tolfo, and Barbara McGillivray. 2021. When time makes sense: A historically-aware approach to targeted sense disambiguation. In *Findings of the Association for Computational Linguistics: ACL-IJCNLP 2021*, pages 2751–2761, Online. Association for Computational Linguistics.

Andreas Blank. 1999. Why do new meanings occur? A cognitive typology of the motivations for lexical semantic change. In Andreas Blank and Peter Koch, editors, *Historical Semantics and Cognition*, page 61–90. Mouton de Gruyter, Berlin/New York.

Terra Blevins and Luke Zettlemoyer. 2020. Moving down the long tail of word sense disambiguation with gloss informed bi-encoders. In *Proceedings of the 58th Annual Meeting of the Association for Computational Linguistics*, pages 1006–1017, Online. Association for Computational Linguistics.

Howard Chen, Mengzhou Xia, and Danqi Chen. 2021. Non-parametric few-shot learning for word sense disambiguation. In *Proceedings of the 2021 Conference of the North American Chapter of the Association for Computational Linguistics: Human Language Technologies*, pages 1774–1781, Online. Association for Computational Linguistics.

Wietse de Vries, Andreas van Cranenburgh, Arianna Bisazza, Tommaso Caselli, Gertjan van Noord, and Malvina Nissim. 2019. BERTje: A Dutch BERT model. *arXiv preprint arXiv:1912.09582*.

Pieter Delobelle, Thomas Winters, and Bettina Berendt. 2020. RobBERT: a Dutch RoBERTa-based language model. *arXiv preprint arXiv:2001.06286*.

Jacob Devlin, Ming-Wei Chang, Kenton Lee, and Kristina Toutanova. 2019. BERT: Pre-training of deep bidirectional transformers for language understanding. In *Proceedings of the 2019 Conference of the North American Chapter of the Association for Computational Linguistics: Human Language Technologies, Volume 1 (Long and Short Papers)*, pages 4171–4186, Minneapolis, Minnesota. Association for Computational Linguistics.

Yingjun Du, Nithin Holla, Xiantong Zhen, Cees Snoek, and Ekaterina Shutova. 2021. Meta-learning with variational semantic memory for word sense disambiguation. In *Proceedings of the 59th Annual Meeting of the Association for Computational Linguistics and the 11th International Joint Conference on Natural Language Processing (Volume 1: Long Papers)*, pages 5254–5268, Online. Association for Computational Linguistics.

Stefan Fischer, Jörg Knappen, Katrin Menzel, and Elke Teich. 2020. The royal society corpus 6.0: Providing 300+ years of scientific writing for humanistic study. In *Proceedings of the 12th Language Resources and Evaluation Conference*, pages 794–802, Marseille, France. European Language Resources Association.

Lauren Fonteyn. 2020. What about grammar? Using BERT embeddings to explore functional-semantic shifts of semi-lexical and grammatical constructions. *CHR 2020: Workshop on Computational Humanities Research, November 18–20, 2020, Amsterdam, The Netherlands*, pages 257–268.

Mario Giulianelli, Marco Del Tredici, and Raquel Fernández. 2020. Analysing Lexical Semantic Change with Contextualised Word Representations. *arXiv:2004.14118 [cs]*. ArXiv: 2004.14118.

Christian Hadiwinoto, Hwee Tou Ng, and Wee Chung Gan. 2019. Improved word sense disambiguation using pre-trained contextualized word representations. In *Proceedings of the 2019 Conference on Empirical Methods in Natural Language Processing and the 9th International Joint Conference on Natural Language Processing (EMNLP-IJCNLP)*, pages 5297–5306, Hong Kong, China. Association for Computational Linguistics.

Thora Hagen, Erik Ketzan, Fotis Jannidis, and Andreas Witt. 2020. Twenty-two historical encyclopedias encoded in TEI: a new resource for the digital humanities. In *Proceedings of the The 4th Joint SIGHUM Workshop on Computational Linguistics for Cultural Heritage, Social Sciences, Humanities and Literature*, pages 112–120, Online. International Committee on Computational Linguistics.

Kenneth Heafield. 2011. KenLM: Faster and smaller language model queries. In *Proceedings of the Sixth Workshop on Statistical Machine Translation*, pages 187–197, Edinburgh, Scotland. Association for Computational Linguistics.

Nithin Holla, Pushkar Mishra, Helen Yannakoudakis, and Ekaterina Shutova. 2020. Learning to learn to disambiguate: Meta-learning for few-shot word sense disambiguation. In *Findings of the Association for Computational Linguistics: EMNLP 2020*, pages 4517–4533, Online. Association for Computational Linguistics.

Kasra Hosseini, Kaspar Beelen, Giovanni Colavizza, and Mariona Coll Ardanuy. 2021. Neural Language Models for Nineteenth-Century English (dataset; language model zoo).

Luyao Huang, Chi Sun, Xipeng Qiu, and Xuanjing Huang. 2019. GlossBERT: BERT for word sense disambiguation with gloss knowledge. In *Proceedings of the 2019 Conference on Empirical Methods in Natural Language Processing and the 9th International Joint Conference on Natural Language Processing (EMNLP-IJCNLP)*, pages 3509–3514, Hong Kong, China. Association for Computational Linguistics.

Instituut voor de Nederlandse Taal. Woordenboek der nederlandsche taal. `https://gtb.ivdnt.org/search/`.

Koninklijke Bibliotheek. Delpher. https://www.delpher.nl/.

Koninklijke Bibliotheek, Taalunie, and howpublished="https://www.dbnl.org/" Vlaamse Erfgoedbibliotheken, title=Digitale Bibliotheek voor de Nederlandse Letteren (DBNL).

Yinhan Liu, Myle Ott, Naman Goyal, Jingfei Du, Mandar Joshi, Danqi Chen, Omer Levy, Mike Lewis, Luke Zettlemoyer, and Veselin Stoyanov. 2019. Roberta: A robustly optimized bert pretraining approach. *ArXiv*, abs/1907.11692.

Daniel Loureiro and Alípio Jorge. 2019. Language modelling makes sense: Propagating representations through WordNet for full-coverage word sense disambiguation. In *Proceedings of the 57th Annual Meeting of the Association for Computational Linguistics*, pages 5682–5691, Florence, Italy. Association for Computational Linguistics.

Fuli Luo, Tianyu Liu, Qiaolin Xia, Baobao Chang, and Zhifang Sui. 2018. Incorporating glosses into neural word sense disambiguation. In *Proceedings of the 56th Annual Meeting of the Association for Computational Linguistics (Volume 1: Long Papers)*, pages 2473–2482, Melbourne, Australia. Association for Computational Linguistics.

Enrique Manjavacas and Lauren Fonteyn. 2021. Macberth: Development and evaluation of a historically pre-trained language model for English (1450-1950). In *Proceedings of the Workshop on NLP4DH @ ICON 2021*, pages 23–36, online.

Enrique Manjavacas and Lauren Fonteyn. 2022. Adapting vs pre-training language models for historical languages. *Journal of Data Mining and Digital Humanities*.

Oxford University Press. Oxford english dictionary. https://www.oed.com/.

Fabian Pedregosa, Gaël Varoquaux, Alexandre Gramfort, Vincent Michel, Bertrand Thirion, Olivier Grisel, Mathieu Blondel, Peter Prettenhofer, Ron Weiss, Vincent Dubourg, et al. 2011. Scikit-learn: Machine learning in python. *the Journal of machine Learning research*, 12:2825–2830.

Michael Piotrowski. 2012. Natural language processing for historical texts. *Synthesis lectures on human language technologies*, 5(2):1–157.

Emily Reif, Ann Yuan, Martin Wattenberg, Fernanda B Viegas, Andy Coenen, Adam Pearce, and Been Kim. 2019. Visualizing and measuring the geometry of bert. *Advances in Neural Information Processing Systems*, 32.

Eyal Sagi, Stefan Kaufmann, and Brady Clark. 2011. Tracing semantic change with Latent Semantic Analysis. In Kathryn Allan and Justyna A. Robinson, editors, *Current Methods in Historical Semantics*. De Gruyter, Berlin, Boston.

Jake Snell, Kevin Swersky, and Richard Zemel. 2017. Prototypical networks for few-shot learning. *Advances in neural information processing systems*, 30.

Nina Tahmasebi, Lars Borin, Adam Jatowt, et al. 2018. Survey of computational approaches to diachronic conceptual change. *arXiv preprint arXiv:1811.06278*.

Ashish Vaswani, Noam Shazeer, Niki Parmar, Jakob Uszkoreit, Llion Jones, Aidan N Gomez, Łukasz Kaiser, and Illia Polosukhin. 2017. Attention is all you need. *Advances in neural information processing systems*, 30.

Oriol Vinyals, Charles Blundell, Timothy Lillicrap, Daan Wierstra, et al. 2016. Matching networks for one shot learning. *Advances in neural information processing systems*, 29.

Thomas Wolf, Lysandre Debut, Victor Sanh, Julien Chaumond, Clement Delangue, Anthony Moi, Pierric Cistac, Tim Rault, Remi Louf, Morgan Funtowicz, Joe Davison, Sam Shleifer, Patrick von Platen, Clara Ma, Yacine Jernite, Julien Plu, Canwen Xu, Teven Le Scao, Sylvain Gugger, Mariama Drame, Quentin Lhoest, and Alexander Rush. 2020. Transformers: State-of-the-art natural language processing. In *Proceedings of the 2020 Conference on Empirical Methods in Natural Language Processing: System Demonstrations*, pages 38–45, Online. Association for Computational Linguistics.

A Appendix

lemma	sense	definition	example	year
RAT	1.a.	Any rodent of the genus Rattus and related genera of the family Muridae, resembling a large mouse, often with a naked or sparsely haired tail.	"Rats and mice purloin our grain" *J. Gay, Fables, II. viii. 74*	1732
	4.a	A dishonest, contemptible, or worthless person.	"No Female Rat shall me deceive, nor catch me by a crafty wild." *in Roxburghe Ballads VI. 106*	1656
RAT	1.	Knaagdier behoorende tot het geslacht Rattus van de familie der Muridae of 'ware muizen'.	"Daar 't katje woond, daar word het huis Gezuiverd van de Rat, en Muis" *Luyken, Besch. d. W. 223*	1708
	2.	Oneig. toegepast op personen. Armoedzaaier, gelukzoeker.	"Dien grootmaecker, die cael Rat" *Ogier, Seven Hoofts. 19*	1644

Table 3: Example lemma and sense with definition and quotation from the Oxford English Dictionary (top row) and the Woordenboek der Nederlandsche Taal (bottom row).

label	sense	example from Royal Society Corpus
N	*mass* or *weight* refers to thing or object	"The mass on the filter was treated with boiling alcohol" (Edward Schunk, 1853) "a flat circular weight nicely turned, and pierced in the direction of its diameter to receive the bar, was slid upon it" (Henry Kater, 1819)
M	*mass* or *weight* refers to MASS (i.e. how much matter is within an object)	"We are thus led to inquire how the stresses are distributed in the earth 's mass and what are their magnitudes" (G. H. Darwin, 1882) "In the third, the weight of the principle bones of a selected number of species (27) is stated" (John Davy, 1865)
W	*weight* refers to WEIGHT (i.e. referring to force, balancing, counterpoises, or the amount of effort required to lift something)	"fig. 3 is only 40 feet from the bow, and that the excess of weight over buoyancy on this length is only 45 tons" (E.J Reed & G.G Stokes, 1871)
W/M	unclear whether the example refers to MASS or WEIGHT	"The Commissioners for the Restoration of the Standards of weight and measure, in their Report dated December 21, 1841, recommended that..." (W.H Miller, 1856)
COL	*mass* or *weight* refers to a collection of objects (e.g. a mass of small fragments)	"A glacier is not a mass of fragments" (James Forbes, 1846)
MET	*mass* or *weight* is used to indicate the importance of a thing (e.g. the weight of authority)	"The next thought is that I may have assigned too great a mass to the doubt" (John Henry Pratt, 1855) "The contact theory has long had possession of men 's minds, is sustained by a greatweight of authority" (Michael Faraday, 1840)

Table 4: Classification scheme of *mass* and *weight* instances retrieved from the Royal Society corpus. In total, 1,500 examples were manually classified in one of these 6 custom categories.

Introducing a Large Corpus of Tokenized Classical Chinese Poems of Tang and Song Dynasties

Chao-Lin Liu Ti-Yong Zheng Kuan-Chun Chen Meng-Han Chung

National Chenghi University, Taiwan

{chaolin,107753037,105753014}@nccu.edu.tw

Abstract

Classical Chinese poems of Tang and Song dynasties are an important part for the studies of Chinese literature. To thoroughly understand the poems, properly segmenting the verses is an important step for human readers and software agents. Yet, due to the availability of data and the costs of annotation, there are still no known large and useful sources that offer classical Chinese poems with annotated word boundaries. In this project, annotators with Chinese literature background labeled 32399 poems. We analyzed the annotated patterns and conducted inter-rater agreement studies about the annotations. The distributions of the annotated patterns for poem lines are very close to some well-known professional heuristics, i.e., that the 2-2-1, 2-1-2, 2-2-1-2, and 2-2-2-1 patterns are very frequent. The annotators agreed well at the line level, but agreed on the segmentations of a whole poem only 43% of the time. We applied a traditional machine-learning approach to segment the poems, and achieved promising results at the line level as well. Using the annotated data as the ground truth, these methods could segment only about 18% of the poems completely right under favorable conditions. Switching to deep-learning methods helped us achieved better than 30%.

1 Introduction

Word segmentation is an important step for understanding Chinese texts because the Chinese language do not include explicit word delimiters, like the spaces in English, in the texts. Different segmentations of the same statements can lead to different interpretations, so segmenting Chinese strings into correct word sequences is crucial for understanding and processing Chinese in computer systems. Classical Chinese poems typically consist of sequences of short verses, so the quality of word segmentation influences the reading of poems significantly. The segmented poems can facilitate further analysis and applications, e.g., poem styles (Jiang, 2008; Qian and Huang, 2015).

The literature has seen a wide variety of approaches to the problem of word segmentation for vernacular Chinese in the past many years, e.g., (Chen and Liu, 1992; Huang et al., 2007; Chen, Zheng, and Chen, 2015; Deng et al. 2016). Annotated corpora have been created for research and competition as well (Ma and Chen, 2003; Sproat and Emerson, 2003; Emerson, 2005).

In contrast, relatively few researchers of Chinese linguistics and literature discussed word segmentation for classical Chinese poems. Wang (1972) examined the problem from both syntactic and semantic perspectives, while Tsao (2004) argued that the perspective of semantic interpretation should be more natural for native speakers. Jiang (2008) inherited and emphasized more on the semantic viewpoints. Relying on modern databases of Tang poems, Hu and Yu (2001) and Lo (2005) can access and compare more poems conveniently, and they adopt the observations discussed in the previous literature for the word segmentation task.

Beyond conceptual discussion, it is harder to segment words in corpora of classical poems in large scale. Lee and colleagues discussed the topics of annotating part-of-speech tags (2012) and of creating dependency trees (2012) for classical Chinese poems. When they analyzed some interesting syntactic patterns in classical poems, they mentioned around one thousand poems (Lee, Kong, and Luo, 2018).

In this paper, we report a relatively larger scale of work for annotating word boundaries in two collections of classical Chinese poems. At the time of writing, we have annotated 32399 classical Chinese poems of the Tang and Song dynasties.[1] We evaluated our annotations in some different ways. First, we conducted inter-rater agreement (IRA) analysis, and the results are convincing. We applied machine learning methods for segmenting words in classical Chinese poems, and have

[1] Tang is a Chinese dynasty that governed China during 618-907CE. Song is a Chinese dynasty that governed China during 960-1279CE. Both dynasties are very influential for the development of Chinese literature. Compared with the availability of linguistic data of modern days, the amount of available data for classical Chinese poems is extremely scarce.

The 2nd International Workshop on Natural Language Processing for Digital Humanities (NLP4DH), pages 135–144
November 20, 2022.

achieved and published some preliminary results when we annotated only thousands of poems (Liu and Chang, 2019). We have improved the quality of our word segmenters significantly by using more annotated data and embracing the technology of deep learning. In addition, we compared our annotations with relevant information in a well-known website, and found that our annotations have a reasonable consensus.

We provide information about data sources, define the task of word segmentation, and discuss some domain-dependent heuristics in Section 2. We explain methods for measuring the quality of word segmentation in Section 3. We introduce our annotation team and their annotations, and report a basic statistical analysis of the annotated poems in Section 4. We explored different perspectives for IRA analysis in Section 5. We introduce the probabilistic classifiers for word segmentation in Section 6. We compared the performances of two different designs of the probabilistic classifier in Section 7, and wrap up this paper in Section 8.

2 Data Sources and Problem Definition

We provide a brief introduction to the forms of classical Chinese poems in Section 2.1, and define the task of marking word boundaries in Section 2.2.

2.1 Data Sources: Three Poem Collections

We present two actual poems so that readers can acquire some basic knowledge and relevant terminology about classical Chinese poems.

We list a poem of a famous Tang poet, Li Bai, in the following.[2]

鳳凰臺上鳳凰遊，鳳去臺空江自流。
吳宮花草埋幽徑，晉代衣冠成古丘。
三山半落青天外，二水中分白鷺洲。
總爲浮雲能蔽日，長安不見使人愁。

This poem has eight lines, each of which has seven Chinese characters. The names of this form of poems are *regulated heptametric octaves* (RHO, henceforth) in English and 七言律詩(qi1 yan2 lu4 shi1) in Chinese. If a poem has only four lines, and each line has seven characters, it is in the form of *heptametric quatrains* (HQ, henceforth) and 七言絕句(qi1 yan2 jue2 ju4). Extended forms of heptametric poems (EFHP, henceforth) may have more than eight lines, e.g., 10, 12, 14 lines. Such poems are called 七言長律(qi1 yan2 chang2 lu4) or 七言排律(qi1 yan2 pai2 lu4) in Chinese.

	items	poets	RPO	HQ	RHO	EFPP	EFHP
CTP1	25990	123	11309	5004	7343	1789	545
CSP1	6409	71			6409		

Table 1: Basic statistics about the annotated poems

We list a poem of another famous Tang poet, Du Fu, in the following.[3]

國破山河在，城春草木深。
感時花濺淚，恨別鳥驚心。
烽火連三月，家書抵萬金。
白頭搔更短，渾欲不勝簪。

This poem also has eight lines, each of which has five Chinese characters. The names of this form of poems are *regulated pentametric octaves* (RPO, henceforth) in English and 五言律詩(wu3 yan2 lu4 shi1) in Chinese. If a poem has only four lines, and each line has seven characters, it is in the form of *pentametric quatrains* (PQ, henceforth) and 五言絕句 (wu3 yan2 jue2 ju4). Extended forms of heptametric poems (EFHP, henceforth) may have more than eight sentences, e.g., 10, 12, 14, etc. lines. Such poems are called 五言長律(wu3 yan2 chang2 lu4) or 五言排律(wu3 yan2 pai2 lu4).

In this research, for the Tang poems, we consider only the poems in volumes 30 through 888 in the *Complete Tang Poems* (CTP, Quan Tang Shi, 全唐詩). CTP has 900 volumes, and is the most representative and important collection of Tang poems for the studies on Chinese literature. Volumes 30 through 888 are the ordinary poems. We also annotated the poems in the *Complete Song Poems* (CSP, Quan Song Shi, 全宋詩).

Due to the limited budget for human annotation, we focus on the word segmentation for poems that have only five-character or seven-character lines. These types of poems represent more than 90% of the poems in the CTP. Similarly, 87% of the poems in the CSP consisted of only five-character or seven-character lines.

As a pioneer work, we did not find known principles to select the poems for annotation. As a consequence, we abide by some basic principles. First of all, we wanted to have reasonably many poems of different types of poems. We annotated the majority of the RPO, HQ, RHO, EFHP, EFPP poems that appeared in volumes 30 through 888 in CTP. Table 1 provides statistics about the annotated data. At this moment, we have annotated only part of the RHO poems in CSP.

Table 1 provides the amounts and types of our annotated poems in CTP and CSP. In total, we have 25,990 annotated CTP poems and 6409 annotated

[2] The poet is 李白. The title of the poem is 登金陵鳳凰臺.

[3] The poet is 杜甫, and the title of the poem is 春望.

CSP poems. Some of the CTP poems were repeatedly annotated by different annotators for IRA analysis. The CTP poems belonged to 123 Tang poets, and the CSP poems belonged to 71 CSP poets. The columns RPO, HQ, RHO, EFPP, and EFHP show the amounts of poems of different types. In Table 1, we use CTP1 to refer to the annotated CTP poems and CSP1 to refer to the annotated CSP poems.

For studying the temporal changes and heritage of the Chinese language, we are working on the annotation of thousands of poems in the *Complete Taiwan Poems* (TWP, Quan Tai Shi, 全臺詩) (Shi, 2011).

2.2 Problem Definition

For human annotators, the goal of word segmentation for classical Chinese poems is to add markers between words. If given a line "吳宮花草埋幽徑", the annotators may produce "吳宮=花草=埋=幽徑", where "=" is the marker for word boundaries.

Technically, we treat the word segmentation problem as a classification problem. Given a line "吳宮花草埋幽徑", an annotator attempts to determine whether or not a character in the string is the last character of a word. If the character is not the last character of a word, we assign it to the category of *non-terminal*. If it is, we assign it to the category of *terminal*. We will use N and T to denote non-terminal and terminal, respectively, in our discussions. Using this notation, the annotators may produce "NTNTTNT" if "吳宮=花草=埋=幽徑" is the correct segmentation for "吳宮花草埋幽徑".

2.3 Domain-Dependent Heuristics

Over the years, based on the experience in studying classical Chinese poems, researchers have proposed practical heuristics about word segmentation that are useful for reading classical Chinese poems. Although the researchers that we cited in the Introduction may not have a consensus on the implications of the popular patterns, they all discussed the high frequencies of the common patterns.

For poems that have 5-character lines, i.e., PQ and RPO, the most common patterns for segmentation are 2-2-1 or 2-1-2. Here, an individual digit represents the number of characters in a segmented word. Hence, the 2-2-1 pattern indicates that we segment a five-character line into three words in the order of a 2-character word, another 2-character word, and a 1-character word. Hence, one may segment "野鶴隨君子，寒松揖大夫" as "野鶴=隨=君子，寒松=揖=大夫", and these are examples of 2-1-2 lines.

Analogously, the researchers believe that 2-2-2-1 and 2-2-1-2 are common patterns for lines in HQ and RHO poems. "雨中=草色=綠=堪染，水上=桃花=紅=欲然" is an example of the 2-2-1-2 pattern.

These heuristic principles are usually right, but there are exceptions. "翻經=謝靈運，畫壁=陸探微" needs the 2-3 pattern to mention person names. One may prefer to read "綠浪東西南北水，紅欄三百九十橋" as "綠浪=東西南北=水，紅欄=三百九十=橋" because of the direction words and the Chinese numbers.

3 Evaluation Measures

3.1 Quality of Word Segmentation

We may measure the quality of word segmentation with four types of measures that are gradually more challenging. Since we are categorizing each character in a poem into two types, it is natural and conventional to measure the classification results with precision, recall, and F_1 measure (Manning and Schütze, 1999; Alpaydin, 2020).

A more practical interest for the task of word segmentation is about word identification. To identify a word, we need to correctly find the beginning and ending of the word, which requires at least two correct classifications. Hence, the percentage of word recovery, PWR, is more challenging than the traditional measures for classification tasks.

We can view the classification of characters as character-level decisions, and view the word recovery as word-level decisions. From here, we can image that there are line-level decisions and poem-level decisions. We may want to measure how well our annotators segment a line completely correct and how well our annotators segment a poem completely correct. Therefore, it should be natural to measure the percentage of perfectly segmented lines, PSL, and the percentage of perfectly segmented poems, PSP. Given a set of L lines and P poems, if our annotators segment L' lines and P' poems perfectly, PSL will be L'/L and PSP will be P'/P.

We can compare the word segmentations produced by our annotators with the word segmentations annotated by human experts, and compute the precision, recall, F_1, PWR, PSL, and PSP to measure the quality of our classifiers.

3.2 Metrics for IRA Analysis

If we have an expert who will annotate the poems and provide the most reliable annotation of the word boundaries, there would not be a very good reason to ask many annotators to repeat the annotation task. We do not have such an expert yet. More importantly, there might not be just one way to segment a poem because it is possible to segment and interpret poems in different ways. Hence, there might not be gold standards for segmenting all classical Chinese poems, at least for some poems.

Therefore, we chose to avoid subjectively decide which annotator is more reliable when comparing the annotators' annotations. We used the Dice coefficient (Dice, 1945) to compare the annotations of a poem that were produced by the annotators.

Let A_1 and A_2 denote the annotations of two annotators. Let C_{12} denote the annotations that both annotators agree. The Dice coefficient for the annotations A_1 and A_2 is defined in (1).

$$\mathrm{Dice}(A_1, A_2) \equiv \frac{2\times|C_{12}|}{|A_1|+|A_2|} \quad (1)$$

Here, $|A_1|$ and $|A_2|$ are respectively the amounts of annotations (for characters in poems) of A_1 and A_2. Since the annotators are annotating the characters of the same collection of poems, $|A_1|$ and $|A_2|$ must be the same. $|C_{12}|$ is the number of agreed annotations, so $|C_{12}|$ must be smaller or equal to $|A_1|$ (and $|A_2|$). The Dice coefficient doubles $|C_{12}|$ to make the coefficient fall into the range of [0, 1]. When two annotations perfectly agree, the Dice coefficient is 1. When two annotations completely differ, the coefficient will be zero.

Take the annotation for the string "ABCDE" for example. Assume that A_1 is NTNTT and that A_2 is NTTNT, i.e., annotator 1 and 2 segment "ABCDE" into AB=CD=E and AB=C=DE, respectively. The annotators agreed on three character-level decisions, so the Dice coefficient for the character-level decisions is $\frac{2\times 3}{5+5}$=0.6. For the word-level decisions, annotator 1 suggests three words, and annotator 2 suggests three words, but they agree on only one word, i.e., AB. Hence, the PWR is $\frac{2\times 1}{3+3} = 0.3\overline{3}$.

We can reuse the definitions for PSL and PSP in Section 3.1 for inter-rater agreement studies. For PSL and PSP, the annotations for a line or for a poem of two annotators either completely agree or do not agree, so there is no need to arbitrarily choose the ground truth, and we may reuse the original definitions of PSL and PSP.

4 Annotated Poems

4.1 Annotating the Poems

We have seven annotators, and all of them major in Chinese Literature. Four of them are affiliated with the University of Taipei (UT, henceforth), and three are with the National Taipei University (NTPU, henceforth). We intentionally recruited annotators from different universities. Annotators who were trained at different universities and did not know each other may add a bit more independence in their annotation-related decisions.

We could not afford to annotate all of the poems in CTP and CSP because of time limits and budget constraints. In total, CTP and CSP have more than 210,000 items of poems. Sometimes, an item contains multiple poems. We have listed the basic statistics about the current annotated poems in Table 1. The 123 poets for the CTP poems were selected because they were the leading contributors to CTP (Liu, Mazanec, and Tharsen, 2018). In addition to considering the amounts of contributions when selecting the CSP poets, we also considered whether the poets lived in the Northern Song or the Southern Song periods.[4] The poets were selected so that we balanced the poems from these two periods, when huge changes took place in China.

Due to some historical reasons, a poem may have different versions (Owen, 2007; Liu, Mazanec, and Tharsen, 2018). For this reason, we keep the poems that were recorded relatively more consistently in different sources in our studies, hoping to enhance the authenticity of our data.

We stated that we annotated 25990 CTP poems in Section 2.1. In fact, we have annotated more than 25990 items of Tang poems, and chose only this amount in our study. Originally, we have annotated 28137 Tang poems. We compared our poems with the Tang poems that were also listed in the Chinese Text project[5], the Scripta Sinica database[6], and the Cold-Spring website[7], and kept only those items that differ at most one Chinese character with a corresponding item in these reference sites. By comparing and filtering our poems, we hope that the remaining Tang poems are qualified to be used in our empirical evaluation. In the following presentation, we will refer to "items of poems" as

[4] The Song dynasty had two main periods. The Northern Song existed during 960-1127CE, and the Southern Song existed during 1127-1279CE.

[5] CTEXT: https://ctext.org/

[6] http://hanchi.ihp.sinica.edu.tw/ihp/hanji.htm

[7] http://skqs.lib.ntnu.edu.tw/dragon/

CTP 5-char poems	**Patterns**	**2-1-2**	**2-2-1**	**2-3**	**1-2-2**	**1-1-2-1**	
	Percentage	56.61	42.11	0.52	0.42	0.19	
	Patterns	**2-1-1-1**	**3-2**	**1-1-1-2**	**1-1-3**	**3-1-1**	**others**
	Percentage	0.06	0.03	0.02	0.01	0.01	< 0.02
CTP 7-char poems	**Patterns**	**2-2-1-2**	**2-2-2-1**	**2-2-3**	**3-1-2-1**	**2-1-2-2**	
	Percentage	58.77	39.05	0.94	0.23	0.23	
	Patterns	**3-1-1-2**	**2-1-1-2-1**	**2-3-2**	**1-2-1-1-2**	**1-2-1-2-1**	**others**
	Percentage	0.20	0.06	0.06	0.05	0.05	< 0.04
CSP RHO poems	**Patterns**	**2-2-1-2**	**2-2-2-1**	**2-2-3**	**2-1-2-2**	**3-1-1-2**	
	Percentage	63.54	34.01	0.96	0.53	0.13	
	Patterns	**1-2-1-1-2**	**2-2-1-1-1**	**3-1-2-1**	**1-1-2-1-2**	**2-1-1-2-1**	**others**
	Percentage	0.11	0.11	0.09	0.07	0.05	< 0.4

Table 2: Distributions of line patterns of annotated CTP and CSP poems ("%" not shown)

"poems" directly because their distinction is not very important for the current study.

4.2 Patterns of the Annotated Poems

We can inspect the patterns of the lines in the annotated poems, and Table 2 shows the distributions of the patterns for the annotated CTP and CSP poems. In the table, we show the percentages of the most frequent 10 patterns for the CTP and CSP poems. We do not show the "%" symbol for succinctness. Based on the statistics in Table 1, we have annotated 13098 (11309+1789) CTP poems that have 5 characters in their lines, and we have annotated 12892 (5004+7343+545) CTP poems that have 7 characters in their lines. We have annotated CSP poems that have 7 characters in their lines.

The experience reported in the literary studies about the common patterns predicts the distributions extremely well (Hu and Yu, 2001; Yu and Hu, 2003; Lo, 2005). More than 98% of the annotated CTP poems that have 5-character lines were annotated as 2-1-2 or 2-2-1 pattern, and we observed 13 patterns for poems that have 5 characters in their lines. More than 97% of annotated CTP poems and CSP poems that have 7-character lines were annotated as 2-2-1-2 or 2-2-2-1 pattern. Both the CTP and CSP 7-character poems have 33 different patterns.

Mathematically, one may have expected that 5-character and 7-character lines may have as many as 16 and 64 different patterns, respectively. A normal classical Chinese poem should follow quite a few phonological, syntactic, and semantic rules, so not all of the patterns are acceptable. Hence, the patterns of the lines are not uniformly distributed. For instance, although possible, the pattern 1-1-1-1-1 for a 5-character line would be very unusual.

	Items	RPO	HQ	RHO	EFHP	EFPP
UT	20495	8879	4376	5276	1684	280
NTPU	5495	2430	628	2067	105	265

Table 3. Workloads of the annotators

Our statistics support a phenomenon that was discussed circa 1700CE but was not mentioned in modern literature for computing technologies (Hu, 2003 reprint).[8] Frequent patterns like 2-1-2, 2-2-1, 2-2-1-2, and 2-2-2-1 can be expected, but the large proportions of these patterns may be surprising. The 2-3 pattern is many times more frequent than the 3-2 pattern in Table 2.

5 Inter-Rater Agreement Analysis

We report results of our inter-rater agreement analysis in this section, and argue that the observed agreements are not just results of the annotators' accepting the heuristics that were explained in Section 2.3.

5.1 Results of the Analysis

To further understand our annotated poems, we conducted an IRA analysis using the annotated Tang poems. Table 3 lists statistics for the annotations that were completed by the UT and NTPU annotators. Hence, the amounts of poems listed in Table 3 must agree with the amounts of poems for the CTP in Table 1. For instance, in Table 1, we have 11309 annotated RPO poems, of which 8879 items were annotated by the UT annotators and 2430 were annotated by the NTPU annotators.

We compared the annotations completed by the UT and by the NTPU annotators. A poem that was annotated by a UT annotator and a NTPU annotator is considered as a pair in the IRA studies, and we have 5217 pairs. We compared these 5217 pairs

[8] Both Tsao (2004, p. 59) and Jiang (2008, p. 166) cited Hu (2003, reprint): "五字句以上二下三為脈，七字句以上四下三為脈，其恆也。有變五字句上三下二者，。。。，皆蹇吃不足多學。" Hu was born in the late 16th century.

	Dice for characters	Dice for words	PSL	PSP
observed	95.2	93.0	87.7	42.8
inferred	82.9	70.8	50.0	0.39*

Table 4: Inter-rater agreement analysis ("%" not shown, 0.39 is for regulated octaves)

and calculated the metrics for IRA analysis as we explained in Section 3.2.

The "observed" row in Table 4 lists the statistics for our IRA analysis. The annotators of UT and NTPU showed very high agreement in their decisions as to character and word level decisions. The Dice coefficient for the character classification is 0.952, and the Dice coefficient for common words is 0.930. The percentage that the annotators perfectly agreed on a line is 87.7%, and the percentage that the annotators agreed perfectly on the segmentation of whole poems is only 42.8%.

5.2 A Theoretical Analysis

In this subsection, we derive theoretical estimators, shown in the "inferred" row, for the "observed" row in Table 4 to show that our annotators must not agree with each other only because they might have common belief on the frequent patterns that we explained in Section 2.3. Instead, the expertise and personal judgements of the annotators have also influenced, for otherwise the statistics in the "observed" row could fall as low as those listed in the "inferred" row. We will show the details about this inference procedure in an extended report.

6 Simple Probabilistic Classifiers

Recall that the task of word segmentation can be viewed as classifying characters as a terminal or non-terminal character for a word.

6.1 Directional Pointwise Mutual Information

If we temporarily assume that all the lines of RPO poems used the 2-2-1 or the 2-1-2 pattern and that all the lines of RHO poems used the 2-2-2-1 or the 2-2-1-2 patterns, word segmentation becomes an extremely simplified task. Given these heuristic principles, a simple-minded word segmenter could randomly choose one of the 2-2-1 and 2-1-2 patterns for an RPO poem and choose one of the 2-2-2-1 and 2-2-1-2 patterns for an RHO poem.

A better method is to rely on the directional pointwise mutual information (DPMI) measure to make decisions. Our DPMI is very similar to the traditional pointwise mutual information. The DPMI measures the strength of the closeness of two characters, and we use DPMI(XY) to denote the DPMI of two *consecutive and ordered* characters X and Y.

We can train the DPMI value of two given characters with unannotated poems easily. We define the DPMI value of X and Y, based on their individual appearances and consecutive collocations in poems.

$$DPMI(XY) \equiv log\frac{\Pr(XY)}{\Pr(X)\Pr(Y)} = log\frac{\Pr(Y|X)}{\Pr(Y)} \quad (2)$$

In (2), $\Pr(X)$ and $\Pr(Y)$ are, respectively, the probabilities of reading the unigrams X and Y in the poems, and $\Pr(XY)$ denotes the probability that we see an ordered bigram XY in the poems. Our definition of DPMI is a slight variation of the original definition of pointwise mutual information (PMI) (Manning and Schütze, 1999; Cover and Thomas, 2006), where the computation typically does not consider the orders of X and Y.

Given a line, say "ABCDE" of an RPO poem, we could compare the DPMI measures of CD and DE to determine whether we segment the line into AB-CD-E or AB-C-DE. If DPMI(CD) is larger than DPMI(DE), we choose AB-CD-E; otherwise, we choose AB-C-DE. Given an RHO line, say "ABCDEFG", we segment the line into AB-CD-EF-G if DPMI(EF) is larger than DPMI(FG) and into AB-CD-E-FG otherwise.

6.2 Weighted DPMI

To actually determine the DPMI for a bigram XY, we need to estimate the probability values of $\Pr(X)$ and $\Pr(Y)$ based on a training dataset. We simply employ the maximum likelihood estimator for this task (Alpaydin, 2020; p. 68).

Although we may determine the probability of the bigram XY, $\Pr(XY)$, with the maximum likelihood estimator as well, we chose to add weights to particular bigrams by considering the domain-dependent heuristics that we discussed in Section 2.3.

Given a line of five characters, say "ABCDE", we could consider two different segmentations, and they are AB=CD=E or AB=C=DE. Under this presumption, we assign a base weight, β, to all of the bigrams in "ABCDE", i.e., "AB", "BC", "CD", and "DE", and we give extra weights to "AB", "CD", and "DE" because of their positions in the line. If the segmentation of "ABCDE" must be either "AB=CD=E" or "AB=C=DE", we essentially have assumed that "AB" is a bigram, so we give a starting weight, σ, to the starting bigram of each line. We give an additional weight, α, to "CD" and "DE" because one of them should be a bigram.

Given a line of "ABCDE", "AB" will gain $\beta+\sigma$ in its total weight, "BC" will gain β, "CD" will gain $\beta+\alpha$, and "DE" will gain $\beta+\alpha$. If the assumptions about the patterns are reasonable, we hope that the values of the weighted DPMI will be more informative than the raw frequency that is used for maximum likelihood estimators.

We set β, σ, and α to 0.3, 1, and 0.5, respectively, in our current study. Obviously, we may try other combinations in our experiments. We set β to a relatively small value because it provides a basic weight to all bigrams. Since "AB" is relatively more certain than "CD" and "DE" to form a bigram, the starting weight is not smaller than the additional weight. We set σ to one because, if accepting the heuristics explained in Section 2.3, the staring bigrams of each line are two-character words. We set α to 0.5 because, in an "ABCDE" line, one of "CD" and "DE" will be a word, so they share the starting weight equally.

We use the total weights of bigrams observed in the training set to calculate the probability of bigrams. Every observed bigram in the training set will accumulate their own total weights, and the probability of a bigram, $\Pr(XY)$, is defined as its total weight, $\mathrm{TW}(XY)$, divided by the overall weights of all bigrams in the training set.

$$\Pr(XY) \equiv \frac{\mathrm{TW}\,(XY)}{\sum_{z\,\in\{the\ bigrams\ in\ the\ training\ set\}} \mathrm{TW}(z)} \quad (3)$$

We will refer to this score function as WDPMI. Note that we establish WDPMI from a probabilistic perspective, but we did not verify whether the resulting weights conform to the axioms of probability properly.

When we apply the weighted DPMI for segmenting the test data, we must be prepared for encountering unseen unigrams and unseen bigrams in the test data. This is because we must strictly separate the test data from the training data (Alpaydin, 2020). As a consequence, we need to handle unseen unigrams and bigrams in the test data. For these cases, we assign them the minimum DPMI for the unigrams or bigrams that we have seen in the training data. This choice is inspired by the Good-Turing smoothing method (Good, 1953).

6.3 Training DPMI and WDPMI

Since we do not need labeled data to train DPMI or WDPMI, we can employ more poems for training the classifiers.

Again, although we do not have theoretical rules to follow and select the poems for training, we do abide by some basic principles. First of all, we wanted to have reasonably many poems for training. We can use all of the PQ, RPO, HQ, RHO, EFHP, EFPP poems that appeared in volumes 30 through 888 in CTP for training. We chose to consider only the RPO and RHO poems in CSP for training because the total of these two types was already more than the CTP poems that we could use for training. Here we also have some TWP poems.

	items	poets	PQ	RPO	HQ	RHO	EFHP	EFPP
CTP2	36562	2257	2183	11859	6960	6970	7222	1368
CSP2	74505	3608		32929		41576		
TWP	58267	99	2220	5451	31614	18982		

Table 5. Statistics about more poems

Table 5 reuses the format of Table 1, but lists the number of labeled and unlabeled poems that we have in the CTP, CSP, and CWP. The Tang and Song poems that we listed in Table 1 are subsets of the poems that we listed in Table 5. We use CTP2 and CSP2 in Table 5 to differentiate the different sets in Tables 1 and 5. Notice that, although we have 6970 RHO items in CTP2, we have 7343 annotated RHO items in CTP1 (Table 1). This is because a CTP poem may be annotated multiple times by different annotators, even when we may not annotate all of the poems in CTP2 and CSP2. A repeatedly annotated poem is counted multiple times in CTP1 and is counted only once in CTP2.

7 Empirical Evaluations

Since we discussed the differences between DPMI and traditional PMI, and we claimed the superiority of weighted DPMI (WDPMI) against DPMI. We conducted a wide variety of experiments to verify this projection.

Since we will use the CTP1 and CSP1 as the test data, we will remove the poems in CTP1 and CSP1 from CTP2 and CSP2, respectively, at training time. We do not indicate this exclusion in Table 6. We can use different combinations of unannotated data (Table 5) as the training data and use different annotated data (Table 1) as the test data to check whether WDPMI indeed prevails.

We list 14 such experiments and their results in Table 6. In Table 1, we have two sets of annotated data. CTP1 and CSP1 are for the Tang (618-907CE) and Song dynasty (960-1279CE), respectively. In Table 5, we have three basic sets of unannotated data. In addition to CTP2 and CSP2, we added TWP. Therefore, we can create seven combinations of these three sets for training in different experiments.

Recall the definition for WDPMI and our discussion in Section 6.2. We set β, σ, and α to 0.3, 1, and 0.5, respectively, for the experiments in

ID	TrainD	TestD	WDPMI						DPMI			
			prec	recl	F_1	PWR	PSL	PSP	F_1	PWR	PSL	PSP
7	CTP2	CTP1	90.25	90.43	90.34	86.27	76.32	16.79	89.19	84.63	73.54	13.42
8	CTP2	CSP1	91.17	91.36	91.27	86.86	73.56	11.11	90.41	85.58	71.05	8.07
9	CSP2	CTP1	90.34	90.53	90.44	86.40	76.55	17.01	89.39	84.92	74.03	13.99
10	CSP2	CSP1	91.97	92.17	92.07	88.07	75.97	13.82	91.24	86.82	73.51	10.38
11	TWP	CTP1	89.30	89.48	89.39	84.93	74.04	14.03	88.42	83.56	71.72	11.79
12	TWP	CSP1	91.06	91.25	91.16	86.70	73.27	10.15	90.41	85.57	71.04	8.05
13	CTP2+CSP2	CTP1	90.73	90.92	90.82	86.95	77.48	18.32	89.84	85.56	75.10	15.25
14	CTP2+CSP2	CSP1	92.09	92.29	92.19	88.24	76.33	14.42	91.44	87.12	74.10	11.06
15	CTP2+TWP	CTP1	90.48	90.67	90.58	86.60	76.89	17.51	89.60	85.23	74.55	14.51
16	CTP2+TWP	CSP1	91.76	91.96	91.86	87.75	75.32	13.16	91.10	86.61	73.08	10.06
17	CSP2+TWP	CTP1	90.45	90.64	90.54	86.56	76.81	17.51	89.57	85.18	74.47	14.60
18	CSP2+TWP	CSP1	92.03	92.23	92.13	88.15	76.12	14.01	91.37	87.02	73.89	10.79
19	CTP2+CSP2+TWP	CTP1	90.76	90.95	90.85	86.99	77.55	18.46	89.89	85.63	75.23	15.41
20	CTP2+CSP2+TWP	CSP1	92.22	92.42	92.32	88.43	76.69	14.91	91.51	87.22	74.29	11.47

Table 6. WDPMI consistently offers better performances than DPMI. ("%" not shown)

	prec	recl	F_1	PWR	PSL	PSP
max	1.15	1.16	1.16	1.64	2.78	3.44
median	0.91	0.91	0.91	1.32	2.34	3.06
mean	0.90	0.90	0.90	1.30	2.38	3.03
min	0.75	0.75	0.75	1.12	2.23	2.11

Table 7. Differences in performance when comparing WDPMI with DPMI ("%" not shown)

Table 6. An unweighted version of DPMI can be considered as a special case of WDPMI without giving special weights. Namely, we could set β, σ, and α to 0.3, 0, and 0, respectively. Due to the limitation of page width, we do not show the values of precision and recall for DPMI in Table 6.

We could verify that using WDPMI indeed led to better performances than using DPMI, if we compare the corresponding statistics in Table 6. Each of the statistics in the shaded area in the WDPMI column is larger than the corresponding statistic in the DPMI column.

We could calculate the differences between the metrics of WDPMI and DPMI by subtracting an item for DPMI from the corresponding item for WDPMI. For Exp. 7, the difference in PSP is 3.37. We can calculate the differences in PSP for 14 experiments, and obtain their maximum (3.44), median (3.06), mean (3.03), and minimum (2.11). The rightmost column in Table 7 shows these results. We repeated such a calculation procedure for precision (prec), recall (recl), F_1, PWR, and PSL for Table 6, and show the results in Table 7. The statistics of 14 experiments in Table 7 consistently suggest that using WDPMI led to better performance than using DPMI.

We can compare the performances of WDPMI and DPMI from other perspectives, and we can include more domain knowledge about the classical poems to improve the performances of our probabilistic classifiers in an extended report of our work. Of course, with the annotated poems, we could apply deep learning (Goodfellow et al., 2016) and other machine learning methods to train and test classifiers that may further enhance the quality of word segmentation.

8 Concluding Remarks

The main purpose of this paper is to report the annotation of word boundaries for 32399 classical Chinese poems. Seven annotators of Chinese literature background carried out the task. To investigate the quality of these human annotation, we conducted inter-rater agreement studies. In fact, we have also compared the annotations with some relevant information extracted from the Sou-Yun website[9], which is a highly recommended website for learning classical Chinese poems, but we cannot provide the details here. Based on these further analyses, we gained confidence on the quality of our annotations.

We have used the annotated data to train classifiers for algorithmically segmenting classical Chinese poems. It was relatively easy to segment the lines in poems correctly, but remained challenging to segment poems completely correct. We understand that there may not be "the" correct answer to segment a poem. "The" correct answer

[9] https://sou-yun.cn/

depends on how a reader interpret the poem. Nevertheless, for the studies of computer science, we used the annotated data as the ground truth in our analysis. The annotators achieved perfect agreement for a given poem 43% of the time. Under favorable conditions when domain-heuristics are applicable, using a traditional machine-learning method, we segment a poem completely correctly 18.46% in Table 6. Switching to deep-learning methods, we could improve the results to slightly above 30%. Details about these new experiments can be provided in an extended paper.

Responses to the Reviewers

Although we briefly discussed the challenges to segment the poems for the "ground truth" that typical experts of computer science background would expect at the beginning of Section 3.2, a reviewer still commented for more discussions on this issue. Almost no one who has reasonable experience in reading Chinese poems would deny that poets might intentionally leave a certain degree of ambiguity in poems for beauty, imageries, hidden intentions, etc. We recognize this level of difficulty as well, but we also hope that it is possible that, for a majority of poems, readers may have an acceptable consensus about the interpretation of a poem. Whether our hope will hold from the perspectives of experts in Chinese literature is subject to more further studies.

A reviewer encouraged us to show the usability of our corpus via higher level of tasks for natural language processing, including named entity recognition and slot tagging (Xu and Sarikaya, 2013). We would like to extend our work in those directions after we first establish the position of the current corpus in the academic world via the discussions in this presentation.

In further experiments, we can elaborate on how using deep learning techniques can outperform the performance of using the heuristics WDPMI. Machines can learn the frequent patterns of classical Chinese poems directly via labeled data, without the need of relying on human's heuristics.

Acknowledgments

We thank the reviewers for their helpful comments on the original submissions. This research was support in part by projects 107-2221-E-004-009 - MY3 of the Ministry of Science and Technology, 110-2221-E-004-008-MY3 of the National Science and Technology Council of Taiwan, and 111H124D-13 of the National Chengchi University in Taiwan.

References

Alpaydin, E. 2020. *Introduction to Machine Learning*, fourth edition, Cambridge: The MIT Press.

Chen, K.-J. and Liu, S.-H. 1992. Word identification for mandarin Chinese sentences, *Proceedings of the Fourteenth Conference on Computational Linguistics*, 101–107.

Chen, Y., Zheng, Q., and Chen, P. 2015. A boundary assembling method for Chinese entity-mention recognition, *IEEE Intelligent Systems*, 30(6):50–58.

Cover, T. M. and Thomas, J. A. 2006. *Elements of Information Theory*, second edition, New Jersey: Wiley-Interscience.

Deng, K., Bol, P. K., Li, K. J., and Liu, J. S. 2016. On the unsupervised analysis of domain-specific Chinese texts, *Proceedings of the National Academy of Sciences*, 113(22):6154–6159.

Dice, L. R. 1945. Measures of the amount of ecologic association between species, *Ecology*, 26(3):297–302.

Emerson, T. 2005. The second international Chinese word segmentation bakeoff, *Proceedings of the Fourth SIGHAN Workshop on Chinese Language Processing*, 123–133.

Good, I. J. 1953. The population frequencies of species and the estimation of population parameters, *Biometrika*, 40(3/4):237–264.

Goodfellow, I., Bengio, Y., and Courville, A. 2016. *Deep Learning*, Cambridge: The MIT Press.

Hu, J. and Yu, S. 2001. The computer aided research work of Chinese ancient poems (唐宋诗之计算机辅助深层研究), *Acta Scientiarum Naturalium Universitatis Pekinensis* (北京大学学报(自然科学版)), 37(5):727–733. (in Chinese)

Hu, Z.-H. (胡震亨, 1569-1645?) 2003. *Tangyin Tongqian* (唐音統籤) (reprint), Shanghai: Shanghai Guji Chu Ban She (上海古籍出版社). (in Chinese)

Huang, C.-R., Šimon, P., Hsieh, S.-K., and Prévot, L. 2007. Rethinking Chinese word segmentation: tokenization, character classification, or wordbreak identification, *Proceedings of the Forty-Fifth Annual Meeting of the Association for Computational Linguistics*, 69–72.

Jiang, S. 2008. *A Linguistic Research for Tang Poems* (唐詩語言研究), Beijing: Language&Culture Press (語文出版社). (in Chinese)

Lee, J. 2012. A classical Chinese corpus with nested part-of-speech tags, *Proceedings of the Sixth EACL*

Workshop on Language Technology for Cultural Heritage, Social Sciences, and Humanities, 75–84.

Lee, J. and Kong, Y. H. 2012. A dependency treebank of classical Chinese poems, *Proceedings of the 2012 Conference of the North American Chapter of the Association for Computational Linguistics: Human Language Technologies*, 191–199.

Lee, J., Kong, Y. H., and Luo, M. 2018. Syntactic patterns in classical Chinese poems: A quantitative study, *Digital Scholarship in the Humanities*, 33(1):82–95.

Liu, C.-L. and Chang, W.-T. 2019. Onto word segmentation of the *Complete Tang Poems*, *Proceedings of the 2019 International Conference on Digital Humanities*.

Liu, C.-L., Mazanec, T. J., and Tharsen, J. R. 2018. Exploring Chinese poetry with digital assistance: Examples from linguistic, literary, and historical viewpoints, *Journal of Chinese Literature and Culture*, 5(2):276–321.

Lo, F. 2005. Design and applications of systems for word segmentation and sense classification for Chinese poems (詩詞語言詞彙切分與語意分類標記之系統設計與應用), *Proceedings of the Fourth Conference of Digital Archive Task Force* (第四屆數位典藏技術研討會論文集) (in Chinese)

Ma, W.-Y. and Chen, K.-J. 2003. Introduction to CKIP Chinese word segmentation system for the first international Chinese word segmentation bakeoff, *Proceedings of the Second SIGHAN workshop on Chinese Language Processing*, 168–171.

Manning, C. and Schütze, H. 1999. *Foundations of Statistical Natural Language Processing*, Cambridge: The MIT Press.

Owen, S. 2007. A Tang Version of Du Fu: The Tangshi Leixuan, *Tang Studies*, 25:57–90, 2007. (DOI: 10.1179/073750307790779469)

Qian, P. and Huang, X. 2015. The statistical modeling and macro-analysis of Chinese classical poetry (中国古诗统计建模与宏观分析), *Journal of Jiangxi Normal University* (Natural Science), 39(2):117–123. (in Chinese)

Shi, Y.-L. (ed.) 2011. *The Complete Taiwan Poems*, National Museum of Taiwan Literature. (https://www.nmtl.gov.tw/publicationmore_149_306.html) (in Chinese)

Sproat, R. and Emerson, T. 2003. The first international Chinese word segmentation bakeoff, *Proceedings of the Second SIGHAN Workshop on Chinese Language Processing*, 133–143.

Tsao, F.-f. 2004. *Some Linguistic Analyses of Chinese Literature: Three Studies of Tang and Song Poems* (從語言學看文學：唐宋近體詩三論), Taipei: Academia Sinica. (in Chinese)

Wang, L. 1972. The Rhymes in Chinese Poems (漢語詩律學), in the *Collection of Wang Li* (王力全集) (reprint), Shangdong: Shangdong Education Press (山東教育出版社) (in Chinese)

Xu, P. and Sarikaya R. 2013. Convolutional neural network based triangular CRF for joint intent detection and slot filling, Proceedings of the 2013 IEEE Workshop on Automatic Speech Recognition and Understanding, 78–83.

Yu, S. and Hu, J. 2003. Word-based statistical analysis of Chinese ancient poetry (唐宋詩之詞匯自動分析及應用), *Language and Linguistics*, 4(3):631–647. (in Chinese)

Creative Text-to-Image Generation: Suggestions for a Benchmark

Irene Russo
Istituto di Linguistica Computazionale "Antonio Zampolli" (ILC-CNR), Pisa
irene.russo@ilc.cnr.it

Abstract

Language models for text-to-image generation can output good quality images when referential aspects of pictures are evaluated. The generation of creative images is not under scrutiny at the moment, but it poses interesting challenges: should we expect more creative images using more creative prompts? What is the relationship between prompts and images in the global process of human evaluation?
In this paper, we want to highlight several criteria that should be taken into account for building a creative text-to-image generation benchmark, collecting insights from multiple disciplines (e.g., linguistics, cognitive psychology, philosophy, psychology of art).

1 Introduction

Creativity is generally defined as the ability to produce new work that departs from existing practices and is appropriate, e.g., "normally fitted or adapted to the resolution of problems or difficulties existing within defined constraints" (Carter, 2004). As a peculiar human feature, creativity has been investigated by multiple disciplines (psychology, aesthetics, linguistics) to find recurring patterns and regularities in the motivated and intentional breaking or bending of rules that every creative act implies.

Creativity varies in time and space as every culturally determined concept. The evaluation of creativity during the Renaissance differed from today's practices because cultural expectations have changed. In Eastern cultures, the focus is on the creative act *per se* instead of on the final result (Lubart, 1990).

The analysis of creativity is also dependent on the media: linguistic and visual creativity are both the result of complex psychological processes in the creator's mind but give rise to radically different perceptual experiences for the receiver. Indeed, linguistic and visual outcomes require different interpretation processes.

To make the understanding of creativity more complicated, the artificial generation of creative instances such as texts, music, images – under the name of computational creativity – poses further challenges to creativity's definition. Sometimes the artist cooperates with the automatic system (as in generative art), while in other cases the result is independent of human agency, such as in text-to-image generation systems.

Today, computational models for text-to-image generation based on unsupervised deep learning methods can output realistic images, translating human written textual descriptions of variable length into images. Text-to-image (T2I, henceforth) generation model aims to generate photorealistic images semantically consistent with the text descriptions.

Starting with the generation of images from single labels or keywords, these models can handle more complex linguistic descriptions. Recent works mainly try to understand how much these images are referentially coherent and complete (Saharia et al., 2022). The evaluation of the referential aptness is more straightforward than the evaluation of creativity, which depends more on subjective variability in judgments and needs well-posed questions to be adequately isolated from other co-occurring variables that influence the aesthetic experience.
The generation of creative images is not under scrutiny at the moment, but it raises interesting questions: should we expect more creative images when using more creative prompts? What is the relationship between captions and images in the holistic process of evaluation? Can we have creativity without agency and authorial responsibility?

In this paper, we want to highlight several criteria that should be taken into account for building a text-to-image generation benchmark that addresses

The 2nd International Workshop on Natural Language Processing for Digital Humanities (NLP4DH), pages 145–154
November 20, 2022. ©2022 Association for Computational Linguistics

those questions, collecting and discussing insights from multiple disciplines (e.g., linguistics, cognitive psychology, philosophy, psychology of art).

The remainder of this article is structured as follows: in Section 2, we describe relevant works from generative art and psychology of art. Section 3 focuses on the definition of creativity in language. We discuss how it is realized at different levels, together with examples that can be included in the benchmark. In Section 4, visual creativity is presented under the lens of the findings from psychology of art. Section 5 introduces the T2I available systems usable at the moment for generating images using textual prompts. Finally, in Section 6, we delineate the key features of human evaluation of creativity for automatically generated images that would help to answer important research questions before concluding in Section 7.

2 Related Work

The definition of a benchmark for creative T2I generation is a practical effort deeply influenced by theoretical questions previously addressed by other disciplines. In this section, we briefly report their relevant findings.

2.1 Generative Art

Generative art is a way to create art that requires a system "set into motion with some degree of autonomy contributing to or resulting in a completed work of art" (Galanter, 2003). It uses agents and is based on unpredictability, a key feature of creativity (Boden and Edmonds, 2009).

Galanter (2003) theorizes the system as self-contained enough to operate autonomously, so the artist's role is to limit this autonomy. For example, an artist could intervene by acting on parameters, filtering the final outputs, or interactively modifying the system through feedback. However, when these systems are black boxes with opaque internal operations, such as deep learning models, it is difficult for the artist to act on them (Dorin et al., 2012). The limitations of deep learning models have been investigated: autonomous deep learning systems created for emulating arts (for example, through style transfer) are not able to reproduce the creative process, and output images with bias (Srinivasan and Uchino, 2021). Another important limitation is that generative art introduces randomness as part of its creative process, while in deep learning methodologies, randomness is a constitutive feature of the design process. However, human intervention can intentionally change the degree of randomness in the training phase or the generation process. Under these premises, we believe that T2I generated images could be perceivable with features attributable to generative art products, e.g., valuable as more or less creative, novel, or pleasant.

Another issue raised by generative art is the role of agency. Creativity is an agential disposition that produces new and valuable things thanks to the know-how of a human agent. Mechanical search and trial and error procedures are not creative. This view is endorsed by Paul and Stokes (2018) who argue that judgments about the creativity of an object implicitly refer to the generative processes involving agency. But computer-based generative art defies or at least causes a rethinking of the notion of agency (Wheeler, 2018).

The output of T2I generation systems is potentially art if the possibility of human interaction is made transparent in this scenario. An appropriate benchmark would go in this direction, investigating the interactions between the types of linguistic prompts and the perceived effects of generated images.

2.2 Computational Aesthetics

Computational aesthetics is a field of study interested in the convergence and generability of aesthetic judgments (Hönig, 2005; Bo et al., 2018). It focuses on the automatic assessment of beauty in human creative products, starting with the datasets of human judgments used to train specialized algorithms. The goal is to develop automatic systems that replicate the evaluation performances of human experts.

It is relevant for evaluating T2I generation outputs because researchers found convergences in the subjects' aesthetic experiences and discover dimensions that constitute regularities manageable with algorithms. Even if the evaluation of creativity is independent of the assessment of aesthetic properties, sometimes the distinction is blurred since aesthetics is an aspect through which creativity is manifested and can be evaluated. A computational approach can illuminate the interplay between an image's perceived creativity and aesthetic value.

We aim to investigate if T2I systems can be globally compared in terms of the aesthetic appreciation of their outputs and how the creativity of the prompt affects the human evaluation of this aspect for the automatically generated images.

2.3 Neuroaesthetics

Reflections about the value and the evaluation of cultural objects such as paintings and pictures have been for centuries the object of study of aesthetics (Carroll, 1999). Human-produced images such as pictures and paintings can be evaluated as creative when presented in a context that clarifies their nature as cultural objects. Throughout history, the predominant criteria defining beauty and pleasure evolved, also influenced by new scientific discoveries in other fields, such as psychology of art. Nowadays, aesthetic theories are deeply influenced by experimental results from psychology, and the emerging field of neuroaesthetics presents promising results about universal regularities in the perception of aesthetic features (Nadal and Chatterjee, 2019).

According to neuroaesthetics, the aesthetic experience is composed of bottom-up perceptual habits (e.g., the tendency to identify objects when viewing artworks) and top-down control mechanisms that involve high-level cognition processes that attribute meanings to images (Cupchik et al., 2009). In general terms, perceptual fluency is enhanced by the amount of information, symmetry, and figure-ground contrast that increases the subjective pleasantness of an image. On the other hand, the complexity of an image is composed of the number of elements, differences in elements, and patterns in their arrangement. From experimental evidence, we know that the relationship between image complexity and pleasantness ratings forms an inverted-U shape graph: people increasingly like art as it goes from very simple to more complex until a peak when pleasantness ratings begin to fall again (Berlyne et al., 1968).
Without denying the influence of social and historical contexts on the perception of such features as beauty, novelty, and creativity, general principles about the perception of complexities in the composition of abstract paintings made clear that too much complexity is negatively correlated with aesthetic appreciation.

These general principles are declined in different ways when the object is a picture, a figurative, or an abstract painting. Evaluating a picture requires comparing the concrete reality that it reproduces and the artist's interpretation of that reality. With paintings, it is sometimes irrelevant the reality portrayed since the artist could deliberately distort it. In those cases, the title of the work acts as a framework for the interpretation. The relationship between the artistic work and the title is essential for evaluating creativity because it sets the boundaries of the evaluation process (see Section 2.4).

At the moment, it is not possible to control high-level properties of the generated images, such as the complexity or the symmetry of the composition, but we are confident it will be possible to a certain degree in the near future. Playing with these parameters will add an interesting dimension to T2I generation models' benchmark.

2.4 Psychology of Art

A series of experiments in the psychology of art investigated title/artwork relationship in the viewer experience (Russell, 2003; Franklin et al., 1993). They agreed on the fact that the title provided by the artist supports the interpretation process, making the image partly dependent on the verbal context. The title is a guide to painting's meaning, affecting attention and interpretation, increasing coherence, and enhancing aesthetic experience.

The viewers use the title to determine the artist's intentions, and different kinds of titles guide the viewer in different ways. Descriptive titles summarise the painting or picture in a short and neutral declarative sentence (e.g., *Woman planting flowers*). In contrast, elaborative titles use abstract words or metaphors not anchored to the image (e.g., *The Satin Tuning Fork*), forcing a metaphorical interpretation. This distinction is easy to understand for representational artworks. In the case of abstract paintings that do not contain a recognizable object, the distinction is between labeling titles void of meaning (e.g., *Studio n.5*) and titles that guide the processing of visual content (e.g., *From Pale Hands to Weary Skies*).

Differences between the two types of paintings (representational vs. abstract) also reflect the interpretation process guided by titles. For representational artworks, elaborative titles increase aesthetic experience more than descriptive titles but not the understanding of them (Millis, 2001). Depending on the time allocated for processing the abstract painting, elaborative titles increased the understanding when the time slot was 60 sec, while in the 1-sec scenario, descriptive titles helped more. The 60-sec exposure did not affect the aesthetic experience (Leder et al., 2006).

To reproduce these results on automatically generated images, we plan to include descriptive and elaborative prompts in the benchmark for evaluating T2I generation systems.

3 Creativity in Language

Linguistic creativity is a multi-dimensional construct, a distinctive trait of human beings not necessarily limited to literary texts but also retrievable in daily conversations (Carter, 2004). Thanks to corpus linguistics, creativity in language uses is an investigable topic: corpora represent the average level against which to measure novelty. Since we know the regularities of language, creative linguistic usages seem something that can be measured and organized along a cline. They gradually outdistance themselves from the norms.

However, very creative usages could not be attested even if the corpus is reputed representative for the language investigated. Moreover, the same corpus could not contain with significative frequency widely used idiomatic expressions that would be wrongly recognized as creative. For this reason, corpus linguistic methodologies should be used with care in the study of linguistic creativity.

The creative exploitation of linguistic means is retrievable at various levels that differ by granularity: if creativity at the morphological level concerns single words or pairs of words, when the focus is on the metaphors, syntagmatic units, or whole sentences are the objects of the analysis. In principle, multiple instances of creative language can be found in a single example: a creative word resulting from blending can be inserted in a metaphorical pattern that the reader recognizes as a flash fiction story (e.g., a very short story, limited in length, see 3.3).

In the following sub-paragraphs, short descriptions of creativity at various levels are reported, with examples and theoretical stances from works on these topics. As an illustrative purpose, we include just metaphors and analogies because they are among the most frequent figures of speeches exploited creatively to illustrate how they can be realized at different linguistic levels.

For each level, we distinguish when possible between denotational and connotational creative exploitations. The first kind aims to introduce new words or collocations that identify a new referent in the world. We produce connotational creative exploitations when we want to communicate about an abstract property, a state of mind, a moral disposition, etc. While with denotational creativity the generated image should keep some of its referential properties (e.g., objects mentioned in the prompt should be identifiable in the image) this is not necessary for connotational creativity that, on the contrary, should produce more abstract images.

3.1 Morphological Creativity

Morphological creativity has been widely investigated to understand when and how morphological rules are exploited (Dal and Namer, 2018; van Marle, 1985). The new coinages can be playful and involve irregular means of word formation (e.g., blends or the import of affixes from other languages). New words are created by the speaker/writer on the fly to cover some communicative needs and are understandable thanks to linguistic and extra-linguistic contexts.

Under the umbrella of morphological creativity – broadly designating the coinage of new words – we posit two distinct morphological processes: the creation of new words with productive morphological rules and the creation of new words with irregular means of word formation, such as blends or the import of affixes from other languages. Neologisms can be created exploiting these paths; the study of *hapax legomena* in corpora can produce a list of attested examples, some of them included in dictionaries at later stages. Cook and Stevenson (2010) created a dataset of recently coined blendings (words such as *staycation, Japanimation*) for English to perform experiments for the automatic identification of source words.

A T2I benchmark could contain a couple of them, but genuinely creative examples are the ones not included for sure in training sets, i.e., non-words or pseudowords used in psycholinguistic experiments as distractors or fillers (words such as *rooned*, *lilf*, *aurene*). As a consequence, we refer to psycholinguistic and computational experiments as a data source.

The ARC Nonword database (Rastle et al., 2002) contains more than 350,000 nonwords and pseudohomophones that are orthographically or phonotactically legal, organized on the basis of several psycholinguistic dimensions such as bigram frequencies and phonological neighbours. Several experiments showed that readers attribute semantic meanings to non-words in proper linguistic contexts (Humphries et al., 2007).

3.2 Syntactic Creativity

In the generativist literature on the topic, syntactic creativity is a deviation that needs to be explained. Multiple studies focus on syntactic creativity in child language, as a sign of imperfect acquisition of syntactic rules (Lieven et al., 2003). Examples that deviate – i.e. are not explainable by – generative models are residually investigated as marked or no standard use, salient from a sociolinguistic point of view.

However, the intentional exploitation of syntactic rules is a common feature also in literary writing. In this case, the violation of rules is functional to some pragmatic effects on the reader/hearer that still need proper experimental investigations (Lecercle, 1990).

As examples of syntactic creativity, Hampe and Schönefeld (2007) propose verbs used with an argument structure much more typically associated with that of other verb classes, as in example 1:

1. *He supported them through the entrance door* (vs. *push through the door*).

The evaluation of creative examples of syntactic usages requires, in several cases, a referential interpretation. With these examples we can not test how much T2I systems can be creative but we can understand if they are good at interpreting and unpacking information from non-standard examples. As such, whether they should be included or not in the benchmark is questionable.

3.2.1 Collocational Creativity

The existence of collocational creativity is a debated issue, especially because if it is associated with rarity in a corpus, there are no decisive methodologies to find creative collocations or rate created ones (Dillon, 2006). Apart from being striking because rare, a creative collocation needs to be apt and tailored for a unique communicative moment.

In order to get conceptually unusual collocations, a good benchmark for the evaluation of creativity in T2I systems could take into account cognitive psychology experiments that use as stimuli adj+noun pairs that are more complex to process (Murphy, 1990). Also adv+verb and verb+complement creative collocations are interesting, but no datasets are available for them. Creative collocations can be metaphorical in nature (e.g., *a diamond-encrusted book*). Metaphors draw analogies between domains not normally linked, treating something as something else by means of similarities, and are more often realized by a sentence (*This book is a gem*). T2I generation systems can produce images that are coherent with prompts containing metaphors when they refer to concrete aspects of the object. In this case, there is denotational creative exploitation. When the function of the metaphor is the evaluation of some abstract properties, the output of the T2I generation systems will signal the lack of understanding, as in Figure 1 and Figure 2:

Figure 1: *This book is a gem* according to DALL·E mini

Figure 2: *A diamond-encrusted book* according to DALL·E mini

3.3 Textual Creativity

Textual creativity is the most complex type of linguistic creativity because it encompasses all the previous levels and is more subject to social and cultural expectations. It concerns the creation of fiction and alternative worlds. The literary language uses involve a complex patterning at the linguistic level, often spanning several pages. At the same time, the interplay with the creativity of the plot – how it violates readers' expectations – is an additional source of perceived creativity. The interplay between phenomena at different linguistic and structural levels and how they contribute to the perception of creativity in texts is an underinvestigated topic.

Since the length of the prompt in T2I systems is limited, one possibility is to use as an example of textual creativity flash fiction (between 250-750 words) (Masih, 2009) or 'Twitter fiction' (140 characters max) (Raguseo, 2010), concise stories that, because of their shortness, are not based on a complex plot.

4 Text-to-Image Generation Systems

In this section, we briefly introduce T2I systems, linking models based on them if available.

GLIDE (Guided Language to Image Diffusion for Generation and Editing) (Nichol et al., 2022) is a system based on a diffusion model and two guidance strategies, e.g., CLIP and classifier-free guidance. The diffusion model is trained with 3.5 billion parameters on the same dataset as DALL-E (Ramesh et al., 2022), using a text encoder to condition natural language descriptions. When compared with other systems, it is preferred by human evaluators for photorealism and caption similarity. GLIDE is able to produce artistic renderings of novel concepts (see Figure 3).

"a painting of a fox in the style of starry night"

Figure 3: Image generated by GLIDE

However, when the text prompt defies world knowledge (e.g., "a mouse hunting a lion"), GLIDE fails (see Figure 4). The system is not able to handle complex textual prompts; for this reason, the model has editing capabilities that allow users to improve model samples until they match the complex prompt.

"a mouse hunting a lion"

Figure 4: Image generated by GLIDE

The authors released a smaller diffusion model on a filtered dataset based on CLIP without editing capabilities [1].

In January 2021, OpenAI introduced DALL·E, a neural network (12-billion parameter version of GPT-3) that creates images from text, using as training set text-image pairs (Ramesh et al., 2021). One year later, DALL·E 2 (Ramesh et al., 2022) was released. It generates more realistic and accurate images with greater resolution using diffusion. Unfortunately, none of those systems is open source, but a smaller model of DALL·E is available online through an online interface[2].

Imagen is a text-to-image diffusion model that does not use only image-text data for training but is based on large transformer generic language models (Saharia et al., 2022) that produce realistic images with a good image-text alignment. It consists of a text encoder that maps text to a sequence of embeddings and a set of conditional diffusion models that map the embeddings to images of increasing resolutions. A Pytorch implementation is freely available [3].

For the evaluation, the authors introduce DrawBench [4], a benchmark of 200 text prompts designed to probe different semantic properties of the models, such as compositionality, spatial relations, rare words, and more creative prompts that, according

[1] https://github.com/openai/glide-text2im

[2] https://www.craiyon.com

[3] https://github.com/lucidrains/imagen-pytorch

[4] https://docs.google.com/spreadsheets/d/1y7nAbmR4FREi6npB1u-Bo3GF\dwdOPYJc617rBOxIRHY/edit#gid=0

to the authors, "push the limits of models' ability to generate highly implausible scenes well beyond the scope of the training data." However, these prompts do not explicitly contain instances of creative language.

Parti (Pathways Autoregressive Text-to-Image model) (Yu et al., 2022) is an autoregressive text-to-image generation model that outputs photorealistic image generation coherent with world knowledge. It is complementary to Imagen because it explores different families of generative models (autoregressive vs. diffusion). For Parti, text-to-image generation is a sequence-to-sequence modeling problem analogous to machine translation: it outputs sequences of image tokens instead of text tokens in another language. Parti uses a powerful image tokenizer, ViT-VQGAN, to encode images as sequences of discrete tokens, and takes advantage of its ability to reconstruct such image token sequences as high-quality, visually diverse images. A Pytorch implementation is freely available [5].

As part of this project, the authors released PartiPrompts (P2) [6], a rich set of over 1600 prompts in English that constitute a holistic benchmark. P2 can be used to measure model capabilities across various categories and challenging aspects. It contains 52 examples such as *A high resolution photo of a chicken working out in a gym* labeled as *Imagination* to test if T2I systems are able to reproduce a not realistic state of affairs.

5 How to Structure the Evaluation Process

The images generated by T2I systems, thanks to prompts included in the benchmark – both paintings and pictures, when it is possible to specify the type of output – should be evaluated by human subjects to answer research questions about the relationship between artificially generated outputs and perceived creativity.

The evaluation of artificially generated images presents both similarities and differences with respect to the evaluation of images – pictures, drawings, paintings – created by humans.

In the following paragraph, valuable criteria for collecting judgments are listed and discussed, reporting, if necessary, how they would impact the selection of prompts included in the benchmark.

[5]https://github.com/lucidrains/parti-pytorch

[6]https://github.com/google-research/parti/blob/main/PartiPrompts.tsv

5.1 Comparative collection of graded judgments on creativity

One of the aims of the evaluation process is to collect converging judgments on creativity. In this case, the search for a good inter-annotator agreement apparently contrasts with the subjective nature of aesthetic judgments that also include the perception of creativity. Nowadays, The gold standard in measuring creativity is the Consensual Assessment Technique (CAT, henceforth) (Amabile, 1982) which concerns the assessment of the creative performance on a real task such as writing a poem or creating a collage. CAT is a product-based subjective assessment technique built on a consensual definition of creativity as the quality of products or responses judged to be creative by appropriate observers.

This technique is based on the availability of experts that know the domain and act as judges that reach good inter-rater reliability, ranging from 0.70 to 0.9 Long and Wang (2022)). There is mixed evidence about the convergence of non-expert raters: their agreement on the evaluation of visual products in art tasks is higher (and more correlated with experts' judgments) than on the evaluation of written output (Kaufman et al., 2008).

CAT was originally designed to compare parallel creative products created in response to the same prompt. Inspired by the design of experiments based on CAT, the evaluation of creativity in T2I generation systems should split the outputs into pairs or small groups of items, rated comparatively by the same annotator with Likert-style evaluation (1-5 or 1-7).

5.2 Collection of creativity judgments that take into account the verbal prompts and their properties

Creativity concerns the meaningful breaking of rules. The recipient of the creative act is in charge of attributing meaning to the creative object, which often requires an interpretation process with a cognitive cost.

Images can not be evaluated out of context. For this reason, it is essential to structure the evaluation phase on linguistic description-image pairs. Therefore, two types of questions are proposed, one addressing the denotational level and another the connotational level of the image:

- How much does the following image represent the content of the associated linguistic description?

- How much does the linguistic description inspire the following image?

These questions aim to force a graded evaluation that compare the results across linguistic prompts with different level of creativity and across different models. One of the working hypotheses testable concerns the idea that more creative connotational linguistic descriptions should generate more creative images.

It is important to include in the prompt connotational and denotational examples, creative and non-creative examples and, among the creative prompts, include examples located along a cline.

5.3 Collection of aesthethic judgments that correlate with creativity judgments

From experimental studies in psychology of art, we know that the perception of aesthetic properties partially influences the perception of creativity. Following Niu and Sternberg (2001), each generated image can be evaluated by asking for comparative judgments on different dimensions of an artistic product: creativity (the degree to which the image is creative), likeability (the degree to which the judge likes it), appropriateness (the degree to which the image is coherent with the textual prompt). There is a correlation between creativity and likeability for drawings and collages produced by humans. We expect that when abstract representations are generated, the influence of likeability on creative judgments would be more substantial.

5.4 Collection of judgments from annotators with different or no expertises

The optimal evaluation process should involve different types of annotators. Instead of involving just people with expertise in art, as proponents of CAT suggest, we plan to ask for judgments from people that are more or less aware of artificial generation in order to understand if technical knowledge influences the evaluation. Also, results from a Turing test scenario, where people do not know which image is artificially generated, could shed light on the limitations of creative T2I generation.

6 Conclusions and Future Work

Creativity is contextually and historically framed and depends on the medium. Nowadays, an unprecedented occasion for investigating the topic is represented by T2I generation models that combine linguistic inputs with visual outputs. However, while the evaluation of the referential quality and coherence of the automatically generated images has been investigated, there are no papers extensively discussing the role and the evaluation of creativity in T2I generation systems.

Is the output of T2I generation systems perceived as creative by humans? Is creativity a property that could be computationally mimicked and empirically increased in models that generate artificial instances? Should we expect more creative images using more creative prompts? What is the relationship between prompts and images in the process of human evaluation?

These are several of the questions that could be addressed with a proper benchmark. In this paper, we critically revised multidisciplinary works that could help to design a good benchmark for the evaluation of creativity in T2I generation systems and highlight several criteria that could shape the evaluation process.

References

T. M. Amabile. 1982. Social psychology of creativity: A consensual assessment technique. *Journal of Personality and Social Psychology*, 43:997–1013.

Daniel E. Berlyne, John C. Ogilvie, and L C Parham. 1968. The dimensionality of visual complexity, interestingness, and pleasingness. *Canadian journal of psychology*, 22 5:376–87.

Yihang Bo, Jinhui Yu, and Kang Zhang. 2018. Computational aesthetics and applications. *Visual Computing for Industry, Biomedicine and Art*, 1.

Margaret A. Boden and Ernest A. Edmonds. 2009. What is generative art? *Digital Creativity*, 20:21 – 46.

Noël Carroll. 1999. *Philosophy of Art : A Contemporary Introduction*. Routledge, New York.

Ronald Carter. 2004. *Language and creativity : the art of common talk*. Routledge, New York.

Paul Cook and Suzanne Stevenson. 2010. Automatically identifying the source words of lexical blends in english. *Computational Linguistics*, 36:129–149.

Gerald C. Cupchik, Oshin Vartanian, Adrian P. Crawley, and David J. Mikulis. 2009. Viewing artworks: Contributions of cognitive control and perceptual facilitation to aesthetic experience. *Brain and Cognition*, 70:84–91.

Georgette Dal and Fiammetta Namer. 2018. Playful nonce-formations in french: Creativity and productivity. In Sabine Arndt-Lappe, Angelika Braun, Claudine Moulin, and Esme Winter-Froemel, editors, *Expanding the Lexicon: At the crossroads of innovation, productivity, and ludicity*. De Gruyter.

George L Dillon. 2006. Corpus, creativity, cliché: Where statistics meet aesthetics. *Journal of Literary Semantics*, 35(2):97–103.

Alan Dorin, Jonathan McCabe, Jon Mccormack, Gordon Monro, and Mitchell Whitelaw. 2012. A framework for understanding generative art. *Digital Creativity*, 23:239 – 259.

Margery B. Franklin, Robert C. Becklen, and Charlotte Lackner Doyle. 1993. The influence of titles on how paintings are seen. *Leonardo*, 26:103 – 108.

Philip Galanter. 2003. What is generative art? complexity theory as a context for art theory. In *In GA2003 – 6th Generative Art Conference*.

Beate Hampe and Doris Schönefeld. 2007. Syntactic leaps or lexical variation? – more on "creative syntax". In Stefan Th. Gries Anatol Stefanowitsch, editor, *Corpora in Cognitive Linguistics: Corpus-Based Approaches to Syntax and Lexis*, pages 127–157. Mouton de Gruyter.

Florian Hönig. 2005. Defining computational aesthetic. In B. Gooch W. Purgathofer L. Neumann, M. Sbert, editor, *Computational Aesthetics in Graphics, Visualization and Imaging*.

Colin J. Humphries, Jeffrey R. Binder, David A. Medler, and Einat Liebenthal. 2007. Time course of semantic processes during sentence comprehension: An fmri study. *NeuroImage*, 36:924–932.

J. Kaufman, John Baer, Jason C. Cole, and Janel D. Sexton. 2008. A comparison of expert and nonexpert raters using the consensual assessment technique. *Creativity Research Journal*, 20:171 – 178.

Jean-Jacques Lecercle. 1990. *The Violence of Language*. Routledge, New York.

Helmut Leder, C. Carbon, and Ai-Leen Ripsas. 2006. Entitling art: Influence of title information on understanding and appreciation of paintings. *Acta psychologica*, 121 2:176–98.

Elena Lieven, Heike Behrens, J. Speares, and Michael Tomasello. 2003. Early syntactic creativity: a usage-based approach. *Journal of child language*, 30 2:333–70.

Haiying Long and Jue Wang. 2022. Dissecting reliability and validity evidence of subjective creativity assessment: A literature review. *Educational Psychology Review*.

Todd Lubart. 1990. Creativity and cross-cultural variation. *International Journal of Psychology*, 25:39–59.

Jaap van Marle. 1985. *On the paradigmatic dimension of morphological creativity*. Foris, Dordrecht.

T. L. Masih. 2009. *Field guide to writing flash fiction: Tips from editors, teachers, and writers in the field*. Rose Metal Press, Brookline, MA.

Keith K. Millis. 2001. Making meaning brings pleasure: the influence of titles on aesthetic experiences. *Emotion*, 1 3:320–9.

Gregory L. Murphy. 1990. Noun phrase interpretation and conceptual combination. *Journal of Memory and Language*, 29:259–288.

Marcos Nadal and Anjan Chatterjee. 2019. Neuroaesthetics and art's diversity and universality. *Wiley interdisciplinary reviews. Cognitive science*, 10 3:e1487.

Alex Nichol, Prafulla Dhariwal, Aditya Ramesh, Pranav Shyam, Pamela Mishkin, Bob McGrew, Ilya Sutskever, and Mark Chen. 2022. Glide: Towards photorealistic image generation and editing with text-guided diffusion models. In *ICML*.

Weihua Niu and Robert J. Sternberg. 2001. Cultural influences on artistic creativity and its evaluation. *International Journal of Psychology*, 36:225–241.

Elliot Samuel Paul and Dustin Stokes. 2018. Attributing creativity. In Berys Gaut and Matthew Kieran, editors, *Creativity and Philosophy*. Routledge.

Carla Raguseo. 2010. Twitter fiction: Social networking and microfiction in 140 characters. *TESL-EJ*, 16.

Aditya Ramesh, Prafulla Dhariwal, Alex Nichol, Casey Chu, and Mark Chen. 2022. Hierarchical text-conditional image generation with clip latents. *ArXiv*, abs/2204.06125.

Aditya Ramesh, Mikhail Pavlov, Gabriel Goh, Scott Gray, Chelsea Voss, Alec Radford, Mark Chen, and Ilya Sutskever. 2021. Zero-shot text-to-image generation. *ArXiv*, abs/2102.12092.

Kathleen Rastle, Jonathan Harrington, and Max Coltheart. 2002. 358,534 nonwords: The arc nonword database. *Quarterly Journal of Experimental Psychology*, 55:1339 – 1362.

Philip A. Russell. 2003. Effort after meaning and the hedonic value of paintings. *British journal of psychology*, 94 Pt 1:99–110.

Chitwan Saharia, William Chan, Saurabh Saxena, Lala Li, Jay Whang, Emily L. Denton, Seyed Kamyar Seyed Ghasemipour, Burcu Karagol Ayan, Seyedeh Sara Mahdavi, Raphael Gontijo Lopes, Tim Salimans, Jonathan Ho, David Fleet, and Mohammad Norouzi. 2022. Photorealistic text-to-image diffusion models with deep language understanding. *ArXiv*, abs/2205.11487.

Ramya Srinivasan and Kanji Uchino. 2021. Biases in generative art: A causal look from the lens of art history. *Proceedings of the 2021 ACM Conference on Fairness, Accountability, and Transparency*.

Michael Wheeler. 2018. Talking about more than heads. the embodied, embedded and extended creative mind. In Berys Gaut and Matthew Kieran, editors, *Creativity and Philosophy*. Routledge.

Jiahui Yu, Yuanzhong Xu, Jing Yu Koh, Thang Luong, Gunjan Baid, Zirui Wang, Vijay Vasudevan, Alexander Ku, Yinfei Yang, Burcu Karagol Ayan, Benton C. Hutchinson, Wei Han, Zarana Parekh, Xin Li, Han Zhang, Jason Baldridge, and Yonghui Wu. 2022. Scaling autoregressive models for content-rich text-to-image generation. *ArXiv*, abs/2206.10789.

The predictability of literary translation

Andrew Piper
McGill University
andrew.piper@mcgill.ca

Matt Erlin
Washington University
merlin@wustl.edu

Allie Blank
Washington University
adblank@wustl.edu

Douglas Knox
Washington University
dknox@wustl.edu

Stephen Pentecost
Washington University
spenteco@wustl.edu

Abstract

Research has shown that the practice of translation exhibits predictable linguistic cues that make translated texts distinguishable from original-language texts (a phenomenon known as "translationese"). In this paper, we test the extent to which literary translations are subject to the same effects and whether they also exhibit meaningful differences at the level of content. Research into the function of translations within national literary markets using smaller case studies has suggested that translations play a cultural role that is distinct from that of original-language literature, i.e. their differences reside not only at the level of translationese but at the level of content. Using a dataset consisting of original-language fiction in English and translations into English from 120 languages (N=21,302), we find that one of the principal functions of literary translation is to convey predictable geographic identities to local readers that nevertheless extend well beyond the foreignness of persons and places.

1 Introduction

Translation plays an important role in the international circulation of stories and ideas. Translations allow for the more widespread circulation of writing that would otherwise be hindered by global language differences. As such, translations can provide insights not only into the global commerce of ideas, but also the ways in which local regional cultures represent world cultures through their selection of works for translation. Research in corpus linguistics has consistently shown that the practice of translation is subject to producing predictable linguistic cues that distinguish translated texts from original-language texts regardless of the source or target languages (Baker, 1995; Volansky et al., 2015; De Sutter et al., 2017). From this perspective translation is understood as a particular "register" of language (called "translationese") governed by the cognitive demands of moving between languages (Liu and Afzaal, 2021; Mauranen, 2004; Xia, 2014).

At the same time, the field of literary translation studies has developed frameworks for understanding the concrete translational practices that arise in different national and historical settings. Relying mostly on smaller case studies, researchers have shown how particular cultural norms, political ideologies, and institutional contexts affect the nature and selection of literary translations within national literary markets (Reynolds, 2021; Heilbron and Sapiro, 2007; Heilbron, 1999). Heilbron (1999) and Sapiro (2010) have illustrated the asymmetry of target and source languages in international translation markets, i.e. the way translations are highly concentrated within a few core languages. Sapiro (2016) and Long (2021) have also shown how translations are often dominated by already highly reprinted canonical literature, where literary translation assumes a function of cultural consecration.

Our aim in this paper is to test the extent to which literary translations exhibit predictable traits similar to translationese but that reside at a deeper level of thematic content. Do translations function in a sense like a distinct literary genre, communicating a predictable set of themes that are otherwise less prevalent within original-language fiction? Understanding this aspect of translations' coherence will help us better understand the cultural functions that translations potentially serve. Our goal in doing so is to bring the affordances of NLP and machine learning into conversation with the work of cul-

The 2nd International Workshop on Natural Language Processing for Digital Humanities (NLP4DH), pages 155–160
November 20, 2022.

tural sociology and translation studies to further our understanding of the larger cultural function of translations in different literary contexts.

2 Data

For this paper, we follow the lead of Toury (1980) and create two equal-sized corpora of fictional texts, one consisting of works originally written in English and one of works translated into English from other languages. Our data is drawn from the NovelTM data-set of English-language fiction, which identifies 176,000 volumes of fiction located in the HathiTrust Digital Library published since the eighteenth century (Underwood et al., 2020). In order to identify a work as a translation, we use a set of regular expressions such as "translated from," "from the [language]," "tr. from," "rendered into English," etc. and match in volume metadata provided by Hathi to identify an initial list of candidates. If an author is included in this initial list, we then include all titles by that author.

In order to identify a volume as an original-language work, we use fuzzy matching against a large set of author names derived from Wikipedia and the Virtual International Authority File (VIAF), a database of author names from 69 library catalogues from around the world and their original language of publication.

We limit publication date between 1950-2008 for two reasons. The period after WWII is often considered a unique period in literary history, and thus these boundaries allow researchers to study translations as part of "post-war" literary culture. Additionally, we found that the diversity of source languages is almost exclusively European prior to this date, limiting the relevance of the data for studying questions concerning geographic space and language. Finally, we also remove all volumes where Underwood's predicted probability of being non-fiction was greater than 85%. Given that the set of original language works was larger than the set of translations, we then downsample each year of our original publications to match the number of translations.

In order to prepare texts for analysis, we concatenate the individual page files from each volume into a single document. We then represent each document as ten randomly selected 1,000-continuous-word samples drawn from the middle 60% of the document to avoid paratextual content in the front and backmatter. In order to avoid instances of low OCR quality, foreign-language passages, and samples that might have non-standard characters, only samples that have 90% of words in an English dictionary comprised of English-language fiction were kept. If a work did not have ten samples that met this criteria it was removed. After final review and cleaning we ended up with samples from 10,657 originals and 10,645 translations published since 1950. Our data contains 9,701 authors and translations from 120 unique languages. Fig. 1 provides the distribution of volumes by decade, while Fig. 2 provides the distribution of volumes by language region. As we can see the Hathi Trust collection is heavily biased towards translations from European languages.

To our knowledge, no existing collection of historically-matched translated and target-language fictional texts approaches the size or linguistic diversity of our corpus, and we hope that it will serve as a resource for additional research.

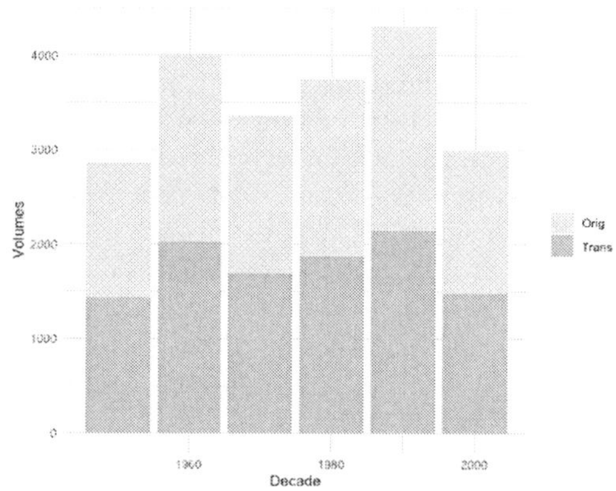

Figure 1: Distribution of translations and originals by decade

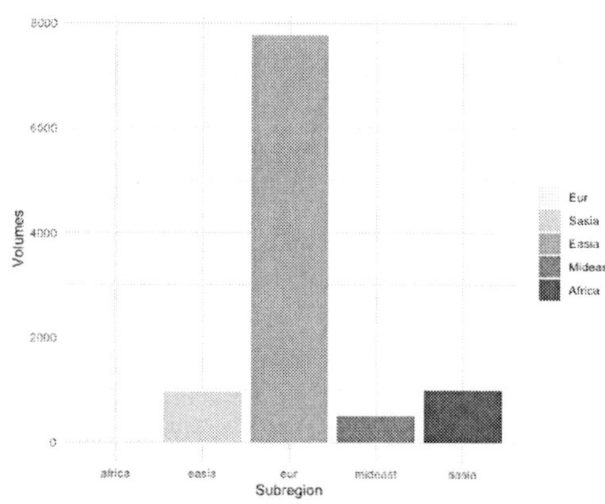

Figure 2: Distribution of volumes by language region

3 Methods

To measure the predictability of translations, we use a process of comparative supervised learning that harnesses different feature representations and different partitions of our data to better understand the conditions under which translations cohere as a distinct class of writing. We focus primarily on two scenarios, between translationese on the one hand and content-level qualities on the other. In each case, we rely on a linear SVM classifier, which has been shown to be robust for numerous text classification tasks (Colas and Brazdil, 2006).

To approximate translationese, we utilize a feature space composed of non-semantically valuable words, also known as "function words." As prior research has shown, numerous qualities of translationese – from the differential rate of pronouns (explicitation) to the recourse to shorter words (simplification) to the misalignment with expected word probabilities due to thinking in two languages simultaneously (interference) – are encoded in function words (Koppel and Ordan, 2011; Baroni and Bernardini, 2006). For our implementation, we use the 153 English stop-words included in the nltk library as our first feature space.

To capture content-level differences between translations and original-language works, we focus on constructing a feature space that is composed of semantically rich words that are not overtly culturally specific. As Volansky et al. (2015) have argued, translations are highly recognizable when compared to originals because they de facto contain foreign places and proper names. The classification task is thus often seen in this regard as a trival undertaking. Our goal is to assess the predictability of translation while masking these overt regional references.

To do so, we first construct a list of the most frequent (non-lemmatized) words that appear in our corpus not including stopwords. We then further manually remove proper names, locations, foreign words, and any obvious references to specific cultures or regions (such as "Madame" or "rupees"). After manual cleaning, we limit the number of words to a total of 2,000.

As an additional step towards masking the effects that individual and culturally-specific keywords may have, we further refine our feature space by adopting the procedure known as "authorless topic modeling" (Thompson and Mimno, 2018). Authorless topic modeling is appropriate for our purposes because it corrects for the tendency of LDA to generate overly source-specific results, especially topics that reflect key terms from a specific author or in this case language. By probabilistically subsampling words and eliminating those that are highly correlated with corpus metadata, this method helps reduce the association between particular topics and source texts, thereby producing more generalizable topics across the whole corpus. After experimentation we settle on a 30 topic model as the optimal representation. We provide samples of our topics in Table 1.

Because we are interested in assessing the extent to which content-level distinctions are potentially geographically dependent, we rerun the above two steps only on the translation data (i.e. we generate new lists of most frequent words, clean and re-apply authorless LDA). We then partition our translation data according to two different scenarios. The first is based on assumptions in the field of world literary studies that models the literary sphere into a European "centre" and non-European "periphery" (Casanova, 2004; Heilbron and Sapiro, 2007). The second subsets texts by each major geographic region as listed in Table 2.

Overall, this results in a total of five prediction tasks, four binary and one multiclass (see Table 2). The binary models allow us to compare the predictive accuracy of our two feature spaces (translationese v. content words) for translations and originals as well as our two larger global regions ("centre" and "periphery"). The multiclass model allows us to assess the regional predictability of translations across four major global areas according to topical distributions. For our binary models, we generate fifty models using a random sample of the data with replacement. For our multiclass model, we use ten-fold cross validation. We report mean F1, Precision, and Recall.

4 Results

We present our results in Table 2. While function words provide a strong level of accuracy, as expected, when predicting translations, surprisingly, our 30-feature LDA model outperforms the translationese model. Despite our efforts to create a set of general-language terms and topics, translations exhibit distinct topical behavior that is independent of proper names, places, or overt cultural references. Such topics also have predictive power for accurately identifying sub-regions according to our

Topic	Mean Coeff	Top Words
17	10.9	house time day village eyes felt face away mind people days started towards body home place water looked today rice
16	1.8	money old good day master hundred thousand pay make business buy shop house time told wife days year men head
0	1.2	woman wife mother husband house old girl daughter father home young child son women family children married sister years day
12	2.1	village old time work horse house good day home road away land long horses farm round men night fields yard
15	2.6	good great time replied day hand make found soon indeed moment order place friend house dear certain cried began long
20	2.9	young eyes old face round girl voice moment hand look white towards hair good smile head room table woman evening

Table 1: Most distinctive topics for non-European and European translations

data.

Translations are thus notably different at the level of content and not just in their reliance on low-level linguistic cues. Indeed, our models suggest that these content-level differences are meaningfully stronger than those indicated by translationese. When we break down our translations by sub-region, we also see that they exhibit very high levels of predictability (with the exception of our Middle Eastern texts though still well above chance). This suggests that translations from different regions are communicating thematically coherent and historically consistent information about those regions that extends beyond superficial markers of places or persons.

Corpus	Feature	F1	Prec	Recall
T/O	function	0.8235	0.8435	0.8267
T/O	LDA	0.8701	0.8707	0.8701
Eur/Non	function	0.7827	0.8163	0.7896
Eur/Non	LDA	0.8752	0.8763	0.8753
Europe	LDA	0.9572	0.9316	0.9844
Sasia	LDA	0.9128	0.9221	0.9048
Easia	LDA	0.7242	0.7893	0.6737
Mideast	LDA	0.3919	0.6566	0.2833

Table 2: Results of classification tasks

5 Discussion

Our paper provides the first ever attempt to use natural language processing to assess 1) whether literary translations exhibit categorically different behavior at the level of content when compared to original-language literature, and 2) whether these differences can be reliably mapped onto specific geographical regions while masking geographic information. We have found that while literary translations do indeed exhibit predictable qualities of translationese, they register even stronger stylistic differences at the level of content. Most notably, this holds even when explicit references to cultural contexts have been removed. Literary translation is distinctive as a class of writing because it talks about different kinds of experiences in different ways than original language literature.

This insight should motivate a good deal of future research into further understanding the particular nature of these differences. While prior work has suggested that literary translation plays a largely hierarchizing function – i.e. reproduces cultural hierarchies by conditioning on already highly reproduced (canonical) works – we find that literary translations are also distinctive because they introduce alternative subject matter into a target language that is geographically predictable even without overt geographical and cultural identifiers.

This suggests to us that one of translation's cultural functions is to encode geographic space, not simply through proper names or locations, but through a more extensive semantic field of references. Translations, in other words, make foreign spaces predictable and familiar to readers.

An exploration of our topic models suggests that translations may indeed be capitalizing on longstanding cultural associations with various geographic regions. One can see this on a superficial level in Table 1 by comparing topic 17 (distinctive

Region	Topic	Z-Score	Top Words
Sasia	17	1.75	house time day village eyes felt face away mind people days started towards body home place water looked today rice
Sasia	24	1.11	doctor read letter book day room years write time books work school name paper written writing wrote professor hospital reading
Easia	16	1.65	money old good day master hundred thousand pay make business buy shop house time told wife days year men head
Easia	6	1.36	right good maybe want time think make tell look old started things sure bit better kind else bad mean anyway
Mideast	28	1.3	god father priest church good people men holy world soul son great poor words heaven tell death devil prayer heart
Mideast	1	1.29	eyes black old world night body light life city white woman death sun people women earth sky time dead men
Africa	7	1.73	people work new party men country government young old women children workers war life meeting city office group political power
Africa	22	1.67	away saw water began day people dog told head old tree eat time men found night ran heard dead boy

Table 3: Most distinctive topics for each region

for non-European translations) with topic 12 (distinctive for European translations). Both of these focus on what we might term "village life," but they include culturally specific elements: farms and horses versus rice. The very stereotypicality of these distinctions reveal how deeply culture is encoded into these texts. One a more interesting level, Topic 0 provides strong evidence of a focus on kinship relations in the non-European translations, possibly one that lines up with conventional narratives of asymmetrical global modernization (Dussel, 1993). Translations into English from non-European languages represent these worlds as shaped by more traditional, kin-driven social structures.

To further unpack the relationship between particular topics and translations from different regions, we use a Z-score calculation to determine which topics were more distinctive for individual regions, as shown in Table 3. The Z-scores are calculated by subtracting the mean of a topic's average probability for all five regions combined from the score for a particular region and then dividing the difference by the standard deviation of the topic's probability across all five regions. While additional research is necessary before any definitive conclusions can be drawn, the top words from the top two topics for each region provide a basis for some preliminary hypotheses.

Topic 17 turns out to be most distinctive for South Asia in particular, suggesting that works from this region that are translated often feature depictions of traditional village life. The East Asian topics prove difficult to parse without additional investigation but suggest a focus on morality (topic 6) and merchantry (topic 16). The relatively high representation of topic 28 in Middle Eastern texts indicates a predictable emphasis on religious matters. And finally, the "African" topic 7 suggests a concern with war and politics, possibly reflecting the postcolonial concerns of post-WWII African fiction. Topic 22 seems rather diffuse, but a glance at the texts in which it has strong representation reveal that it is associated with folk and fairy tales, which again suggests a stereotypical approach to translations from African languages.

Measuring the predictability of translation at the level content allows us to better understand the ways in which different regions and languages are represented in English. Studying translation at this level of scale can offer insights into how different regions consume and portray the world beyond their borders. While our work offers an initial insight into the function of translations into English, future work will want to compare these results with other regional and linguistic contexts. How do different regions represent world cultures differently when compared to each other? Our work offers a framework that can be applied to future parallel datasets to further understand the role that translation plays in shaping the global literary marketplace.

References

Mona Baker. 1995. Corpora in translation studies: An overview and some suggestions for future research. *Target. International Journal of Translation Studies*, 7(2):223–243.

Marco Baroni and Silvia Bernardini. 2006. A new approach to the study of translationese: Machine-learning the difference between original and translated text. *Literary and Linguistic Computing*, 21(3):259–274.

Pascale Casanova. 2004. *The world republic of letters*. Harvard University Press.

Fabrice Colas and Pavel Brazdil. 2006. Comparison of svm and some older classification algorithms in text classification tasks. In *IFIP International Conference on Artificial Intelligence in Theory and Practice*, pages 169–178. Springer.

Gert De Sutter, Marie-Aude Lefer, and Isabelle Delaere. 2017. *Empirical translation studies: New methodological and theoretical traditions*, volume 300. Walter de Gruyter GmbH & Co KG.

Enrique Dussel. 1993. Eurocentrism and modernity (introduction to the frankfurt lectures). *boundary 2*, 20(3):65–76.

Johan Heilbron. 1999. Towards a sociology of translation: Book translations as a cultural world-system. *European journal of social theory*, 2(4):429–444.

Johan Heilbron and Gisèle Sapiro. 2007. Outline for a sociology of translation. *Constructing a sociology of translation*, pages 93–107.

Moshe Koppel and Noam Ordan. 2011. Translationese and its dialects. In *Proceedings of the 49th Annual Meeting of the Association for Computational Linguistics: Human Language Technologies*, pages 1318–1326, Portland, Oregon, USA. Association for Computational Linguistics.

Kanglong Liu and Muhammad Afzaal. 2021. Syntactic complexity in translated and non-translated texts: A corpus-based study of simplification. *Plos one*, 16(6):e0253454.

Hoyt Long. 2021. Chance encounters: World literature between the unexpected and the probable. *Journal of Cultural Analytics*, 6(3):25525.

Anna Mauranen. 2004. Corpora, universals and interference. *Translation universals: Do they exist.*

Matthew Reynolds. 2021. *Prismatic translation*. Legenda.

Gisèle Sapiro. 2010. Globalization and cultural diversity in the book market: The case of literary translations in the us and in france. *Poetics*, 38(4):419–439.

Gisèle Sapiro. 2016. How do literary works cross borders (or not)?: A sociological approach to world literature. *Journal of World Literature*, 1(1):81–96.

Laure Thompson and David Mimno. 2018. Authorless topic models: Biasing models away from known structure. In *Proceedings of the 27th International Conference on Computational Linguistics*, pages 3903–3914.

Gideon Toury. 1980. *In search of a theory of translation*. Porter Institute for Poetics and Semiotics, Tel Aviv University.

Ted Underwood, Patrick Kimutis, and Jessica Witte. 2020. Noveltm datasets for english-language fiction, 1700-2009. *Journal of Cultural Analytics*, 5(2):13147.

Vered Volansky, Noam Ordan, and Shuly Wintner. 2015. On the features of translationese. *Digital Scholarship in the Humanities*, 30(1):98–118.

Yun Xia. 2014. *Normalization in translation: Corpus-based diachronic research into Twentieth-century English–Chinese fictional translation*. Cambridge Scholars Publishing.

Emotion Conditioned Creative Dialog Generation

Khalid Alnajjar
University of Helsinki
Finland
Khalid.alnajjar@helsinki.fi

Mika Hämäläinen
University of Helsinki
Finland
mika.hamalainen@helsinki.fi

Abstract

We present a DialGPT based model for generating creative dialog responses that are conditioned based on one of the following emotions: *anger, disgust, fear, happiness, pain, sadness* and *surprise*. Our model is capable of producing a contextually apt response given an input sentence and a desired emotion label. Our model is capable of expressing the desired emotion with an accuracy of 0.6. The best performing emotions are *neutral*, *fear* and *disgust*. When measuring the strength of the expressed emotion, we find that *anger*, *fear* and *disgust* are expressed in the most strong fashion by the model.

1 Introduction

Dialog systems and different kinds of natural language interfaces are all around us. When we seek information or contact customer support, we are increasingly more often first greeted by a bot rather than a person. Bots are typically stiff and not lifelike making communication with them an awkward experience. This is because their goal oriented nature typically sets some constraints in terms of how creative a system can be.

We can perceive a gap between dialog systems that are designed to convey a certain message in a goal oriented fashion and dialog systems that generate chit-chat. Chit-chat can be generated rather freely because any topical response is valid, where as a certain degree of factual correctness is to be expected from a goal oriented system.

In this paper, we seek to bring the two lines of dialog generation research closer together. We implement a system that can generate topical responses (in the sense of chit-chat) with a fixed emotional content. Thus the goal of the system is to convey a desired emotion in its response, no matter what the actual textual content ended up being. This means that part of the semantics of the out is fixed, while a part as to how to contextually adapt the emotional content. is still up to computational creativity.

We base our experiments on a recently published dialog dataset that contains sentiment annotations[1]. The dataset is based on a video game called Fallout New Vegas and it has dialog where each line of the dialog is annotated as containing one of the following emotions: *anger, disgust, fear, happiness, neutral, pain, sadness* or *surprise*. This dataset makes for an optimal training data for the task we seek to solve.

2 Related Work

In terms of computational creativity and natural language generation, there are several papers out there that present work conducted on a variety of different creative language generation tasks such as poem generation (Hegade et al., 2021; Hämäläinen et al., 2022), humor generation (Weller et al., 2020; Alnajjar and Hämäläinen, 2021), news generation (Shu et al., 2021; Koppatz et al., 2022) and story generation (Vicente et al., 2018; Concepción et al., 2019). In this section, we will take a closer look at the work conducted on dialog generation.

Xie and Pu (2021) present work on generating empathetic dialog. Their model deals with the following categories of empathetic intent: *questioning, agreeing, acknowledging, sympathizing, encouraging, consoling, suggesting* and *wishing*. They base their model on the transformer architecture and they use RoBERTa for input encoding. In addition, they train a classifier that predicts the salient empathetic intent.

Dialog generation has also been tackled in a context-controlled and topic-aware manner (Ling et al., 2021). Their model consists of four parts: a hierarchical context encoder, a contex dependent topic representation module, a context guided topic

[1]https://zenodo.org/record/6990638

The 2nd International Workshop on Natural Language Processing for Digital Humanities (NLP4DH), pages 161–166
November 20, 2022.

	Anger	Disgust	Fear	Happy	Neutral	Pained	Sad	Surprised
Sentences	3 335	932	1 620	4 029	8 802	994	1 055	1 649

Table 1: Number of sentences per emotion

Prompt	Response	Emotion
I hear you've been causing trouble.	Oh yeah? Fuck off, asshole.	Anger
I was hoping you'd be that stupid.	What? Hey, guys! Help me here!	Surprise
I've dealt with those newcomers.	I take care of those who help with that. Here, you earned it	Happiness

Table 2: Examples of the training data

transition module and a joint attention based response decoder.

Chen et al. (2021) present their work on multi-turn dialog generation. They use a cross-hierarchical encoder that encodes a sentence for an answer selector model, after this a response generator model is used to generate the final output. The initial encoding is done by a transformer based model while the final genration is done by an LSTM model.

Dialog adaptation has been studied before in the context of video games (Hämäläinen and Alnajjar, 2019). The authors use an LSTM model to paraphrase the syntax of existing dialog to introduce diversity and a word2vec model to adapt the meaning of the sentence towards a desired player attribute.

3 Creativity and Emotion

There are several takes on creativity in a computational setting. In this section, we cover some of these theoretical ways of understanding computational creativity. Theoretical foundation has been, for a long time, at the very core of computational creativity to combat systems that do mere generation. That is generation for the sake of outputting something by any means necessary.

A computationally creative system should exhibit skill, imagination and appreciation according to Colton (2008). He argues that all of these three components are a strict requirement for creativity to exist in a system. Skill refers to the system's capability of producing a creative artifact whereas appreciation means that the system should also know why its creation is good. Imagination requires the system to be capable of garnering a lot of diverse output for one input.

Creativity can also be modeled through the FACE theory (Colton et al., 2011). This theory states creativity comes from the interplay between framing, aesthetics, concept and expression. Expressions are the creative output produced by the system. The system itself is called concept. Aesthetics is similar to appreciation in the previous theory; it means that the system should be able to appreciate the creative value of its output. Framing highlights the fact that creativity does not take place in a vacuum but is presented in a context. In our case, framing would be the entire dialog between a human user and the machine.

Boden (1998) identifies three types of creativity; exploratory creativity, transformational creativity and combinatory creativity. In combinatory creativity, a system forms new artifacts by combining old ones in novel ways. In exploratory creativity, a system is conducing a search in a conceptual space discovering new creative artifacts. A system that can achieve transformational creativity can change its search space.

A system is considered to be autonomously creative if it can change its own standards without being explicitly told to do so Jennings (2010). The change cannot occur at random either because a simple random change at random intervals would otherwise be enough to satisfy the criterion.

Emotion is considered as a higher level cognitive phenomenon than a feeling (see Shouse 2005). Feelings are seen to be universally felt in a similar fashion as a response to some external or internal stimulus. Emotions, on the other hand, are culturally and socially represented and their existence in all cultures in a similar way is not a given thing (see Lim 2016).

One way of seeing emotions is that they rely on affect (see Russell 2003), which is a state our mind is continuously in. An affect can move across two axes: positive-negative and arousal-relaxed. The affect we feel is contextually resolved to a higher level emotion based on the context we find ourselves in. For instance, a high arousal and negativity could be interpreted either as anger or disgust among others.

Ekman (1992) has identified six basic emotions: *anger, disgust, fear, happiness, sadness* and *surprise*. These emotions are also present in our dataset, which makes this theory optimal to build upon. The basic emotions are considered to be universal across cultures based on studies conducted on facial expressions.

4 Data

Our dataset consists of dialog in English where each line is annotated with an emotion label. Table 1 shows the data size and how many sentences were there in the dataset for each emotion. The dialog is from a video game called Fallout New Vegas[2] by Obsidian Entertainment. The game is set in a post-apocalyptic world inhabitet by creatures that were born as a result of nuclear radiation such as mutants, ghouls and feral ghouls in addition to humans.

The game dialog consists mostly of player prompts that result in a response by an NPC (non-player character). In Table 2 we can see some examples of the dialog. In our case, we train our model by using the prompt and the emotion label as an input to predict the response.

Fallout New Vegas is a relatively large video game because it is an open world RPG (role-playing game) where the player can roam freely from one place to another. As a result of this, the game has a variety of different scripted characters which means that there is no bias in terms of having the same characters speaking with each other all the time. There is, however, a bias in the topic of conversations given that they take place in a fictional world. Many of the dialogs deal with fictional places, characters, items and so on.

5 Dialog Generation

In this section, we outline our approach to emotionally conditioned dialog generation. We conduct our experiment using Transformers (Wolf et al., 2020) and Datasets (Lhoest et al., 2021) Python libraries. We base our model on a pretrained model called DialoGPT medium[3].

DialoGPT (Zhang et al., 2020) is based on the GPT-2 (Radford et al., 2019) architecture, which in turn is based on the generic transformer language model (Vaswani et al., 2017). The transformer model leverages a stack of masked multi-head self-attention layers to train on large datasets. DialoGPT employs a maximum mutual information scoring function (Li et al., 2015; Zhang et al., 2018) during the training phase optimizing the reward with a policy gradient (Williams, 1992) with a sample averaged baseline (Zhang et al., 2018).

We changed the format of the data to be as "EMOTION_1: SENTENCE_1. EMOTION_2: SENTENCE_2 [EOS]", where EMOTION_n indicates the emotion of the nth sentence in the conversation. This way, the model is exposed to emotional knowledge regarding the preceding locution of the response, as well. We use 90% of the data for training and 10% for validation. We train the model for 5 epochs.

6 Results and Evaluation

In order to evaluate our model, we sample dialog from an unrelated open-world RPG called The Witcher 3: Wild Hunt[4] by CD Projekt. The dialog is extracted using a w3strings decoder tool[5]. By using dialog from a different video game, we can see whether our model works in a different domain. The Witcher 3 is set to a medieval fantasy world inhabited by magical creatures. Some of the generated output can be seen in Table 3.

We sample randomly 15 sentences for each emotion, and produce emotion conditioned replies. In the input, "EMOTION_1:" was not present as the dialogs in The Witcher did not include emotion labels. These are then evaluated by crowd-workers on a crowd-sourcing platform called Appen[6]. For every output we evaluate, we show the input sentence and the output to the user and ask them if the output expresses the desired emotion as a simple yes/no question. In case, the user selected "yes", we also asked how strongly the line expressed the desired emotion on a 5-point scale (the stronger, the higher), the scale is 0-based from 0 to 4. Each generated output was evaluated by 5 different judges.

All in all, the judges agreement with the emotion label was **0.6**. In Figure 1, we can see the judges' agreement per emotion label. The worst performing emotion is *pained* and the best performing ones are *neutral, fear* and *disgust. Sad, surprise* and

[2] https://fallout.bethesda.net/en/games/fallout-new-vegas

[3] https://huggingface.co/microsoft/DialoGPT-medium

[4] https://www.thewitcher.com/en/witcher3

[5] https://www.nexusmods.com/witcher3/mods/1055/

[6] https://appen.com/

Prompt	Emotion	Output
Doesn't look like the talkative type.	Anger	What the fuck are you looking at?
Wait a minute! I ain't done nothin' to you!	Fear	I don't want any trouble, okay?
Asked you a question. How many?	Sad	I'm sorry, but I don't have the time to talk right now.
Need coin, fast? Those blasted nonhumans at the Vivaldi Bank say your credit's no good? Come see me!	Surprise	I've never heard of that before.

Table 3: Examples of the results

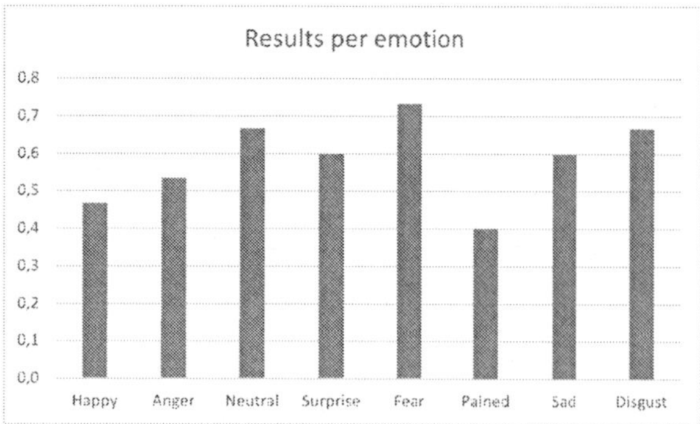

Figure 1: Percentage of "yes" answers per emotion

anger are all rated expressing the emotion over half of the time. These results are based on the aggregated results provided by Appen.

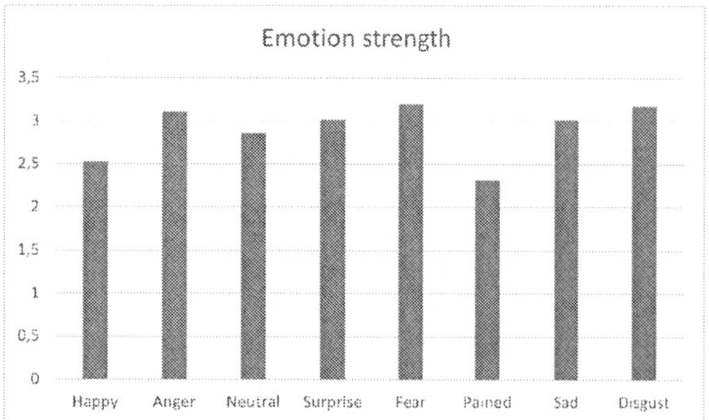

Figure 2: Strength of each emotion

Figure 2 shows how strong the judges rated each emotion to be. 0 indicates not strong at all and 4 very strong. As we can see, all emotions achieve above mid-level performance. *Anger, fear* and *disgust* being the most strongly expressed emotions. All in all, based on the results, it seems that the model is capable of producing emotional responses in a suitably strong manner.

7 Conclusions

Emotion conditioned dialog generation remains a challenge. In this paper, we have shown the viability of using a DialoGPT model for this task. The results are promising especially given that the evaluation was run on out-of-the-domain data.

The video game that was used in this paper also comes with audio files for each line of dialog. This is an interesting direction for future research because we could generate emotion conditioned dialog with audio as well. The same sentence can be said with multiple different tones and intonations to express different emotions. Building a system that can express emotion in generated speech as well would have great application potentials in speech oriented dialog systems.

Acknowledgments

This work was partially financed by the Society of Swedish Literature in Finland with funding from Enhancing Conversational AI with Computational Creativity, and by the Ella and Georg Ehrnrooth Foundation for Modelling Conversational Artificial Intelligence with Intent and Creativity.

References

Khalid Alnajjar and Mika Hämäläinen. 2021. When a computer cracks a joke: Automated generation of humorous headlines. In *Proceedings of the 12th International Conference on Computational Creativity (ICCC 2021)*. Association for Computational Creativity.

Margaret A Boden. 1998. Creativity and artificial intelligence. *Artificial intelligence*, 103(1-2):347–356.

Xiuying Chen, Zhi Cui, Jiayi Zhang, Chen Wei, Jianwei Cui, Bin Wang, Dongyan Zhao, and Rui Yan. 2021. Reasoning in dialog: Improving response generation by context reading comprehension. In *Proceedings of the AAAI Conference on Artificial Intelligence*, volume 35, pages 12683–12691.

Simon Colton. 2008. Creativity versus the perception of creativity in computational systems. In *AAAI spring symposium: creative intelligent systems*, volume 8, page 7. Palo Alto, CA.

Simon Colton, John William Charnley, and Alison Pease. 2011. Computational creativity theory: The face and idea descriptive models. In *ICCC*, pages 90–95. Mexico City.

Eugenio Concepción, Pablo Gervás, and Gonzalo Méndez. 2019. Evolving the ines story generation system: From single to multiple plot lines. In *ICCC*, pages 220–227.

P Ekman. 1992. Are there basic emotions? *Psychological review*, 99(3):550–553.

Mika Hämäläinen and Khalid Alnajjar. 2019. Creative contextual dialog adaptation in an open world rpg. In *Proceedings of the 14th International Conference on the Foundations of Digital Games*, pages 1–7.

Mika Hämäläinen, Khalid Alnajjar, and Thierry Poibeau. 2022. Modern french poetry generation with roberta and gpt-2. In *13th International Conference on Computational Creativity (ICCC) 2022*.

Prakash Hegade, Rajaram M Joshi, Vibha G Hegde, Tejaswini Kale, and Srushti Basavaraddi. 2021. Pominer: A web mining poem generator and its security model. *SN Computer Science*, 2(5):1–14.

Kyle E Jennings. 2010. Developing creativity: Artificial barriers in artificial intelligence. *Minds and Machines*, 20(4):489–501.

Maximilian Koppatz, Khalid Alnajjar, Mika Hämäläinen, and Thierry Poibeau. 2022. Automatic generation of factual news headlines in finnish. In *15th International Natural Language Generation Conference (INLG)*.

Quentin Lhoest, Albert Villanova del Moral, Yacine Jernite, Abhishek Thakur, Patrick von Platen, Suraj Patil, Julien Chaumond, Mariama Drame, Julien Plu, Lewis Tunstall, Joe Davison, Mario Šaško, Gunjan Chhablani, Bhavitvya Malik, Simon Brandeis, Teven Le Scao, Victor Sanh, Canwen Xu, Nicolas Patry, Angelina McMillan-Major, Philipp Schmid, Sylvain Gugger, Clément Delangue, Théo Matussière, Lysandre Debut, Stas Bekman, Pierric Cistac, Thibault Goehringer, Victor Mustar, François Lagunas, Alexander Rush, and Thomas Wolf. 2021. Datasets: A community library for natural language processing. In *Proceedings of the 2021 Conference on Empirical Methods in Natural Language Processing: System Demonstrations*, pages 175–184, Online and Punta Cana, Dominican Republic. Association for Computational Linguistics.

Jiwei Li, Michel Galley, Chris Brockett, Jianfeng Gao, and Bill Dolan. 2015. A diversity-promoting objective function for neural conversation models. *arXiv preprint arXiv:1510.03055*.

Nangyeon Lim. 2016. Cultural differences in emotion: differences in emotional arousal level between the east and the west. *Integrative medicine research*, 5(2):105–109.

Yanxiang Ling, Fei Cai, Xuejun Hu, Jun Liu, Wanyu Chen, and Honghui Chen. 2021. Context-controlled topic-aware neural response generation for open-domain dialog systems. *Information Processing & Management*, 58(1):102392.

Alec Radford, Jeffrey Wu, Rewon Child, David Luan, Dario Amodei, Ilya Sutskever, et al. 2019. Language models are unsupervised multitask learners. *OpenAI blog*, 1(8):9.

James A Russell. 2003. Core affect and the psychological construction of emotion. *Psychological review*, 110(1):145.

Eric Shouse. 2005. Feeling, emotion, affect. *M/c journal*, 8(6).

Kai Shu, Yichuan Li, Kaize Ding, and Huan Liu. 2021. Fact-enhanced synthetic news generation. In *Proceedings of the AAAI Conference on Artificial Intelligence*, volume 35, pages 13825–13833.

Ashish Vaswani, Noam Shazeer, Niki Parmar, Jakob Uszkoreit, Llion Jones, Aidan N Gomez, Łukasz Kaiser, and Illia Polosukhin. 2017. Attention is all you need. *Advances in neural information processing systems*, 30.

Marta Vicente, Cristina Barros, and Elena Lloret. 2018. Statistical language modelling for automatic story generation. *Journal of Intelligent & Fuzzy Systems*, 34(5):3069–3079.

Orion Weller, Nancy Fulda, and Kevin Seppi. 2020. Can humor prediction datasets be used for humor generation? humorous headline generation via style transfer. In *Proceedings of the Second Workshop on Figurative Language Processing*, pages 186–191.

Ronald J Williams. 1992. Simple statistical gradient-following algorithms for connectionist reinforcement learning. *Machine learning*, 8(3):229–256.

Thomas Wolf, Lysandre Debut, Victor Sanh, Julien Chaumond, Clement Delangue, Anthony Moi, Pierric Cistac, Tim Rault, Remi Louf, Morgan Funtowicz, Joe Davison, Sam Shleifer, Patrick von Platen, Clara Ma, Yacine Jernite, Julien Plu, Canwen Xu, Teven Le Scao, Sylvain Gugger, Mariama Drame, Quentin Lhoest, and Alexander Rush. 2020. Transformers: State-of-the-art natural language processing. In *Proceedings of the 2020 Conference on Empirical Methods in Natural Language Processing: System Demonstrations*, pages 38–45, Online. Association for Computational Linguistics.

Yubo Xie and Pearl Pu. 2021. Empathetic dialog generation with fine-grained intents. In *Proceedings of the 25th Conference on Computational Natural Language Learning*, pages 133–147.

Yizhe Zhang, Michel Galley, Jianfeng Gao, Zhe Gan, Xiujun Li, Chris Brockett, and Bill Dolan. 2018. Generating informative and diverse conversational responses via adversarial information maximization.

Advances in Neural Information Processing Systems, 31.

Yizhe Zhang, Siqi Sun, Michel Galley, Yen-Chun Chen, Chris Brockett, Xiang Gao, Jianfeng Gao, Jingjing Liu, and William B Dolan. 2020. Dialogpt: Large-scale generative pre-training for conversational response generation. In *Proceedings of the 58th Annual Meeting of the Association for Computational Linguistics: System Demonstrations*, pages 270–278.

Integration of Named Entity Recognition and Sentence Segmentation on Ancient Chinese based on Siku-BERT

Sijia Ge
University of Colorado-Boulder
Sijia.Ge@colorado.edu

Abstract

Sentence segmentation and named entity recognition are two significant tasks in ancient Chinese processing since punctuation and named entity information are important for further research on ancient classics. These two are sequence labeling tasks in essence so we can tag the labels of these two tasks for each token simultaneously. Our work is to evaluate whether such a unified way would be better than tagging the label of each task separately with a BERT-based model. The paper adopts a BERT-based model that was pre-trained on ancient Chinese text to conduct experiments on *Zuozhuan* text. The results show there is no difference between these two tagging approaches without concerning the type of entities and punctuation. The ablation experiments show that the punctuation token in the text is useful for NER tasks, and finer tagging sets such as differentiating the tokens that locate at the end of an entity and those are in the middle of an entity could offer a useful feature for NER while impact negatively sentences segmentation with unified tagging.

1 Introduction

The Chinese classics is the invaluable legacy for both public and academia. The study of ancient classic texts involves various disciplines such as religion, arts, literature, politics, etc. The public can learn about the diverse aspects of ancient China and enhance their knowledge of history; the ancient Chinese texts provide evidence for research areas like the diachronic evolution of the Chinese characters and so on. Besides, handling languages like ancient Chinese is also significant to multi-language processing as the grammar, vocabulary and other linguistic categories are strongly different from those in other languages, including modern Chinese. For example, "之" (zhi) was used to express the possessive in ancient Chinese while "的" (de) replaces it to become the major word to express possessive in modern Chinese.

Two related downstream tasks are sentence segmentation and named entity recognition since most ancient texts were not punctuated originally and the entity information would be the foundation for further research, only if we know the names of the official positions we could know the hierarchy of the administrative systems in ancient China.

For the above two tasks, we can consider both of them as sequence labeling tasks (i.e. token classification tasks), which means the model would classify each token in the input sequence to a pre-designed category. For the NER task, the model would identify which tokens would be components of a named entity, and identify the relative position to the entity. In other words, it would determine the span of the entity from the input sequence. In the sentence "**As of now, Twitter is still a publicly-traded company on the New York Stock Exchange.**", there are two named entities: "**Twitter**", we can tag it as "S" to represent this is an entity consists one single token, but an entity can also consist of several tokens, like "**New York Stock Exchange**". We can tag "New" in "New York Stock Exchange" as "B", which signifies that "New" is part of an entity and is the beginning of that entity; for sentence segmentation, we can tag the token which is followed by punctuation as a special tag and tag the rest as the other label. So in the previous instance, "now" and "exchange" can be tagged as special tokens to represent there is punctuation followed by these tokens.

Considering these two tasks as token classification makes it possible to combine them and tag each token for the two tasks simultaneously, which is efficient. The advancement of deep learning especially the development of BERT-based models improved the performance of token classification tasks (Devlin et al., 2018). Some scholars have tried pre-trained the BERT-based model on raw ancient Chinese texts and fine-tuned them on the specific downstream tasks such as word segmen-

The 2nd International Workshop on Natural Language Processing for Digital Humanities (NLP4DH), pages 167–173
November 20, 2022.

tation, part-of-speech tagging, and so on, which verified the feasibility of applying the BERT-based model to ancient Chinese datasets (YU Jingsong, 2019; Hu et al., 2021; Chang et al., 2021). However, most current works just focus on one specific sub-task resulting in a lack of comparison between separate tagging and unified tagging.

In our project, we want to answer the question: whether unified tagging on ancient Chinese texts would be better than separate tagging in terms of NER and sentence segmentation when training with a BERT-based model. we adopt the siku-BERT model as our pre-trained model which was pre-trained on the unlabeled ancient Chinese raw text and then fine-tuned on the *Zuozhuan*, comparing the performance of the separated tagging scheme and the integrated tagging scheme.

2 Related Work

Sentence segmentation on ancient Chinese: Tang et al. (2021) applied the incremental training approach to the pre-trained model and got an improvement of 1.83% and 2.21% respectively compared to the model without incremental training on sentence segmentation and punctuation tasks. Hu et al. (2021) developed a BERT+CNN model to perform sentence segmentation on poems, lyrics, and prose text, which was 10% higher than the Bi-GRU model on all of these three text styles. An LSTM-CRF model was employed (Xu et al., 2019), with the assistance of a radical embedding, the performance of this model improved compared to the typical LSTM-based model in sentence segmentation, and the result from the epitaph text of the Tang dynasty arrived at a F-1 score of 81.34%.

Named entity recognition for ancient Chinese: Wu et al. (2015) developed a deep neural network to generate word embeddings and conducted a named entity recognition task. The results showed that this model performed better than the state-of-the-art CRF model, arriving at the highest F-1 score of 92.80%. A Bi-LSTM-CRF model was proposed and applied to the traditional Chinese medicine patents' named entity recognition problems (Deng et al., 2021). The paper verified that context semantic information can be learned without feature engineering, and the performance was better than the baseline methods, arriving at an F-1 score of 94.48%. Chang et al. (2021) applied a BERT-Bi-LSTM/IDCNN-CRF model to the NER task and performed better than the Bi-LSTM-CRF benchmark model, which was 4.79% higher in F-1 score when CLUENER dataset was applied. A radical-level-based Bi-LSTM-CRF model with a self-attention mechanism was employed (Yin et al., 2019), solving the problem of how to deal with hidden information due to the properties of Chinese characters, and arriving at a F-1 score of 93.00% in CCKS_2017 dataset and 86.34% in TP_CNER dataset.

Our work is different from previous literature as we integrate the two sequence labeling tasks into one by merging labels and comparing the performance of the integrated tagging approach with the performance of the separated tagging approach.

Unified char-based tagging for ancient Chinese: YU Jiangde (2015) developed a Max-Entropy model with a unified character-based label set to perform word segmentation, part-of-speech tagging, and named entity recognition tasks. The experimental results showed that training with the unified char-based label set would be better than training in three separate turns. Cheng et al. (2020) developed a Bi-LSTM-CRF model to conduct word segmentation, part-of-speech tagging, and sentence segmentation tasks with a unified char-based label set, which also proved that labels integration with mixed corpus would get better performance. Qi et al. (2021) constructed a model unifying the word segmentation and part-of-speech (POS) tagging tasks and got the F-1 scores of 95.98% in the word segmentation task and 88.97% in the POS tagging task.

Compared to these works, although we also adopt the unified char-based tagging, our work adopts the BERT-based model to perform on the NER and sentence segmentation tasks, which is expected to extract the features better and get better performance.

3 Methods

Model: we adopt the Siku-BERT (Wang et al., 2021) as the pre-trained model, it was trained on SiKuQaunShu (a collection of ancient classics, including 536,097,588 tokens, all characters were written in traditional Chinese). Such a huge corpus will cover most ancient Chinese characters so that it would be sufficient for training. The pre-trained model architecture is based on the Chinese BERT-base model. Besides the BERT model, we add one CRF (Conditional Random Field) layer to get the global optimized label sequence.

Hardware: all experiments are trained on a Tesla V80 GPU.

Pre-processing on tagging scheme: as mentioned in the introduction part, we convert the NER task and sentence segmentation into sequence labeling tasks. To do that, we adopt the char-based labeling (Ng and Low, 2004) as the annotation scheme. That means, for the NER task, we would annotate each token (character) with one label, to signify whether this character is a part of an entity, and if so, what is the position of the token concerning the entity. We use "B" (beginning), "I" (internal), "S" (single token as an entity), and "O" (outside) to represent the position of the current character concerning an entity.

For example, "Twitter" and "New York Stock Exchange" are two named entities in the sentence "**As of now, Twitter is still a publicly-traded company on the New York Stock Exchange.**" Since "New York Stock Exchange" is an entity, we would tag the sequence as "B I I I", the "B" corresponds to "New" and mirrors that it is the beginning of an entity, and "I" means the corresponding token inside an entity, "Twitter" is a single token entity, so it is tagged as "S". Other characters that are not a part of an entity are tagged as "O" (outside of the entity).

An ancient Chinese example is

九O 月O 晉B 惠I 公I 卒O 懷B 公I 立O

(In September, Jin Hui Gong died and Huai Gong inherited the throne.)

"晉惠公"（Jin Hui Gong）is a person's name, so it is tagged as B I I .

Since our purpose for the sentence segmentation task is exactly to find out the position where punctuation occurs, we wipe out all tokens that are punctuation in our experiments, otherwise, the model just needs to tag the special label for the token that is followed by punctuation to get a good result, but this is too easy for this task. We tag the character which is followed by punctuation as "P" and those are not with "L", so like the above sentence:

As of now, Twitter is still a publicly-traded company on the New York Stock Exchange .

We will tag "now" and "exchange" as "P" and others as "L" since only these two precede punctuation.

For our ancient Chinese example:

九月, 晉惠公卒, 懷公立.

We tag the sequence as followings:

九L 月P 晉L 惠L 公L 卒P 懷L 公L 立P

That means "月""卒""立" are followed by punctuation. If there are two continuous punctuation in the original raw text, we just tag "P" once for the token before this punctuation since we just need to segment the sentence instead of recovering each punctuation.

Besides tagging these two tasks separately, we also merge the labels of each token for these two tasks into one so that we can train two tasks in one experiment. If we join the label for NER and sentence segmentation tasks with "-", the above example would be like

九O-L 月O-P 晉B-L 惠I-L 公I-L 卒O-P 懷B-L 公I-L 立O-P

So "晉 B-L" signifies that "晉" locates at the beginning of an entity but this character is not followed by punctuation.

The purpose is to compare the performance of these two tagging approaches (one is tagging for specific tasks separately and the other is tagging for both two tasks by merging the label set) with the Siku-BERT model.

Training data: Our training data is *Zuozhuan*, a chronicle of general history records during the Spring and Autumn (770-476 BC) and Warring States (475-221) periods in China. The number of tokens in the training data is 244,345, and including 25,005 entities, 33,775 punctuation. The split ratio for the training and validation sets is 8 : 2.

Hyperparameters setting: Our main purpose is not the absolute score of each task but the relative difference between the two tagging approaches, thus we keep all settings the same across experiments.

We set up 10 epochs for the training in total and the batch size for each epoch is 8, the learning rate is 0.001, and the scheduler step is 600. We adopt cross entropy as our loss function and AdamW as the optimizer; the drop-out rate is 0.2.

4 Experimental Design

4.1 The separate training for NER and sentence segmentation

First, we conduct experiments for NER and sentence segmentation separately to compare the result with the training through the unified tagging approach. Noticed that in our experiments we ignore the type of the entities (person names, place names, etc) and the type of the punctuation (colon, comma, period, etc) to make the experiment simpler while it would be worthwhile to explore with different types of entities and punctuation on a finer granularity level.

The evaluation metric for both the NER task and the sentence segmentation task would be the F-1 score mainly since the distribution of the frequency of the labels is imbalanced, but for the NER task, we count the number of samples that the model hits based on the entity level rather than based on the token level. To make it clearer, for the above examples, if the correct label sequence is

New B York I Stock I Exchange I

And the model predicts it as :

New B York I Stock O Exchange B

We don't count this as one correct prediction even if half tokens are labeled correctly.

The evaluation metric for the task of sentence segmentation is the F-1 score as well, for this task, we count the correct samples just based on the token so that we count the number of "P" and "L" labels in the gold labels and the model predictions.

4.2 Integration training for NER and sentence segmentation

To compare the effect of the integrated tagging scheme on both tasks, we train with the integrated label tagging on these two tasks together but evaluate each task separately as in 4.1. All settings are the same as 4.1 except for the tagging approach.

It's impossible to feed all texts as one into the model and thus we have to segment samples. The length of a sample cannot be the original sentence length that is segmented by punctuation, because if we do so, the model would know that only if it tags a punctuation marker "P" for the token at the end of each sample (that is a segmentation point), then the model can perform well. We don't allow the model to "cheat" in this way, so we segment each sample into a fixed length of 128, and apply it to both tasks and both tagging approaches for the sake of fairness.

Besides the major experiments, we add two groups of ablation experiments to explore the role of other factors. One of the two main factors is the pre-process approach for the NER task specifically, in this factor we can divide into two sub-factors, one is whether preserve the punctuation on the data, and the other is whether segment the sample based on a fixed number or the original sentence length, we conduct such experiments only for the NER task side without impacting the sentence segmentation; the second main factor is the label set for NER, besides "BIOS", we can also use "BIOES" to tag the entity. The only difference is that we use "E" (end) and "I" (internal) to differentiate whether the current character is the end of an entity or just inside an entity but not at the end, this increases the number of the classes. We compare the two label sets for both the NER and sentence segmentation tasks.

metric	sep tagging	uni tagging
test_accuracy	0.934	0.907
test_f1	0.869	0.867
test_precision	0.881	0.901
test_recall	0.894	0.86

Table 1: The result of NER task on separate tagging and unified tagging

5 Results

5.1 The NER task results on two tagging approaches

We conduct the NER task first and compute the F-1 score of tagging NER only and that of unified tagging. The result in table 1 ("sep tagging" means the data only includes the NER label, "uni tagging" means the data includes both NER and sentence segmentation tags) illustrates that there is no big difference between the two tagging approaches and both get an F-1 score of 0.87, while the separate tagging is a little bit better than the unified tagging one in terms of accuracy. It seems that the model does not improve with the additional sentence segmentation tags in the unified tagging approach.

5.2 The sentence segmentation task results on two tagging approaches

The result of the sentence segmentation task is the same as the NER task, with the F-1 score on both tagging schemes arriving at 0.97. The reason why the performance on the sentence segmentation task is so high is that we evaluate it on a token level, which would be high since much more non-punctuation markers than punctuation markers. Such a task is a binary token classification, for each token, the model has a 50% chance to hit the correct tag. While for the NER task the model only has a 25% probability to tag the correct token, the result would be even lower when evaluating the performance on the entity level.

5.3 The impact of punctuation on NER task

There is no difference in terms of the NER task when training with separate tagging and unified tagging, it seems that the label of punctuation does not offer any clue for the named entity identification. While we find out that the punctuation token benefits the NER task from the ablation experiment. What we do is conducting two more NER experiments on the same data but pre-process the data in different ways. One is changing the length of the samples, there is no punctuation in the data, but keep the original length of each sentence as the length of each sample, which means each sample is segmented by the original punctuation but removes all punctuation tokens; the other one not only keeps the original sentence length for each sample but also preserves punctuation. Comparing the performance of the former one and the initial experiment can infer the impact of the length of the sample on the NER task and comparing the performance of these two additional experiments can get the impact of the punctuation token on the performance.

The result is shown in table 2, "N" means there are no punctuation tokens in the sample while "Y" means preserving punctuation tokens, so "N+128 length" refers to the initial experiment setting. We can observe that the first one and the second one are almost the same, which shows that the length of the sample would not impact the NER result, while the third one is better than the first two, which shows the role of punctuation tokens for the NER task. It makes sense since there are some frequent structures such as the place names are followed by a period and the person names often occur before a colon when quoting the sentence from the speaker.

We also wonder why does the unified tagging not work better from our results in 5.1 as it at least offers the punctuation information to some extent by the label set. One possible explanation is that in our experiment, the model cannot learn the relationships between the entity labels and the different types of punctuation, in other words, whether a token follow by punctuation makes less sense than what type of punctuation follows it, consequently, it doesn't work if the entity information is related to a type of punctuation specifically.

5.4 The impact of granularity of label sets

Another ablation experiment is comparing the impact of the granularity in terms of different label sets for NER. Besides the "BIOS" label set, the other popular label set to tag the named entity is "BIOES". Compared to the "BIOS" tag set, it has one "E" label to represent the end of the entity. For "New York Stock Exchange", it would be tagged as "B I I I" with "BIOS" label set but tagged as "B I I E" with "BIOES" label set. Such a change makes the model to further figure out whether the current token is the end of the entity or just inside the entity. We reproduce the experiments in the same way as our initial experiments except for the NER tagging labels. The result is shown as table 3.

From the table, we can conclude that the performance improves a bit for both tagging approaches with the "BIOES" label set compared to the "BIOS" tagging set, and the separate tagging approach is slightly better than the unified tagging approach, which is opposite to the previous work (e.g. Cheng et al., 2020). The finer label set is a double-edged sword. On the one hand, finer labels offer more information and features for the models; on the other hand, more labels make it harder for the model to make a correct prediction. The model doesn't need to differentiate the tokens locate at the end of entities and ones locate at the middle of entities with "BIOS" labels.

For the sentence segmentation task, the performance on the separate tagging does not change while the performance decreases obviously on the integrated tagging approach, decreasing from 0.97 to 0.915, which is surprising for us since the previous work reported it improved by 3.5% compared to separated tagging (Cheng et al., 2020).

6 Conclusions

In our project, we adopt a BERT-based model to evaluate the performance of the named entity recognition task and the sentence segmentation task on ancient Chinese text with a unified tagging approach and a separate tagging approach respectively. We find out that there is no difference when we take different tagging strategies, both strategies get an F-1 score of 0.87 on the NER task and 0.97 on the sentence segmentation task, which poses a challenge to the conclusion that unified tagging is always better concluding from the previous works; we also conclude that punctuation marker is im-

process method	N + 128 length	N + original length	Y+ original length
test_f1	0.867	0.869	0.881

Table 2: The result of NER task on different pre-process approaches

tasktagging approach	separate tagging	unified tagging
NER	0.891	0.882
sentence segmentation	0.97	0.915

Table 3: The F1 score compared with two tagging schemes on BIOES label

portant for the NER task from our ablation experiments, training on the data with punctuation would be better on the NER task; moreover, finer tagging set like "BIOES" is better than "BIOS" for the NER task for both separated and unified tagging approaches, but performs worse on the sentence segmentation task if apply unified tagging.

Our experiment shows an inconsistent result to the previous research that also compared the unified tagging scheme with the separate tagging approach (YU Jiangde, 2015; Cheng et al., 2020; Shi et al., 2010); the further exploration we need to do is tagging the types of the entity and punctuation as well and count the performance based on different types of entities or punctuation, in addition, we want to try different model architectures and different pretrained models, we want to verify whether what we observe from our current experiments is specific for the model and architecture.

Our work pays attention to the ancient Chinese data which is low-resource and being ignored. The shortage of annotated data and the relatively fewer application scenarios make it a minority field in NLP, which is required more research. The usage of advanced deep learning techniques for automatic sentence segmentation and named entity recognition of ancient Chinese not only facilitate readers to read, but also can be of great significance to the arrangement of ancient books, and the intelligent application of ancient Chinese.

References

Yuan Chang, Lei Kong, Kejia Jia, and Qinglei Meng. 2021. Chinese named entity recognition method based on bert. In *2021 IEEE International Conference on Data Science and Computer Application (ICDSCA)*, pages 294–299. IEEE.

Ning Cheng, Bin Li, Liming Xiao, Changwei Xu, Sijia Ge, Xingyue Hao, and Minxuan Feng. 2020. Integration of automatic sentence segmentation and lexical analysis of ancient chinese based on bilstm-crf model. In *Proceedings of LT4HALA 2020-1st Workshop on Language Technologies for Historical and Ancient Languages*, pages 52–58.

Na Deng, Hao Fu, and Xu Chen. 2021. Named entity recognition of traditional chinese medicine patents based on bilstm-crf. *Wireless Communications and Mobile Computing*, 2021.

Jacob Devlin, Ming-Wei Chang, Kenton Lee, and Kristina Toutanova. 2018. BERT: pre-training of deep bidirectional transformers for language understanding. *CoRR*, abs/1810.04805.

Renfen Hu, Shen Li, and Yuchen Zhu. 2021. Knowledge representation and sentence segmentation of ancient chinese based on deep language models. *Journal of Chinese Information Processing*, 35(4):8–15.

Hwee Tou Ng and Jin Kiat Low. 2004. Chinese part-of-speech tagging: One-at-a-time or all-at-once? word-based or character-based? In *EMNLP*, pages 277–284.

Zhang Qi, Jiang Chuan, Ji Youshu, Feng Minxuan, Li Bin, Xu Chao, and Liu Liu. 2021. Unified model for word segmentation and pos tagging of multi-domain pre-qin literature. *Data Analysis and Knowledge Discovery*, 5(3):2–11.

Min Shi, Bin Li, and Xiaohe Chen. 2010. Crf based research on a unified approach to word segmentation and pos tagging for pre-qin chinese. *Journal of Chinese Information Processing*, 2(24):39–45.

Xuemei Tang, Qi Su, Jun Wang, Yuhang Chen, and Hao Yang. 2021. (automatic traditional Ancient Chinese texts segmentation and punctuation based on pre-training language model). In *Proceedings of the 20th Chinese National Conference on Computational Linguistics*, pages 678–688, Huhhot, China. Chinese Information Processing Society of China.

Dongbo Wang, Chang Liu, Zihe Zhu, Jiang, Feng, Haotian Hu, Si Shen, and Bin Li. 2021. Construction and application of pre-training model of "siku quanshu" oriented to digital humanities.

Yonghui Wu, Min Jiang, Jianbo Lei, and Hua Xu. 2015. Named entity recognition in chinese clinical text using deep neural network. *Studies in health technology and informatics*, 216:624.

Han Xu, Wang Hongsu, Zhang Sanqian, Fu Qunchao, and Liu Jun. 2019. Sentence segmentation for classical chinese based on lstm with radical embedding. *The Journal of China Universities of Posts and Telecommunications*, 26(02):1–8.

Mingwang Yin, Chengjie Mou, Kaineng Xiong, and Jiangtao Ren. 2019. Chinese clinical named entity recognition with radical-level feature and self-attention mechanism. *J. of Biomedical Informatics*, 98(C).

YU Zhengtao YU Jiangde, HU Shunyi. 2015. A unified character-based tagging approach to chinese lexical analysis. *Journal of Chinese Information Processing*, 29(6):1.

ZHANG Yongwei YU Jingsong, WEI Yi. 2019. Automatic ancient chinese texts segmentation based on bert. 33(11):57.

(Re-)Digitizing 吳守禮 Ngôo Siú-lé's Mandarin – Taiwanese Dictionary

Pierre Magistry
INALCO, ERTIM
pierre.magistry@inalco.fr

Afala Phaxay
INALCO, ERTIM

Abstract

This paper presents the efforts conducted to obtain a usable and open digital version in XML-TEI of one of the major lexicographic work for Taiwanese bilingual dictionaries, namely the 《國臺對照活用辭典》 *Practical Mandarin-Taiwanese Dictionary*, (吳, 2000). The original dictionary was published in 2000, after decades of work by Prof. 吳守禮 (Ngôo Siu-le/Wu Shouli).
We publish the resulting TEI files on Zenodo[1]

1 Introduction

This paper describes the efforts, the issues and some proposed solutions to conduct the re-digitization of the two volumes (over 2800 pages) of the 《國臺對照活用辭典》 *Practical Mandarin-Taiwanese Dictionary*, a masterpiece of Taiwanese lexicography authored by Prof. 吳守禮 (Ngôo Siu-le/Wu Shouli) in the last decades of the 20th century and published in 2000.

The author started its work before the Unicode was founded, at a time when commercial sinographic word processing softwares were designed mostly for Mandarin. He had to come up with workaround solutions to print sinograms and phonetic symbols specific to Taiwanese, involving the creation of thousands of glyphs.

As a result, our work was not strictly speaking a digitizing project, since the original document was already digital-born. But we had to face a number of challenges to turn the original files from their obscure proprietary format into a more modern, open and standard format (we choose XML-TEI) in order to make it easily usable in future projects.

1.1 Context

This project begun after 吳 Ngôo's family members, as right holders of the dictionary, decided to release the work of their ancestor under a permissive and open license. They were willing to provide a larger access to this work and ensure the continuity of this legacy. Their first choice was to turn to the Wikimedia Foundation and target WikiSource to host a public version of the dictionary. Volunteers from Wikimedia Taiwan worked out all the legal aspects of this project and enabled Ngôo's family to release the original data under a Creative Commons license, allowing us to conduct our work. Unfortunately, due to typographic and other technical difficulty which will be described below, the conversion to mediawiki was all but straightforward. Wikimedians turned to the g0v community (involving one author of this paper) for technical support and we finally took the decision to first convert the document into a more standard XML-TEI file so it would be easier to work on it and later to provide all sorts of browsing interfaces. This work was also slowed down by inevitable limitation of time available to volunteers from Wikimedia and g0v, and is now being conducted in a more academic environment. We hope it can return to the public and NGO sphere once we achieve a good level of felicity to the original author's work.

1.2 The author and the Dictionary

Prof. 吳 Ngôo (1909 – 2005) was born in Tainan and received a primary education in Taiwanese. He later graduated from the Taihoku Imperial University, continued his research and work as a translator and lexicographer in Japan where he learned Mandarin before this language was brought to Taiwan by the Kuomintang. He came back to Taiwan to conduct research and teach at the Taihoku Imperial University which later became National Taiwan University (NTU) where he became professor and dedicated is research to the study of Taiwanese.
The 《國臺對照活用辭典》 dictionary is only one of his numerous publications. He finished it

[1] https://doi.org/10.5281/zenodo.1308746)

The 2nd International Workshop on Natural Language Processing for Digital Humanities (NLP4DH), pages 174–178
November 20, 2022.

after he retired from NTU. It was published in 2000 and the next year it obtained the *presidential price for culture* 總統文化獎.

2 Structure of the dictionary

This massive piece of work covers over 12,000 sinograms and 40,000 lexical entries, providing information including traditional phonology, syntax, meaning (bilingual) and semantic relations. In this section we describe how the dictionary was organized.

2.1 macrostructure

The macrostructure of the dictionary presents two layers of information, which is typical of sinitic languages dictionaries. The first layer focuses on Mandarin syllables, ordered according to the canonical order of the 注音符號 (*zhuyin fuhao*) transcription.

Under each syllable section, one can find the list of corresponding sinograms, ordered following the number of strokes in the sinograms. Under each sinogram entry, lexical entries (words) which include this sinogram, ordered by the number of sinograms in the word and following the order of *zhuyin fuhao* for words of the same length.

2.2 microstructure

Each sinogram entry comes with a description of its various readings. It includes the traditional phonological description (the 反切 *fanqie*), possible readings in Mandarin and possible readings from the *bân-lâm* group, drawing from many sourcing, notably William Campbell's dictionary (Campbell, 1913) for Taiwanese and the *Pumin* dictionary representative of Xiamen (Amoy) readings (University, 1982). These descriptions include the customary distinctions between literary and popular readings (a traditional distinction in ban-lam studies, 文白異讀).

Word entries represent actual lexical items. They can be numbered in cases of homographs. The author provides the part of speech, definition in Mandarin and translation or translation of the term and/or the definition in Taiwanese. Interestingly, all the text written in Taiwanese comes with phonetic transcription in the form of *zhuyin fuhao*, on the side of each character (just like the *furigana* in Japanese). Possible regional variations in pronunciation or orthography are indicated with a slash / character. See Figure 1 for an example.

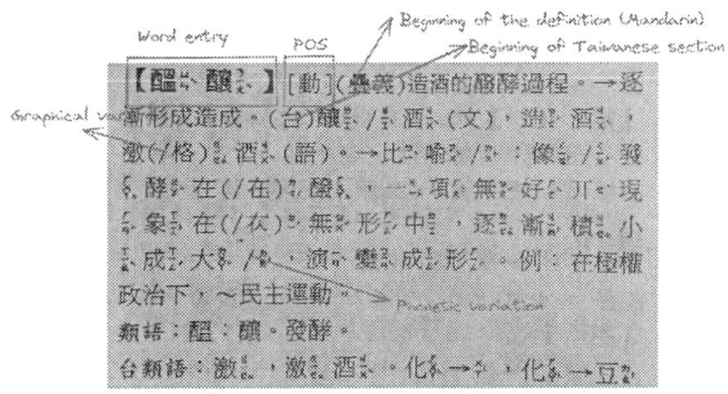

Figure 1: example of a word entry, with some annotation of the types of information provided

3 Digitization stages

The starting point was a set of floppy disks. It required a succession of steps involving various tools and strategies to obtain a usable dataset out of it.

One of the main issues we had to face was to understand how Prof. Ngô managed to include thousands of glyphs which were specific to Taiwanese texts and absent from the encodings of that time.[2]

3.1 Recoding

The first step was to figure out how to read the files, especially in terms of encoding. Prof. Ngô started his work on his dictionary before the Unicode even existed. Knowing this work had been done on a word-processing software for traditional Chinese in Taiwan, Big5 encoding was a safe guess. However, Big5 was only a *de facto* standard, with various vendors extensions, and the use of the Private Use Area (PUA) for new glyphs may differ from one vendor to another.

After a few trials, we wrote a small Perl script to perform the conversion from CP950 (Microsoft version of Big5-ETEN) to UTF-8, and at the same time converting Big5 PUA codes into Unicode PUA, keeping a simple mapping between the two so we can later go back to the original value.[3]

3.2 Reverse engineering the format

Once the text was in an easily readable UTF-8 encoding, we could investigate how to parse the syntax of the text formatting software. The file

[2]with the noticeable exception of the CCCII encoding, but it seems that text processing softwares of that time, being more focused on Mandarin, did not support it.

[3]The script can be read here, kudos to Audrey Tang `https://github.com/g0v/koktai/blob/master/a-tsioh_sandbox/recode_utf8.pl`

format relies on a set of control expressions written in plain text. We were able to guess the most important ones by comparing the content of the file to the printed version of the book.

One important command to find out was the switch between different fonts. The author had to add so many new glyphs that the PUA space available on Big5 was too small. To be able to print all the desired characters, he had to fill it twice, with two different font. As a result, some original Big5 PUA codes are ambiguous and we need to know the font intended for rendering to know which character it corresponds to.

To ease the parsing and XML output, we wrote this part in Scala, which provides convenient parser combinators[4] to describe the grammar of the file format and can natively and elegantly deal with XML as it is part of the language basic syntax.

3.3 Characters in the Private Use Area

At this stage we could face the issue of the thousands of characters encoded in the PUA.

We had the list of codes, associated with a font name and were also provided the font files from which we could extract the images of each glyph. This left us with thousands of images to map to their code.

There were two main cases for these glyphs. Some represented syllable transcriptions in *zhuyin fuhao*. These glyphs are actually the combination of smaller characters transcribing subcomponents of the syllable (typically initial and final, sometime a simple phoneme). We choose to transcribe these glyphs into their decomposed form, which is easy to type and process.

The other type of glyph is actual sinograms, which are specific to Taiwanese or too rare in Mandarin to have been included in Big5 encodings. For some of them, they were later included in Unicode, in which case we could recode them into the new non PUA Unicode code point. Some other were still missing and we could only provide the original image and the description of its composition as a Unicode Ideographic Description Sequence IDS.

3.4 Crowdsourcing the mapping

In order to obtain the mappings described in the previous subsection, we relied on the strong online community of g0v followers to launch a crowd-

[4]https://index.scala-lang.org/scala/scala-parser-combinators

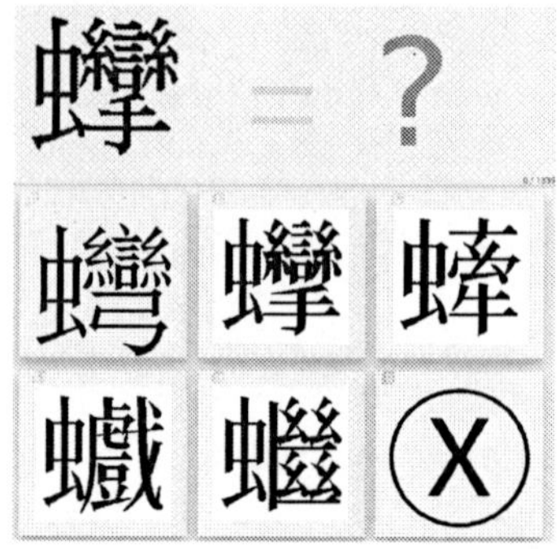

Figure 2: screenshot of the crowdsourcing interface. A simple click or tap on the match will take the user to another character

Figure 3: glyph for a Taiwanese syllable (typically romanized as *bih*)

sourcing campaign during a hackathon. The description of the syllable glyphs could simply be keyed in by Taiwanese netizen familiar with *zhuyin fuhao*. On the other hand, the missing sinograms were mostly obscure and often unknown characters for nonspecialist of Taiwanese script (Mandarin being the language of education in Taiwan).

To make it easier and faster for the netizen to help us, we pre-processed the data with an image similarity algorithm based on Python's OpenCV library. By doing so, we could provide a simple online interface presenting a targeted glyph and a few similar glyphs (extracted from a Unicode font of similar style). In that way, participants in the crowdsourcing just had to click on corresponding characters when present.

Same glyph was presented multiple times (at least 3 participants had to agree on the mapping), and we proceed in multiple waves, to remove already mapped characters and focus on missing data. We counted over $13,000$ user sessions in about 30h.

3.5 OCR for missing pages

Once we obtained a first usable version of this dataset and started working on a web interface, we noticed some discrepancies between our data and the printed version. We soon realized that missing entries were a result from corrupted files on one of the original floppy disks. Some hundred pages of entries were therefore not available. In order to recover those data, we decided to use Optical Character Recognition (OCR) on the scanned version of the missing pages. Granted we had enough data in our hands to train a model. It would have been way too time-consuming and tedious to retrieve them manually rather than limiting the manual work to post-correction of the OCR.

From the numerous OCR tools available, we chose eScriptorium [5], which claim to "focus on pre-typographical and/or non-alphabetic cultures." It is based on Kraken [6] which is "optimized for historical and non-Latin script material." Our situation was a good test case to see how it would fare against sinograms.

eScriptorium's web interface was not too difficult to handle thanks to its tutorial. With eScriptorium, we had two major steps : document segmentation and characters' recognition. All the information is saved into a PAGE [7] schema file. At first, we directly performed the models' training on the original scanned page of the dictionary. The document segmentation gave quite good results with errors such as recognizing one long line of text instead of two lines from two separate columns or not recognizing the entirety of the vertical *zhuyin fuhao* as part of the text's region. On the other hand, the character recognition step would be the difficult part, especially with the specific typography of this dictionary, we would have to train a model from scratch. But the XML we already built could serve as the basis to create training data.

This led us to not only generate our own images of lines from the TEI output of the existing data, with corresponding PAGE files. Our images consist of one single line per images of similar length and police size compared to what was in the original data, however, the police and size used would randomly be chosen among several ones to ensure a more robust model. Sadly, eScriptorium could not correctly recognize and segment our generated images, perhaps it was because the model was trained on the original pages which structure was not the same as ours : a one line image. When the police size was smaller, we didn't come upon this issue.

The result on generated data reached over 95% of accuracy, But it did not perform as well on actual pages from the scanned version. At this point the model could rarely recognize one line entirely. We had to add some original pages during the model's training to introduce the structure of what we wanted the model to be used on, so that it would not be encountering it for the first time. That allowed the new model to now recognize several lines entirely.

4 TEI output

To distribute the dataset in a format as standard as possible, we do our best to follow the TEI guidelines with specific sections for dictionaries. We use **entryFree** elements to describe sinograms and **entry** elements for words. Special characters mapped from the original PUA are described inside the **teiHeader** element as many **charDecl**.

For the moment, we count $6,900$ **charDecl**, $11,805$ **entryFree** and $43,926$ **entry** elements. These figures do not include data from the OCR which is still a work in progress. The exact XML schema is also subject to evolution as we plan to deeper analyze the content of the entries, so we invite the readers to refer to the current version released on the Zenodo repository.
`https://doi.org/10.5281/zenodo.1308746`

5 Conclusion and Future Work

We hope to achieve a high degree of felicity to the original work by Prof. 吳 Ngôo. We will then be able to provide easier and broader access to this valuable material, with full-text search and reverse index. Our experiment with eScriptorium also encourages us to address other volumes, such as the handwritten Taiwanese Dictionary published in 1986 by the same author(吳 , 1986).

Acknowledgments

Part of this work was funded by a *Taiwan Fellowship* grant from Taiwan's MOFA. We express our gratitude to prof. 吳 Ngôo's family who initiated this work by sharing the data openly. We also thanks all the participants from Wikimedia Taiwan and g0v at the initial hackathons, especially Chou Soichi and Audrey Tang for their contributions on legal and technical aspects of the work, as well as the numerous yet anonymous netizens who kindly contributed to the crowdsourcing.

[5] `https://escriptorium.fr/`
[6] `https://kraken.re/master/index.html`
[7] `https://github.com/PRImA-Research-Lab/PAGE-XML/blob/master/documentation/XML%20File%20Structure.pdf`

References

William Campbell. 1913. *A Dictionary of the Amoy Vernacular spoken through out the prefectures of Chin-chiu, Chang-Chiu and Formosa*. Fukuin Printing Co., Yokohama.

Xiamen University. 1982. 普通話閩南方言詞典 . 福建人民出版社 *Fujian People's Publishing House*, Xiamen.

守禮 吳 . 1986. 綜合閩南臺灣語基本字典初稿 . 文史哲出版社 *The liberal arts press co., ltd.*, Taipei.

守禮 吳 . 2000. 國臺對照活用辭典 , *Practical Mandarin-Taiwanese Dictionary*. 遠流出版事業股份有限公司 Yuan-Liou Publishing Co., Ltd., Taipei.

Author Index

Association for Computational Linguistics
209 N. Eighth Street
Stroudsburg, Pennsylvania 18360

ISBN 978-1-7138-6317-5

CURRAN ASSOCIATES INC.
proceedings.com